Technology
and
Social Change

Technology
and
Social Change

Edited by

H. RUSSELL BERNARD
and
PERTTI J. PELTO

The Macmillan Company, New York
Collier-Macmillan Limited, London

This is for Captain George Tsakalotos,
who started it all.

The Macmillan Company
866 Third Avenue, New York, New York 10022

Collier-Macmillan Canada, Ltd., Toronto, Ontario

Library of Congress catalog card number: 70–160373

First Printing

PREFACE

In 1967 the editors met fortuitously in Mexico. During our conversations we discovered we had a similar concern for the role of technology in culture change. Moreover, we had arrived independently at this concern from very different field experiences : Pelto had been studying the effects of snowmobiles on Lapp reindeer herdsmen, whereas Bernard had been following the effects of synthetic sponge production on Greek sponge-fishing industries. In these two cases we saw a common theme. In both situations the lives of the people we had studied were irreversibly altered by modern Western technology. The Lapps found the snowmobiles were as much fun as they were work aids. They also found out that machines break and that repairs can be costly. The Greek sponge divers just found themselves rendered obsolete. We were struck by the profound chainlike effects on local culture that had occurred (and were continuing to occur) as a direct result of technology. This volume, then, grew from our discussions of the consequences of technological change for social change. As the book developed we saw that many of the general questions we had raised could not be answered, given the present state of our knowledge ; but as the authors who had been invited to submit manuscripts did so, we also saw that many new questions were being brought out. Thus, applying the principle that any work should raise at least twice as many new questions as it answers, we must say that putting the volume together has been a gratifying experience.

Our students in various courses have enjoyed reading the case material. From them we feel this book should be useful for classes in economic anthropology, applied anthropology, culture change, and development.

We have incurred many debts and wish to express our gratitude to those who helped us, especially Mr. Charles Smith of The Macmillan Company for his foresight in contracting the book and patience in seeing it through production. We were aided greatly in our thinking by the participants in a symposium on technology and culture change held at the AAA meetings in San Diego, 1970. Most of those contributing are also authors in this volume, with two notable exceptions: Deward Walker of the University of Colorado and Peter Usher of the Northern Sciences Research Group in Canada. Their contributions on the general effects of hydroelectric dams and snowmobiles were particularly useful in clarifying issues with regard to the differences between mini- and maxi-technology. Carole Bernard typed and retyped the manuscripts of the ten different authors and deciphered ten different interlineating handwritings. Dr. Gretl Pelto lent her superb editing talents to the venture.

H. Russell Bernard
Washington State University
Pullman

Pertti Pelto
University of Connecticut
Storrs

CONTENTS

Technology
and
Social Change

1

INTRODUCTION

The study of technological innovation and its effects on social and cultural systems remains one of the most neglected areas in anthropological research. Very few anthropological field studies have concentrated on the analysis of particular technological innovations or changes, even though field workers are constantly reminded, in the course of research, of the penetrations of roads, dams, air travel facilities, new types of vehicles, medical systems, new cultivation techniques, and other technical modifications into previously "untouched" areas. Even in the most isolated areas rapid technological changes are touching and changing people's lives to an unprecedented degree.

The neglect of technological data in contemporary anthropological field research is surprising when we consider the very large role of technological factors in macrotheories of biocultural evolution. Sherwood Washburn and others have suggested complex interactions between earliest tool making and the growth of hand and brain in the development of increasingly *sapiens* forms of *Homo*. M. F. Ashley Montagu and others have discussed the role of the invention of fire in shaping the physical evolution of man. Clifford Geertz has shown in a more general way how cultural (especially "technological") and biological evolution in man are inextricably linked in a feedback system. Coming down to later periods of human evolution, V. G. Childe has dealt extensively with the role of such major technological breakthroughs as the wheel, smelting, the plow, and the sail in man's social development. Technology, by all odds, has been the main focus of prehistoric archaeology, and is of central concern to most other fields of anthropology whenever the broad outlines of human culture history are examined.

In the early days of cultural anthropology there was a widespread interest in primitive technology and its relation to other parts of culture. Somewhere

1

along the way, probably at the same time that "ethnology" became more fashionable than "ethnography," American anthropologists became less concerned with material technical culture and more with values, social structure, and other ideational data. Only in most recent times is there a discernible countertrend.

Marvin Harris has recently discussed some of the reasons for anthropologists' neglect of "materialistic" studies of technology and the environment. He points out that there appears to be a strong "idealistic bias" in anthropology. Most anthropologists have preferred to study ideational systems—values, cognitive systems, ritual enactments, and (*ad nauseam*) kinship systems, with little regard for what Harris calls the technoenvironmental side of human lifeways. A psychologistic, ideational, and sociological bias has pervaded anthropology during most of the twentieth century.

It is Harris' view that the nonmaterialistic bias in anthropology had its origins in the early part of the century, in the Boasian–Kroeberian reaction to evolutionist thinking, and it was tinged with a bit of fear of Marxist ideological associations. We should not ignore, also, the powerful impact of Freudian thought during these same decades—for Freud's influence on anthropology has been strong and was certainly a contributor to a mentalistic approach to human behavior. In *The Rise of Anthropological Theory* Harris concludes that the leading intellectual figures in anthropology during the first half of the twentieth century "stressed the inner, subjective meaning of experience to the exclusion of objective effects and relations. They denied historical determinism in general, and above all they denied the determinism of the material conditions of life. By emphasizing inscrutable values, vain prestige, irrational motives, they discredited the economic interpretation of history" (Harris, 1968 : 2).

Of course, anthropologists have not been unanimous in their neglect of the material conditions of man. In 1936 Julian Steward was laying foundations for a "cultural ecology" frame of reference, in terms of which the natural environment, and man's tools and equipment for exploiting the environment, took on central importance. Although Steward has not assumed anything like a technoenvironmental and technoeconomic determinism, such as that proposed by Harris, his major research efforts have aided in a reassessment of the material side of man's adaptational situation.

The more extreme technological evolutionists, led by Leslie White, have been the strongest forces advocating a more heavily materialistic orientation in anthropological research and theory building. Unfortunately, even these "materialistic" anthropologists have seldom carried out systematic analyses of technological features. Steward has been concerned with the interaction of nature and tools among preindustrial peoples. His latest work, the three-volume collection on *Contemporary Change in*

Traditional Societies, reflects his thinking on the transformation of pre-industrial societies in the modern world. However, not one of the chapters in those three volumes is devoted to the role of technology in bringing about that transformation. Leslie White's theory of cultural evolution, of course, is based on technological determinism, but the theory is very general and never addresses itself to the role of the Levallois technique or the four-wheel-drive automobile. As Robert Spier has recently pointed out, the theory is "like many of White's theoretical positions, one which is generally true but not specifically applicable."

The mentalistic, relatively antimaterialistic, attitudes of anthropologists are evident in the collection of papers on *Human Problems in Technological Change*, edited by Spicer (1952). This is one of the very few books in the past thirty years of anthropology that is addressed to technological data. Interestingly, many of the papers in the book deal with cases in which technological innovations were either rejected outright or at least sharply modified by local populations—thus implying that values, beliefs, personality traits, and social arrangements are somehow causally superior to material and technological factors. It is also interesting to note that five of the cases in Spicer's book do not deal with technological innovations at all, but are concerned with general social and economic introductions.

Somehow the strain toward writing in the ethnographic present, concern with functional analyses of social institutions, and pretending that *massive* technological change is not going on in tribal and peasant societies are all still with us as they were in Lowie's day, when, as Professor Casagrande points out, the profession was interested in the "status Crow." To read much of the anthropological literature from 1930 to 1960, the environments of peasants and tribesmen contain no roads, no airplanes, no hydroelectric dams, and no railroads. For most of the communities and populations studied during that period we are unable to find out when the first automobiles and bus lines were introduced, or what, if any, "modern" kitchen and household utensils were in use during the period of the anthropologist's stay in the area. Only anecdotal, fragmentary mention is made of any large-scale modifications of the local physical environment—in the form of buildings, new means of travel and communication, and other installations.

During the 1960's, however, several trends emerged which have redirected anthropological attention to the long-neglected technological "side" of human behavior.

1. The continuing growth of interest in ecological studies, as seen, for example, in the work of Rappaport, Vayda, and others in the techno-environmental conditions of life in the New Guinea highlands, draws attention to man's tools and material equipment.
2. The equally important rebirth of interest in human origins—spurred

by the rich paleoanthropological finds at Olduvai Gorge—has reasserted the great significance of tools and equipment in man's increasingly complex modes of adapting to, and modifying, physical environments. One of the important consequences of these new studies is, as noted above, the realization that man, indeed, does "make himself," as Childe so aptly phrased it. The discovery that man's own adaptation device, swidden agriculture, probably created the ecological conditions favoring the development of sickle-cell anemia has been instrumental in furthering this realization.

3. Popular and scientific concern about environmental deterioration suddenly, during the late 1960's, thrust upon us the realization that man's technology is somehow "out of control." All of a sudden we find that the air and water all around us is polluted, and that we have "destroyed" large portions of the environment. From "A man on the moon by 1970!" we are hearing cries of "A man in Lake Erie by 1980!" Our attention is thus directed to the ways in which large-scale environmental modifications—dams, roads, air travel systems, massive buildings, factories—have drastically altered our life space. Anthropologists and other social scientists are waking up to the fact that technological changes and innovations *must*, after all, have massive effects on social relations, cultural values and attitudes, and psychological functioning.

This collection of empirical studies is offered, then, as a small step toward lessening the disparity between anthropological work and the technical–social realities of the world today. Nothing in these papers is intended to assert a completely materialistic determinism, however. In all of these cases social relationships, cultural values, economic arrangements, ritual patterns and other nonmaterial facts are interrelated with technoenvironmental things in ways that make it unproductive to argue the priority of one or the other "side" as prime mover of human culture history.

Most but not all the papers in this book fall into two main categories of technological innovations. Several cases deal with large-scale environmental modifications—dams, factories, and "new cities." These are highly visible technical developments that thrust investments of energy, money, and materials into specific locations. Their effects—social, economic, and cultural—begin even before the first breaking of ground or the first hiring of labor, for they often involve planned dislocations of populations as well as alienation of land (and other resources). As will become clear in several of these papers, the governmental or private planners who make the decisions about large-scale physical structures often do not make much attempt to weigh or predict the effects of their constructions on the surrounding populations. The purposes of large-scale modifications are usually regional and national in scope, so that dislocations of local life styles are incidental to the main goals of the planners. If, on the other hand, these planners were to ask anthropologists and other social scientists for help in studying and predicting the future effects of these structures, they would probably not be much better off, for as already mentioned, anthropologists and their fellow colleagues have not studied these kinds of problems. The great lesson of applied anthropology, as we see it, is that concern is no substitute for knowledge and competence. We may be aware of the possibilities for dislocation and disorientation of human cultures faced with massive technological input, but this is simply no guarantee that we will know how to modify their effects. In today's world little heed is paid to the social scientist who cries doom at every turn and offers trivial solutions to significant problems. There is a need for knowledgeable anthropologists who are aware that all technological progress is not inherently evil, who are not doctrinaire relativists to the point of making living museums of isolated peoples in the name of sparing them the agonies of contact with "modern" ways of living.

A second kind of technological innovation that has far-reaching effects takes the form of gadgets, tools, weapons, vehicles, houses, and other "microtechnology" that usually become the private property of individual persons and families. Microtechnological items usually arrive in a particular community or region through the efforts of commercial operators who seek to sell the things for a profit to large numbers of people. No social planning is involved, other than the commercial planning of the trader, huckster, or other operator who introduces the hardware. This set of papers discusses the snowmobile (Pelto and Müller-Wille) as a new transportation device in the arctic; items such as flashlights, radios, and other equipment in Uganda (Robbins and Kilbride); the house and its effects on Indians and Eskimos in new arctic towns (Honigmann). These cases illustrate some of the ways in which even seemingly minor and commonplace items can have significant social and cultural effects.

One significant aspect of the difference we see between micro- and macrotechnology can be expressed (from the point of view of the affected local populations) by the question "Do you have a piece of it, or does it have a piece of you?"

Three of the papers in this volume do not fit neatly into either the microtechnology or the large-scale environmental modification categories. Kiste's paper, to be sure, does involve a large-scale environmental modification but of a bizarre sort. It is a case of massive technological and social encounter between a non-Western community (Bikinians) and their powerful political and economic keepers—the Americans. The forced dislocation from Bikini, because Americans needed that real estate for testing nuclear weapons, put the Bikinians into environmental situations where their old technological inventory was both unsuited and unavailable. Much of the technical stuff available from the American masters has been poorly suited to the local conditions in which the Bikinians must try to adapt. This large-scale technoenvironmental dislocation resulted in marked social changes and the creation of a deepening dependence relationship, as the Bikinians find adaptation to a welfare recipient role more possible and more rewarding than the hopeless struggle to reconstitute a successful technology.

Bernard's paper on the sponge divers of Kalymnos, like the story of the Bikinians, deals with the complexity of interrelations between a small local population and the wider world. But the impact of the world on Kalymnos is not so much concerned with political–military facts as it is with the effects of commercial and technical developments at the world's trade centers. Far from the shores of Kalymnos the fluctuations of the commercial sponge market, the development of synthetic sponge substitutes, and inventions of new kinds of diving apparatus all send their shock waves to the Greek spongemen, who react to each of these changes in the rules of the game with a tenacious and flexible adaptive style. Like a yo-yo on the end of an invisible string, the fortunes of the sponge industry go up and down in response to events in the world's capitals. Of course the same sorts of dependencies are evident in every human community to greater or lesser degree, but the sponge-diving industry seems especially sensitive to influences from the outside, at the same time maintaining a seeming inner equilibrium based on the strong social, economic, and psychological investments many men have put into this activity.

The description of what synthetic sponges have done to Kalymnos makes one wonder about an entire class of similar cases. What have been the effects of nylon on the silk industry? How have plastics changed the life styles of people who used to make shell buttons? What role will nuclear power play in transforming the communities of Appalachia which depend on the mining of fossil fuels? What is the future of Mexican potters in the face of cheap plastic and metal kitchenwares?

Burton Benedict's paper, too, is different. Here the complex interrelations of social policy, medical technology, and rampant partisan politics interact in the population explosion that is Mauritius. Mauritius is possibly a microcosmic adumbration of the fate of our world island, as the long shadow of overpopulation reaches over more and more of the globe. No single technological item and no single social policy cuts to the heart of the matter. The interrelations are highly complicated, but the role of technology both as a "cause" and as a potential alleviator of the population crisis is forcefully described.

It is apparent that all of these papers constitute the barest fiddling with the surface of very complex matters. Little in the way of definitive "causal" statements can be drawn from these studies. In each case, though, the writers have taken as part of their task the raising of significant questions, for which future research may provide some answers.

Two of the most important questions raised concern (1) the role of the individual in social change and (2) the visceral (but perhaps empirically testable) issue of whether or not technology is "good for" people. The first is an area of profound neglect. One of our students recently undertook as a master's problem to describe a Jesuit priest who was initiating economic reform projects among American Indians. After two months of research the student was still writing *apologias* on why it is acceptable anthropology to study one human being's innovative activities. Why spend so much time justifying the work instead of getting on with it? "Just in case the faculty decides it's not real anthropology," was the reply. Some of the papers in this volume (notably Doughty's and Scudder and Colson's) address themselves to this issue. Their descriptions of individual entrepreneurs and technological innovators in their analysis of social change leave little doubt that this area needs to be carefully researched.

The question of whether technology is "good for" people is more difficult. Because few of us would prefer to give up our "civilized" comforts to return to a hunting and gathering existence, it would be fatuous to assert that all technological change throughout history has been "bad." On the other hand, some tales of technical modification can be real horror stories. The range of variation, even with a particular type of technological change in different environments, is great. The snowmobile, for example, would appear to be a fairly uniform type of technical development—and it can only be important in a certain type of environment, one with quite a lot of snow and a long winter. Yet the introduction of this device in some areas appears on the whole to be either beneficial or inconsequential. In other areas the evidence points to the possibility of serious dislocations.

The studies in this collection were solicited by the editors on the basis of intrinsic interest, availability of material, geographical balance, and "gross type" of innovation. By having a typology in mind before we started, we admittedly biased our sample. We wanted a dam or two, a native craft or industry replaced by a synthetic industrial product, a few chapters on gadgetry, and so on. We even toyed with the idea of having new management systems and their effects as an example of "nonmaterial" technological innovation. We wanted some studies of mechanical rice mills in village Asia or tortilla factories in Mexico so we could see how technology has affected societies through the release of women from household work.

We have not, of course, been able to include all the various types of technological change that are currently taking place. The cases presented here are but a sample of these changes and indicate the need for further research in a variety of areas. Among the topics that should be explored with in-depth case studies we suggest the following :

1. The interaction and differences between material and nonmaterial innovations.
2. The differences between micro- and macrotechnology.
3. The major areas of technology, such as housing, power production, manufacturing, education, recreation, health, communications, transport, and so on.
4. The differences between cases where the following variables are considered:
   a. Is the innovation introduced by the choice of the natives?
   b. In the case of government or "big business," have those who control the introduction of a new item planned for the possible social consequences?
   c. Was the innovation introduced by an entrepreneur?

The examples of technological change examined in this collection pertain to essentially rural environments. These are the kinds of settings which anthropologists have thus far studied most extensively. Study of technological developments in rural regions is important because these are situations and populations in which the effects of individual innovations are usually easier to sort out than they would be in the complex entanglements of highly technological urban settings. At the same time these rural environments are increasingly threatened by massive technical expansion and exploitation in ways that could have powerful and irreversible consequences for urban populations as well.

Most of the people in the impact areas discussed in these cases are still living in essentially preindustrial conditions. They are increasingly drawn into relationships with industrialized urban systems, but their quality of living, and their reactions to their environments, are not yet "contaminated" by the full impact of modernization. Thus the cultural, social, and psychobiological characteristics of these people as they encounter the advance of technological transformation provide us with a much needed comparative perspective for interpreting and understanding modes of adaptation of urban peoples to technological change. The importance of this last point comes sharply into focus if we consider seriously Jacques Ellul's comments in *The Technological Society*, where he notes that man's technical–material artifacts may have so taken over the course of cultural adaptation that the processes of technological change have become irreversible. It is crucial that anthropologists study human adaptations to technological change among peoples for whom technology has not yet "become an end in itself, to which men must adapt themselves."

Future anthropological research must, of course, include full attention to effects of technological change in *all* of man's environments—rural and urban.

2

We usually associate studies of factories and industrialization with developments in urban areas. "Modernization" in rural agricultural areas, on the other hand, is most often concerned with agricultural improvements, or else the secondary impacts—the reflected culture change—resulting from migrations of able-bodied men to the places where factory wage earning is possible. It has been rare for the factories and related industrial changes to be placed in the agricultural hinterlands.

But in many areas of the world the principal cities are overcrowded, increasingly deteriorated environments, with all the problems that seem to accompany densely populated communities in which the traditional, kinship-based, social controls are not operative. In the next decades many parts of the world—in both "postindustrial" and "developing" areas—are likely to experiment with dispersal of factories into rural areas to rejuvenate sagging agricultural economies and to alleviate the increasingly intolerable congestion in the cities.

In this study of a new industrial city, Ciudad Industrial, John Poggie presents materials that deal with the effects of an experiment in rural industrialization.

CIUDAD INDUSTRIAL:
A New City in Rural Mexico[1]
John J. Poggie, Jr.

John J. Poggie, Jr., is Assistant Professor, Department of Sociology and Anthropology, University of Rhode Island. He received his Ph.D. from the University of Minnesota and he is now preparing several publications on his field work in Veracruz and Hidalgo, Mexico.

During the 1950's the new city of Ciudad Industrial[2] was built in the midst of the maguey fields and agricultural villages of south Hidalgo, Mexico. This technological experiment has created an interesting "field laboratory" for the study of the social impact of rural technification. The three major factories in Ciudad Industrial have created a selection of employment opportunities and occupational roles that were previously unknown in the region. At the same time the modern homes, new schools, special facilities, and middle-class life style of the city could have a strong impact on the aspirations of the nearby villagers.

In this paper we will examine the impact of the new city on the lives of the people in the surrounding towns and villages.

[1] My field work in the region of Ciudad Industrial during 1966–1967 was supported by the National Institute of General Medical Sciences, Graduate Training Program in Anthropology (Grant No. GMO1164) at the University of Minnesota. I wish to thank Fernando Cámara Barbachano, Reuban Hill, Luis Leñaro Otero, Gastón Martinez Matiella for scholarly advice and assistance in making field arrangements. I am also grateful to Frank C. Miller for his suggestions in the early analysis of these data. I wish particularly to thank Pertti J. Pelto for sharing with me his creative insights into the processes of modernization Finally, I thank the people of the Los Llanos region for their friendly cooperation.
[2] We have used pseudonyms for the names of communities, in order to protect the anonymity of the research population.

The region of Los Llanos, located some 60 miles northeast of Mexico City, is a dry, elevated (8,000 feet) intermontane valley. There is a rich history to this semiarid region that extends back to pre-Conquest occupation by the same peoples that dominated the valley of Mexico. Ceremonial pyramids that appear related to the great city of Teotihuacan, and numerous other archaeological sites, give evidence of the importance of this region in pre-Columbian times.

The Spanish Conquest was followed by the formation of numerous haciendas in the Los Llanos region. These haciendas were quasifeudal organizations with a "nobleman–serf" class structure and are considered by some to be part of the famous Black Legend of the Spanish Conquest vividly described by Las Casas. The economic base of the haciendas at first was cattle, but in time they evolved into the well-known pulque haciendas which produced some of the highest quality pulque (a native fermented beverage) in all Mexico. Most of the pulque produced in the area was shipped by railroad to the *cantinas* and other drinking spots of Mexico City.

The Revolution brought an end to the hacienda system of the region and was the beginning of land reform under the new Agrarian Code (*Codigo Agrario*). Most of the hacienda lands were given to peasant communities in the form of *ejidos* (cf. Simpson, 1937). The *ejido* farmers own and control their allotted lands as a corporate community, and their lands cannot be sold to outsiders. Each member of the community is allotted his share of land, and these parcels of land are farmed individually. People who emigrate from the *ejido* lose their rights to lands. The once affluent haciendas remain, stripped of their lands and wealth. Some of them are practically abandoned, but others are still operated as pulque enterprises on the reduced land holdings allowed to them.

During the heyday of the haciendas in the nineteenth century, the well-being of the area was tied to the single-crop (pulque) economy, although maize has always been the subsistence mainstay in the homes of the peasants. Pulque is fermented from the sweet sap (*aguamiel*) of the maguey (century plant). Throughout south Hidalgo, and much of the rest of central Mexico, these spiny plants are ubiquitous in the courtyards, around the maize fields, and up and down hillsides too steep and rocky for the cultivation of other food plants. The maguey is a xerophytic plant well suited to the caprices of rainfall in these dry regions. Thus, as long as there was an assured demand for pulque in Mexico City, the economy of the region remained fairly stable, though the level of living among the peasants is lower in south Hidalgo than in many other, more productive regions.

In recent decades the people of Mexico City have increasingly turned to beer and Pepsi Cola to quench their thirst, and pulque drinking continues to decline despite some "nativistic" attempts to revive interest in this national drink. For example, in the ten-year period from 1943 to 1953 (Martinez, 1966) the consumption of pulque in the states of Hidalgo, Tlaxcala, and Mexico dropped 25 per cent, whereas beer consumption increased by 73 per cent.

Peasant delivering maguey sap for *pulque* in Malapan, a rural town. (*Photo by John Poggie.*)

Undoubtedly the transition to modern beverages has been even more rapid since that time. As the market for pulque has declined, the general economic situation of south Hidalgo has worsened over the years.

Pulque is still produced in the Los Llanos region, but on a greatly reduced scale. Barley and maize are now the main agricultural products; but, because of the marginality of the climate and lack of irrigation, productivity is low. Thus, since the beginning of the Mexican Revolution (1910), the region has experienced a steady economic deterioration. Until the 1950's there was no development of industrial activity to offset the decline in agriculture.

In response to the worsening economic situation in south Hidalgo, Mexican governmental officials decided to establish a new industrial complex in the region. This involved some very complicated economic, political, and social motives (cf. Blair, 1964), which resulted in a decision to build the three major factories as government-controlled enterprises; the new city itself was to be built and administered by the Mexican government.

THE NEW CITY

The site chosen for the new Ciudad Industrial is in the middle of the Los Llanos valley, where, as informants put it, "there was nothing but maguey

View of Ciudad Industrial (administration building on the left). (*Photo by John Poggie.*)

fields before." Land was acquired from the neighboring *ejido* communities through a variety of agreements, in terms whereby the communities were to receive new roads, favorable access to factory jobs, and other compensations for the loss of their lands.

The first of the three major factories in Ciudad Industrial was an automobile plant manufacturing Fiat automobiles and Dina (Diesel Nacional) buses and trucks. Construction of the plant began in 1952. At the same time, the government created an agency, Constructors Industrial Irolo S.A. (often referred to as CIISA), for the planning and construction of the new city. By 1958 there were three factories and about 3,000 workers in Ciudad Industrial producing railroad cars in the Carros plant, automobiles and trucks at Dina, and textile machinery in the third factory (Sidena). Textile machinery was later discontinued and Sidena now produces Fordson tractors as well as some parts for the other two plants (cf. Young and Young, 1960, 1962a, 1962b, 1966; Poggie, 1968).

The design of most of the areas of the new city does not strike one as particularly innovative or artistically splendid. There is a modest plaza, flanked by a movie house, post office, and telephone exchange, with the two-story administration building at one end. Nearby are several large "*collectivos*"—apartment buildings with rooms for single workers as well as some modest family quarters. The large primary school is a short distance away. Across the street from the plaza is a very small and inconspicuous Catholic church.

The main street of Ciudad Industrial has several small store buildings, and at the north end of the avenue there is a large market building, flanked by an

13

Fish seller in weekly market in Ciudad Industrial. (*Photo by John Poggie.*)

open-air market place with cement tables for the vendors, who come to sell their wares at the weekly Saturday market.

The residential area of the city—consisting mainly of rows of one-story, single-family houses—is to the east and up the hill from "main street." There was little variation in the design of the first group of houses built in the area, except for the fact that executives' houses further up the hill are larger and more attractive. The houses are all constructed of concrete.

A few years after the initial construction of the city, a new residential area, the "Colonia Nueva" was built, this time in very attractive brick. The homes are for the most part duplexes and triplexes, with an architecture resembling some of the more aesthetically interesting sections of Mexico City. School buildings, a small commercial pavilion, and some other non-residential units were integrated into the plan of the "Colonia Nueva."

Since the completion of the "Colonia Nueva" very little has been added to the city, which by 1966 had a population of about 14,000 people. Residence in Ciudad Industrial is limited to factory workers, administration employees, and the small number of commercial operators. This restrictive policy has prevented the growth of a slum area such as is usually found in new industrial cities with open residential possibilities (cf. Peattie, 1968; Moore, 1963).

14

Also, the administration has been strict in the issuance of commercial permits. Thus the growth of the business district of Ciudad Industrial is quite retarded in comparison to other cities of comparable size.

Cantinas and other drinking establishments are not allowed in Ciudad Industrial, making it unique among Mexican cities in its dearth of "night life." This administrative policy has far-reaching consequences, for it means that the citizens must confine their drinking and other recreational activities to their homes or else seek entertainment in the other towns of the region.

More than half of the factory labor force is resident in Ciudad Industrial, but large numbers of workers commute daily from their homes in the nearby villages and towns. Many of these people have no desire to find housing in the new city, for life is freer in many respects in their home towns, and many of these workers also have agricultural holdings to look after. Because we are mainly concerned with the effects of the new technological situation on the traditional local population, we shall focus on the farmers and workers in the communities surrounding Ciudad Industrial.

THE NETWORK OF COMMUNITIES IN THE LOS LLANOS REGION

The approximately thirty communities of the Los Llanos region range in size from Xalpan, an important commercial center with about 8,000 inhabitants, to little hamlets of fifty or sixty people, such as the former hacienda Santa Rosa.

The town of Xalpan is the largest community in the area, and is the major commercial center. Xalpan is the only place in the area where farm equipment, tractors, and automobiles are sold, and it also has two or three small factories. Most of the villages of the region fall into the several-hundred-inhabitants category, with at least two or three small stores and a corn-grinding mill. Atlaquilpan, Malapan, and Benito Juarez are head towns of their respective *municipos*, and have populations in the 1,500 to 4,000 range. All three of these towns are within six miles of Ciudad Industrial.

The old and new history of the area is in part reflected in the names of these communities. Atlaquilpan's history extends back over a thousand years, to the time of the Teotihuacan empire. The cathedral of the town, dating from colonial times, was built on the site of a pre-Columbian pyramid, and there are numerous other archaeological signs of its Indian past. Early chronicles report that the town and its immediate environs had a population of over 10,000 at the time of Cortez' arrival.

On the other hand, communities like Benito Juarez represent the new, postrevolutionary history. As a new *ejido* community on the site of the former hacienda San Felipe, even the names of the two mirror the shift from "sacred to secular" that accompanied the Revolution. Some older people of the area have apparently not made this "cognitive shift," for they continue to refer to the place as San Felipe. A large proportion of the inhabitants are immigrants from other towns and villages in the Hidalgo–Tlaxcala region, and many of the latest in-migrants are factory workers in Ciudad Industrial, five and a half miles away.

Before the new industrial city was planted in their midst, the villages and towns were linked together in a network of relationships with the commercially active Xalpan as the sociometric center. Beyond the edges of the crescent-shaped valley, there are towns with relatively less articulation to Los Llanos and more active ties with other valleys and regions. The total area of the Los Llanos community net is not large; a half hour bus ride takes one out of the valley into other similar clusters of communities.

THE IMPACT OF THE NEW CITY ON INDIVIDUALS: COMPARISONS OF FARMERS AND WORKERS

In studies of industrialization it is usually suggested that the new occupational roles of factory workers, together with their enlarged earnings, bring about a relatively sharp differentiation between workers and the supposedly more traditional farmers. Naturally, the specific ecological contexts in which the technological (and other) changes occur have important influences on the degree of such differentiation. Nash (1958) has described the effects of a factory on a rural Guatemalan Indian community, in which the new wage labor opportunities and related aspects of industrialization seem to have brought about very little differentiation between the wage workers and their neighbors. Nash does report that in some aspects of culture—especially in political involvements and personal aspirations—there are important differences between workers and farmers, though these were quite slow to develop. Inkeles, in a study of the effects of factory experience in a number of different parts of the world, has found that, "Each year in the factory contributes to significant change, and the process is continuous, so that after ten years in a factory, the typical worker will, on our measures of individual 'modernity,' far outscore his compatriot who continued in his native village" (Inkeles, 1967: vi).

Most cases of growing industrialization involve migration to factory centers at some distance from the agricultural hometowns of the workers. The fairly rapid "modernization" of factory workers' attitudes and behavioral patterns represents the combined effects of occupational roles, loosening of kinship and community ties, and exposure to already developed urban cultural complexity. As Rogers has noted, "The task before researchers is not an easy one, for it will be difficult to separate the effects due to industrialization and those due to urbanization, both are intricately entangled. . . . Is it the effect of the occupation, or of residence in the city, which produces changes in the traditional individual?" (Rogers, 1969: 376).

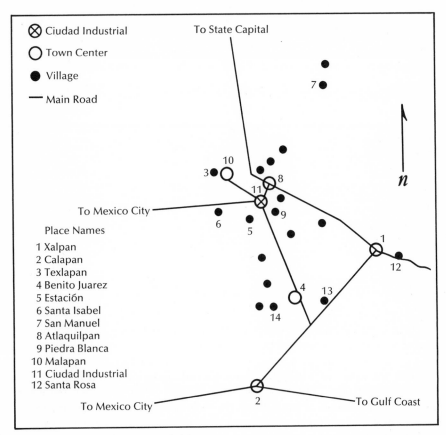

FIGURE 1. Network of communities.

In the case of Ciudad Industrial we can separate different factors if we concentrate our analysis on those factory workers who live in the agricultural towns and villages, mingling with their co-resident farmer kinsmen and neighbors. That is the strategy in this study.

During extensive research operations in the Ciudad Industrial area in 1966–1968, we selected seven of the communities of Los Llanos region for more intensive study, part of which included detailed interviews with samples of householders in each community. The communities in which the survey was carried out are numbered 4, 5, 7, 8, 9, 13, and 14 on the map (Figure 1). Community 8 is Atlaquilpan, 4 is Benito Juarez, and 7 is San Manuel, a village that, at the present time, has no factory workers in its local population. The other three communities in the survey were generally intermediate in population size, geographical relationship to the industrial city, and number of factory workers. The populations of these communities are given in Table 1.

Table 1

Population (1960) of Seven Sample
Network Communities*

Community No.	Population
8	3,076
4	2,059
5	888
13	800
7	714
14	447
9	103
Total	8,087

Mean of sample = 1,155.
* VIII Censo General de Población
1964.

These communities were selected for study because they are fairly representative of several different kinds of variations in the region. They vary from
"high" to "low" in the number of workers at the factories; they represent
most of the range of variation in commercial elaboration and institutional
complexity (cf. Gold, 1968; Young and Young, 1960), and they represent
several different kinds of positions in the sociometric network of communities
(see Young, 1964; Poggie, 1968; and Poggie and Miller, 1969 for further
discussion of the community network of Los Llanos).

Our structured interviews were administered by field workers from the
Instituto Mexicano de Estudios Sociales (IMES), in close consultation with
several anthropologists, including the author. Quota samples of forty farmers,
forty workers, and forty "others" were obtained in the two largest communities, and sampling in the smaller communities generally consisted of forty
farmers plus all the workers and "others" to be found. (The "other"
category consists chiefly of storekeepers and artisans.) Thus in San Manuel
the sample consisted of forty famers only, because no other occupational
types were found residing in that semi-isolated village.

Interviews were carried out during the period July 19 to August 8, 1967.
The total number of women interviewed (spouses of household heads) was
562 and the total male sample was 492. For 477 families we have interviews
with both household head and his spouse. Of these, 114 are worker households, 247 are farmers, and 116 are "others."

In order to compare the worker families with "pure farmers" as nearly as
possible, we removed from the sample all those farm households which
contained *any* individuals who were servants or other kinds of employees in

Ciudad Industrial. Also, incomplete and defective schedules were eliminated, so the adjusted sample consists of 97 workers and 185 farmers.

Because the worker households tend on the whole to be much younger than the farmers, the farmer sample was divided at a fifty-year-old cut-off point into "young farmers" (114 households) and "old farmers" (71 households). Table 2 shows the age distribution of these groups. The mean age among the workers is thirty-two, and the mean age of "young farmers" is thirty-five.

Table 2
Age Distribution Within the Occupational Groups

| | Age | | | | | | | | |
	15–19	20–24	25–29	30–34	35–39	40–44	45–49	50–54	55+	Total
Workers	4	17	19	18	21	10	7		1	97
Younger farmers	1	11	15	27	21	19	20			114
Older farmers								14	57	71

There are significant differences in education levels among the three groups. Table 3 shows that the workers have, on the average, twice as many

Table 3
Mean Education in Years of Groups of Respondents

Group	Mean Education in Years
Workers (15–49 years)	3.9
Younger farmers (15–49 years)	1.8
Older farmers (50 years and older)	0.7

years of education as the young farmers, and the older farmers have very little schooling. These differences will be taken into account in the analysis of values and attitudes.

Another potentially significant difference between workers and farmers is that more of the workers have come into the villages from other regions outside the Los Llanos valley area. In several statistical checks we found that "origin in communities outside the region," did not appear to have a significant influence on people's attitudes and values, so places of origin are not controlled in the following analysis.

MATERIAL STYLE OF LIFE

Factory workers have much greater cash incomes than their farmer neighbors. In 1967 the lowest rungs of the occupational ladder in the factories received at least $2 per day, and many workers were earning $4 and $5 per day. Farmers, on the other hand, were estimated to have annual incomes of only $250 to $350 annually (based on computing the cash values of their net crop yields). This means that the lowest-paid factory workers had annual incomes at least twice that of the farmers. Income figures are extremely difficult to estimate among farming peoples, but even in the best years the harvests of maize, barley, and beans (plus income from the maguey plants) are relatively meager in this area.

The availability of cash among the factory workers should be reflected in their acquisition of material possessions. The people of Los Llanos, like the

Table 4

Guttman Scale of Material Style of Life

Scale Step	Item Content	Percentage of Respondents at and Below This Step	Scale Errors in Step
I	Absence of all scale items	100	10
II	Wool or cotton blankets	98	3
III	Bed sheets	96	5
IV	Own their home	94	24
V	Wool mattress	88	26
VI	Radio	81	60
VII	Cupboard	68	51
VIII	Wardrobe	57	50
IX	Electric lights	44	15
X	Electric iron	41	30
XI	China or porcelain dishes	35	31
XII	Sewing machine	30	28
XIII	Piped-in water	23	22
XIV	Cook with gas	20	34
XV	Bath or privy	14	34
XVI	Four or more rooms	9	45

Coefficient of reproducibility = 0.90.
Coefficient of scalability = 0.62.

people of most other areas of the world, want to have at least some of the material symbols of modernity, and the factory workers have a better chance to acquire these than do the farmers.

In the household interview a number of questions were asked about possession of material goods. Among these marks of "modernization" we selected twenty-one types of possessions for analysis. These items include china or porcelain dishes, blankets, sheets, wool mattress, car or truck, telephone, television, record player, refrigerator, wardrobe, cupboard, sewing machine, blender, radio, electric iron, gas cooking, electric lights, piped-in water, bath or privy, four or more rooms in the house, and home ownership. Several of these items did not aid in sorting out "high" and "low" material style of life, in Guttman scalogram terms, because possession of, for example, piped-in water depends more on the state of the town water system than it does on individual efforts.

A Guttman scalogram of fifteen items was constructed for our index of a "material style of life." This index of material goods is shown in Table 4. Although the coefficient of reproducibility at 0.90 is acceptable as a scalogram, it should be noted that the step-by-step levels of ownership of these items have many exceptions. Many families with relatively few material possessions have acquired some rather costly and unusual possessions, perhaps because a son or daughter in the city has been able to send the articles home as gifts. In the right-hand column of Table 4 we have listed the number of "errors" in the scalogram.

In order to use our "material style of life" scale as conservatively as possible at this stage of analysis, we simply divided the entire population at the midpoint of the range of distribution. Thus the following statistical comments are based on comparisons of "high" and "low" material style of life in our three sample groups (see Table 5).

Table 5

Material Style of Life

Material Style of Life	Workers (15–49 Years)	Younger Farmers (15–49 Years)	Older Farmers (50 Years and Older)
High scale steps (IX–XVI)	72	29	19
Low scale steps (I–VIII)	21	73	49
Totals	93	102	68

Workers vs. younger farmers $\chi^2 = 24.4$, 1 df, $P < 0.001$, lambda $= 0.19$.
Workers vs. older farmers $\chi^2 = 38.9$, 1 df, $P < 0.001$, lambda $= 0.43$.
Younger farmers vs. older farmers $=$ N.S.

As predicted, we find that the workers, even though they are on the average younger than the farmers, have in general a higher percentage of households in the "high" category of material goods. Although many of the workers have not been employed in the factories for very long, and they are, on the whole, younger than the farmer group, they nonetheless have converted some of their cash income advantages into household furnishings and equipment. When we control for educational level (Table 6) this pattern still holds. Thus the significant variable related to higher material style of life appears to be the factory worker status, with its associated income, although there is also a relationship between higher education and material style of life, especially among the farmers.

Table 6

Material Style of Life
(Controlling for Education of Occupational Groups)

Material Style of Life	Workers* (15–49 Years)		Younger Farmers (15–49 Years)		Older Farmers (50 Years and Older)	
Educational Level 0–1 Year						
High scale steps (IX–XVI)	8	72.7%	5	12.1%	12	24.0%
Low scale steps (I–VIII)	3	27.3%	36	87.9%	38	76.0%
Subtotals	11	100.0%	41	100.0%	50	100.0%
Educational Level 2–4 Years						
High scale steps (IX–XVI)	32	72.7%	19	36.5%	6	42.9%
Low scale steps (I–VIII)	12	27.3%	33	63.5%	8	57.1%
Subtotals	44	100.0%	52	100.0%	14	100.0%
Educational Level 5 Years or More						
High scale steps (IX–XVI)	32	86.5%	5	55.6%	1	100.0%
Low scale steps (I–VIII)	5	13.5%	4	44.4%	0	0.0%
Subtotals	37	100.0%	9	100.0%	1	100.0%
Totals†	92		102		65	

* The exclusion of the six cases where the worker is a son does not change the pattern of these results.

† Several cases had to be discarded because of technical difficulties.

Because the older farmers have presumably had a longer time to accumulate material possessions than the young farmers, we would expect that they would be intermediate between workers and young farmers in material goods. This is not the case, however. Young farmers and older farmers are quite similar in their relative "material affluence" (both groups have 28 per cent "high" and 72 per cent "low" material style of life indexes). This suggests that the younger farmers are acquiring material items much more rapidly at their stage in the life cycle than did the older generation. Apparently these younger men are enjoying some of the new prosperity of the region.

For four of the communities in our survey sample we have some comparable data on material possessions collected by Frank and Ruth Young in 1958.[3] (The four towns are Atlaquilpan, Benito Juarez, Estación, and Piedra Blanca.) Table 7 shows the percentage of change in these material possessions during the time period from 1958 to 1967. Already in 1958 workers had more

Table 7

Changes Between 1958 and 1967 in the Percentage of Farmers
and Workers Owning Seven Household Items

Farmers (four communities): 1958 (*N*) 168, 1967 (*N*) 135.
1958–1967 changes (per cent change)

Petates	Mattress	Sheets	Gas stove	Electric iron	Blender	Radio
−13	+21	+28	+10	+34	+6	+30

Workers (four communities): 1958 (*N*) 95, 1967 (*N*) 87.
1958–1967 changes (per cent change)

Petates	Mattress	Sheets	Gas stove	Electric iron	Blender	Radio
−29	+30	+24	+43	+39	+27	+38

of these material goods than did the farmers, but it is quite significant that *both groups* have recorded significant increases in ownership of the items. Mattresses, sheets, gas stoves, electric irons, blenders, and radios are now much more common in the Los Llanos region than they were in 1958. The use of the traditional *petates* for sleeping purposes has declined. For some items the workers have advanced more rapidly than the farmers, e.g., in ownership of gas stoves and blenders, but it appears that at this time there is not a drastic and overriding differentiation occurring to separate workers from their agricultural neighbors. A certain "sharing of the wealth" is evident.

[3] We wish to thank Frank and Ruth Young for generously sharing with us their unpublished data.

ASPIRATIONS FOR SONS' CAREERS

One of the changes that has often been noted in studies of "moderniza-tion" is in people's aspirations for more education and more rewarding and prestigeful occupations for their sons and daughters. Related to these is the question of future residence for sons and daughters. Traditional farming peoples are often thought to insist on sons following in the older generation's footsteps in occupation and other aspects of life style.

In our interviews we included the following questions:

1. What level of education do you think your sons should have?
2. What type of work would you like your sons to have?
3. Where would you like your sons to live when they are grown up?

(Similar questions about daughters were asked, but will not be examined here.)

Workers clearly have higher educational aspirations for their sons than do the farmers (Table 8). This pattern holds when we break down the samples by years of education (Table 9). Apparently educational aspirations have risen quickly in response to contact with new occupational roles at the factories.

Table 8

Aspirations for Sons' Education

Education Desired for Sons	Workers (15–49 Years)	Younger Farmers (15–49 Years)	Older Farmers (50 Years or Older)
Primary	15	71	42
Secondary	13	9	8
Professional	59	21	7
Other	8	10	6

Workers vs. younger farmers $\chi^2 = 60.7$, 3 df, $P < 0.001$, lambda = 0.37.
Workers vs. older farmers $\chi^2 = 50.9$, 3 df, $P < 0.001$, lambda = 0.38.
Younger farmers vs. older farmers = N.S.

The factory workers would like their sons to get semiprofessional- or professional-level educations (very difficult to achieve in rural Mexico), whereas the model pattern for young farmers is the wish that their sons complete primary school. This tendency is even more clear when we note the attitudes of the older farmers.

Table 9

Aspirations for Sons' Education
(Controlling for Education of Occupational Groups)

Education Desired for Sons	Workers (15–49 Years)		Younger Farmers (15–49 Years)		Older Farmers (50 Years and Older)	
Educational Level 0–1 Year						
Primary	4	33.4%	26	62.0%	30	56.6%
Secondary	1	8.3%	4	9.5%	6	11.3%
Professional	6	50.0%	6	14.2%	5	9.5%
Other	0	0.0%	4	9.5%	6	11.3%
No answer	1	8.3%	2	4.8%	6	11.3%
Subtotals	12	100.0%	42	100.0%	53	100.0%
Educational Level 2–4 Years						
Primary	8	17.4%	31	58.5%	8	61.5%
Secondary	9	19.6%	3	5.7%	2	15.4%
Professional	23	50.0%	14	26.4%	2	15.4%
Other	5	10.9%	4	7.5%	0	0.0%
No answer	1	2.1%	1	1.9%	1	7.7%
Subtotals	46	100.0%	53	100.0%	13	100.0%
Educational Level 5 or More Years						
Primary	2	5.4%	6	66.7%	1	100.0%
Secondary	3	8.1%	1	11.1%	0	0.0%
Professional	29	78.4%	0	0.0%	0	0.0%
Other	3	8.1%	2	22.2%	0	0.0%
No answer	0	0.0%	0	0.0%	0	0.0%
Subtotals	37	100.0%	9	100.0%	1	100.0%
Totals*	95		104		71	

* Several cases had to be discarded because of technical difficulties.

Table 10

Aspirations for Sons' Occupation

Occupation Desired for Sons	Workers (15–49 Years)	Younger Farmers (15–49 Years)	Older Farmers (50 Years and Older)
Worker	24	56	31
Farmer	0	6	14
Semiprofessional and professional	59	25	8
Other	11	20	11

Workers vs. younger farmers $\chi^2 = 24$, 3 df, $P < 0.001$, lambda $= 0.26$.
Workers vs. older farmers $\chi^2 = 35$, 3 df, $P < 0.001$, lambda $= 0.25$.
Younger farmers vs. older farmers = N.S.

The same pattern appears when we examine the aspirations for sons' occupations. In Table 10 it is especially interesting that most of the people, even the farmers, want their sons to have nonagricultural occupations. Thus *none* of the workers suggests, an agricultural occupation for sons. Instead, their goals are set very high; a large majority would like to see their sons achieve professional, or at least semiprofessional, careers. One of the most frequently mentioned choices is that of "engineer," a natural choice, considering the kinds of high-prestige role models they encounter at the factories.

Table 11

Aspirations for Sons' Occupation
(Controlling the Education of Occupational Groups)

Type of Work Desired for Sons	Workers (15–49 Years)		Younger Farmers (15–49 Years)		Older Farmers (50 Years and Older)	
Educational Level 0–1 Year						
Worker	3	25.0%	21	51.2%	22	40.7%
Farmer	0	0.0%	2	4.9%	12	22.2%
Semiprofessional and professional	5	41.7%	7	17.1%	6	11.1%
Other	2	16.6%	8	19.5%	9	16.7%
No answer	2	16.6%	3	7.3%	5	9.3%
Subtotals	12	99.9%	41	100.0%	54	100.0%
Educational Level 2–4 Years						
Worker	15	32.6%	26	47.3%	6	46.2%
Farmer	0	0.0%	3	5.5%	2	15.4%
Semiprofessional and professional	24	52.2%	13	23.6%	2	15.4%
Other	7	15.2%	11	20.0%	2	15.4%
No answer	0	0.0%	2	3.6%	1	7.6%
Subtotals	46	100.0%	55	100.0%	13	100.0%
Educational Level 5 Years or More						
Worker	5	13.5%	5	55.6%	1	100.0%
Farmer	0	0.0%	1	11.1%	0	0.0%
Semiprofessional and professional	30	81.0%	2	2.2%	0	0.0%
Other	2	5.4%	0	0.0%	0	0.0%
No answer	0	0.0%	1	11.1%	0	0.0%
Subtotals	37	99.9%	9	100.0%	1	100.0%
Totals*	95		105		68	

* A few cases had to be discarded because of technical difficulties.

The younger farmer's aspirations are not quite that high, but they would like their sons to get jobs at the factories. Even older farmers give very few votes to the category "farmer" (see Table 11).

If we follow Whiteford's (1964) classification of occupations in Mexico, these results show that farmers aspire toward lower- and middle-class occupations, whereas the workers exhibit aspirations for middle- and upper-class careers for their children. Each group names goals that are a step up from the father's present occupations.

When we turn to the responses concerning preferred residential locations for sons, we find no significant differences among the three groups. Only a minority of the people wish for their sons to live in or near their present communities. On the other hand, only about 10 per cent of the people suggest that Ciudad Industrial would be a desirable place for their sons to live. The mobility and "modernization" aspirations of both workers and farmers is visible in the rather strong tendency to name Mexico City or some other larger industrial center as a suitable location for their sons' careers (see Table 12). These data suggest that *all* sectors of the village populations are desirous of significant socioeconomic changes, at least for their children.

Table 12

Preferences as to Where Sons Should Live

Location	Workers (15–49 Years)		Younger Farmers (15–49 Years)		Older Farmers (50 Years and Older)	
Same town or a local community	40	41.2%	58	50.9%	30	42.3%
Ciudad Industrial	11	11.3%	11	9.6%	6	8.4%
Federal District or city or state outside region	38	39.3%	29	25.4%	21	29.6%
No answer	8	8.2%	16	14.1%	14	19.7%
Totals	97	100.0%	114	100.0%	71	100.0%

Workers vs. younger farmers = N.S.
Workers vs. older farmers = N.S.
Younger farmers vs. older farmers = N.S.

VARIATIONS IN FAMILY ATTITUDES

Many social scientists have noted that attitudes toward sex roles and intra-family interactions are among the more important indicators of social change in modernizing populations (cf. Kahl, 1968). To examine some aspects of family attitudes we included items from Joseph Kahl's research in Latin

American countries. The items of special interest in our interview include the following:

1. Divorce can be accepted.
2. A wife should obey her husband in everything.
3. Married women should stay at home and not work to earn money even though they need it.
4. Parents should limit the number of children they have.
5. *Children should always obey their parents.
6. A person in difficulties should expect help only from his relatives.

Following Kahl, we defined "yes" answers on items (1) and (4) to be "modern," whereas the other four are considered to be "modern" when a person answers them negatively. Four of these items (questions 6, 3, 1, and 2, in that order) form a Guttman scalogram with an acceptable level of patterning (see Table 13, in which the scalogram has a "coefficient of reproducibility" of 0.91). Because there are so few items in this scalogram,

Table 13

Guttman Scale of Modern–Traditional Values

Scale Step	Item Content	Cumulative Percentage of Respondents	Scale Errors In Step
I	Traditional answers to all questions	100	30
II	Modern answer to (6), A person in difficulties should expect help only from his relatives	65	2
III	Modern answer to (3), Married women should stay at home and not work to earn money even though they need it	45	28
IV	Modern answer to (1), Divorce can be accepted	23	33
V	Modern answer to (2), A wife should obey her husband in everything	6	16

Coefficient of reproducibility = 0.91.
Coefficient of scalability = 0.64.

we felt it best to use this range of variation quite conservatively. In the comparison of workers and farmers on family attitudes we have simply divided the response patterns into "traditional family attitudes" and "modern family attitudes" (Table 14). There is a tendency for the workers to show a higher frequency of "modern family attitudes" than do the farmers, but the amount of this tendency is not impressively large. In general we can say that both workers and farmers have relatively conservative attitudes toward sex roles and other aspects of family life. For example, 94 per cent of the total sample answered "yes" to the item "A wife should obey her husband in everything." Also, only 23 per cent of the population see divorce as possibly acceptable.

Table 14

Modern–Traditional Values Toward Family

	Workers (15–49 Years)	Younger Farmers (15–49 Years)	Older Farmers (50 Years and Older)
Traditional scale scores (I and II)	44	68	41
Modern scale scores (III, IV, and V)	50	45	29
Totals*	94	113	70

Workers vs. younger farmers $\chi^2 = 3.68$, 1 df, $P < 0.05$ (one-tailed).
Workers vs. older farmers $\chi^2 = 2.20$, 1 df, $P < 0.20$, N.S.
Younger farmers vs. older farmers $\chi^2 = 0.47$, 1 df, $P < 0.80$, N.S.
* A few cases had to be discarded because of technical difficulties.

GENERAL WORLD VIEW

Traditional peasant populations are generally thought to exhibit a pattern of attitudes about the world, and their place in it, that limits their possibilities for social change. Everett Rogers' recent work on Modernization Among Peasants (1969) includes the following attitudes under the heading "the subculture of peasantry":

> *mutual distrust in interpersonal relations*
> *perceived limited good*
> *dependence on and hostility toward government authority*
> *familism*
> *lack of innovativeness*
> *limited aspirations*
> *lack of deferred gratification*
> *limited view of the world*
> *low empathy*

(See also Foster, 1967, 1969.)

In our interviews in the villages of the Los Llanos region we included several questions which were intended to reflect some of the ideational characteristics discussed by Rogers. For example, we asked the people to select an answer to the question, "What helps most to succeed in life?"

1. To be born into an important family.
2. To keep the teachings of the older generation.
3. To be very popular with people.
4. To have a good education and special knowledge.

The results of this question, shown in Table 15, show that farmers and workers alike are committed to a belief in the efficacy of getting an education and special training as against the other, more fatalistic or traditionalistic alternatives.

Table 15

Belief in the Efficacy of Personal Effort

Success in Life Comes from	Workers (15–59 Years)		Younger Farmers (15–49 Years)		Older Farmers (50 Years or Older)	
1. Being born into an important family	1	1.0%	4	4.3%	3	4.2%
2. Keeping the teachings	10	10.3%	16	14.0%	12	17.0%
3. Being very popular with people	1	1.0%	1	0.9%	0	0.0%
4. Education and special knowledge	84	86.6%	89	78.1%	53	74.6%
No answer	1	1.0%	4	3.5%	3	4.2%
Totals	97	99.9%	114	100.0%	71	100.0%

Workers vs. younger farmers = N.S.
Workers vs. older farmers = N.S.
Younger farmers vs. older farmers = N.S.

A similar pattern appears in response to the question, "Do you think it is important to make plans for the future?" Table 16 shows that the workers have a tendency to answer "yes" to this question more frequently than the farmers, but the differences are not great. Even among the older farmers 61 per cent respond affirmitively to this future-oriented question.

As a measure of optimism about the future we asked our respondents, "Five years from now do you think your situations will be (1) better, (2) worse, (3) the same?" Table 17 demonstrates that a general optimism about the future is the majority view in Los Llanos. As in each of the preceding items, the workers respond with higher percentages of future-oriented

Table 16

Belief in Plans for the Future

Important to Plan for the Future	Workers (15–49 Years)		Younger Farmers (15–49 Years)		Older Farmers (50 Years and Older)	
Yes	82	84.5%	84	73.7%	43	60.6%
No	13	13.4%	26	22.8%	26	36.6%
No answer	2	2.1%	4	3.5%	2	2.8%
Total	97	100.0%	114	100.0%	71	100.0%

Workers vs. younger farmers = N.S.
Workers vs. older farmers = N.S.
Younger farmers vs. older farmers = N.S.

or "modern" attitudes than do the farmers, but especially when compared with agriculturalists who are their age peers, the differences are completely insignificant, both statistically and practically.

If we were to combine these items about modern versus traditional attitudes into a "modernization index," we would no doubt demonstrate that "workers are different from farmers." We have chosen instead to look at the pattern of responses to several individual items in order to see more clearly the details of people's response patterns. The world view of the factory workers, in light of these interview items, does not seem strikingly different from that of the farmers. Even the older farmers seem to take a fairly optimistic and future-oriented view of life in the Los Llanos region.

Table 17

Optimism

Five Years from Now Your Situation Will Be	Workers (15–49 Years)		Younger Farmers (15–49 Years)		Older Farmers (50 Years or Older)	
Better	80	82.5%	88	77.2%	39	54.9%
Worse	10	10.3%	13	11.4%	20	28.2%
The same	5	5.1%	9	7.9%	9	12.7%
No answer	2	2.1%	4	3.5%	3	4.2%
Totals	97	100.0%	114	100.0%	71	100.0%

Workers vs. younger farmers = N.S.
Workers vs. older farmers = N.S.
Younger farmers vs. older farmers = N.S.

All these materials suggest that the experience of working in the factories and having more money for purchase of luxury goods has an impact on the people, but it has not led to a striking cleavage between "moderns" and "traditionals." It would seem that the experience of working in the factories does not automatically lead people to become sharply different from the agricultural peasants, if both remain in their traditional villages. An important reason for this state of affairs in the Los Llanos region is that changes in attitudes, world view, and other aspects of culture are apparently affecting all sectors of the population. This is quite a different situation, then, from those many places in the world where the industrializing urban centers are the scenes of modernization, while the agricultural villages remain rather isolated from most of the transformations taking place in the people's life styles and ways of thought.

SOCIAL CHANGES IN THE LOS LLANOS VILLAGES AND TOWNS

One of the most interesting aspects of the present situation in the Los Llanos region is the way in which the entire area is changing in response to the presence of Ciudad Industrial. In order to understand the impact of this massive technological innovation, we need to examine regional and community processes as well as the behavior and attitudes of individuals.

Ciudad Industrial has now established itself as a major influence in the region, and more and more communities are oriented to primary contact with the industrial center. Whereas in 1958 the industrial city appeared to be in some ways a foreign body in the organic unity of the region (Young and Young, 1960), by 1966 the structure of intercommunity relationships had been rearranged to accommodate the obviously significant impacts of the new city. The communities of the region have become increasingly specialized in the past few years, and a number of them have made significant institutional changes in response to the influences of the new agents and models of modernization in their midst (see Table 18).

One important element of change in the region is the series of "assists" that Ciudad Industrial has granted to surrounding communities, some of which originated in the agreements reached concerning the lands given over to the new city. The town of Malapan, for example, obtained its electricity and an artesian-well system in accordance with the agreements reached in the original negotiations. The nearby town of Texlapan received a new school and electricity in exchange for the lands that it gave up to the new city. These agreements, which led to some modernization of the villages, were only a beginning. The villages and towns began to petition the city for aid in other improvements as well. Malapan was granted a paved road connecting it with Ciudad Industrial, two thirds of which was paid for by the Carros factory. In addition, the telephone exchange in the industrial city was linked to Malapan, thus improving their contacts with the outside world.

Texlapan was loaned materials for road reconditioning; Santa Isabel was connected by road to Ciudad Industrial; and Benito Juarez received aid in the construction of a church, better streets, and expansion of the local school system (cf. Fishel, 1964). In other programs the administrative head of the industrial city attempted to establish adult education classes and other development projects in the surrounding communities. In all, twelve communities of the region have received some kind of direct aid from the administration and factories in Ciudad Industrial.

In addition to aid given by the factories and the administration of the new city, there has been a considerable influence from the activities of the factory workers as they have taken a stronger hand in the political–social activities of their home communities. In many cases the new factory workers are the sons of farmers with no great influence in community affairs. As these "new men" of the region find themselves with additional financial means, but with a level of social prestige that is not commensurate with their present incomes (cf. Simon, 1968), they have in part spent their money to improve the status-giving aspects of their homes, but they have also taken an active interest in community affairs, adding their newly acquired technological expertise to town water projects, electrical systems, and other community improvements (Mundale, n.d.; Simon, n.d.).

It may be argued that one of the effects of the new occupational roles in Ciudad Industrial is to promote the translation of new money and ideas into local prestige—in the traditional communities—through new political and social participation, backed up by technicians and other help from the factories. In some instances the engineers from the city have come into places like Benito Juarez to advise and assist in technical matters of water lines, electrical systems, and construction of public buildings.

These developments are of far-reaching importance, for the feedback of technical expertise and pressures for modernization are much less evident in those situations where the factory workers are in the cities, far from their native agricultural hinterlands.

The factory workers, as we noted earlier, have rather high—perhaps unreasonably high—aspirations for their sons' levels of education. As growingly influential members of the local communities, they constitute a force that is increasingly pressing for additions to the school facilities. Most of the communities of the area have added significantly to their school facilities in recent years. It is certain that the very low levels of education reflected in Table 3 have already been significantly altered in the present generation, and that the years to come will see greatly increased pressures put on the educational system of the region.

There are other ways in which the workers have "spread the wealth" to their home communities. In seeking to better their living standards, many of the factory workers have been building new homes. In the spring of 1969 there were forty-three new houses under construction in Benito Juarez—most of them for factory worker families. The work on the houses is done mainly with local labor, the masons and carpenters who are part of the "other" category in our survey sample of the area. Previously these artisans have eked out a modest living standard by combining their trades work with family agriculture. Now there are some increased opportunities to earn cash—part of the "spin-off" from the factory payrolls. Some of the non-factory workers also find employment from their wage-earning neighbors and relatives in the form of hired agricultural activities on the lands that the workers do not have time to cultivate themselves.

The communities of the Los Llanos region have become increasingly specialized as the entire network has adjusted itself to the presence of the factory city. Some of this adjustment seems to be directly caused by the policies in the administration of the new industrial center. The work-seeking populations of the region cannot move into the industrial center to swell the local population while they search for jobs, because housing in Ciudad Industrial is tightly restricted. It is much easier for the people to remain in their home communities, even *after* they get jobs in the factories.

The restrictive commercial policies of the city have worked to the benefit of the other larger towns, especially Xalpan, with its already well-developed commercial houses. These businesses have continued to increase in scope and affluence in response to the new money now flowing in the regional economy. On the other hand, commercial elaboration has continued in the other towns as well; the noncommercial orientation of Ciudad Industrial pushes local purchasing power into other communities in addition to Xalpan.

Residential development has naturally spread to the towns nearest Ciudad Industrial—especially Atlaquilpan, Estación, and Benito Juarez. These seem in part to be developing into "bedroom suburbs" of the industrial city. Atlaquilpan, in addition, is a town with a rich tradition of fiestas and other public celebrations. Many of the people of the area report that fiestas in that town are a regular part of their annual activities.

During the summer of 1967 we asked panels of key informants in each of the communities to tell us "where the people of this town go for . . ." medical services, sports events, sales of produce, weekly markets, and a number of other activities. The data from these key informant interviews give quantified support for the general impression our field workers have gathered concerning the "functional specialization" of the communities of the region. These data show that the entire area is becoming integrated into a regional system in which the people of the different communities depend on particular towns for a complex array of services and activities. Table 18 gives a breakdown of the major specializations among the communities.

From the key informants' descriptions we find that the industrial city is a notable center of sports activity and medical services, in addition to its chief characteristic as employment center of the area. Fairly extensive medical

Table 18

Community Specialization

Selling of crops	Xalpan
Commercial activity	Xalpan, Calapan
Fiestas	Atlaquilpan, Xalpan, Calapan
Medical aid	Ciudad Industrial, Xalpan, Calapan
Schools	Ciudad Industrial, Xalpan
Sports	Ciudad Industrial, Xalpan
Political	Xalpan, Atlaquilpan
Industrial jobs	Ciudad Industrial, Calapan, Xalpan
Weekly markets	Xalpan, Ciudad Industrial
Social diversions (cantinas, bars, coffee shops, houses of prostitution)	Xalpan, Calapan
Residential areas (especially for workers)	Benito Juarez, Estación, Atlaquilpan

services are, to be sure, available in Xalpan and Calapan, especially convenient for the people down at the southern end of the valley system. Because the attractions of Ciudad Industrial do not include much in the way of night life, social diversion is to be found particularly in Xalpan, which even has a modest house of prostitution to serve the needs of the regional populace.

The community which is most important for both sacred and secular fiestas in the valley of Los Llanos is Atlaquilpan. It is in Atlaquilpan that the events of the Mexican Revolution are re-enacted each year and where major religious holidays are celebrated with considerable vigor. Not many sleep on the night of the fiesta of the Virgin of Guadalupe (December 12) with the many loud aerial bombs that rock the area every few minutes throughout the night. Atlaquilpan is also important as a political administrative center for the communities in the region. Its importance has increased in recent years because it has political jurisdiction over Ciudad Industrial, so that in terms of population the *municipio* of Atlaquilpan is the largest in the region, even though Xalpan is the district political center.

To a certain extent specialization of functions among individual communities existed before the coming of the industrial city. However, our data indicate that this differentiation of functions has increased in the past decade—there is now more money and a wider array of interests in terms of which diversity is structured.

LOS LLANOS: A DISPERSED CITY

The growing economic and social differentiation within the Los Llanos region, together with the intensification of interdependences, suggests that it may be useful to conceptualize the entire region as quite different from the usual rural scene. We suggest that in many respects the region can now be considered as a very special social system that might be labeled a "dispersed city."

Compared to most other rural regions of Mexico, the differentiation of functions, as outlined above, is striking. It is indeed curious to encounter a situation where the "city" of 14,000 people has manifestly less commercial, professional, and entertainment activity than the other communities of the region, of which the largest is only about half the size of the industrial center. Ciudad Industrial is, in its style of organization, a kind of "industrial park," dependent on the rest of the region for housing, commercial activity, enter- tainment, and other services. On the other hand, the other communities of

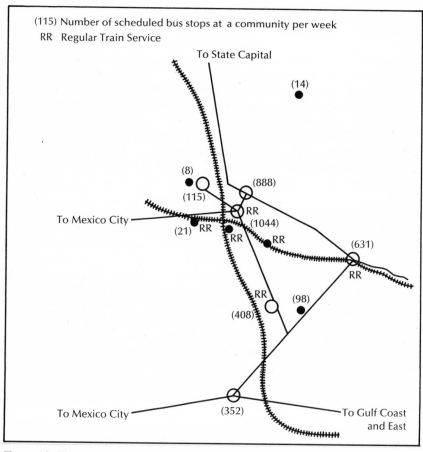

FIGURE 2. Transportation in the Los Llanos region.

the region are now highly dependent on the cash input of the factory complex. Without this source of money in the region, many stores and other enterprises would close their doors.

One feature of the valley system that is essential to the "dispersed city" character of Los Llanos is the transportation system. There are a large number of private automobiles in the area, purchased on very favorable terms by the workers in the Dina factory. But the network of bus transportation truly approaches metropolitan proportions in its number of routes and frequency of operation. There surely can be few towns of comparable size to Xalpan in rural Mexico that are served by 1,044 scheduled buses per week. In fact, this figure—which amounts to approximately 150 buses per day—is probably higher than the comparable figures for many districts in Mexico City itself. Towns the size of Benito Juarez in other parts of Mexico generally have excellent bus services, but fifteen or twenty buses per day usually provide quite adequate service to all points from a typical rural *cabacera*. Benito Juarez (see Figure 2) has 408 scheduled bus stops per week, or an average of fifty-eight buses per day!

The network of bus services in the Los Llanos region is so thick in part because of the circular structure of the traffic pattern. As Figure 2 demonstrates, the route from Atlaquilpan to Ciudad Industrial to Benito Juarez to Xalpan to Atlaquilpan is a circle, which incidentally touches the main feeder points of the valley system. Only the people out toward San Manuel (see Figure 1) are cut off from very frequent bus service, because the dirt road into that arm of the valley is in very poor condition and is nearly impassable in the rainy season.

The railroad network adds to the density of transportation within this "rural metropolis." People from places such as Santa Isabel and Estación often go by train the few kilometers across the valley to Xalpan, particularly to the Sunday market day. This railroad network is, of course, a legacy from the old *pulque* era and provided one of the sound economic reasons for locating the industrial city in Los Llanos rather than in any one of several alternative locations.

SUMMARY AND CONCLUSIONS

The technological innovation of a factory complex and new city in a rural hinterland provides a natural experimental situation in which it is possible to separate the social and cultural effects of factory work from the complex of other change-inducing features of urbanization and migration. In the region of Los Llanos it is possible to compare factory workers with their farmer kinsmen and neighbors, "holding constant" the effects of place of residence.

In this experimental situation it appears that the usually expected gulf between the traditional ways of life of farmers and the new aspirations and activities of the wage earners has not occurred—at least not nearly as dramatically as has been the case in some other areas. There have been changes in the life styles and cultural values of both workers and farmers in the region. This "spreading of the wealth" and cultural influence seem to result from the nature of Ciudad Industrial as a rather controlled and special environment. The administrators in Ciudad Industrial may have been mainly concerned with developing a particular kind of industrial environment in the city itself, but the effect has been to diffuse the workers and their influences—as well as some of their payrolls—into other parts of the valley system. The various towns and villages of the valley thus all partake to some degree of the economic inputs of the factory complex, rather than simply giving up portions of their populations through outmigration. And the workers, seeking to enhance their well-being and prestige in their home towns, feed back new knowledge and new money into the places that are becoming the several differentiated segments of a semimetropolitan complex. At least for the time being this is one urban area that has neither traffic problems nor air pollution.

3

There have been many irrigation and power projects on the world's great rivers ; and these have had extensive effects on the peoples who live along those rivers. In this chapter Professors Scudder and Colson take an in-depth look at the effects on the Gwembe Tonga of the Kariba Dam Project. The problems confronting the Gwembe were enormous. They were resettled, taught new skills, given an entirely new subsistence base on several different occasions. In spite of the difficulties, the Gwembe actively embraced each new experiment in cash production. And in each case we see the crucial roles played by native entrepreneurs and innovators. The effect of the innovative personality in culture change has never been generally assessed. In this chapter, however, as in those by Doughty and Henderson, we get a rare and intimate glimpse into just how important a factor it is.

THE KARIBA DAM PROJECT:

Resettlement and Local Initiative

Thayer Scudder and Elizabeth F. Colson[1]

Thayer Scudder is Professor of Anthropology, Division of Humanities and Social Sciences, California Institute of Technology. He received his Ph.D. in Anthropology from Harvard University and did postdoctoral study at the London School of Economics. Since 1966 Dr. Scudder has been a member of the National Academy of Science's Committee on the Development of African Water Resources; he has been doing research and consultation on that subject in Africa for over fifteen years.

Elizabeth F. Colson is Professor of Anthropology at the University of California, Berkeley, and Fellow, Center for Advanced Study in the Behavioral Sciences. She received her Ph.D. from Radcliffe College and was a Research Officer, then Director of the Rhodes–Livingstone Institute. She has been involved in long-time field research among the Plateau and Gwembe Tonga.

INTRODUCTION

In March, 1955, the government of the Federation of the Rhodesias and Nyasaland announced that it was preparing to accept bids for the construction of a major hydroelectric dam at Kariba Gorge on the Zambezi River. A little over three years later, in December, 1958, the dam was completed and the world's largest artificial reservoir began to form behind its wall, rising

[1] This article is based on field work carried out in Gwembe District by Scudder in 1956–1957, 1962–1963, 1967, and 1970; and by Colson in 1949, 1956–1957, 1960, 1962–1963, 1965, and 1968. All work through 1962–1963 was done under the auspices of the Rhodes-Livingstone Institute (now the Institute for Social Research in the University of Zambia),

Kariba Dam. (*Photo by Thayer Scudder.*)

over the Zambezi river plain and the lower hills of Gwembe Valley (the name given to this portion of the Middle Zambezi Valley). In July, 1963, Lake Kariba filled its basin, an area of some 2,000 square miles. It covered all of Gwembe Valley south of Kariba Gorge, which lay below the 1,600-foot elevation.

This region had been occupied by some 57,000 Gwembe Tonga, all of whom had to be resettled above the shoreline of the lake or in the country below Kariba Dam. They were moved from old established neighborhoods, usually centered on deposits of alluvial soils laid down close to the Zambezi. These soils had been under cultivation for generations. Those subject to annual flooding were cropped twice a year, year in and year out. Those lands above the usual flood line were subject to periodic bush fallow and were becoming increasingly marginal as population pressure led to a reduction

which also gave substantial assistance during the 1965 and 1967 visits of Colson and Scudder. Colson's 1965 visit was financed by a grant from the joint committee on Africa of the Social Science Research Council and the American Council of Learned Societies; her 1968 visit was made while in Zambia under other auspices. Scudder's 1967 and 1970 visits were largely financed by the California Institute of Technology, and by FAO, for whom he served as a consultant on the Kafue and Kariba fisheries. Assistance in processing data has been given by the University of California, Berkeley, and the California Institute of Technology, Pasadena. Special thanks are due Mrs. Nancy Pine and Miss Leanne Hinton. The authors also wish to thank Professor Ray F. Smith and Mrs. Smith for their comments on the section dealing with cotton cultivation.

41

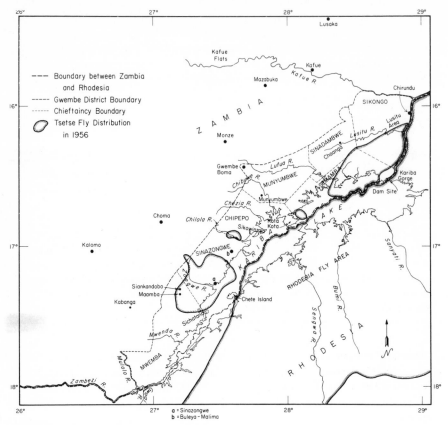

FIGURE 1. Gwembe district and the Kariba Lake basin. (*Data courtesy of W. S. Steel.*)

of the fallow period. In the early 1950's river villagers had begun to clear new gardens in bush areas several miles inland from the Zambezi, and these were providing a temporary relief to a land-hungry people. Beyond the Zambezi margin there was only a scattered population concentrated on the small alluvial deposits associated with the upper courses of the tributary rivers. For the most part these people depended upon shifting cultivation. The absence of reliable water supplies through the dry season left much of the Gwembe uninhabitable.

The people of the Gwembe were cut off from the rest of Central Africa by rough escarpments which were penetrated by roads only at the beginning of the 1950's. They had much freedom from official supervision despite the fact that they first came under European administrators in the 1890's. The dense population of the Zambezi River margin favored the growth of a vigorous rural social life, and difficulties of transport meant that people had to rely upon themselves for both daily necessities and those things which gave color to their lives. They had, for example, clothing fashions of their own, and distinctive drum and flute orchestras which represented neighborhood communities as corporate organizations. On the other hand, it was difficult to generate any cash income in the Gwembe, because they could export little, except for a limited amount of tobacco. To earn cash, men had to leave the Gwembe. Officials for Gwembe District, that portion of the area which fell within what was then Northern Rhodesia, estimated that at any one time 41.5 per cent of the able-bodied men between the ages of 18 and 62 were away at work. Most of them went to work in the towns of what was then Southern Rhodesia, where their lack of education confined them to the lowest-paid jobs available to unskilled labor. The majority of them continued to alternate between periods spent as labor migrants and periods in the village where they merged easily back into village life. While they were gone, their wives cultivated the fields and provided for the family subsistence. Men went to work to earn money for tax, for clothes and blankets, and for a few other items. They also went to relieve the dwindling family food supplies in years when the crop failed and they foresaw hunger.

Gwembe was a recurrent hunger area. Low rainfalls, erratic floods, and insect pests were among the factors which in any year might bring hunger to some neighborhoods, or at times, to all neighborhoods (Scudder, 1962:215–47). In the southwestern portion of Gwembe, population had grown beyond the ability of the region to supply its food requirements under existing agricultural techniques, and here there was apt to be an annual shortage. This was met by a lowering of standards of living, with people accepting the fact of hunger, and by an increase in long-term migration which removed many men from dependence upon local resources. Here, too, men had begun to take their wives with them to the towns, releasing their fields to other kin or allowing the fields to be placed in fallow.

Until the mid-1940's Gwembe emigrants to the plateau west of the valley had also reduced the strain on local resources. They had gone to areas close enough to the railway line so that cash cropping was feasible. They had also gone to areas free from tsetse fly where plows had become standard agricultural equipment by the 1940's.

Much of the Gwembe Valley remained a tsetse area into the 1950's (Figure 1). The dense population in the southwestern portion of the valley had eliminated a habitat favorable to the spread of the tsetse fly, and here cattle herds were large and supplemented the flocks of sheep and herds of goats which were the principal capital investment of other portions of Gwembe. Some men owned plows, but the pressure on land made it difficult for them to use the plow to open up additional acreage. In the central portion of the Gwembe, the tsetse fly began to recede in the late 1940's at a time when new drugs against trypanosomiasis also gave injected cattle a better chance to survive contact with infected areas. In Gwembe District, the first injections of cattle appear to have been carried out in 1948 (Scudder, 1962:165–72).

Cattle then began to spread into neighborhoods in the Central Gwembe. At the time the decision to build the dam was made, the majority of Central Gwembe men and women still owned no cattle. Cultivation was usually hoe cultivation, and those who attempted to plow with oxen or to handle cattle in any fashion did so awkwardly and with considerable trepidation. In neighborhood after neighborhood they were also attempting to spell out the various responsibilities of cattle owners and cultivators in the protection of crops from free-ranging cattle. Many Gwembe men and women were prepared to regard the animals as an unmitigated nuisance.

Economic organization was embryonic. Gwembe Tonga value their independence highly, and each man is ambitious to have control over his own activities and to direct a work team composed of his wives and children. Work was carried out either individually or by the immediate family group working under the direction of husband and father. If more hands were needed, then they were recruited through a work party rewarded with beer or a small feast. Work parties were used for clearing land, weeding, building purposes, and the making of dugout canoes. Communal hunting or fishing parties were very much spur-of-the-moment affairs, joined by anyone who liked, and with little visible sign of leadership. A little direct trade took place, principally in the exchange of grain for stock, but most goods were exchanged and other services obtained as part of the reciprocal obligations of the kinship system, the clan system, and the system of clan joking relationships. The largest exchanges of property were in the form of bridewealth transaction, including the payment of elopement damages. This meant that much of the savings in wages of labor migrants eventually found its way into the hands of the elders who had marriageable daughters. They also held the bulk of the alluvial soils and were the ones most likely to have an income from tobacco sales.

One other institution provided for assistance and for economic transactions. This was bond friendship (*bulongwe*), a contractual arrangement entered into usually by two men who had no other basis of interaction and who could see some mutual benefit in their association. The most important bond friendships were probably those created between Gwembe men and certain traders who visited Gwembe in search of tobacco. They received tobacco on consignment from their bond friends and the following year returned to complete the transaction with a substantial gift in the form of blankets and cloth and hoes, the necessities of Gwembe life. If this was satisfactory, they received a new consignment of tobacco (Colson, 1962). Other bond friendships were made with men living on the western plateau to provide a refuge and a source of food in hunger years. Trading stores were few in number, given the lack of transport and the absence of roads. Cash was therefore seen as useful principally for the payment of taxes and fines and had little relevance to daily life. Men liked to contrast Gwembe with the towns as the place where one could live without money.

They also liked to contrast Gwembe with the towns as the place where a man was free from most authority. They had not developed a centralized organization of their own or delegated controls to any set of offices. Although an administrative hierarchy composed of headmen, chiefs, and council had been imposed upon them from above and they were also subject to the rule of a district commissioner with his district messengers and other assistants (at least in Gwembe District), they evaded these as much as possible and resented attempts to regulate their lives. In 1953, men in Gwembe District stoned the district officials who were attempting to force a cassava-growing scheme upon them as a measure against famine.

THE KARIBA RESETTLEMENT

The decision to build Kariba Dam was taken by a government unpopular among the majority of Africans, who regarded it as representative of the European settlers. Prior to 1953 the territories of Northern Rhodesia and Nyasaland which were administered under the British Colonial Office could be seen as developing eventually toward independent African nations, and over-all Colonial Office policy called for the encouragement of African participation in government and in general social advancement. Southern Rhodesia, the third member of the Federation, had been settler-dominated from the beginning of its existence as a political unit and had been given a special status in 1923. It had never been treated as a colony or placed under the Colonial Office. The Federation was brought about largely at the insistence of Southern Rhodesian settlers with the assistance of some of the settlers in Northern Rhodesia. The Federation government saw Kariba Dam as a symbol of the emergence of a new nation which was to dominate the Central African scene. The dam, built on the Zambezi River, which here formed the boundary between Northern and Southern Rhodesia, would closely link the economics of the two territories. It was the first, and also the last, major economic undertaking of the Federation. The dispossession of the Gwembe Tonga which resulted from the construction of the dam also helped lead to the downfall of the Federation. African public opinion was confirmed in its belief that the Federation was for the benefit of the Europeans, who would not hesitate to take whatever the Africans had if they could profit from so doing. Increasing political action eventually led to the break-up of the Federation in 1963 and the emergence of three new countries: Zambia (Northern Rhodesia), Rhodesia (Southern Rhodesia), and Malawi (Nyasaland). We will write of Zambia and Rhodesia, although for a portion of the period covered by this article the terms are anachronisms.

Gwembe Tonga lived on either side of the Zambezi River and both Rhodesia and Zambia were involved in the resettlement problem. Each country was responsible for relocating its own people. Because we had little time to work in Rhodesia and know the situation largely from work within

Zambia, we are confining ourselves to a discussion of its impact upon the people who lived within Gwembe District in the Southern Province of Zambia. Population estimates for 1958 show 55,106 people living in the district. The final estimate of the total number resettled as a result of Kariba is 34,000, that is, over 60 per cent of the total population.[2] Six thousand were resettled in the Lusitu area of Sikongo Chieftaincy below Kariba Dam; 1,600 were sent to Choma District on the plateau; the rest were moved into unoccupied bush country above the projected lakeshore. The resettlement was carried out over the strong opposition of the people, who argued that talk of a lake was a blind behind which the Europeans planned to steal their land. Many refused to move. In September, 1958, a confrontation between a gathering of men in Chipepo Chieftaincy and the mobile police who had been brought down to quell the resistance led to a charge and the opening of fire by the police. Official records show eight men killed and some thirty-two others wounded (Government Report, 1958). This broke the open massive resistance.

People moved to the resettlement areas designated for them and began the work of re-establishing themselves. This was a major enterprise, as it meant the rebuilding of 199 villages and the rehousing of 34,000 people. It also meant the clearing of fields, usually in areas covered with timber. A substantial portion of the land available for resettlement was in mopane (*Colophospermum mopane*) woodlands. Gwembe men are good axe men, but mopane is a hard wood which markedly increased the labor of clearance.

In planning for resettlement the government decided that the major work would have to be done by the Gwembe people themselves. They would be responsible for the rebuilding of their homesteads using local materials, and for the clearing of new fields. Government, on the other hand, would build roads to provide access to the new areas, dig wells or otherwise provide water resources, rebuild schools and dispensaries, and undertake to control game and to clear resettlement areas of tsetse fly so that people could bring in their stock. It would provide lorries to move property and those persons who had to travel any distance. It would provide for future development by increasing expenditures for agricultural experimentation and veterinary services and by providing for the development of a commerical fisheries. For this last it would build various lakeshore installations, create training programs for potential fishermen, and provide a loan fund which fishermen could use for outfitting themselves with nets and boats. It also agreed to limit commercial fishing on the Zambian side of the lake initially to Gwembe residents and to allow the Gwembe Local Government the right to license and so receive fees from new commercial development on the lakeshore. Finally, direct compensation was to be paid to the Gwembe in the form of a payment of £200,000 to the Gwembe Local Government to be used for general

---

[2] Estimates of total population and population resettled were supplied by the District Commissioner, Gwembe.

development. In addition those people who were resettled were to be compensated in the form of individual payments. The cost of this program was to be borne by the Federal Power Board, which paid to the Zambian government:

£   913,000—direct resettlement expenses
    200,000—"tribal" compensation
    372,000—individual compensation
1,115,000—fund for Gwembe rehabilitation
              (Colson, 1960:218–22)

The individual compensation ultimately took the form of three payments. The first was assessed on the huts which had to be abandoned and usually amounted to £10 per hut. The second and third payments of £5 and £2 10s. per person were sometimes referred to as compensation for loss of production because of the move, but in fact were made on a per capita basis for every man, woman, and child who appeared on the village counts carried out by district officers shortly before the move. The Gwembe villagers spoke of them as payments for "the body" and regarded them as per capita payments to individuals. This generated a good deal of discussion and much hostility as to who had rights over the money. Men usually claimed the total allocated to all members of households dependent upon them. The first distributions were made in late 1958; the last appear to have been made in 1960. A young man with a wife and baby might receive as little as £27 10s. Polygamists with a number of wives, numerous dependents, and a homestead with a number of huts usually received something in the neighborhood of £100 if they lived in those sections of Gwembe where storage of grain was made in large clay bins. These were *not* counted as structures for purposes of compensation, although they might well represent a greater investment of labor than the family dwelling hut and were on occasion used as additional sleeping quarters. In the southwestern end of the district, in Mwemba Chieftaincy, people built both regular dwelling huts and huts on raised platforms (*igazi*), which were used both as granaries and as sleeping quarters. These *were* counted as huts, doubling the hut compensation received by most Mwemba families. In this chieftaincy some payments received by family heads rose as high as £170.

All told, these years saw a massive input of liquid capital into Gwembe District, especially into villages chosen for resettlement. There was also much local wage work. This was associated with bush clearance as contractors worked to clear 126,000 acres of projected fishing grounds, and with work carried out by government in building roads, in rebuilding schools and other public structures, and in various other tasks associated with the attempt to make the diminished area viable for its people. The total input probably did not pay people for what they lost in the way of permanent assets. Compensation was not paid for granaries, stock pens, field shelters, drying platforms, or all the other structures essential to a farming community. They suffered serious losses in stock. We calculate from district livestock estimates for the period just before and just after resettlement that something like £48,000 in cattle, sheep, and goats were lost either in accidents in transit or through conditions associated with the new area. Such conditions included an increased number of predators, poisonous plants, lack of suitable browse, water shortages, epidemics, and the continued presence of tsetse in some regions. Villagers' comments on their loss in chickens suggested that the loss here was substantial, but we cannot estimate it in monetary terms, as little information exists on the size of poultry flocks. There was also the loss of alluvial soils, which meant that many tobacco growers lost their cash crop. Finally, there was a great deal of breakage of household equipment in transit to the new regions.

Compensation payments were also offset by a loss in earnings from labor migration, because men who normally would have gone out to work stayed in Gwembe to rebuild homesteads and clear new land. We cannot estimate the loss incurred in this fashion, but the migration rate for the district is estimated to have dropped from 41.5 to 34 per cent for the years in question. Because those villages which were not being resettled probably maintained their normal rate, or may even have increased the outflow of workers because of crop failures in 1957 and 1958, the loss in wages to resettled villages may have been even greater than the percentage drop indicates.

Nevertheless, for the time being there was a good deal of money introduced into the Gwembe economy. Some of it was immediately seized by the Gwembe Local Authority for fines on those who had resisted the move or as arrears in taxation. Much of the money also had to be spent simply for maintenance in the years before enough land could be cleared so that families could once more grow their own food (see Scudder, 1966:101). Their need moreover was aggravated by the fact that the district had two bad harvests just prior to the move, and food had to be imported in 1957, 1958, 1959, and 1960. The District Commissioner reported that £76,925 5s. was received for maize distributed through government depots during the years associated with the move. Much of this came from Kariba compensation payments, in the form of bags of grain being credited against the payments due to the family unit of the man who purchased food. Private traders also imported and sold grain either by the bag or in small quantities appropriate to the resources of the people. We have no figures on their sales. Gwembe informants, when asked about the use of Kariba money, were firm in their assurances that most of them had had to spend the greater portion of what was due to them on the food which allowed them to survive until fields came into production in 1960. There is also good evidence that much money was spent on new clothing and blankets, as the craving for clothes and warmth could for once be satisfied. It was standard practice for the man who received compensation money to allot £1 to each woman and child above the toddler stage to be used for the purchase of clothing or such other luxuries as they desired.

The rest the men kept in their own hands for the purchase of food, equipment, stock, and other major items. They also used the money for bridewealth payments, and some was saved against future need.

Our quantitative data on the use of compensation money are poor because people were reluctant to admit that they had profited in any fashion from relocation. They therefore usually insisted that compensation money had been used only for food and denied that they had had a surplus for other items beyond a minimum of clothing. In fact, however, much of the money was used for re-establishing the people on the land and in equipping them for an expansion of farming activities.

In the emergency of a forced move, people did not experiment with new social forms. They used the old work organizations they had developed prior to the move. It was a period when they required a massive input of labor and they knew only one way to mobilize the workers required for clearing and homestead building. Much of the grain bought with Kariba money went for food, but a good deal of it was made into beer used to reward workers mobilized either from the neighborhood or from previous inhabitants of nearby areas. These workers were usually short of grain during the crucial years because of the failures of the rain harvest and were glad to trade their work for the chance to share in the provisions made possible by compensation. Men were also able to use either money or the grain it bought to create bond friendships with old residents. In some instances this gave them access to particularly desirable land. One therefore has the paradox that although the resettlement years were a time of hunger, they were also a time of a great deal of beer and trade in grain.

A few men had begun to open tiny fields in 1957, a year before the final move was forced upon them. The majority did not begin to clear land until they had been forced into the resettlement areas. This left them little time before the beginning of the rains of 1958 brought a halt to clearance. They also proceeded with the caution typical of the subsistence cultivator who knows he has no margin of capital or energy to risk in experimentation. The first fields opened on new soils, whose potential was doubtful, were therefore only tiny plots, and even where men could have planted large fields in areas opened by the bush clearance operation which were still unflooded, they were unwilling to waste seed until the soil was proved. Most men waited until their own or their neighbors' experiments gave them some assurance before they began clearing and planting on any large scale. Some, especially in Lusitu, also hung back for political reasons, arguing that if they refused to clear and plant the government would ultimately have to give way and permit them to return to their old homes of whose flooding they remained doubtful.

It was in the cold season of 1959 that the first large clearance began, when the lake flooding had covered the former fields of the most populous villages and the first experimental plots had shown the value of the new soils. That year there was still hunger. In 1960 most people planted enough land that with good rains they had a sufficient harvest. Clearing continued through 1961.

Thereafter it dropped off as men extended old fields or as individuals pioneered new areas to replace fields whose declining yields were already signaling soil exhaustion after four years of continuous cultivation.

In the same years, people rehoused themselves and built new field shelters, granaries, and shelters for stock, using the same work party organization as in the clearing of fields. The majority of men had spent some time in the resettlement areas in 1957, beginning the building of homesteads; but the failure of the government to make water supplies available to them brought building operations to a halt late in the dry season and disgusted the majority with the project. Little therefore was done in the normal building period during the dry season of 1958. The majority of people arrived in their new areas to find themselves faced with the task of housing themselves and their stock in the month or so before the rains would set in, at a time when thatching grass had already been burned off, and with little time to cut the poles required for huts. They settled for building one or two huts for each homestead, where they huddled together until the next dry season, when building could once more begin. Stock pens also had to be built at once because of the large number of hyenas and other predators. The major building program took place in 1959, and by the end of that dry season most married women were provided with their own huts. Granaries were constructed in 1960, as only then was there sufficient grain to require a major invest-

Oxen and scotch cart being used to bring in the sorghum harvest from the fields. It will be stored in the newly made village granary. (*Photo by Thayer Scudder.*)

ment in its storage. By the end of 1960, homesteads were complete and differed little from those of the earlier era save that the abundance of timber made it possible for men to build on a larger scale than in the old areas where building materials had become scarce. Thereafter building could again continue at a normal pace as homesteads were shifted or old buildings had to be replaced.

Kariba compensation money therefore, though it may not have offset capital losses, played a major role in re-establishing the population on the land and in provisioning it through the first hard years after the move. Clearing and rebuilding took place with a minimum of government involvement. After this surplus funds went into a variety of other ventures, although probably the immediate impact upon the economy is seen in the inflation of bridewealths which was a marked feature of the period. The average bridewealth rose from £30 to £42.[3] In part this may be accounted for by the rise in wages also occurring during this period, but the major inflationary influence was the compensation money. The rise is not unexpected. A large increase in fluid resources is almost certainly going to be diverted first into customary channels and so cause inflation. Only secondarily does it go to finance an expansion of new wants.

The next most common use of funds after bridewealth appears to have been the purchase of stock, which again is a customary form of investment. In this case, however, the major purchase appears to have been of cattle rather than small stock. Men bought cattle not only as a form of savings but also as plow animals and as a source of plow animals. They also bought plows. Initially the men who were equipped with plows were able to open up larger fields than their fellows, and so benefited from considerable grain surpluses. In one neighborhood where only 18 per cent of the men over twenty had owned plows in 1956, some 28 per cent owned plows in 1962. In another neighborhood which had been in closer proximity to the tsetse belt in 1956, only 6 per cent of the men had owned plows. In 1962, 28.5 per cent owned plows. In one of these neighborhoods three men had also invested in ox carts, the first in their neighborhood.

Livestock figures and figures on major agricultural equipment for the whole of Gwembe District show the same trends, although the effect upon resettled villages is masked by the inclusion of chieftaincies in upland valleys unaffected by the move. These chieftaincies had been outside the 1956 tsetse belt and had early obtained sizable cattle herds. They had also introduced plowing well in advance of the rest of Gwembe, before any serious attempt was made by government to encourage agricultural change. The stocking of the resettlement areas, especially those settled by people from former tsetse areas, drew upon the upland chieftaincies and upon the herds of the Plateau

[3] In computing averages, payments (including stock) were first expressed in money terms. Averages were calculated for those payments made in respect of marriages entered into for the five years before resettlement and the five years after resettlement. Information comes from census data we collected in three central Gwembe neighborhoods.

Before the Kariba Dam, most villagers were sufficiently unfamiliar with cattle and plowing that up to four people might be involved. By 1963, villagers could take care of all operations alone. In this photo the plow is being turned to start a new furrow. Note the control with one arm and whip in the right hand. (*Photo by Thayer Scudder.*)

Tonga of Mazabuka and Choma Districts. Gwembe men had, in many instances, invested in cattle in earlier years but had left the animals with kinsmen or bond friends on the plateau. Those who acquired cattle through inheritance or the marriage of kinswomen in upland chieftaincies or plateau neighborhoods also left the stock on the plateau out of the tsetse area. Now that it was considered safer to bring the cattle into Gwembe they began to draw upon these reserves. Nevertheless a good deal of the increase in Gwembe herds in the years associated with resettlement is due to new purchases based on the cash provided by the Kariba payments. Later it reflects the profits made from commercial fishing in the lake.

One other frequent purchase had a direct bearing on the changing economy of Gwembe. This was the purchase of large cast-iron pots and water drums which were used primarily in the brewing of beer. With better equipment and large grain surpluses in the first years after the new fields began to produce, brewing for sale became an important source of income in most of those Gwembe neighborhoods still handicapped as exporters of grain by their distance from the railway line. We have brewing records for one village over a seventy-six-day period in 1967. It is a small village with perhaps 200 persons, yet its

Table 1

Increase in Number of Oxen, Plows, and Ox Carts,
Gwembe District, Years 1957–1963
(based on information supplied by the District Commissioner,
Gwembe District)

Year	Trained and Untrained Oxen	Plows	Ox Carts
1957	5,674	1,736	30
1958	5,536	1,868	32
1959	5,619	2,116	60
1960	6,276	2,116	60
1961	6,947	2,146	88
1962	7,895	2,152	97
1963	8,924	2,287	102

women brewed fifty-four times. On thirty-six occasions they brewed for sale.

We have little evidence that Gwembe cultivators in the early years of re-location experimented with new agricultural techniques other than plowing. They were also conservative in their adoption of new crops. One of the conditions made by the Gwembe Local Government in its negotiations with the government of Zambia over the question of resettlement had been that people were not to be required to adopt new agricultural methods. Although they had preferred to cultivate long-term alluvial soils, they were already familiar with shifting cultivation and the use of bush fallows. They had some idea of the various soil types they encountered and chose to apply existing techniques to them. Though technical officers of the Department of Agriculture had been of the opinion that *mopane* soils were not suitable for cultivation until the pioneering work of Crichton Mitchell in the Gwembe, Gwembe villagers were already aware that some of these soils could be used. They had seldom used them in the years just prior to resettlement because they had been able to clear thickets where the returns were higher and the labor of clearance less (Scudder, 1962:18–21). Now, in the absence of preferred soils, they brought *mopane* woodlands into cultivation, apparently quite independently of the agricultural workers in the district.

By 1961 the villagers had largely re-established themselves on the land, had begun the preliminary buildup of new agricultural equipment, and had done much to restock themselves after the losses associated with the move. They were ready to experiment with new opportunities, given that the basic necessities of life were once more assured.

This re-establishment had been bought at considerable social cost, some of which could have been avoided. The enormous demand for labor immediately after the move led men to make major demands upon their dependents, especially upon their wives and adolescent sons, who were needed in clearing, building, herding, and plowing. Women had been pushed into greater efforts in coping with the much harder task of working the new soils filled with stumps and roots and often had to hoe larger acreages now that a single harvest was to support the family through the year. They were also called upon for much work in the brewing of beer to pay the many work parties of the era. In 1962 both boys and women showed the strains they were under. The particular form taken by the Kariba compensation payments increased family dissension. Gwembe villagers think of themselves as working for particular rewards, and of support coming to them as a reward for work. A young man planting in his mother's field explains his labors not as due to her as a mother but as working for some promised reward. A child leading the plow team in his father's field may say he is working for a shirt. It is accepted that a child owes work to its parents for the gift of life, but the parents in turn owe support to the child because of its work. People are very conscious that food is produced through work, as are the other good things of life.

Government officials visualized the compensation payments as a mechanism for assisting Gwembe cultivators to re-establish themselves and to tide them through the difficult years, and this in fact the payments did. But because of the per capita basis of their computation, the Gwembe villagers visualized the money as direct payments to each person. Even a tiny child was therefore seen as working for its family by earning Kariba compensation money. The child had done as much for the family unit as had the man who headed it, for it could be argued that only the hut payment and the per capita payment in his name belonged fully to him. The fact that he received the total amount due the family meant that he accumulated a large reciprocal debt to wives and children which he had no way to repay. He was now using land which they had helped him to clear, instead of supporting them on land which came to him from his ancestors. The cash income that supplied clothing and other luxuries came from the Kariba money which had been earned by everyone in the family, rather than from his labor in a distant city.

Even though men might seem more prosperous in 1962 than in 1956 in terms of stock, equipment, size of homestead, and general style of expenditure, they seemed to have lost status within their family units. Some change in status was perhaps inevitable when their efforts to halt resettlement had revealed them as powerless. It need not have been as drastic if compensation payments had been based on a system that recognized adults as property owners and primary producers and recompensed them for the loss of their capital assets. This would have been a complicated business, requiring staff to make the additional assessments. It would also have given rise to numerous arguments as men fought hard to increase their compensation. It would no doubt have been more expensive because it would have led to a more realistic appraisal of the real assets of the people and their losses. It is therefore understandable why the Zambian government decided that the per capita basis was the easiest to administer and so the most desirable way of computing compensation.

FISHING

Once re-established after relocation, the Gwembe Tonga responded to a number of new local opportunities in the 1960's, of which the most important were fishing the new lake, marketing cattle, and cash-cropping cotton. In each case the government provided assistance while the people, after a cautious start, adopted new techniques and attitudes. Unfortunately in regard to both fishing and cattle husbandry, and perhaps even in the cultivation of cotton, the combination of government assistance and local initiative was insufficient to maintain the initial momentum. Unfavorable ecological consequences intervened, the consequences of which were largely unforeseen.

At the time of relocation it was obvious to all concerned that there was insufficient land in the resettlement areas to support the people unless new skills and new agricultural techniques were introduced. This was especially the case in the southwestern portion of the Gwembe. It was the hope of the government that fishing, in particular, would be able to support a significant portion of the relocated villagers. On the basis of what little was known about the Zambezi fisheries and artificial reservoir in the tropics, the estimates of the potential of the new lake ranged between 10,000 and 20,000 short tons per years. At 1963 prices, this would have a retail value of approximately $1.4 million and $4.2 million, roughly one third of which would go to the fishermen. Provided the Tonga showed the initiative, that amount should be more than enough to support thousands of fishermen plus their dependents.

The new fisheries were to be based on the use of gill or tangle nets. Because trees decay very slowly after they are submerged, an ambitious program of bush clearing was initiated in the late 1950's. Approximately 234,000 acres were cleared in what would be the shallower areas on both sides of the lake. This was slightly over half of those forested areas of highest potential, with cleared areas scattered among uncleared stretches of bush.

Although fishing had long been a respected part-time activity among the Gwembe Tonga, the rapid flow of the Zambezi and the narrow flood plains had precluded the development of an important riverine fishing industry prior to the construction of Kariba. Because the people were unfamiliar with gill nets as well as with the type of boat and outboard engine suitable to a large lake, an ambitious training program was essential. This began in a small way in 1956, when the first two junior fisheries staff members were assigned to Gwembe District to teach villagers how to use and repair gill nets. Nets were also issued to various Europeans working in the valley, including Scudder, with the understanding that they would assist in the training program. Though few people were involved prior to relocation, those in the program quickly learned the essential skills. A few purchased their own nets, and most of them were able to repay their purchase price within a few months.

When the dam was sealed late in 1958, training was intensified and the lake was closed to all but local fishermen. By the middle of 1959, there were 407 fishermen using 748 gill nets, according to a census carried out by government personnel. Though most of their boats were dugouts (which would be too dangerous to use in open waters once the lake was filled), the first fishermen were already making use of a government loans program to purchase more suitable craft. Late in 1961 the first fisheries training center in Zambia was opened on Lake Kariba at Sinazoongwe. After some experimentation, a standard one-month course was developed; with 336 Tonga attending courses during 1962. More specialized courses were also started to train local boat builders and to teach boat and outboard handling and maintenance.

The build-up in the number of fishermen and in the annual catches during these initial years was impressive: 2,000 Zambian fishermen marketed an estimated 3,000 short tons of fish during 1962, and the yield increased to an estimated 4,000 short tons in 1963. Though personnel in the Department of Fisheries grumbled about what they considered to be the haphazard techniques of the Gwembe Tonga, practically everyone agreed that the Kariba Lake fisheries was a success. The manager of the national development corporation praised the fishermen for their excellent repayment rate on equipment loans, and the Gwembe Rural Council received an estimated £4,716 during 1963 from the tax levied against the traders who marketed Kariba fish to the major urban centers. As for the fishermen themselves, the better ones were upgrading their equipment and setting aside over £100 per year in savings, and a much larger number were investing in cattle, plows, and consumer goods. At the same time the more successful younger men were initiating plural marriages and completing their payments at an earlier date than would have been the case in the past. Not only were they wealthier, but they were also achieving their independence from grasping elders at an earlier date. The future looked good indeed.

In 1964 yields fell off to 2,100 short tons with the decline continuing through 1967, when less than 1,000 short tons were recorded. The number of fishermen plummeted to fewer than 500, of which an unknown number were not Tonga, because the fisheries had been opened to strangers in 1964. Unlike the optimistic fishermen of 1963, many were in debt with little hope of being able to pay off their government loans.

Though the fisheries boom had collapsed, there was little the local fishermen could do about it short of seeking another occupation. Though the Middle Zambezi has always been poor in species in comparison to the rivers of West Africa, the existing fish population found itself in a most favorable environment during the years immediately after the dam was sealed. "Not only were predators dispersed, but herbivores profited from a greatly increased food supply, including flooded vegetation in the shallower waters and a bloom of phytoplankton. According to Coulter, not only were the 1958–1959 and 1959–1960 breeding seasons apparently longer, but survival rates among fry were 'very high.' As they matured, it was these that formed the basis for the new fisheries" (Scudder, in press, and Coulter, 1967). Succeeding generations were not so fortunate. Though the reasons behind the drop in

Construction of the type of fish basket used before Kariba Dam was built. (*Photo by Thayer Scudder.*)

Gill net mounting by one of the new Lake Kariba Tonga fishermen. Gill nets were not in use at all on the middle Zambezi prior to 1956. (*Photo by Thayer Scudder.*)

productivity are not yet clear, a number of factors appear to be involved. During the period of initial flooding when nutrients were released from the soil, vast quantities of vegetation were flooded, and the waters were colored by quantities of tiny nonvascular plants. With the biological and chemical stabilization of the lake fish populations found less nutrients. Another factor may have been the buildup of predators, and especially the tiger fish, *Hydrocynus vittatus*. The most important commercial species, a riverine cichlid known as *Tilapia mortimeri*, has not adapted to a changed habitat as successfully as the tiger fish. Along with other commerical species, *T. mortimeri* also has moved out of the cleared areas, either into deeper uncleared waters (which formerly were deoxygenated) or into adjacent shallow areas from which the bush was not cleared. Here fish are much harder to catch because mats of aquatic water fern, *Salvinia ariculata*, clinging to the crowns of semisubmerged trees, interfere with boat handling and the setting of nets, and the many submerged snags tear the nets to pieces.

As soon as the fisheries began to decline, hundreds of Tonga left the fish camps to return to the villages or once again to seek jobs on the plateau. Some remained as poor as they had been before they began fishing. Others used their savings to set themselves up in new enterprises. In Lusaka two young men from the same village were able, for £127 and £675, respectively, to build small houses with extra rooms to rent out at £2 15s. to £3 per month each. Within the Gwembe, a number of the new village stores were capitalized with fishing profits. A still larger number of former fishermen returned to farming. Those that had converted their profits to cattle were able not only to cultivate larger holdings through the use of ox traction, but also to partake in the cattle sales that began to increase during the early 1960's.

THE CATTLE INDUSTRY

Visitors to the Gwembe Valley have frequently commented on the excellent condition of the cattle there in comparison with those on the Zambian Plateau. Not only is there more food (both grazing and browsing), but the water supply is also better. Lake Kariba has improved the situation in regard to both these factors. On the other hand, the major constraint to the development of a cattle industry in the valley is the presence of tsetse fly (Figure 1), which is the carrier of animal sleeping sickness. Before Kariba, Munyumbwe was the only tsetse-free chieftaincy. Here local residents had been willing to sell excess stock to other Tonga and to butchers from the plateau at least by 1951. The same had been true in Sinadambwe up to that time, with these two chieftaincies together accounting for approximately two thirds of the Gwembe cattle at that time (11,561 out of 19,906). During the middle of the 1950's, however, tsetse expanded into Sinadambwe from Simamba, with the result that the number of cattle there had declined drastically, from 6,141 to 1,881 in 1959.

Prior to the 1955 decision to construct the Kariba Dam there were no government livestock or tsetse personnel stationed in the Gwembe Valley. By the end of 1956, however, three Tsetse Control Supervisors had been transferred to the valley along with supporting staff. Their job was to make sure that those areas being chosen for relocation would be free from tsetse at the earliest possible date. During the same year three junior veterinary personnel were also assigned to Gwembe District, and a livestock officer was stationed locally in 1960. Through 1962 all personnel were optimistic; it seemed to be only a matter of time before the tsetse threat was either eliminated entirely from the valley or contained within known areas whose margins could be treated whenever necessary.

As for the Tonga, by the end of 1962 they had over 24,000 cattle, which was more than ever before, with the largest concentrations in Munyumbwe and Mwemba, followed by Sinadambwe. In Mwemba at least eighty-one cattle (a record number to date) had been driven up to the plateau for sale at the Cold Storage Board's Kabanga scale. The average price was £18 10s., which compared well with other sources of cash available to Mwemba residents. In Munyumbwe, at least 148 cattle were sold to butchers during the year, and another 133 were sold to residents elsewhere in the valley; still another fifty-six were sold to unspecified buyers. In Sinadambwe, on the other hand, sales were few because people there had only begun to rebuild their herds after the tsetse encroachment of the late 1950's. Nonetheless, the desire to sell cattle as a cash crop still existed. Awareness of the sales potential of Gwembe stock had also spread to Old Chipepo and to the Lusitu. Knowledgeable government personnel became increasingly aware of the possibility of cattle as an export crop.

Aside from a major program to eradicate the tsetse fly and to protect cattle through the use of prophylactic and curative drugs, the government assisted the villagers with stock improvement, with marketing, and subsequently with loans. Though the first government-sponsored sales in the Gwembe were organized in 1951, private butchers operating from the plateau were the main buyers through 1963. In 1964 the Cold Storage Board became the main buyers of Gwembe cattle when it organized, in Munyumbwe and Mwemba, its first sales in the valley. Between October, 1963, and the end of September, 1964, a minimum of 408 Gwembe cattle were sold for butchering, as opposed to 141 during a twelve-month period in 1961–1962. Of these, 303 were sold to the Cold Storage Board, with 222 of them marketed through the Munyumbwe and Mwemba scales.[4] Cash paid out to Gwembe farmers was £3,963, as opposed to £1,293 received from private butchers. The following year Cold Storage Board sales were held in Sinazongwe and villagers in the Lusitu requested that sales also be organized there, although facilities were not completed until 1967.

Once again the Gwembe Tonga were showing initiative by responding,

[4] The remainder were marketed through CSB scales on the plateau to which Sinazongwe and Mwemba residents drove their cattle as they had done in the past.

after their usual cautious start, to a new opportunity. And once again their expectations, as well as the government's, were set back as a result of ecological factors. This time the "ecological boomerang" was the unexpected expansion of the tsetse fly into Munyumbwe for the first time in recorded history. The first cattle deaths were reported in 1963; by 1964 the total number of cattle had decreased from over 8,000 (or slightly over one per capita) to under 5,000. The decline continued during 1965 and 1966, although at a slower rate. During 1966 and 1967 the Cold Storage Board reported no sales from Munyumbwe, for the villagers no longer had sufficient cattle to meet their own ox traction needs; some in fact were observed plowing with cows. The same tsetse encroachment also hit Sinadambwe during 1964, wiping out the meager gains in cattle which had been achieved between 1960 and 1962. Three years later an epidemic of sleeping sickness broke out in the Lusitu, with at least 454 cattle dying out of less than 3,500. This was a catastrophe because the Lusitu people were just beginning to use their oxen for cotton cultivation and to sell their small surpluses to government and to private traders.

Ironically, there was a correlation between the fly encroachment into Munyumbwe and Sinadabwe in 1964 and the creation of Lake Kariba. Not only did the filling lake push some fly populations inland, but along its now stabilized margin it created a favorable fly habitat. As a result, tsetse expanded rapidly along the eastern edges of the lake, with formerly isolated pockets coalescing. Movement inland was then facilitated by traveling fishermen and fish traders who unwittingly carried the fly on their bundles of fish into formerly tsetse-free cattle areas.[5] Though the threat was less along the western margin of the lake, disturbing reports of flies in isolated portions of both Mwemba and Chipepo were made between 1963 and 1967, while sporadic flies were reported along the lakeshore margin in Sinazongwe— apparently imported by fishermen from fly-infested islands in Rhodesia. Though the major threat, the lake was not solely responsible. In the Lusitu there were three potential sources of reinfection. One was from across the Zambezi in Rhodesia. The other two were unpopulated areas on either side of Lusitu, one of which is exceedingly rugged and was the most likely origin point of the 1967 epidemic.

In spite of massive and well-organized tsetse control operations since the completion of the Kariba Dam,[6] the future of the Gwembe cattle industry is questionable. Even if the fly is completely eliminated from the lakeshore margin (which was one tsetse control goal during the 1960's), the danger of reinfestation from Rhodesia is a continuing problem. To combat it periodic surveys at either end of the lake and at danger points in between are essential

---

[5] Although tsetse pickets were established along the main routes, and all vehicles were regularly sprayed, it was not possible to cover bicycles moving on small trails through fly-infested areas. See Scudder, in press, for a detailed discussion of the expansion of tsetse during the 1960's.

[6] In 1965, for example, over 1,300 lineal miles were sprayed at a cost of £43,552.

so that reinfestation can be stopped before the fly has the opportunity to build up and expand its populations. The residual, more isolated pockets of tsetse flies within Gwembe District itself are easier to control simply because their locale is known. Although there is little hope that present techniques can actually eliminate the fly in the most inaccessible areas, it is possible that this end can be achieved by releasing large numbers of laboratory males which have been sterilized through the use of radioactive isotopes. Meanwhile, the risk of fly encroachment into cattle areas continues, as do deaths from sleeping sickness.

COTTON

If fishing was the big opportunity for Gwembe residents in 1962, in 1967 it was cotton. Archeological evidence suggests the possibility that cotton was first cultivated in the Gwembe Valley prior to 1500 A.D. At Ingombe Ilede in the Lusitu spindle whorls occur throughout the stratified site, and remnants of cotton cloth are associated with the rich central burials "preserved by the oxidizing effects of the copper bangles" that were buried with the deceased (Fagan, 1967:678). Although it is of course possible that the fiber was imported, the climate and soils of the Lusitu are exceptionally favorable for cotton cultivation.

The status of cotton in the Gwembe between the fifteenth and twentieth centuries remains a mystery. During the 1920's favorable world conditions encouraged a "minor boom" on the Zambian plateau "accompanied by the erection of a ginnery at Mazabuka and the planting of over 11,000 acres of cotton by 1925–1926" (Prentice, 1963:13). Success was short-lived, however, because of falling prices and insect damage. Although some villagers in the Gwembe continued to grow cotton in small quantities during the 1930's, in 1939 there were only about 150 growers. Their yields ranged from under 50 pounds of seed cotton per acre to over 1,820, with an average of 463 pounds. Supervision of the small plots (0.05 to 1.7 acres) was the responsibility of three cotton assistants whose supervisor resided on the plateau. During the war years even this junior staff was withdrawn and the number of growers dropped to one. Remembering the history of hunger in the valley, government officials on their infrequent tours emphasized self-sufficiency in food production rather than cash crops. By 1953, however, the vision of the Gwembe as a cotton area was revived, this time by the District Commissioner, who drew up his own development program. Its agricultural aspects became the responsibility of the Department of Agriculture, which had appointed its first senior staff member, an agricultural supervisor, to the Gwembe in 1952. Subsequently, a Principal Agricultural Supervisor, Crichton Mitchell, was appointed, who more than anyone else laid the groundwork for the resurgence of cotton within the Gwembe.

For a start, Mitchell carefully selected and nurtured a small number of local farmers in Munyumbwe's chieftaincy. Avoiding the use of both insecticides and chemical fertilizers,[7] he placed cotton within a grain–legume rotation, with manure to be added to the cereal crop. The stress was on quality. Those who followed Mitchell's advice were called improved farmers and received an incentive payment of £1 per acre. Their achievement was closely watched, and their failures were rebuked and their successes reported with pride in carefully kept monthly and annual reports. During 1956, however, there was serious discussion within the department as to whether or not the extension work in cotton should be stopped. There were only five producers whose total crop came to a meager 1,474 pounds of lower-grade cotton. Furthermore, without departmental pressure, even they might stop growing the crop. And once again pest control was becoming a major problem.

The following year the picture brightened, as the first Grade A cotton grown by villagers was exported from the valley. Though total sales amounted to only £24 of seed cotton, a milestone had been passed. With regard to the insect problem, a major decision was made—to provide DDT to those growers who needed it.

The first growers during the 1950's were not involved in Kariba resettlement, because they lived at the base of the escarpment inland from the future lake basin. After relocation was completed, a small peasant farming scheme was initiated in the two most favorable resettlement areas. These were Buleya-Malima and the Lusitu. Selected in 1959, the first ten peasant farmers were supposed to lead the way by demonstrating the correct procedures for growing cotton. Initially each was restricted to 20 acres and required to follow a four-crop rotation which would include in any one year a maximum of five acres of cotton. Credit was supplied up to £150 for the purchase of cattle and ox traction equipment. Though the total number of peasant farmers has never exceeded twenty, without doubt their initial success was a major stimulus behind the rapid build-up in cotton production during the 1960's.

During 1961, 8,515 pounds were sold through government channels, with slightly under £200 distributed to the growers, most of whom were peasant farmers. By 1963 the number of producers, the acreage, and the yields had all increased significantly, with forty-three Tonga cultivators exporting 55,000 pounds from somewhat over 50 acres. During the next four years the number of growers and the acreage sown in cotton nearly doubled annually, so that there were at least 400 growers with approximately 900 acres during the 1966–1967 season. Exports had risen above 700,000 pounds of seed cotton. There was every reason to expect that during the next season both the total number of growers and the acreage would again increase significantly.

As with fishing in 1962, many Gwembe Tonga were ready to experiment

---

[7] In barring insecticides at first, Mitchell wished to keep the standard of husbandry among his farmers as simple as possible. As for fertilizers, he questioned their value under Gwembe conditions.

Using only family labor (three wives), a peasant farmer harvests his cotton crop. (*Photo by Thayer Scudder.*)

with cotton as a cash crop by 1967. In the Lusitu several farmers in most villages either had grown cotton during the previous season or were intending to during the season ahead. Although the Lusitu was the pacemaker, the tempo was picking up throughout the rest of the valley, with cotton growers now found in every chieftaincy with the possible exception of Simamba. Although we know nothing about the backgrounds of the pioneer cultivators in Munyumbwe during the 1950's, the picture is relatively clear elsewhere. In Sinazongwe, Sinadambwe, and the Lusitu the first cultivators were usually the small number of peasant farmers. These were individuals who were prepared to leave their villages and who had been selected by the government to pioneer a new system of land use involving a four-crop rotation, animal manuring, cash cropping, ox traction, and the use of credit. In Mwemba there were no peasant farmers partly because the chieftaincy was isolated from the main road system until 1967 when an all-weather road was opened up to the new coal mine at Maamba. During the 1966–1967 season, however, six individuals initiated cotton cultivation. All were local elite, familiar with the ways of the outside world. Either educated beyond primary school or with educated sons, they also had access to local transportation to carry their cotton to the nearest depot of the government marketing board. Because of their initial success, the Department of Agriculture had received numerous requests for information from villagers who now wished to follow their example. Enough of these had signed up as potential growers to convince the marketing board to establish a depot during the 1967–1968 season within Mwemba itself.

In Chipepo the innovators were prominent villagers with a history for initiating new enterprises. This does not mean that their participation in the cotton industry could have been accurately predicted, because others with a similar history of innovation were still pursuing a wait-and-see attitude. On the other hand, the type of person involved could be characterized as having succeeded, on the one hand, in traditional village activities such as building up a herd of livestock and, on the other, in pioneering such new occupations as fishing and storekeeping.

Like the Mwemba innovators they were also familiar with the outside world, and some of their number were sufficiently at ease with government officials to visit them in their offices in order to demand or otherwise arrange transport. Though all were married, most fell in the age category of "junior elders." Turning to Simamba, there are several factors that could explain the delay within this chieftaincy. Of these the most important would appear to be the presence of bovine sleeping sickness, which restricts the use of extraction for cotton cultivation. Furthermore, Simamba was as isolated as Mwemba prior to the construction of the Kariba Dam. It was also the last chieftaincy to obtain schools, there being none prior to relocation. Isolated, with virtually no cattle, and less familiar with the ways of the outside world, the inhabitants of Simamba are only just beginning to catch up with their neighbors.

By 1967 cotton was seen as a valuable cash crop by both village and peasant farmers. An example of each, both living in the Lusitu, is given in Table 2. The peasant farmer, Samuel, started growing cotton in 1961 when he experimented with $\frac{1}{4}$ acre. In 1962 he planted a full acre, selling the crop for nearly £52. When Scudder visited him in May, 1963, his acreage had tripled and he was anticipating a gross income of approximately £150. Gross income in 1965 and 1966 was £400 and £513, respectively. During this six-year period, his farm as a whole had prospered and his standard of living had gone up. His homestead was well built of permanent materials and new building was continuing. Total acreage in crops had increased from less than 10 to 32, and a variety of ox traction implements recently had been replaced by a tractor complete with disk plow and trailer.[8] Looking to the future

[8] This is not the place to discuss the pros and cons of tractor versus ox traction within the Gwembe. Because of inexperience, the first tractor users may well incur major losses. On the other hand, the careful introduction of tractors may prove the best alternative for certain cooperative and peasant farmers because of the threat of tsetse to ox traction.

Table 2

Expenses and Income of Two Cotton Growers
During the 1966–1967 Season

Samuel: A Peasant Farmer* with Approximately 20 Cotton Acres	Miles: A Villager with Approximately 1¼ Cotton Acres
Cash costs as calculated by the farmer†	£ *s.* *d.*
Seed 5	11 6
Insecticides 21 (three applications)‡	4 18 4 (eight applications)
Transport 56	2 5 0
Other —	1 (spray-pump rental)
Total £ 82	8 14 10
Gross income	
45 bales Grade A	975 lb. Grade A
£675	27 16 12
Net income as calculated by the farmer	
£593	19 2 6
Net income per acre	
approximately £27 approximately 16	
Yield per acre	
approximately 850 lb. approximately 800 lb.	

* Names are fictional.

† Both farmers use only family labor, Samuel having three wives and Miles one. Because of the slow pace of picking by unskilled laborers, the relative success of different farmers may depend in large part on their ability to use only family labor.

‡ Ten or eleven applications are recommended.

Samuel intended to continue his present stress on both maize and cotton, expanding his acreage to 25 and 30 acres, respectively, during the coming season.

Like most villagers, including the Chipepo pioneers, Miles had spent a number of years working outside the Gwembe Valley as an unskilled labor migrant. This phase ended in the mid-1950's when he began to expand his fields and his livestock holdings. At the time he was slightly over thirty. When Scudder mapped his holdings in 1957, they included two bush gardens which Miles had cleared during recent years. In spite of the fact that he had inherited little land, only one member of his village controlled a larger acreage. Along with three other members, Miles had also begun to experiment with cattle. Following relocation, he again showed his enterprise by clearing fields that were among the largest in the neighborhood. By 1963 he had purchased his first plow, and his four cattle included two trained oxen. By 1967 his herd had increased to seventeen, four of which were trained oxen. In the future Miles intended to expand his cotton effort by increasing his acreage from 1¼ to 2 during the coming season. He also planned to purchase his own back-pack sprayer, with the aid of a 50 per cent government subsidy.

When Scudder left the Gwembe Valley toward the end of 1967, the rapid increase in cotton production among both villagers and peasant farmers had the markings of a success story. The resemblance to the lake fisheries in 1963 and to the rising interest in cattle sales prior to the spread of tsetse fly in 1966 and 1967 was striking. Within the Gwembe, soils were suitable for cotton; the valley's remoteness had also been alleviated partially by the development of new roads and the improvement of old ones in connection with the Kariba project and more recently by the commencement of coal mining in the southwestern portion of the valley. Transport had been initially provided by the District Government, local storekeepers, elite, and missionaries, with the Grain Marketing Board stepping in during the 1966–1967 season. Though a significant number of villagers already had the land, the labor, and the equipment in the form of oxen and plows to grow cotton, local resources were supplemented by a program of agricultural credit initiated during 1965 under the auspices of the Credit Organization of Zambia. During 1966, 505 applications were processed in the district, of which 196 were approved for £12,932. Most of these were for the purchase of oxen and plows, with repayment to be phased over three years. During 1967 the total number of applications had increased, although at the time of Scudder's departure in November the District Loans Committee was still reviewing some so that data on the number of approvals were incomplete.

In spite of an excellent start the future of cotton among the Gwembe Tonga is not assured. And again the most serious threat is not unsatisfactory farmer attitudes or lack of government assistance, but rather ecological risks.[9] A major constraint is the perennial threat of drought in a semiarid land. Another problem concerns the distribution of tsetse and the danger of encroachment into cattle areas. Cotton cultivators in the valley prefer either ox traction or tractor mechanization. The total number of privately owned tractors was under ten in 1967. It is hard to imagine this number doubling within the next five years unless cooperative farms are heavily financed under government auspices. This means the increasing number of village farmers must rely on the ox plow at a time when the total number of cattle within the Gwembe has been decreasing because of outbreaks of bovine trypanoso-miasis.

In addition to the tsetse problem there is the general problem of cotton pests. The Gwembe Valley is one of the few areas in Zambia where three species of bollworms occur (Table 3). Of these the Afro-American is considered the most important at the moment. Most damage is done by the larvae, seven or eight of which, according to one estimate, "can destroy all bolls and fruiting points of a large cotton plant" (Department of Agriculture, 1965:5). In addition to the bollworms, stainers abound while termites and harvester

---

[9] We do not mean to imply here that farmer attitudes or government assistance are entirely satisfactory. On the contrary, the refusal of the Gwembe farmer to carry out conservation measures has serious long-term implications, and the government loans program has a number of deficiencies.

Table 3

Common Cotton Pests of the Gwembe

Latin Name	English Name	Recommended Insecticide*
Heliothis armigera	Afro-American bollworm	DDT
Earias biplaga	Spiny bollworm	Sevin
Diparopsis castanea	Red bollworm	Sevin
Empoasca spp.	Jassid	Sevin, DDT
Lygus sp.	Lygus	DDT
Aphis gossypii	Aphid	Rogor 40
Tetranychus spp.	Red spider	Rogor 40
Dysdercus spp.	Stainer	Sevin
Various genera	Leaf-eating caterpillars	DDT and/or Sevin
Unidentified genera	Termites and harvester ants	DDT

* These recommendations are contained in a departmental circular (October 1, 1965) on Cotton Growing in Zambia. On page 9 the following hypothetical spraying program is presented as an illustration: (1) four weeks after germination: Sevin; (2) seven weeks after germination: Sevin; (3–6) four DDT applications; (7) Sevin + Rogor; (8–10) three DDT applications; (11) Sevin and (12) Sevin + Rogor. After the first two sprays, weekly applications are suggested until the rains end; then fortnightly.

ants have been observed toppling young cotton seedlings like minuscule beavers. Leaf-sucking insects include aphids, red spiders, and jassids.

Pesticides were first used on Tonga cotton during the 1957–1958 season, with DDT issued by the Department of Agriculture to the needy grower. Noting that pest control was the main cotton problem, Mitchell questioned the effectiveness of DDT alone in his 1958 annual report, adding that during the next season it would be mixed with B.H.C. Subsequent reports continue to mention the insect problem. Hence quality was down in 1960 because of stainer, whereas red spider was first observed in 1962. In 1964 local farmers were advised to spray their crop between five and seven times. By 1967 eleven applications of insecticides were recommended during the Gwembe growing season, the farmer applying this to his crop with a hand pump attached to a back-pack sprayer.

Although eleven sprayings during the growth season is relatively low by international standards, the continued use of broad-spectrum insecticides like DDT can have a number of negative consequences. Because DDT acts indiscriminately against both pests and their natural enemies, what were formerly secondary pests can build up their populations to the point where they have a detrimental effect on cotton yields. At the same time, certain primary pests may become insecticide resistant, as has happened in parts of Latin America and the United States and in Turkey, Israel, Egypt, and Australia (Smith, 1969:5). The usual response in such a situation is to increase the number of spray applications, with the capital and labor costs to the farmer also increasing. If yields then drop drastically, owing to a pest problem, irregular rainfall, or a combination of the two, the small farmer could quickly find himself with an uneconomic crop.

Within the Gwembe, the potential risk to the small cotton grower of a significant drop in yields should be considered a major one. Drought is recurrent and pests there have already been a partial cause for the cessation of cotton production in the past. Though present acreages are very small in comparison to those areas of the tropics where resistance to insecticides has occurred, and though they are also dispersed, the government of Zambia is pushing cotton as a cash crop. In 1970 the first textile factory in Zambia commenced production with an initial capacity to process 20 million pounds of seed cotton. Although this exceeds present national yields, the gap is rapidly closing, with production jumping from under 500,000 pounds in 1963 to approximately 15 million in 1969 (*Zambia Mail*, 1970). During this same period acreage rose from under 2,000 to over 20,000. At least one twentieth of this is within the Gwembe and this proportion probably will increase simply because the Gwembe is considered to be an area of high potential for cotton. Provided ecological catastrophe does not intervene in the next few years, we can expect both the number of growers and the size of holdings to increase rapidly. If present government policy continues, particular stress will be placed on cooperative farms on which a group of enterprising villagers will be assisted with credit and advice. The first two cotton cooperatives in the Gwembe were to commence operations during the 1967–1968 season. By October the eleven members of one had cleared and stumped over 100 acres, of which they planned to plant twenty in cotton. Using government credit, they had already purchased a tractor and hired a driver to handle it. The members of the other cooperative planned to start with 25 acres of cotton. Agricultural staff were directed to work closely with the members of both in order to increase their chances of success.

Increasingly, integrated pest control is being advocated by entomologists to reduce the ecological dangers inherent in the massive application of broad-spectrum insecticides. This is defined as a "pest management system that utilizes all suitable techniques and methods (e.g., biological, cultural, genetic, and chemical control) in as compatible a manner as possible to keep pest populations below economic injury rates" (Smith, 1969:3). Although this approach makes both ecological and economic sense, to date it has been most successfully used in connection with large-scale agriculture. How successfully it can be applied to village farmers, most of whom are still illiterate, remains to be seen. One difficulty concerns the implementation of better techniques among thousands of smallholders. Just as early planting is necessary to increase yields, so the postharvest destruction of plants is mandatory to reduce the carry-over of insect pests to the next season by providing a cotton-free period. In Zambia the mandatory eradication date is October 1, yet as Scudder traveled around the Gwembe throughout that month in 1967, he observed fields in which the piling and burning of plants had been either delayed or ignored. Furthermore, very few farmers were willing to rotate cotton, preferring to grow it year after year in the same fields, or at best alternate it with maize, which shares with cotton a number of pests. Early planting also tended to be neglected, with the stress placed first on the sowing of food crops.

The proper application of insecticides is another serious problem because it requires the village farmer not only to delay the first application as long as possible, but also to know when to apply what agent. In 1967 three insecticides (DDT, Sevin, and Rogor) were used to control different cotton pests. If the farmer is to use these chemicals selectively he must not mix them for uniform applications, but rather base their use on the observation of insect populations within his field. This, of course, requires not only a knowledge of the specific pests but also a knowledge of those stages in their life cycles which are potentially dangerous.

In order to better educate the farmer, greater reliance will have to be placed on short courses and on an enlarged staff of cotton demonstrators. Though Gwembe farmers understand the general need to control insect pests, few follow exactly the advice given. During the 1966–1967 season, for example, Samuel applied insecticides only three times on his 20 acres of cotton, whereas Miles, with a much smaller holding, completed six applications. With a program of integrated pest control a much more detailed program will have to be conscientiously followed. In part the need for this could be taught within the framework of short courses for cotton culture, the precedent for which was set in 1967 when a number of village growers attended a one-week course on the plateau. At the same time the number of cotton demonstrators was increasing. Educated through grade 7, with only two weeks of training in agriculture before accepting their rural assignments, this staff may easily be criticized for its inadequacies. On the other hand, they have already helped the village farmer in a major way through advice and record keeping. Though further education in the form of refresher courses is, of course, desirable, it is certainly important that the numbers of these demonstrators increase proportionately at least as fast as the number of growers.

As in the case of fishing and cattle husbandry, the Gwembe villager has responded favorably to a new economic opportunity in the form of cotton as a cash crop. In 1967 the future looked bright to the grower. Although the pest control situation looks ominous against the background of recent developments elsewhere, cotton researchers in Zambia are well aware of the problems. In spite of this awareness, however, and as an on-going research program, it remains to be seen whether or not a system of cotton cultivation can be developed and maintained which is suitable for the Gwembe smallholder.

4

When the government of Zambia undertook to relocate the Gwembe Tonga they did so under a special set of circumstances : the relocated were citizens of the same country as the relocators ; the area being evacuated was destined to become an enormous productive center by virtue of the lake being formed behind the Kariba Dam ; the people who were moved were recipients of specialized programs of economic development.

The case described here by Dr. Robert Kiste is entirely different. The people of Bikini Atoll were relocated after World War II because they happened to live in an area chosen for atmospheric nuclear testing by the United States. Those who were evacuated were thus wards of the evacuators ; the area being cleared was to become deadly poisonous, perhaps irreversibly (no one knew at the time how long the radiation danger would last) ; and the people affected were virtually abandoned on several occasions until it became apparent that government intervention was their only means of survival. Thus, the Dam and the Bomb, though causing population relocation, had few similar effects.

Nevertheless, one of the consequences of massive development projects seems to be population resettlement. And as Dr. Kiste shows, if this task is undertaken without proper planning and involvement of the local community in determining their own destiny, the effects can be devastating.

RELOCATION AND TECHNOLOGICAL CHANGE IN MICRONESIA[1]

Robert Kiste

Robert C. Kiste is Associate Professor, Department of Anthropology, University of Minnesota. He received his Ph.D. from the University of Oregon and has done extensive field research among the Bikini and Eniwetok communities in the Marshall Islands. He is currently writing an ethnological study of the Eniwetok Marshallese.

INTRODUCTION

In early 1946 the community inhabiting Bikini Atoll in the northern Marshall Islands was relocated when its homeland was selected as a nuclear test site. The initial resettlement of the Bikinians on Rongerik, another northern atoll, ended in less than two years. Rongerik's resources were not adequate, and the Bikinians were evacuated to a naval base at Kwajalein Atoll. Later they were resettled on Kili, a small single island in the southern Marshalls.

[1] My 1963–1964 field work with the Bikini people was conducted within the framework of a larger research effort, the Project for the Comparative Study of Cultural Change and Stability in Displaced Communities in the Pacific. The project was directed by Dr. Homer G. Barnett, Department of Anthropology, University of Oregon, and was funded by the National Science Foundation. My 1969 research with the Bikinians was made possible by a grant from the Office for International Projects, University of Minnesota.

In addition to the Bikini people, who have always done their utmost to assist my research efforts and have been generous with their hospitality, I am particularly indebted to several individuals. The training and guidance provided by Dr. Homer G. Barnett during my tenure as a graduate student at the University of Oregon have been greatly appreciated. I owe

The Bikini community was organized upon principles of kinship that were similar to those of other Marshallese communities. Their material culture, technology, and economic system were relatively simple but well adapted to the northern islands. Subsistence was gained by fishing and gathering food crops which required little care. Most items comprising their inventory of material culture were manufactured from resources local to Bikini.

The Bikinians' responses to the events and circumstances of their relocations have precipitated alterations in many facets of their culture and community. This paper is primarily concerned with those modifications which have occurred in the realm of material culture, technology, and related facets of the traditional economic system. Extensive changes in social organization have been described elsewhere (Kiste, 1967, 1968; Mason, 1950, 1954) and are noted only as they relate to the interests of this paper.

With resettlement on Kili, the Bikinians were faced with the problem of adapting to an unfamiliar environment. Novel agricultural practices and techniques, changes in the form and use of surface vessels, and adoption of other material and technological innovations were required if the Bikinians were to make a satisfactory adjustment to Kili.

In the course of the Bikinians' resettlements, welfare measures and development programs have been implemented by the government of the United States Trust Territory of the Pacific Islands. The Bikinians' responses to these efforts have not been those intended or anticipated by the Americans. The islanders have adopted certain material items and techniques that were not planned or foreseen, and many of the innovations deliberately introduced by development projects have been rejected or not fully accepted. The variables determining the Bikinians' responses have been several. Failure to perceive the potential advantages of adopting unfamiliar techniques, the incompatibility of those techniques with traditional work habits, and discouragement resulting from natural catastrophe have influenced the islanders' receptivity to innovations.

Two other integrally related variables have been far more significant in shaping the Bikinians' responses: a fervent desire to return to their ancestral homeland and a stance of dependence upon agencies of the United States government. A return to Bikini could only be accomplished with the consent and assistance of the United States, and the islanders' desire to return has been partially responsible for the status of dependence that they have established with the United States. Their stance of dependence has more origins and is rooted in at least three other sets of historical circumstances. First, prior to relocation, the Bikinians were a people subject to the authority

a special debt to Dr. Leonard Mason, formerly of the Department of Anthropology, University of Hawaii, who introduced me to the Bikini community on Kili Island, guided my field work efforts, and made available his unpublished data from his previous researches among the Bikinians. Several conversations between 1964 and 1969 with Dr. Jack A. Tobin, Marshall Islands District Community Development Advisor, have given me numerous insights pertaining to the Bikinians' responses to their several relocations.

of personages and groups external to their community upon whom they were dependent for the gratification of a few of their wants. Secondly, soon after their initial relocation, they became convinced that the United States had caused them to suffer a great injustice and was obligated to provide for their wants and needs. Thirdly, they have been exposed to dramatic manifestations of the wealth and technological power of the United States. The Bikinians' exposure to the wealth and technology of the United States has created wants that they cannot satisfy and has led them to draw unfavorable comparisons between the efficacy of their own material culture and technology with that of the Americans. From their point of view, Americans have conclusively demonstrated that with their vast resources and technological prowess they could easily provide for the Bikinians' every want and need. These factors and the Bikinians' conviction that the United States is morally obligated to them have caused them to conclude that it would be both just and advantageous for them to become wards dependent upon agencies of the United States government. That the Bikinians were accustomed to a limited stance of dependence prior to the relocation predisposed them to adopt such a stance.

ENVIRONMENTAL AND HISTORICAL SETTING

The Marshall Islands lie on the eastern margin of Micronesia, some 2,000 miles southwest of Hawaii in the central Pacific a few degrees north of the equator (see Figure 1). They and the islands to the west, the Carolines and Marianas, were seized from Japan during World War II. In 1947 the area became the United States Trust Territory of the Pacific Islands within the framework of the United Nations. Under Article 73 of the United Nations Charter, the United States pledged to "promote to the utmost the well-being of the inhabitants," while it reserved the right to establish military sites of strategic value to its own national security. The islands were governed by the United States Navy until 1951, when their administration was transferred to the Department of Interior and civilian control.

In former times European powers competed for influence in Micronesia. Traders and missionaries were well established in the area by the late nineteenth century. A lucrative copra trade brought conflict between Germany, Spain, and England, resulting in German control over the Marshalls in 1885. Thirteen years later Germany extended its hegemony over the Carolines and most of the Marianas.

The German administration, which encouraged further development of the copra trade, ended with the outbreak of World War I, when Japan seized Germany's Micronesian possessions. Large numbers of Japanese colonists expanded the copra trade and initiated other economic enterprises. In the late 1930's Japan fortified a number of islands in the series of events which culminated in World War II. Military bases on the Marshallese atolls of Kwajalein and Eniwetok were among the first in Micronesia to be invaded by American forces.

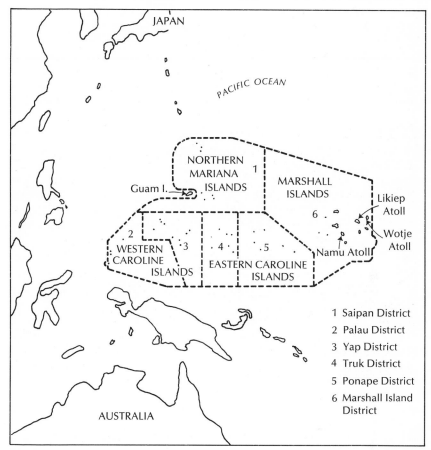

FIGURE 1. Trust Territory of the Pacific Islands; Northern Mariana, Caroline, and Marshall islands.

The Marshalls consist of thirty-four atolls and single islands and are arranged in two roughly parallel chains on a northwest–southeast axis (see Figure 2). The western chain, *Ralik*, consists of fifteen atolls and three islands; it is divided by Marshallese into northern and southern seas. The northernmost atoll in the northern sea is Bikini; the sea includes Rongerik and extends south to Kwajalein Atoll and Lib Island. *Ralik* atolls and islands in the latitudes to the south of Lib are in the southern sea. Kili Island, Jaluit Atoll (the center of German and Japanese governments), and Majuro Atoll (the American administrative center) are located in the southern sea.

All of the Marshalls are formed of coral built up from submerged volcanic peaks. The elevation of most atolls and islands ranges from 8 to 20 feet above low-tide level; there are no high islands such as those found in the Carolines and Marianas. The discrepancy between land and sea area is

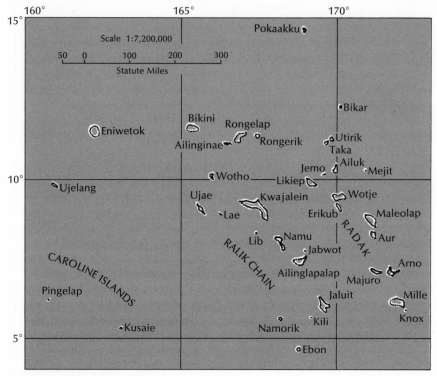

FIGURE 2. Marshall islands.

striking. The Marshalls are scattered over 375,000 square miles of ocean (an area about one and a half times the size of Texas); the total land area of all islands and atolls is a meager 69.86 square miles (about one twentieth the area of Rhode Island).

Because of their position in the low latitudes and small land area, the Marshalls have a tropical marine climate. Temperatures (mean annual temperature is 81°F.) and humidity (relative humidity averages about 85 per cent, with little variation) are high and uniform over the archipelago. The islands have a heavy precipitation, but significant differences in the amount and monthly distribution of rainfall distinguish the northern from the southern atolls. Bikini and other atolls in the far north receive an annual rainfall of about 60 inches (Wiens 1962:154). The northern atolls lie within the belt of the northeast trades, and from December to April the winds blow strong and steady, bringing clear skies but little rain. In contrast, the southern atolls have an annual rainfall of about 180 inches, and as they are on the southern margin of the tradewind belt, rainfall is distributed more evenly over the year.

Reflecting the differences in precipitation patterns, the southern atolls have richer soils, a more luxuriant vegetation cover, and a greater number of subsistence crops than the northern atolls. The largest populations have always been located in the south. Europeans were first attracted to the more favorable environment of the south, and it was there that trading and mission activities were commenced in the 1850's and 1860's. Foreigners did not make a substantial penetration into the far north until after the turn of the century.

Bikini is not only the northernmost atoll in Ralik, it is also distant and isolated from others; its closest neighbor, Rongelab, lies 80 miles to the east. Bikini is composed of twenty-six islands. The largest covers 0.66 square miles and all twenty-six have a combined land area of 2.32 square miles. The reef upon which the islands are built encloses a lagoon that is approximately 243 square miles in area; the lagoon is roughly oval in shape and is 26 miles long and a maximum width of about 15 miles (see Figure 3).

The Bikinians had some contact with the people of Rongelab, but because of their isolation they had less contact with outsiders than most other Marshallese. Bikini was included in the realm of one of the paramount chiefs who resided in the south. The atoll was his possession, and the people were subject to his authority. They were obliged to render him tribute and send domestics to serve in his household. The paramount chief was obligated to reciprocate with gifts and to come to their aid in times of need or disaster. He seldom called or sent representatives to the distant atoll, however, and his contact with them was infrequent.

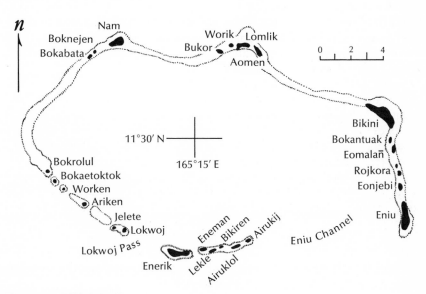

FIGURE 3. Bikini Atoll.

Few German vessels had ever called at Bikini, and the islanders were not missionized until 1908. During most of the Japanese era, a field-trip vessel which combined administrative and trading operations visited the atoll only twice a year. The relations between the Japanese officials and islanders were quite formal and emphasized their superordinate–subordinate statuses. The officials were uniformed, carried swords, and demanded deferential behavior from the people.

Because of their limited contacts with outsiders, the Bikinians had little opportunity to learn from foreigners and they were among the least acculturated Marshallese. Southern islanders thought of them as a backward people not unlike their own ancestors of the precontact era, and Bikinians who ventured away from home were subject to ridicule. A small unit of Japanese soldiers established a weather station on the atoll. They informed the Bikinians that Japan was the most powerful nation in the world and was at war with weaker powers. The soldiers imposed a strict regimen, conscripted Bikinian labor, established curfews, and suspended Christian services. The Bikinians believed the soldiers' claims and had no alternative but to acquiesce to their demands.

The Bikinians' image of the Japanese was shattered with the American invasion of the Marshalls in 1944. The soldiers at Bikini committed suicide rather than face a small contingent of American troops. The Americans assured the islanders that they had nothing to fear, and they turned over all Japanese food supplies and equipment to them.

The United States soon imposed an order of its own. A Navy vessel called every third month with administrative officials, doctors, and traders. A small store, an elementary school, and a medical dispensary were established in the community for the first time. Each was staffed by Bikinians who attended brief training sessions. The Bikinians were pleased to be relieved of the harsh rule imposed by the Japanese military and were delighted that the Americans thought them worthy of so much attention.

In late 1945 United States political and military leaders planned nuclear tests under controlled conditions which would contribute to military and scientific knowledge. Attention was soon focused on the question of the effects of nuclear weapons employed against naval vessels (Hines, 1962:21). A pair of tests given the code name Operation Crossroads was planned, and a search for an appropriate site began. It had to be within an area of the world controlled by the United States and was to be uninhabited or have a small population which could be relocated. The site had to be located in a climatic zone free from storms and cold temperatures. A protected anchorage was required for a fleet of target vessels. Dangers of radioactive fallout required that the site be distant from heavily populated areas and all sea and air routes.

Bikini fulfilled all climatic and geographic conditions required for Operation Crossroads. The community which inhabited Bikini also met the specifications; it numbered less than 170 inhabitants.

THE BIKINI COMMUNITY

Social Organization

Most of the islanders at Bikini were divided among three matriclans which had a long history on the atoll. Other clans were represented by a half dozen islanders from other atolls. The clan was an exogamous unit, and each of the three Bikini ones were comprised of related matrilineages which were ranked according to the relative age of their founding ancestresses. Usually the eldest male of a matrilineage was its *alab*, or head. The senior lineage of one of the clans was the Bikini chiefly lineage, and its *alab* was the hereditary *iroij*, chief, of the community. All Bikinians, including the *iroij*, were subject to the authority of the paramount chief in the southern Marshalls.

Because of its scarcity land was the most valued resource, and political authority was associated with its control. The typical landholding was a strip of land traversing the width of an island from lagoon to ocean sides. Matrilineages were the common type of landholding unit, and the *alabs* supervised the use of land and the distribution of its resources and were entitled to a disproportionate share of income and food from the land. A patrilateral alternative to matrilineal inheritance was common, and patri-centered groups comprised of individual males with their own children were another type of landholding group. Males heading such units were also known as *alabs* and enjoyed the same status and authority over land and people as the lineage *alabs*. In the majority of cases the holdings of an *alab* and his landholding group were dispersed, as they had parcels on more than one island in the atoll.

The *alabs*, including the *iroij*, were eleven in number, and they were the community's traditional leaders. *Alabs* represented their own interest groups in community affairs. The *iroij* provided leadership in communitywide affairs, mediated disputes, and was the Bikinians' main spokesman in dealing with outsiders.

Soon after their arrival the Americans introduced a council form of government. In theory the council was a democratic body composed of popularly selected elders headed by a magistrate. In reality this innovation produced little change. The *alabs* comprised the council, and the *iroij* was named magistrate. At the suggestion of the Americans, the council met regularly and a greater degree of formality was thereby introduced to the traditional leaders' deliberations.

The Bikinians' residences were dispersed over the central part of the largest island in the atoll. The *alabs* headed household units. With two exceptions each unit was situated on a land parcel over which the household head was *alab*. Households varied greatly in size and composition. Smaller ones were little more than nuclear family units of a half-dozen members. Larger ones sometimes counted two dozen members and were most often bilateral extended families which included some of the *alab*'s married children.

Households were commensal units which accomplished the domestic tasks of everyday life.

Technology and Economics

The Bikinians' subsistence economy was based on a minimal agricultural effort and extensive exploitation of marine resources. The inventory of subsistence crops consisted of only three plants; all were well adapted to the northern islands. The coconut was important because it provided a thirst-quenching drink and edible meat. The pandanus tree provided a seasonal fruit of substantial nutritional value which could be preserved and stored against lean times. Arrowroot yielded small tubers that were of minor significance in the diet.

None of the subsistence crops required much care, and the Bikinians had a very casual attitude toward agricultural endeavors. Seed coconuts were simply planted at random in shallow holes and were left untended. Pandanus was propagated by cuttings from mature trees and required no further care. When arrowroot was excavated with a simple digging stick, a future crop was ensured by a few tubers left in the ground.

The small inventory of subsistence plants never provided the Bikinians with more than a marginal subsistence. The few coconuts that could be spared were processed into copra, which was sold to traders upon whom the Bikinians were dependent for cloth, fishhooks, tools, utensils, and kerosene lamps. Other goods and imported foods were rare, and most items in the inventory of their material culture were manufactured from local resources. A variety of baskets was produced from coconut fronds. Fiber from coconut husks was the raw material for a high-quality sennit that was used in houses and canoe construction. Pandanus leaf was processed into mats and thatch panels for house roofs and walls. The pandanus thatch was quite durable in the northern islands and lasted from two to three years. A variety of hardwoods was available for house frames and canoes.

Outrigger canoes played an important role in Bikinian life, and the people shared with other Marshallese a strong tradition of sailing and seamanship. The outriggers were of two types. Eight of the Bikinians' canoes were sailing vessels with hulls approaching 30 feet in length and lateen sails rigged on 20-foot masts. The sailing canoes required a crew of three and could transport a sizable load of cargo and as many as seven or eight passengers. The large canoes were used for travel within the lagoon and were less frequently employed in the open sea. Small one-man paddle canoes were less important and were seven in number. These smaller craft were used off the shore of the main island but were not designed for sailing or lagoon crossings.

Canoes of both types were used to exploit Bikini's abundant marine resources. A great variety of fish, including large deep-water game fish such as tuna, was caught by trolling the lagoon and ocean waters in the sailing canoes.

Large sailing canoes similar to those which were employed by the Bikinians prior to their relocation. (*Photo by Robert C. Kiste.*)

Men also sailed to distant points in the atoll where schools of fish were caught by the surround method and spear fishing. Turtles and a variety of shellfish were also collected during such ventures. Of less importance was the drop-line method of fishing with a weighted line from the small paddle canoes.

The sailing canoes were also used to collect subsistence crops. Families often sailed from the main island to their holdings on other islands, where they remained for several days collecting and processing their crops. The islanders enjoyed these expeditions which broke the monotony of life on the main island and provided them with an opportunity to get away from their fellow Bikinians, with whom they had daily face-to-face contact. Sailing the lagoon's waters was in itself a form of recreation. Young men sometimes sailed for the pure joy of it, and fishing expeditions were seldom devoted entirely to work. Men took pleasure in their fishing ventures; they often stopped at small islands in the atoll to refresh themselves with coconut and to explore for driftwood and other objects cast up by the sea.

Paddle canoes were the property of individual males. Each of the eight sailing canoes fell under the authority of an *alab* and was referred to as the canoe of the people who formed his household and lived on the land over which he had authority. An *alab's* brothers, sons, and sons-in-law who resided elsewhere commonly sailed with the males of his household; it does not appear that males formed discretely delineated canoe groups.

Men devoted a considerable amount of time and energy in constructing and maintaining the large canoes. Canoe hulls were fashioned from hand-shaped planks which were lashed together with sennit. Maintenance was a never-ending task because canoes frequently required caulking, renewal of sennit lashings, and replacement of broken or deteriorated planks. Men took great pride in their canoes; a craft that was swift and easily maneuverable was especially prized.

RONGERIK RELOCATION

Decision to Relocate

The Bikinians first learned that their atoll had been selected for Operation Crossroads on Sunday, February 10, 1946, when the ranking officer of the military government in the Marshalls, a Navy Commodore, flew to Bikini with members of his staff and the paramount chief, who had consented to the plan to move his people. After their morning church services the Bikinians were addressed by the Commodore. According to his own report, he drew upon the Bible and "compared the Bikinians to the children of Israel whom the Lord saved from their enemy and led into the Promised Land. He told them of the bomb that men in America had made and the destruction it had wrought upon the enemy" (Richard, 1957:510). He explained that Americans were trying to learn how to use nuclear power for the good of mankind and to end all wars and how the Navy had searched the entire world for a test site and had decided Bikini was best. He asked if the Bikinians would sacrifice their homeland for the welfare of all men.

After the Bikinians had deliberated, the *iroij* of the community reported their decision. According to the Commodore's description, the iroij indicated, "If the United States government and the scientists of the world want to use our island atoll for furthering development, which with God's blessing will result in kindness and benefit to all mankind, my people will be pleased to go elsewhere" (Mason, 1954:263).

Another official report indicated, "Of the eleven family heads (*alabs*), nine named Rongerik Atoll as their first choice for the resettlement" (Meade, 1946). The Bikinians apparently selected Rongerik because it was uninhabited and because it is relatively close to Bikini (135 miles to the east) and is only a few miles from Rongelab and its people, with whom the Bikinians were familiar. The administration initially feared that the islanders might experience some difficulties on Rongerik because it is much smaller than Bikini (Rongerik has ten islands which have an area of 0.63 square miles and a small lagoon of only 55 square miles) and its resources had never been developed by a permanent population. Two other sites were briefly considered and rejected before the Americans agreed with the Bikinians on Rongerik.

Government sources indicate that the Bikinians willingly agreed to relocate because they understood that their sacrifice would benefit all mankind.

It seems plausible, however, that other factors were more important in determining the Bikinians' response. The islanders were accustomed to authority imposed from the outside, that is, the paramount chief and the colonial governments which preceded the Americans. The Bikinians in 1946 were still impressed by the decisive defeat of the Japanese by the United States, and the Americans' descriptions of the nuclear weapons convinced them of the power and technological superiority of the United States. Further, they felt indebted to the American Navy, which had evidenced more concern for their welfare than any of the previous foreigners. By his own report the Commodore also appealed to their Christian beliefs and values, which had been introduced by the American-sponsored missionary effort. Considering these circumstances it is not surprising that the Bikinians consented to abandon their homeland, and it would not be unlikely to suggest that they felt it would be to their disadvantage or beyond their power to resist.

The negotiations with the Bikinians in early 1946 were filtered through interpreters, and it is impossible to determine what impressions were actually conveyed. The Commodore was instructed that he could "promise them no more than the opportunity to submit claims for damages" (Richard, 1957: 509), and he later reported that he made no other commitments (Mason, 1954:263). The Bikinians, however, have always maintained that they always understood that their relocation was to be a temporary measure "if the atoll was not destroyed by atomic holocaust." They have claimed that Navy officials assured them that they had no cause for alarm because they would suffer neither want nor discomfort as a consequence of relocation. In the event that a return to Bikini was impossible, the islanders indicate, "we were told not to worry and that we could even live on a sandbar because the Navy would be like a father to us."

The Move to Rongerik

Less than three weeks after the first visit of the Commodore to Bikini, the islanders witnessed the beginnings of the massive preparations of Operation Crossroads. Ships began entering the Bikini lagoon bringing oceanographers, geologists, botanists, biologists, and engineers who conducted surveys of the atoll and blasted a deep-water channel through the reef off the main island. The blasts killed large numbers of fish, and the Bikinians feasted while they watched the scientists busy with all their paraphernalia. More vessels arrived and the tempo of activities increased. The Bikinians were introduced to motion pictures, which were shown on deck of naval vessels each evening. They understood little of what they saw, but they were reportedly engrossed with the films (Markwith, 1946:108). It seems certain, however, that they did perceive the wealth and material riches of America through the Hollywood offerings.

A great amount of publicity and fanfare attended the relocation of the

Bikinians. The *iroij* became known as the King of Bikini in the world press. Commercial newsreel teams and Navy photographers taught the people the meaning of the motion picture camera. Re-enactments of the Commodore's initial visit, farewell ceremonies, and certain facets of Bikini life were staged for the photographers' benefit. One of the Navy photographers reported that the people were in the process of becoming movie actors and noted,

> *The young girls were especially susceptible and giggled and posed as soon as a lens was turned their way. However, by the third day of our stay, there were so many photographers around, all shooting at once, that the girls hardly knew whom to pose for. As soon as one of the professionals settled on an angle, several of the amateurs fell in around him, and after much discussion of exposure, film speed, etc., there was a fusillade of shutter clicks.*

> *[Ibid.: 109]*

The preparations for Operation Crossroads were totally beyond the experience and imagination of the Bikinians. They were delighted with their place in the spotlight and were flattered that they seemed of such great importance to the Americans who could mobilize such an operation.

The move to Rongerik was swiftly accomplished. In early March the Bikinians loaded vast quantities of thatch, their canoes, and personal possessions on board a Navy vessel. They departed from Bikini on March 6, and arrived at Rongerik the next day. Temporary dwellings had been prepared by an advance party. The Bikinians moved ashore with several weeks supply of food provided by the Navy and began the task of building permanent quarters. Within a few days all Navy personnel departed.

The first weeks on Rongerik were a honeymoon period. Food supplies were plentiful because the Navy stores were supplemented by substantial quantities of fruits from the atoll's unexploited coconut and pandanus trees. Rongerik became something of a sideshow for Americans who shuttled to and from Bikini, and the people grew accustomed to the seaplanes which brought their visitors. The community was presented with a radio receiver and loud-speaker system powered by a generator so that they could follow the events at Bikini. All appeared well on the surface; Navy officers congratulated themselves on a job well done.

The optimism was short-lived. Even before the first test at Bikini in July, 1946, it became apparent that the islanders were not happy at Rongerik. Some varieties of fish which were edible at Bikini proved toxic at Rongerik. The people complained that the coconuts were too small and were of poor quality. The raw materials for sennit and thatch were lacking in quality and quantity. The people recalled a Marshallese myth which told how an evil spirit contaminated Rongerik, and they wanted to return to Bikini.

Operation Crossroads occupied the Americans, however, and it was thought that the Bikinians were not making an effort to adjust to their new home. The nuclear tests were completed in July, and as the operation drew to a close, the flow of visitors to Rongerik ceased. The regular field-trip vessel called every second or third month during the latter part of 1946 and early 1947. Administrative officers reported that the people were finding it increasingly difficult to maintain an adequate subsistence level. In mid-1947, a medical officer concluded that the Bikinians were "visibly suffering from malnutrition resulting from inadequate food resources on Rongerik" (Mason, 1954:314).

During the latter part of 1947 several alternative plans for another relocation were explored. Ujelang Atoll, also in the northern Marshalls, was selected as the only site which could support the population. Ujelang had been developed as a commercial copra plantation by the Germans and Japanese and had been uninhabited since World War II. The Bikinians agreed to resettle there, and in late November a number of Bikini men and Seabees arrived at Ujelang with materials to construct a village. In less than two weeks the Bikinians' hope of quitting Rongerik was ended. Officials in Washington, D.C., advised the Trust Territory administration that Eniwetok, another northern atoll, was to be utilized for a second series of nuclear tests and that its inhabitants had to be moved within the month. Operations in the Marshalls changed accordingly. The Eniwetok people were moved to Ujelang and the Bikinians remained on Rongerik (Kiste, 1968:4–9).

Conditions on Rongerik worsened. Houses and canoes fell into disrepair because of the lack of raw materials of sufficient quality. Food resources continued to decrease in quantity. The Bikinians' traditional form of social organization, work groups, and system of distribution was abandoned in favor of a communal system and effort directed by the council. The council oversaw all collecting and fishing activities and delegated tasks to men on the basis of their age and ability. A rationing system was implemented to ensure every individual an equal share of food. Community morale declined. The islanders were fearful and pessimistic about their future as they believed that the Americans had ceased to be concerned about their welfare and had abandoned them.

In early 1948 Leonard Mason, an anthropologist from the University of Hawaii, flew to Rongerik at the request of the administration to conduct an investigation. His arrival coincided with the most critical food shortage ever experienced by the Bikinians (Mason, 1950:10). Emergency rations and a medical officer were immediately flown to Rongerik. The physician reported the Bikinians' condition to be that of a starving people and plans were formulated to abandon Rongerik. An emergency evacuation was quickly mobilized, and as a temporary measure, the people and their personal possessions and dilapidated canoes were moved to Kwajalein in mid-March. The Rongerik resettlement had lasted two years and one week.

SOJOURN AT KWAJALEIN

The preparations for Operation Crossroads, the Americans' ability to mobilize the resources and equipment necessary to move whole populations, and the failure of the Bikinians' own cultural and technological resources to meet the crisis at Rongerik further convinced the Bikinians of the superiority of the wealth and technological might of the United States. Their experience at Kwajalein served to reinforce these observations and conclusions.

Prior to their arrival at Kwajalein, a tent village was prepared for the Bikinians next to a labor camp which housed Marshallese who served the military as laborers. The Bikinians were moved into their quarters, provided medical attention, and issued blankets and clothing. For the duration of their stay meals were provided in a common mess with the laborers. The fare was plain by American standards but it was a great contrast with Rongerik and was richer and more varied than the Bikinians' traditional diet. Rice, coffee, tea, bread, and canned meats, stews, and fruit were standard items on the menu.

The military base was a marvel to most of the Bikinians. Kwajalein had been denuded of vegetation and leveled during the invasion of 1944. From the debris of war the Americans had constructed a large airstrip, quonset huts, temporary wooden structures, offices, shops, churches, and a variety of other buildings. The lagoon side of the main island was equipped as a docking area for naval vessels and was cluttered with marine equipment. The military community was complete with streets, electric lights, water distilled from the sea, sewage and disposal systems, telephones, radios, movie theaters, refrigeration units, laundries, and a variety of motor vehicles. The Bikinians' quarters were equipped with electric lights.

At the end of a month and after the Bikinians had recovered from their Rongerik ordeal, those who desired work were employed in janitorial duties, boatbuilding, laundering, carpentering, and other tasks related to the maintenance of the base. With their earnings they bought new clothing and sampled widely from the great variety of goods at the post exchange; they were especially attracted to such exotic items as wrist watches, costume jewelry, and perfumes. They attended movies regularly and found candy, soft drinks, and ice cream much to their liking.

The Bikinians' sojourn at Kwajalein was never considered more than a temporary measure, and the search for another site for relocation began shortly after the abandonment of Rongerik. Officers of the administration, the Bikini *iroij*, some of the *alabs*, and the paramount chief evaluated several potential sites. The choice was narrowed down to a small northern atoll that was inhabited by a small population and uninhabited Kili Island in the southern Marshalls. The atoll was part of the paramount chief's domain; Kili had been a commercial copra plantation under the Germans and Japanese and had passed to the United States as public domain and was not the possession of any paramount chief.

The Bikinians' paramount chief encouraged them to settle on his atoll and attempted to persuade the administration that this would be the most satisfactory choice for all concerned. The Bikini *iroij* and several *alabs* visited both places and shared their observations with their fellow islanders. They considered their paramount chief's wishes, but considerable sentiment against him had developed. At Rongerik some Bikinians had charged that the chief had not fulfilled his obligation to aid them during their time of need. They suggested that because he had failed them, it would be to their advantage to have the United States serve as his surrogate. Other Bikinians were more conservative and feared that something terrible might happen if they attempted to sever their tie with the paramount chief.

Events at Kwajalein strengthened the negative feeling toward the paramount chief. He hurt his own cause and irritated the Bikinians on several occasions when he visited them and acted in a highhanded fashion by demanding that they serve in his household without compensation. Some Americans ridiculed the idea of a hereditary chief and talked to Bikinians about self-determination and democracy. The islanders in the labor camp were among the most acculturated Marshallese, and many of them were openly critical of the traditional social system which divided people into privileged and subservient classes. They advised the Bikinians to cast their lot with the Americans. The Bikinians were fully aware that the paramount chief wielded little power in comparison to the United States, and a majority voted to resettle on Kili when a plebiscite was held to determine where they would relocate.

In the fall of 1948 an advance party of Bikini men and American Seabees began preparations on Kili for the settlement. The Bikinians once again loaded their personal possessions onboard a Navy vessel for transport to a new home. Their canoes had further deteriorated during their seven-and-one-half-month sojourn at Kwajalein and were not worth moving. The main body of the community went ashore on Kili in early November. A store of foodstocks and building materials was landed with great difficulty because of rough surf conditions. The number of islanders on Kili was about twenty more than the size of the prerelocation community. A few people who had been absent from Bikini in 1946 had rejoined the community and the medical dispensary provided by the Americans had begun to have its effect; medicines had reduced the high infant mortality rate and births had far outnumbered deaths.

KILI RESETTLEMENT

Environmental Challenge

Kili has an elongate configuration with a fringing reef shelf which extends unbroken around its entire perimeter (Figure 4). Its area of one-third square mile is one half the size of the main island at Bikini and one sixth of the total land area of Bikini's twenty-six islands. In contrast to Bikini, Kili has a rich soil cover. A central depression in the island's center contains a humus-laden black muck forming an excellent taro swamp. Kili's soils and favorable location in the wet belt of the southern Marshalls offer considerable agricultural potential.

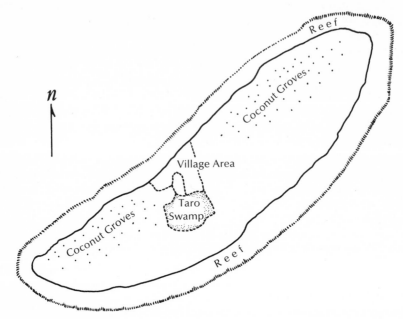

FIGURE 4. Kili island.

The development of the island as a copra plantation was begun by German traders before the end of the century. Japanese improved the plantation, and by the end of their reign well-ordered rows of excellent-quality coconut palms covered 95 per cent of the island. Few pandanus trees and no arrowroot had been allowed on the plantation. Plants with which the Bikinians had little familiarity—breadfruit trees, papaya, bananas, sweet potatoes, and taro—remained from the plantation, but they were not sufficient in quantity to support the Bikinian community.

In marked contrast to Bikini, Kili has a paucity of marine resources. The island has no lagoon or sheltered fishing area, and the reef shelf provides meager feeding grounds for marine fauna. The long axis of the island tends in an east-northeast to west-southwest direction. In the absence of a lagoon the axis of the island is quite unfavorable because it runs almost parallel to the northeast trades. No side of the island can be described as leeward. There is no protected anchorage for vessels which might otherwise be used for trolling the ocean waters. Landing at Kili is hazardous because the reef shelf is strewn with coral boulders, and heavy surf is generated by the reef's configuration. Conditions are worst from November to late spring of each year, when the tradewinds create sea swells that crash upon the reef, isolate the island, and curtail fishing except for infrequent calm spells. During Japanese

Bikini men attempting to launch a boat through a channel in the reef which surrounds Kili. (*Photo by Robert C. Kiste.*)

times vessels based at Jaluit Atoll some 30 miles away took advantage of the calms in the winter sea and made the short run to Kili to take on copra and unload supplies.

Skills and work habits different from those of the Bikinians were required on Kili. To achieve an adequate subsistence level they would have to rely less on marine resources and make the most of the island's agricultural potential. They would have to abandon their casual attitude toward agricultural endeavors and learn and practice the techniques required to cultivate the subsistence crops that were unfamiliar to them. All of these crops, at least in their immature stages, require more attention and care than the plants common to Bikini. The cultivation of taro is especially arduous and involves long hours of back-straining labor and continuous crop maintenance.

It was assumed by the administration that the excellent palm groves would yield a coconut crop far in excess of the Bikinian's subsistence needs and that the surplus would be processed into copra and a substantial cash income for the purchase of imported foods. With efficient planning and management of resources, imports could be stored up against the winter season, when they were cut off from the sea and fishing. As the Bikinians had minimal experience in trading and commercial operations, they lacked the managerial and planning skills that were requisite to the task.

In brief, the Bikinians had to change the entire basis of their economic system and acquire new skills and work habits if they were to make a successful adaptation to the island. No one in 1948 appreciated the extent to which the islanders would have to modify their lives if the Kili resettlement were to be a success.

The First Years of the Resettlement

Among the immediate tasks confronting the Bikinians on Kili was the construction of dwellings, the clearing of the dense overgrowth that had engulfed the palm groves and taro swamp since their abandonment, and a rigorous program of planting subsistence crops. The construction of a village came first, and again the Bikinians experienced a honeymoon period during the initial phase of a new settlement. The administration supplied foodstuffs during the construction period and the island's long-unexploited trees and crops yielded an abundance of food. The islanders worked hard during their first six months on Kili as they concentrated on clearing land for a village and building new dwellings. A Navy carpenter remained with them to supervise construction, and the administration provided tools, nails, sawed lumber, and tar-paper roofing material for the construction of dwellings. In contrast to Bikini's dispersed settlement pattern, dwellings were laid out in a compact area along 200 yards of roadway paralleling one of the island's shores.

The communal organization that had developed at Rongerik was continued for the first five and one-half years on Kili. As at Rongerik, the council directed the communal effort. The system was advantageous when a concentrated effort was required for the construction of the village. After the village was finished, two or three days of each week were set aside for communal labor. The council met on those mornings and divided all able-bodied men into groups that were put to work clearing brush from the groves, opening trails, weeding the swamp, and planting pandanus and breadfruit. Copra making, when scheduled, proceeded through the week and was not limited to communal workdays.

Few difficulties and no subsistence problems were experienced during the first months of the settlement. Crops were collected and distributed among households under the direction of the council. These local resources and the food supplied by the administration were distributed among households by the council. American officials judged that the settlement was off to a good start and terminated the food subsidy in the belief that it was no longer needed.

As at Rongerik, such initial optimism was premature as a number of setbacks were soon encountered. Field-trip vessels lagged far behind schedule, and the islanders were unable to trade their copra for food and other supplies. Unseasonably stormy weather churned the seas and prevented the pickup of copra. Foodstuffs were extended to the community on credit and men had to swim the goods ashore. Copra deteriorated ashore while the community's store sank into debt.

The second year of the settlement began with a low stock of imported foods. Rough seas continually hampered the landing of cargo. By early 1950 food became extremely scarce. Few fish could be caught, and the people mainly subsisted on immature coconuts. The shortage was not as critical as that experienced at Rongerik, but it reminded the people of their ordeal there, and they were distraught at the thought of remaining on Kili.

To help the Bikinians secure more food from the sea the administration had Marshallese at Kwajalein construct six large sailing canoes to replace those that had been left behind. Two of the canoes were shipped to Kili before it was realized that the large craft had no utility on the island. The Bikinians assembled one of the canoes only to learn that during calm weather it was exceedingly difficult to raise it from the sea and carry it undamaged across the reef to the beach. In rough weather the task was impossible. The second canoe was never assembled.

Although they found no use for the large sailing canoes, men constructed eleven of the one-man paddle canoes. Two men could lift one of these small craft over the reef, and they soon became quite skilled in managing their canoes in all but the worst of surf conditions. Drop-line fishing from the paddle canoes, which had been relatively unimportant in the past, replaced trolling from the larger vessels. The drop-line method is far less productive than trolling, and only tuna and a few other varieties of deep-water fish are caught with the technique.

The loss of the large sailing canoes from the Bikinians' inventory of material culture and resettlement on a single island altered more than economic sectors of their traditional life style. All of the islanders, young and old alike, missed the diversions and pleasures of sailing and the relief from the monotony of life in a small community that was formerly afforded by sailing expeditions to nearby islands within an atoll. All the islanders complained of their confinement on Kili and compared the island to a prison.

The replacement of sailing canoes by paddle canoes also affected traditional patterns of cooperation and the allocation of time and effort given to certain tasks. Men no longer formed the cooperative work groups that were required for the sailing and maintenance of the large canoes. The smaller craft required less care, and the time and effort that was formerly devoted to the larger canoes could have been rechanneled toward agricultural endeavors. Such was not the case, however.

Concerned about the success of the settlement, the administration commissioned its staff anthropologist, Dr. Philip Drucker, to assess the situation on Kili in the late spring of 1950. His report gave no reason for optimism. Outside the village area only several acres of coconut groves had been cleared of brush. Copra production had been adversely affected by the poor condition of the groves and the islanders' consumption of nuts. Little progress had been made toward the development of other crops. Breadfruit trees away from the village were engulfed with vines and were bearing poorly. The people had made a small effort to extend the planting of breadfruit, but most of their plantings had failed because of their inexperience with the plant. Southern Marshallese usually plant breadfruit near their dwellings, where it is convenient to gather the fruit and where young trees may be easily cared for. Most commonly, young shoots from mature trees are planted in holes which have been filled with mulch and humus. The Bikinians were not familiar with these procedures and had attempted to plant breadfruit away from the village, where they failed. Instead of breadfruit, pandanus, which would thrive almost anywhere, was planted in and around the dwellings, as had been their custom at Bikini.

The taro that was left in the swamp from the plantation was largely depleted. The large tuberous roots had been eaten, but little attempt had been made to replant the healthy tops which would have provided a continued crop. A young Marshallese male from one of the southern atolls assigned to the community as a school teacher had attempted to advise the Bikinians on taro cultivation. On his own initiative he had developed a demonstrative plot. It was weeded and boasted a healthy stand of taro, but the Bikinians had not followed his example. They complained that working in the swamp, digging in the mud, and constantly weeding required too great an effort. Further, they resented an outsider giving advice. The teacher did not attempt to provide instruction in the cultivation of other plants unfamiliar to the Bikinians, and their attempts to propagate them were not successful.

The Bikinian's failure to respond to the well-meant advice of the teacher and their lack of success in planting could be accounted for partially by their traditional casual attitude toward agricultural endeavors and their unfamiliarity with plants that were not cultivated at Bikini. A more significant factor, however, was their attitude toward Kili and their resettlement. Their attitude toward the island was "almost completely and unanimously negativistic" (Drucker, 1950), and they were convinced that they had been promised that they could return to Bikini if its islands were not "burned up or sunk." They knew that Bikini was intact, and they expected that sooner or later they would be returning.

The Bikinians had no desire to make a commitment to Kili and to adopt agricultural techniques which would have enhanced their chances of achieving an adequate subsistence. Only two people of consequence, the *iroij* and one of the *alabs*, conceded that the island could be made livable. Otherwise, the Bikinians presented a "united front" to outsiders. They elaborated upon the negative aspects of the island: its small size, the absence of a lagoon, the reef, and the rough winter surf. In retrospect, Bikini was remembered as an atoll of bountiful resources and "an oceanic land of milk and honey" (*ibid.*). A song reflecting their feelings and nostalgia for Bikini had been composed:

> Nothing can be right for me, I cannot be happy.
> As I sleep on my sleeping mat and pillow, I dream
>   about my atoll and its beloved places.
> My dreams remind me too painfully
> About all those places I used to know.
>
> When in dreams I seem to hear the sounds I once knew
> My memories make me "Homesick."

It is then that nostalgia overwhelms me and makes me weep
Because it is more than I can stand.
[A translation from Marshallese prepared by P. Drucker
for the naval historian Richard, 1957:541.]

The communal organization that had been advantageous and effective
when a concentrated effort was required for the construction of dwellings
had ceased to be effective. It was observed that council meetings were taking
up a good part of each morning, and the day was well advanced by the time
the work was planned. Some men gave little effort to their assigned tasks; as
shirkers were not penalized by the communal distribution system, they had a
negative effect on other workers. Further, the people had no incentive to
make an effort to develop land that was not theirs, and in the event of a land
division, no one had any assurance that he would receive sections that had
been improved.

In order to provide some relief from the confinement of Kili, to assist the
Bikinians' efforts and fishing, and to help them transport copra to Majuro,
the administration commissioned boatbuilders at Kwajalein to convert a
40-foot whaleboat for their use. The vessel had a 10-ton capacity and was
outfitted with both sails and engine. It was christened the *Crossroads*, and a
group of Bikini men were taken to Kwajalein to sail the craft to Kili. It
was assumed that having been sailors in the past that the Bikinians would
have little difficulty in navigating and managing the vessel. The reverse was
true.

The *Crossroads* required different skills and organization of personnel
than those involved in sailing an outrigger canoe. The Bikinians could
manage the *Crossroads*' sailing apparatus, but none was qualified to operate
and maintain a marine engine. In contrast to the past, when each of the
sailing canoes fell under the authority of one of the *alabs*, the *Crossroads*
belonged to the entire community, and it was uncertain as to who was to be
charged with the responsibility of managing the vessel's operation. An
elderly Bikinian who had had some experience in sailing canoes between
northern atolls was named captain of the vessel because he knew celestial
navigation and methods of determining position by wave and swell patterns
(Winkler, 1899; Kramer and Nevermann, 1938; Davenport, 1960). In
reality, his authority as master of the vessel was never clearly established, and
it immediately became apparent that he was not familiar with navigating
the waters of the southern atolls. As one Bikinian summarized the situation:
"Everyone was telling him to go this way or that way. We really had too
many captains."

On the *Crossroads*' maiden voyage, the Bikinians missed Kili altogether and
stopped at several atolls before finding the island. Similar difficulties were
encountered on other voyages; on one occasion the Bikinians ended up at an
atoll in the *Ratak* chain. The Bikinians did not have the opportunity to
develop the skills and organization of personnel to master the operation of

the *Crossroads*. In January, 1951, heavy surf washed the vessel upon Kili's reef and it sank with a full load of copra onboard.

The loss of the *Crossroads* further convinced the people that Kili was uninhabitable. The communal effort became even less effective, and community morale sank lower and lower. On more than one occasion from 1951 to 1953 food supplies ran critically low and rough seas prevented the launching of the small canoes and the landing of cargo. Copra deteriorated in the warehouse, and the community sank into debt. At one time the situation became so critical that an air drop of emergency food rations was required (Leysne, 1952).

Some individuals found occasional relief from Kili by traveling to Kwajalein and rejoining the ranks of the wage laborers. A few remained there, but most returned to their relatives and community after an absence of a few months. Those who made the journey to Kwajalein observed changes that were occurring there. Temporary structures hastily constructed during the late and immediate postwar years were being replaced with larger and more permanent facilities. The military base was being expanded, and such luxuries as swimming pools and a small golf course were added. All that the Bikinians saw there further convinced them of the magnitude of American wealth and power.

As the Bikinians on Kili continued to experience discomfort and deprivation, they became certain that they had suffered a great wrong and that they were being neglected by those who were responsible for their relocation. Promises to protect their health and welfare that purportedly had been made by Navy officers were frequently recalled. If a return to Bikini was not possible, the islanders suggested that they be relocated someplace other than Kili. In any event they wanted more help from the United States, and they were convinced that it would be but a small matter for the Americans to provide for all their wants and spare them from further hardship.

Initiation of the Development Project

Concerned about the Bikinians' growing stance of dependence and dissatisfaction with Kili, the administration briefly considered relocating them once again, but the idea was rejected when a proposed site was judged less adequate than Rongerik (Tobin, 1953). The administration then attempted to persuade the islanders that they had no alternative but to remain on Kili, and they were encouraged to divide the island into separate land parcels in the hope that they would be motivated to develop land in which they held some personal interest. The Bikinians resisted for a variety of reasons. They had been discussing a land division for some time but could not agree about a divisional scheme. They did not wish to make any commitment to Kili, and they feared that a land division would be interpreted as a sign that they were resigned to remaining on the island.

The legal status of Kili also posed a problem. The island remained public domain under the authority of the Trust Territory government. The paramount chief who held Bikini claimed that he should be given title to Kili as compensation for his loss of Bikini. By then the Bikinians were quite firm in their desire to sever their ties with the chief and have the United States function as his surrogate. They wanted to place themselves under the sheltering arm of the Americans and resisted dividing Kili until the issue with the paramount chief was settled to their satisfaction.

In early 1954 the administration initiated an extensive development project to facilitate the Bikinians' adjustment to Kili. The project team was comprised of a Micronesian trained in community development and tropical agriculture at the University of Hawaii and his two assistants. The manager shared the administration's belief that a land division would serve to motivate the islanders to make a greater effort on Kili and he strongly encouraged them to effect such an action.

The inauguration of the project apparently convinced the Bikinians that they would remain on Kili. This factor and the islanders' own discontent over the failure of the communal system precipitated action. The *iroij* devised a land-division scheme, which was implemented. Land was allocated among households in proportion to their relative sizes. The former landholding groups—that is, the matrilineages and patricentered units—were not considered in the division of land on Kili. The creation of the households as corporate landholding groups was an innovation which has had numerous repercussions upon the entire social organization of the community which have been described elsewhere (Kiste, 1968:240–65).

Still fearing that the land division would be interpreted as an indication that they had resigned themselves to Kili, the Bikinians attempted to conceal what they had done. The administration soon learned of the division, however, and was pleased because it had the effect that had been desired; each of the household units began to clear its land and produce its own copra. The land division also helped launch the development project on a positive course. The project's goals were (1) to teach agricultural techniques, with special emphasis on taro cultivation; (2) to clear the groves and increase copra production; and (3) to develop a cooperative to manage trading operations.

The *iroij* gave his full support to the project team and encouraged the people to work under its guidance. Cooperating with the council, the project manager organized, scheduled, and supervised all work activities. Men were organized into work teams and began to develop the taro swamp and plant other subsistence crops. The Bikinians were taught how to plant, mulch, and care for those crops with which they had little experience. The most productive methods of coconut palm cultivation were also introduced. The Bikinians were instructed as to the reasons and necessity for keeping the groves brushed, and they learned how the proper spacing of trees ensured a maximal crop.

Within five months substantial progress had been made. It was reported "it is obvious that the people have worked hard under the manager's direction, and the results are obvious to the eye everywhere" (Riesenberg, 1954). Part of the taro swamp had been cleared and properly planted. The planting of other crops had been greatly increased. For the first time a number of people indicated that if progress continued to be made, they would be willing to remain on the island.

The majority of the islanders, however, were still pessimistic. At least three of the *alabs*, one of whom stood in the direct line of succession to the *iroij* and was especially influential, were withholding their support, and they led a group of dissidents, which dampened the morale and optimism of others. The dissidents were skeptical and critical of any effort to improve their lot on Kili (Tobin, 1954). Many believed that they should be given subsistence and wages by the government. From their point of view the success of the relocation was the responsibility of the Americans, and the United States should compensate them for any effort they expended.

Rapid progress in the development of a cooperative, however, helped to alleviate some of the influence of the dissidents. When the project began, the accumulated debts of the community's store amounted to several hundred dollars. In conjunction with the efforts to increase copra production, the project manager initiated an imaginative program in which Bikinians manufactured items to be exported and sold to Americans and Marshallese. Using traditional skills, women produced handicraft items and older men made wooden bowls and fathoms of coconut fiber sennit. The store purchased all copra and manufactured items, and the project manager made private arrangements for a trader to call frequently and transport their goods. The handicraft items found a ready market with the Americans, and the sennit was sold to other Marshallese. Profits were substantial; within a year the store had assets of over $4,000. It was reorganized as the Kili Cooperative, in which every Bikinian held an equal share. It was hoped that in time the Cooperative would pay dividends, and even the most skeptical of the dissidents were pleased with the prospects.

In late 1955 the project manager resigned and the export business declined, because the private shipping arrangement was ended with his departure. He was replaced by another islander with equal qualifications. No Bikinians had received sufficient training to manage the Cooperative, and the new manager assumed the responsibility of supervising the business. The capital accumulated by the Cooperative provided it with a good financial base, and it continued to handle copra and trade goods. It appeared that the Bikinians were adopting the agricultural techniques introduced by the project team, and progress in agricultural development continued to be made.

By the mid-1950's the dwellings on Kili were in need of repair. The sawed-lumber walls and floor were still in fair condition, but the tar-paper roofs had deteriorated in the more than six years since the dwellings were built. On several occasions the Bikinians asked for materials to repair their houses, but the administration responded by encouraging them to use pandanus leaf thatch, as they had in the past. The Bikinians countered that the amount of pandanus on the island was not sufficient. There was some basis for their claim. The quantity of pandanus trees that remained from the plantations had not been increased sufficiently by the Bikinians' plantings to provide thatch for the entire community.

It was clear, however, that the islanders had come to prefer imported building materials to thatch and locally available woods. Some of the pandanus leaf that was available was left unused at the same time that the islanders were requesting materials from the administration. They had learned to appreciate the fact that the imports were more durable and required less time and effort than the processing of pandanus leaf thatch panels. Nails and hammers were easier to use and more efficient than the manufacture and use of sennit in house repair and construction.

The administration eventually relented and provided the Bikinians with corrugated iron roofing and nails. It was probably hoped that the provision of the materials would help sustain the positive attitude that had developed among some of the islanders. The administration's action, however, only served to reinforce the Bikinians' belief that the Americans could easily provide for them.

The Project's Second Phase

In 1956 the development project entered a new phase. Japanese prewar holdings on nearby Jaluit were provided for the development of a colony of Bikinians. A village of a half dozen dwellings and warehouses was constructed by the administration. It was planned that colonists would develop the Jaluit land to supplement Kili's copra and subsistence resources. Following the Japanese practice, the colony was also to provide a permanent base from which a vessel could service Kili, and a 50-foot motorized sailing vessel, the *Libra*, was acquired. An experienced captain and engineer, both islanders, were hired to operate the vessel and train Bikinians. It was thought that within a short time the Bikinians could assume the full responsibility of managing the vessel.

The Bikinians were enthusiastic over the *Libra* but were quite reluctant about the colony. They had gained a greater sophistication and knowledge of the world beyond their community as a consequence of their experiences associated with their relocations, but many were still hesitant to interact with the more acculturated southerners. Further, they did not want to divide their community, and they feared that the Jaluit people would view the colony as an encroachment upon their territory. Resistance to the colony was overcome by pressure applied by the administration and by an agreement pertaining to the legal status of the Bikini, Kili, and Jaluit lands. The Bikinians granted the United States indefinite use of Bikini in exchange for monetary compensation and full and legal use rights to Kili and the Jaluit lands. A one-time payment of $25,000 was given the Bikinians and a $300,000 trust fund was established which yielded them an interest payment of about $5,000 every six months. The paramount chief was not included in the settlement, and the people's future relationship with him was left for them to determine.

The Bikinians were quite pleased with the agreement. The exclusion of the paramount chief was interpreted as official confirmation of their desire to terminate his claim to Kili and hegemony over them. The size of the financial settlement convinced them that they had made the right choice in casting their lot with the United States. Much of the one-time payment was soon expended in the purchase of clothing, food, utensils, tools, and other material items.

The *Libra* and the agreement had a positive effect on the Bikinians' morale and attitude. They were more secure over their right to the Jaluit lands and a mood of optimism prevailed. The project manager moved to Jaluit with a small body of colonists to supervise the colony's development. The initial work went well. Land was cleared and planting begun. Radio equipment was provided and colonists frequently communicated with their relatives on Kili. The *Libra* sailed between the colony and Kili and occasionally to Majuro. A branch of the Cooperative was established at the colony.

The absence of the project manager from Kili was noticed. The people became lax in their maintenance of the taro swamp and coconut groves. Without experienced management, the Cooperative showed minor losses. The over-all progress of the project, however, was quite encouraging. For the first time it seemed that the Bikinians might make a satisfactory adjustment to the island (Mason, 1958), and they were beginning to feel secure in the belief that the Americans would not abandon them after all.

Typhoon Disaster

The project suffered an irreversible setback in November, 1957. The *Libra* was caught off Kili in the fury of a typhoon. No loss of life was incurred, but the vessel sank with several hundred dollars of cargo. Much of the agricultural work was undone. Seawater was washed into the taro swamp. Breadfruit trees were stripped bare, large numbers of palms were downed, and other subsistence crops were greatly depleted. Two months later another typhoon caused even greater damage on Jaluit and another southern atoll. None of the colonists was lost but the colony was devastated. The colonists were returned to Kili.

The destruction caused by the typhoon brought an end to almost all that had been accomplished. A survey on Kili indicated that copra and food resources would be drastically reduced for months and that the islanders would have to depend heavily upon imported foods for at least a year. With the losses it had suffered it was clear that the Cooperative's resources would soon be depleted, and relief foods were provided by the administration.

After the typhoons the Bikinians were little better off than they had been during the initial years of the resettlement. The quantity of subsistence crops was somewhat greater than in the first years on Kili, but this gain was offset by an increase in the size of the community. The modest medical program initiated by the Navy in the mid-1940's had continued to have effects that had not been anticipated. The reduced infant mortality and general improvement in the people's health had swelled the community's size over 240 individuals, almost eighty more than the population that was relocated in 1946. To worsen their prospects, the rehabilitation of Jaluit required most of the administration's attention, and the Kili project team was transferred there. It was hoped that the Bikinians would take the initiative and employ the skills they had learned from the project and would rehabilitate Kili with little supervision or guidance from the outside. Such hope was unwarranted. The emergency food supplies were soon exhausted, and in mid-1958 the Bikinians were placed on a food relief program. At three-month intervals over the next year and a half they were provided with substantial quantities of rice and flour.

The optimism that had developed among Bikinians during the project was completely dissipated, and their morale was quite low. Two years after the typhoon most of the damaged trees had recovered and were bearing fruit. A few individuals planted breadfruit, but most planted the coconut and pandanus trees with which they had always been familiar. Some effort had been made to keep the coconut groves free from brush, but the planting and spacing techniques introduced by the project team were not employed. The saline content of the taro swamp had decreased and taro could again be cultivated. No effort had been made to replant the swamp, however, and it was abandoned to weeds.

The lack of activity in agricultural endeavors made the winter seasons more difficult than they otherwise might have been, and the islanders were again reduced to a diet of immature coconuts on more than one occasion. Their earlier conviction that Kili was not habitable was reaffirmed by these experiences. They had realized no lasting return from the efforts they had expended during the development project, and they were unwilling to commit themselves to such an effort again without substantial assistance from the administration.

The Early 1960's

In 1961 the administration once again considered relocating the Bikinians, and their hopes were raised only to be disappointed. No adequate site for the community could be found. Those *alabs* who had led the dissidents during the early phase of the development project again emerged as vocal critics of the Americans and as potent forces influencing public opinion. All past grievances were recalled, and it was claimed that the development project had been without any value. A few individuals charged that the project managers had never been interested in aiding the Bikinians and that they had stolen some of the Cooperative's capital. The project managers had become scapegoats against whom the islanders could direct their feelings of frustration and discontent.

Almost all the islanders still harbored the hope that eventually they would be returned to Bikini. Memories of the atoll had become increasingly distorted with the passage of time. The past at Bikini became something of a Golden Age in the stories told by elders, and young Bikinians came to believe that no one had ever experienced want or discomfort at Bikini. The administration attempted to discourage the people's hope of returning to Bikini and to convince them that they had no alternative but to remain on Kili and commit themselves to agricultural development. The Bikinians responded that the Americans had been the cause of their relocation and that, in their opinion, the Americans were clearly responsible for their future. A number of Bikinians frequently traveled to the district center at Majuro to appeal for more aid and to request that they be returned to Bikini or be moved elsewhere. Often they also asked that the administration provide them with subsistence and housing while they were at Majuro, and their appearances there became so frequent that they were referred to as the "usual Kili reaction."

When surf conditions allowed cargo to be unloaded at Kili, the semi-annual interest payments from the trust fund enabled the Bikinians to supplement the island's subsistence resources. The payments had other consequences, however. A substantial amount of each payment was expended for material items. The Bikinians acquired a greater quantity of those trade goods which they had always purchased and ready-to-wear clothing became more common. Some people bought small camp-style kerosene stoves, transistor radios and other novel items. The payments also had a negative effect on copra production. Even in the calm summer months, the Bikinians produced little or no copra in the weeks prior to the receipt of a payment. The $5,000 was much greater than income derived from a few weeks of copra production and allowed the Bikinians to care for their immediate needs. In the long run the Bikinians lost income, however, as nuts not processed into copra deteriorated on the ground. It is also likely that the interest payments influenced the Bikinians' attitude toward agricultural endeavors. Had they not had a substantial income to supplement Kili's resources, they might have been more inclined to rehabilitate the swamp and expend greater effort toward the cultivation of other crops.

As the preceding data indicate, the interest payments reinforced the Bikinians' stance of dependence. Their appetite for imported goods increased with their purchasing power, and during the early 1960's they made requests to draw substantial sums from the trust fund's principal or to have it increased. Other Marshallese offered the opinion that the Bikinians had been unwise and should have held out for a larger trust fund. Financial settlements paid to other Marshallese populations soon convinced the Bikinians that they had indeed been content with too little. In 1964 the islanders of Kwajalein received approximately $1 million for a ninty-nine-year lease on land occupied by the military. A similar sum was paid to the people of Rongalab Atoll as compensation for injuries and discomforts caused by radioactive fallout from one of the tests conducted at Bikini. Both settlements were one-time payments which did not provide a perpetual income, but the Bikinians were only impressed with the amount of the settlements, and they felt that they had suffered another injustice, and they renewed their appeals for an increase in their trust fund.

The continued expansion of the population on Kili made it increasingly difficult for the Bikinians to achieve a minimum subsistence level during the winter seasons. By the time of the author's first field work with the community in 1963–1964, it had grown to 280 individuals. As in earlier years, some people occasionally return to Kwajalein to find relief from Kili and supplement their cash income. Kwajalein in the early 1960's was a well-established part of the military's ballistic missile testing program. Bikinians and other Marshallese working there witnessed missile launches and the interception of intercontinental missiles fired from the west coast of the United States. Bikinians who remained at home learned of the United States' rocket and space program from those who traveled to Kwajalein and from radio broadcasts. Satellites orbiting the earth are quite visible in the clear night sky of the Pacific. Having heard of manned space flights, the Bikinians assumed that all the satellites observed from Kili were space craft piloted by Americans.

American space technology was further evidence of the wealth and capabilities of the United States and reaffirmed the Bikinians' belief that it would be but a small matter for the Americans to remedy their plight on Kili. On numerous occasions the Bikinians recounted to the author the problems posed by Kili's reef and heavy surf, the increasing pressure of the population on the small island, and the discomforts they had endured. The wealth and technological know-how of the United States and the Americans' moral obligation to them were frequently mentioned. On one such occasion and after all opinions had been voiced, the author sat with a group of Bikinians on Kili's beach and watched a glowing satellite traverse the night sky. One old Bikinian asked, "Why is it you Americans are so smart and powerful that you can send men to the moon, but you can't help us with our problems here on Kili?"

The islanders' stance of dependence that had developed over the years was manifest in other ways and was reinforced by a program sponsored by the administration during the writer's 1963–1964 residence on the island. A school lunch program was initiated for the benefit of students throughout the Marshall Islands. The program was modeled after similar efforts in the United States. It was assumed that foodstuffs could simply be delivered to communities and that their consumption would be limited to school children. Accordingly, in the fall of 1963 several hundred pounds of U.S. Department of Agriculture surplus rice, flour, and other commodities were unloaded at

Bikini men on Kili Island today. They are making the small paddle canoes which they now use. (*Photo by Robert C. Kiste.*)

Kili. For a time adult volunteers prepared a noon meal for students each day. The program precipitated a large increase in school enrollment; children under the normal school age swelled the ranks of first graders, and adolescents who had previously dropped out of school returned. An abundance of food was prepared each noon and students took leftovers home.

As usual, November brought rough seas and the lean winter season. By December the council began distributing the U.S.D.A. food among the households. Supplies were exhausted when a calm spell coincided with the arrival of a field-trip ship. More U.S.D.A. food and other cargo were gotten ashore. With a second supply of U.S.D.A. food on hand, people purchased little foodstuffs with their own cash. Within a short time the U.S.D.A. food was again being distributed throughout the community. The surplus food prevented the annual winter period of shortages from reaching critical proportions, and from the Bikinians' point of view it was another piece of evidence which supported their earlier conclusion; the United States could well afford to provide them the support they so much desired.

The author's observations on Bikinians' agricultural endeavors did not differ from the reports of earlier years. During the calm summer months men fished almost every day, and some extended their plantings of coconuts and pandanus. Although men could describe in some detail the agricultural techniques advocated by the outside specialists, they were not practiced; planting was done in the casual manner of the past. The islanders' disdain

Bikinians rethatching the roof of a dwelling house on Kili Island. (*Photo by Robert C. Kiste*.)

for taro cultivation was made quite explicit when a few individuals planted coconuts in the overgrown swamp.

When fishing was curtailed with the advent of the winter season, there was only a small increase in agricultural activity. Some men brushed sections of their coconut groves, but most of the hours that had been devoted to fishing were spent in and about the village. The paddle canoes were repaired and stored away; a few men devoted the winter months to the construction of two new canoes. Many hours were spent in conversation, and it was plain that men were bored with their lot. Their discussions often focused about their grievances, their dislike of Kili, and the injustices inflicted upon them by the Americans.

Dwellings were again in much need of repair. The metal roofing provided in the 1950's had largely rusted away, and the original wooden floors and walls were badly deteriorated. Out of necessity and contrary to their wishes, many of the islanders had reroofed their dilapidated dwellings with pandanus thatch. They made requests for building materials, but the administration encouraged them to utilize their interest payments to purchase quantities of building material for house repair. The Bikinians rejected the suggestion and countered that the income derived from the trust fund was compensation paid for their loss of Bikini, and that it was unfair to request them to utilize the interest payments for the necessities of life on Kili. They further argued that the interest payments were needed for the purchase of food and other trade goods and that it was the Americans' responsibility to provide housing on Kili because they had moved them there; some claimed that they had

103

never wanted to resettle on Kili and that the plebiscite at Kwajalein in 1948 had been rigged by the Americans.

Return to Bikini

Conditions on Kili did not improve during the latter part of the 1960's and the administration renewed its efforts to find a solution to the problem of the Bikinians which had plagued it for over twenty years. No nuclear tests had been conducted at Bikini since 1957, and the High Commissioner requested that the Atomic Energy Commission evaluate the possibility of returning the Bikinians to their homeland. In August, 1968, the President of the United States announced that radiation levels at Bikini were low enough that most of the atoll could be reinhabited safely. The Bikinians were reportedly elated at the announcement, and shortly thereafter several of them accompanied the High Commissioner, other administration officials, and a corps of newsmen to Bikini for a reconnaissance. The atoll was not as the Bikinians had remembered it. A massive amount of debris and equipment cast aside after the tests cluttered its islands and beaches. Two or three small islands and portions of others had disappeared as a consequence of the nuclear experiments, and the atoll was engulfed by a dense layer of scrub vegetation.

In early 1969 a joint task force comprised of A.E.C. and military personnel began a rehabilitation program for Bikini. A tent village with electrical power plant, water-distillation system, and other modern conveniences was created. An airstrip constructed and used during the test period was reconditioned. The task force of men outfitted with heavy equipment and a variety of vehicles began the task of removing debris and clearing vegetation. In June eight Bikini men were flown to the atoll to aid with the work.

The administration planned to phase the resettlement over a six- to eight-year period to allow for the maturation of newly planted coconut palms before returning the community to Bikini. Initially, work crews of men from Kili would begin the planting. The crew were to be employed by the administration and rotated every three months between Bikini and Kili so that men would not be separated from their families for long periods of time. At an unspecified date, family units would be relocated gradually until the bulk of the community was returned. The Bikinians were consulted as plans for dwellings, a dispensary, school buildings, a church, council house, and warehouse were developed. To avoid the problems encountered with housing on Kili plans specified that all buildings be constructed of concrete block and aluminum roofing. As an interim measure, $95,000 was budgeted for the renovation of dwellings on Kili. The estimated cost of the over-all project was estimated at a sum far in excess of $3 million.

By the summer of 1969, when the writer returned to Kili to conduct further research, much of the enthusiasm that had been generated by the news that they would return to Bikini had dissipated, and the Bikinians were not altogether pleased with the administration's plans. The number of Bikinians on Kili had increased to about 300, and they had just experienced one of their more difficult winters on the island. The resources of the Cooperative had been completely exhausted and it was bankrupt; the U.S.D.A. school foods had not been sufficient. Rough seas prevented the landing of cargo, and the Bikinians had suffered weeks of famine before additional relief foods could be gotten ashore.

Many of the Bikinians wanted to return to Bikini immediately and have the administration provide subsistence until newly planted trees matured. Men were demanding wages higher than those normally paid to agricultural laborers for the work that they would do at Bikini, and they were not satisfied with the prospect of new housing on Kili; they wanted to be paid for their labor if they were required to construct their own dwellings. A re-evaluation of Kili was also occurring. Most of the islanders felt that they had too great an investment in the island to relinquish it entirely, and they admitted that for all its disadvantages, Kili was valuable because of its excellent coconut groves. Everyone wanted to keep Kili, as well as have Bikini returned to them.

The Bikinians' discontent with the size of their trust fund was exacerbated by an announcement that the displaced Eniwetok people were to receive financial compensation in excess of $1 million. The Eniwetok people have remained on Ujelang since their resettlement there in 1947. They too received a trust fund in the later 1950's as compensation for discomforts caused by relocation, but they were awarded a smaller fund than the Bikinians because Ujeland has fewer disadvantages than Kili. Like the Bikinians, they have often asked to be returned to their homeland. The news that the Bikinians were to be returned to Bikini caused considerable unrest among the Eniwetok people, and they protested the fact that they had to remain on Ujelang. In a move that can only be interpreted as an effort to pacify them, "undisclosed agencies" of the United States government provided $1.02 million as further compensation. The sum was to be invested for the benefit of the Eniwetok community. The settlement caused considerable agitation on Kili. The Bikinians believed that they too should receive additional money, and they renewed their pleas for an increase in their trust fund. Some individuals suggested that they should demand restitution for the Bikini land which had been destroyed by the nuclear experiments.

In August, 1969, a shipment of seed nuts was taken to Bikini and the Bikinians there began a planting program under the supervision of an agriculturist. The clean-up phase of the rehabilitation program was completed in October, and all A.E.C. and military personnel departed. A crew of twenty-three workers from Kili and a second load of seed nuts were taken to Bikini in December to continue the planting.

During the winter of 1969–1970, the Bikinians' unrest over monetary compensation increased, and they demanded that the United States pay them $100 million for their sufferings and the damages done to Bikini and that they be allowed to return to Bikini immediately (Micronitor, 1970).

In April, 1970, members of the administration met with the Bikinians on Kili to explain why the resettlement must be phased over a number of years. As an interim measure the Bikinians were assured that the administration will attempt "to make living conditions on Kili more pleasant until Bikini is fit for habitation" (ibid.). The sum of $10,000 was provided to re-establish their Cooperative, and the Bikinians were assured that they would be employed by the administration for the construction of new dwellings on Kili.

CONCLUSIONS

During the 1970's the Bikinians will realize their desire to be resettled at Bikini. Few if any of them are aware that problems of adjustment not unlike those which they have experienced on Kili will reoccur. The majority of the islanders today were either children or not yet born at the time of the community's initial relocation in 1946. They have grown up on Kili and are not familiar with lagoon fishing, sailing, or life on an atoll. Like their elders twenty-five years ago, young islanders will experience resettlement in an unfamiliar environment and will be faced with the task of learning and adopting new skills. Although older Bikinians are familiar with atoll life, the Bikini of today is not the Bikini that they knew prior to relocation, and they will have to reconcile the realities of today with their memories of the past.

It may be suggested that many of the variables which have determined the Bikinians' responses to past resettlements and innovations introduced by the administration will continue to shape their future relationship with the government and their reactions to the rehabilitation and resettlement program at Bikini. Under the administration's supervision the planting program at Bikini is designed to develop coconut groves which will be of better quality and will cover a greater portion of the atoll than the stands of palms that were destroyed by the nuclear operations. Other subsistence crops will be developed in locations selected by agriculturalists after the planting of palms has been completed. The Bikinians have not manifested any indication that they are convinced of the value of or are willing to employ the planting and cultivation techniques that have been introduced to them, nor has their casual attitude toward agricultural endeavors been substantially altered. It is doubtful that they will commit themselves to the continued agricultural development of Bikini after American supervision is withdrawn and when they are no longer paid for their labor.

Related to the last point, and far more important than the Bikinians' attitudes toward agricultural work, however, is their stance of dependence upon agencies of the United States government; dependence will be a pervasive and crucial variable which will greatly influence their responses to the current resettlement program. The factors that have been instrumental in shaping their stance of dependence are clearly still present. As evidenced by their recent demands for monetary compensation for damages to Bikini and wages for their participation in the resettlement program, the Bikinians' belief that the United States has caused them a great injustice and is obligated to make restitution is very much alive and manifest today. The Bikinians' exposure to American military and scientific operations, and the programs of assistance, welfare measures, and monetary compensation provided by the administration in the past have all been interpreted by the Bikinians as evidence that the United States has great wealth and technological power at its disposal and that it could easily allocate more of its resources to ensure their well-being. The current resettlement program at Bikini and the housing project on Kili constitute further evidence to support the conclusions which the Bikinians have already drawn.

5

One of the few things we know for certain about vast developmental projects is that they will have unplanned, unpredictable effects on the culture and social structure of the regions around them. In Ciudad Industrial Poggie described the consequences for a region of Mexico of the building of a rural industrial city. Scudder and Colson dealt with the effects of the massive Kariba Dam and the efforts of the government to stimulate the local economy. In this chapter Professor Paul Doughty describes the building of the vast hydroelectric power complex at Huallanca, Peru, and demonstrates through case studies both the immediate and the long-range, unpredictable effects on the people of the area. Professor Doughty asserts, in fact, that as far as the local people are concerned, the "ripple effects" (as he calls them) of a project are often more important than the formal goals set forth by planners, engineers, and the like. Thus, if social scientists could make the ripple effects more predictable, they could contribute significantly to the process of development.

ENGINEERS AND ENERGY IN THE ANDES

Paul L. Doughty

Paul L. Doughty is chairman of the Department of Anthropology at the University of Florida. He received his Ph.D. in Anthropology from Cornell University, where he was also Coordinator of the Cornell–Peru Project. He has been doing extensive work in Peru for over ten years; among his many articles and several books is Huaylas: An Andean District in Search of Progress.

The traditional thrust of development programs undertaken in the Third World has centered upon the introduction of new technologies affecting economic behavior. Programs are therefore designed to achieve their impact specifically in these areas under the assumption, often unelaborated, that there will be "ripple effects" which enlarge the total consequences beyond those conceived and predicted in the initial planning. Rarely, however, are these secondary effects contemplated to the degree they warrant, nor are they usually anticipated so that the potentially positive trends can be enhanced and the negative results counteracted through the application of specific policies and remedies.

It is the hypothesis of this presentation that the ripple effects are often more important to the people involved than the announced goals of development projects, and that the waves produced will touch many shores. It is likely, however, that the far-reaching consequences of technological change will not be "evenly" felt or experienced by the population, but rather, that various segments of the society will respond and participate differently and therefore benefit accordingly.

110

ENGINEERS AND ENERGY

In the remoteness of the Andean valleys and peaks one often finds conditions and events which seem incongruous in the twentieth century. It is ironic that in many of these areas one of man's oldest mechanical inventions, the wheel, and the great modern power source, electricity, are being introduced almost simultaneously. Their advent is of great consequence for the traditionally stagnant social and economic conditions found in the Andes. Aside from the abundant and spectacular remains of the Incas and other ancient Andean civilizations, the visitor finds Quechua Indian peasants living as serfs on great quasifeudal estates, with ways of life which reflect the traditions of the sixteenth century as much as those of the present. Life in the Andean highlands of Peru is quite directly based upon the exploitative and authoritarian colonial model established by the Spanish empire after its conquest of the Incas in 1531. These features of Andean life have long been the concern of many scholars and students.

Perhaps less well known, although equally interesting, has been the recent history of technological change and its growing impact upon the traditional ways of life. It is not surprising that along with an archaic social structure and culture one finds an equally antique technology. Thus, in a land where subsistence agriculture absorbs the energies of most of the people who live on the slopes and plateaus of the rugged Andes, modern tools have yet to receive wide endorsement. The ancient Inca "foot plow" (*chakitlla*) and the simple wooden scratch plow brought by early Spanish settlers are the principal instruments for tilling the soil. Work is, by and large, a manual task performed by the impoverished men, women, and children of the lowest social classes without the benefit of the mechanical, motorized, or electrical devices upon which Euro-american society so greatly depends.

Indeed, it is the mark of the lower classes that they work with their hands, which become dirtied, callused, and thickened by the exigencies of their daily tasks. In the Andes persons of lower social standing dramatize this role by "shaking hands" in a peculiar manner with those who are perceived to be of greater social status. An Indian peon or *cholo* worker offers his wrist to be grasped by his superior so that the other might avoid the discomfort of contacting a tarnished hand. In matters of work and occupation the contemporary social structure of highland Peru can be roughly dichotomized between those who work with their hands and those who, essentially, do not. The Spanish-speaking (although often bilingual) mestizo townsmen who control local economics indeed frequently refer to the Quechua-speaking lower class as "brute-Indians," a further reflection upon the "manual" as opposed to "mental" character of their respective activities.

A more sophisticated and far less onerous extension of the traditional distinction between these categories lies in the legal and functional differences established between *obreros* (blue-collar workers) and *empleados* (white-collar workers) in the urban–industrial context. The *obrero* performs manual tasks in an "industrial" setting, whereas the *empleado*, wearing white shirt and tie, earns his living behind a desk or in other "clean" activity. The status of *empleado* is sought, therefore, because it automatically confers greater social respect and in many cases, but not all, means higher salaries and better fringe benefits than *obreros* receive. The aspirations of the youth whose interests have been stimulated by what they find attractive in the world beyond their villages therefore involve the acquisition of new skills and knowledge and a chance to achieve socioeconomic mobility through their application. Most would prefer to achieve *empleado* status.

The persons who have access to labor-saving devices and who can employ them to enhance their productive efforts enjoy greater social status and respect as well as the possibility of economic enrichment. It is not surprising, therefore, to discover that modern technology, when introduced, comes first under the control of the dominant social groups, who utilize it to maintain the structural status quo. With the introduction of a mechanical tool or machine the person of high social status will first demonstrate his knowledge of its operation to an underling and then step back, his position of superiority established, and let the other perform the actual work in normal day-to-day affairs. Because of the high cost and scarcity of machines (their ownership is of great prestige value), modern tools may serve to symbolize the traditional dominant–subordinate social hierarchy. Such implements are therefore not seen as something the masses could employ independently; consequently, one finds in the Andes little effort expended in their dissemination among the people at large. As witness of this fact sales outlets for farm implements have usually been found in the big cities, where the large landowners (*hacendados*) congregate and not in the smaller rural towns, where independent small farmers and peasants might have ready access to them. By the same token, the dealers who sell modern machinery attempt to profit on unit sales rather than volume of sales because their assumption is that only a select and wealthy few are able to or will need to acquire such items.

This situation tends to thwart modernization processes in rural areas particularly. Rurality is associated with the lower-class peasantry and the Indian underclass, so that up until now, these people (perhaps 40 per cent of the national population) have not been the targets for developmental efforts on any appreciable scale.

Peru, like many countries in the Third World, is characterized by extreme centralization and a consuming focus upon large urban centers, particularly Lima, the capital located on the central coast.

The population of Lima has been swelled by the constant influx of highland migrants over the past twenty years and now holds a fifth of the nation's inhabitants. It is a classic primate city which inevitably draws people into its sphere of influence. By the same token, Lima tends to absorb the lion's share of investments for industrial development, public infrastructural projects, and salaried employment. This, of course, is not a new pattern, because

Lima was the former seat of the Spanish vice-royalty in colonial times and was similarly dominant and prestigeful then. However, the uneven process of modernization has accentuated the situation.

Relationships between the capital city (and other more developed coastal centers) and the highland population have, therefore, always evinced a strained character. The highlanders are often considered rustics, too unsophisticated for participation in higher-level events, and national and foreign investments in the Andes have been limited to labor-intensive extractive industries employing manual laborers. Andean people who wished to participate at a more advanced level in national life have been forced to migrate to the coast, for only there can sufficient opportunity be found. The migratory process in Peru, as elsewhere, tends to be highly selective, involving those who aggressively seek to achieve a change in their lives. The lowest-class highlanders, monolingual Quechua and Aymara Indians, are largely excluded from this process because they lack the social and cultural knowledge required, as well as the motivation. It is the bilingual *cholo* population and small-town mestizos from both rural and urban sectors of highland society who comprise the vast majority of migrants. Thus, in the instances when major development projects have been undertaken in the Andes, it is not surprising that interest and ambition are galvanized in those yearning for alternatives. This was the case when the Peruvian government, in 1943, began a fourteen-year construction project creating for that time the largest hydroelectric plant in the country in the district of Huaylas of the department (state) of Ancash.

HUAYLAS, CRADLE OF "ILLUSTRIOUS PERSONAGES"

The Santa River flows from a glacial lake in a northerly direction through the Callejón de Huaylas, a 100-mile-long valley flanked on the east by the 20,000-foot snow-capped peaks of the Cordillera Blanca and on the west by the dry, lesser mountains of the Cordillera Negra. The District of Huaylas occupies a handsome tributory valley at the northern end of the Callejón de Huaylas at an altitude of 9,500 feet, a mile above the Santa River as it plunges abruptly through a deep and spectacular canyon on its way to the ocean. The Cañon del Pato, as it is called, is as narrow as 70 feet in places, and over a relatively short distance provides a fall of 415 meters.

At its northern extreme the canyon opens into a mile-deep void, at the bottom of which, on the precipitous banks of the Santa, rests the village of Huallanca, at an altitude of 4,500 feet. This village had been formed in the 1920's and 1930's during the construction of the railroad which terminates there; at the time of the 1940 census it had a population of 299 persons and was part of Huaylas district. The climate is hot. In 1943 bananas, mangoes, chirimoyas, and other tropical products were being cultivated there in small plots along the banks of the river by Huaylinos who lived in the safety of the valley above the canyon, for Huallanca was the focal point at the time for the dreaded *verruga*.[1]

Though they lived some 200 miles northeast of Lima in the "heart of the Andes," the people of Huaylas had developed a considerable respect and desire for technological change.[2] Despite the seeming remoteness of their district, the Huaylinos (people of Huaylas) over the previous half century had sought to transcend the bucolic rurality of their lives by integrating themselves into the national life. Beginning in the latter part of the nineteenth century they had created primary schools in all areas of the district, largely staffed by Huaylinos, they built a handsome municipal office in the town plaza in 1901 and in the decade of the 1920's they began two vehicular roads to connect their valley with the rail head at Huallanca and the main highway 17 kilometers to the south. Improvements were made in the pre-Columbian irrigation system and other lesser projects were undertaken. All told, the people of Huaylas had distinguished themselves for their collective energy and "progressive" outlook, characteristics that they valued highly and that seemed to be much admired in the region. By 1940 Huaylinos, in short, thought well of themselves and viewed life with a certain degree of optimism and openness, unlike some neighboring areas dominated by archaic haciendas which cast a stagnant pall over the entire social and economic structure around them.[3]

The town of Huaylas, with a population of 1,246 in 1940, was the capital of the district which bore its name. Here resided most of the "illustrious personages" in their typical abode, tile-roofed houses along cobbled streets radiating out from the plaza. The white plastered buildings also held the numerous small stores and many specialized shops of carpenters, shoemakers, and the like. The sixteenth-century parish church and local hotel bordered the plaza, where a newly installed water fountain played, a gift of the colony of Huaylas' migrants in Lima. The Huaylinos living in Lima had also been influential in obtaining the diesel generator which, in 1940, provided the first electric lighting in the town.

Although they liked to think of themselves as "urban," the townsmen were also farmers exploiting their dispersed family plots. The rural residents of the district, numbering 4,368 in 1940, lived on their own land, forming tiny hamlets here and there which constituted the centers of the rural barrios or wards of the district. They were relatively well housed and lived comfortably, but not with affluence. In contrast to many Indians living on the haciendas, no one in Huaylas was suffering from hunger; the general economic and nutritional level was somewhat above the regional average.

[1] Bartonellosis, or Carrion's Disease, is a crippling affliction transmitted by a tiny mosquito found only in certain Andean valleys.

[2] The data presented here have been gathered over a period of many years. Specific recent material was obtained in 1969, when the author went to Peru under a Summer Faculty Research grant of the Latin American Studies Program of Indiana University. For a full description of Huaylas life see Doughty, 1968.

[3] See Mario C. Vasquez, No. 1.

Huaylinos were proud of their agricultural products, which consisted principally of wheat, maize, barley, alfalfa, potatoes, and other grains and tubers. "There is no other maize like ours," they would say, and indeed people today in neighboring towns corroborate this opinion. Successful farming, however, depends upon the careful use of irrigation waters which are husbanded in numerous small reservoirs scattered throughout the district from which it is distributed in accord with intricate arrangements that the cultivators make among themselves in each area.

THE AGE OF STEEL AND POWER IN HUAYLAS

The dramatic geography of Cañon del Pato made possible the realization of the hydroelectric project, designed to provide power for the industrial development planned for the region near the mouth of the Santa River in the best natural harbor on the Peruvian coast.[4] Here the tranquil fishing town of Chimbote, with a 1940 population of less than 5,000, was to be converted into an industrial center featuring that most desired of all developmental "holy of holies," a steel mill. The public and engineering eye was on this target, whose achievement was thought to be of "transcendental importance for Peru," the means of catapulting the country into the modern age. To accomplish this task the government created a semipublic agency known as the Peruvian Corporation of the Santa in 1943, with far-reaching executive and financial powers. This agency was to have complete operational and developmental control of the steel mill, Chimbote port facility, the railroad to Huallanca, and the hydroelectric plant in the Cañon del Pato. Initiated during World War II with exclusively Peruvian personnel and resources, the project lapsed after a short time, to be revived by international capital in 1946. The complicated financial arrangements led to difficulties and in 1950 a disastrous flood destroyed a large portion of the partially completed work. The project was again refinanced and finished in 1957. When the patriotic declaration of the President introduced what the newspapers proclaimed as Peru's "Age of Steel," the project had cost over $68 million to produce 50,000 kilowatts of energy and 66,000 tons of steel annually.[5]

After the great men had been praised by their peers and the "technicians

[4] I should point out an ironic and devastating fact concerning the region. This paper was written just prior to the terrible disaster of May 31, 1970, when an earthquake and avalanche resulted in the destruction of most towns and villages in the Callejón de Huaylas. Not the least of these casualties was the hydroelectric complex at Huallanca, the railroad, and the district of Huaylas itself. The infrastructural investments of a half century were either obliterated or severely damaged. These events are too recent for us to begin to assess their full meaning, but one thing is certain: that which we now discuss in retrospect and achievements which were made at such a deliberate pace against great obstacles will need to be redone. In essence, like a grisly laboratory experiment, the demonstration table was swept clean. It is well for us to think, as we read, how we might better address ourselves to this task in light of this historic experience.

[5] See *Corporación Peruana del Santa*, 1958.

and engineers" lauded for their ingenuity, few words were left for the others, the 14,000 who had actually performed the work. The project had been arduous and dangerous, factors which local people often mentioned, because work on the canyon was considered a test of one's mettle to the lower class as much as it was a test of engineering ability in the eyes of the others. For the working man the Cañon del Pato had been a fearful place in which to work because of past experience there. In the decade of 1920, when the government was constructing tunnels for the railroad, hundreds of men had worked and perished on the monumental and stony cliffs. According to one man who worked there:

> *in those times the work was very different, not as it is now, see, there were no benefits: the boss just wrote down your name and that was it! Then they paid you, but if an accident happened, no one had responsibility: there were no police, authorities, nothing. . . . If I died, for example, the company gave the family ten pounds [100 soles], buried me and that was it! . . . all the hills are full of cadavers, one could say, no? Just where they died, God knows where they were interred, that's all. In those days the work was all by hand and death was as nothing . . . .*

In the intervening years the geographical condition of the canyon had not changed, of course. To work in the canyons, niches and paths had to be carved from the rock cliffs; cable foot bridges were built and communications networks established along the 9-kilometer tunnel route between the dam and the power generators which were to be located a quarter mile inside a mountain in a great artificial cavern. Although the benefits and pay were better, the danger remained. Little wonder that the task was seen as impressive and awe-inspiring. What the dignitaries left unsaid at the inauguration, the people themselves commemorated in such songs as the following *huayno*.

Cañon del Pato	Canyon del Pato
Cañon del Pato,	Cañon del Pato,
Catarata poderoso,	Awesome cataract,
Todos te tema	Everyone fears you.
Te aborrecen	They abhor you
Por tu fama.	For your fame.
Eres la causa de la muerte	You are the cause of the death
Que fue librado	That was liberated
Por la naturaleza	By nature
Y obreros ancashinos.	And the workers of Ancsh.
La lucha verdadera de obreros	The real struggle of workers
Con el barreno	With the drill
Y el martillo	And hammer
En la mano.	In hand.
Recuayinos, Chacasinos y Huaylinos	Men of Recuay, Chacas and Huaylas
Dominaron a las rocas	Dominated the millenarian

Cañon del Pato	Canyon del Pato
Milenarias.	Rocks.
Esto es el homenaje	This is the homage
A todos los valientes	To all the valiant
Trabajadores	Workers
De la maravillosa obra	Of the marvelous work
Del gran Cañon del Pato.	Of the great Cañon del Pato.

Fewer voices still drew attention to the actual and future impact upon these men and their families. In design and concept, aside from investments conceived as being directly related to construction, there had been no consideration of what fruits might ripen for later harvest. Consequently, the input and output terminology of the national planners left a great deal to the imagination, despite implicit assumptions that jobs and "development" would occur. Was this correct?

Given the nature of the Peruvian social structure at the time, particularly with regard to the highlands, it is understandable that those in power at the national level were not particularly concerned in any explicit way with the impact upon the peasantry. The president, both at the time of the project initiation and conclusion, happened to be the same man, Don Manuel Prado y Ugarteche, an archtypical oligarch whose lack of interest in the needs of the highlands was well known. The head of the Santa Corporation was his nephew, a civil engineer, under whom labored a remarkably dedicated group of engineers devoted to promoting technological progress. These were men of great prestige, for not only were they the relatives and representatives of the national elite, but they possessed sophisticated knowledge separating them, figuratively, by centuries, from the workers under their direction. They were the epitome of progress, its spokesmen and creators, to be treated with deference and respect in many ways surpassing that accorded to the traditional landlord or *patrón*, whose strength resided in ascribed status and sheer power. The engineer, however, represented achievement and his knowledge could be acquired by others. Moreover, most of this technical elite came from outside the area, particularly the coast and even from other countries. As such, they evinced different behaviors and themselves had little stake in local events or, indeed, interest as to what impact might be produced in the local sociopolitical realm. But they also had little knowledge of local tradition, social structure, important men, or other aspects of the regional cultural setting, a fact which opened the gateway to numerous changes. Because of their positions of power and the fact that there was no local control over their activities, the engineers became the new "gatekeepers," dominating the economy through the payroll and permitting social mobility and talent development through the assignments of jobs and rank changes. In short, as the high priests of the cult of technology, the engineers came to personify progress in the most real terms for the villagers of Huaylas and surrounding area.

In order to pursue its task the Santa Corporation found it necessary to create living and working facilities considered adequate for its employees. Large investments were therefore made in both Chimbote and Huallanca, including the construction of housing, planting of trees, installation of shops and equipment, improvement of the railroad, and construction of hotels for visitors. This construction completely altered the character of the tiny railroad depot of Huallanca and produced dramatic changes in its population and in the region.

In order to make the canyon habitable, it was at once necessary to liquidate and continue to control *verruga*-carrying mosquitoes in the area. International public health consultants supervised the intensive spraying of the Huallanca environs and the district of Huaylas in general. In short order the result of this effort was felt. The extreme infant mortality rate (435 deaths per 1,000 live births) was halved within six years and continued to drop thereafter, producing a minor population "explosion" in the district. In addition, general modern health facilities were introduced for the care of the workers, who, with their families, were entitled to such treatment under Peruvian industrial law. This was an entirely new dimension, because there was no facility anywhere in the Department of Ancash at the time equipped for the practice of modern medicine. In addition to this, a dental office was also opened under the aegis of the corporation, making this service available for the first time to most of the people.

As work proceeded thousands of workers were attracted from over the entire country, but particularly from the Callejón de Huaylas. In Huallanca a new residential pattern took shape. The *obreros*, who constituted the vast majority of new workers, were housed in barracks-type structures along the river's edge or in precarious and spectacular canyon-side locations near work sites. White-collar employees were provided with somewhat better housing in different sections, further away from the rushing river, in the higher sections of the rough terrain occupied by the corporation installations. The best housing was reserved for the professional and engineering staff and their families. This consisted of comfortable bungalows clustered on high ground overlooking the rest of the inhabited area. Here pleasant tropical gardens were nurtured and a canopy of flowering trees and bougainvillaea created an oasis in the otherwise starkly barren canyon bottom. The roadways in the corporation area were the only paved roads in the Callejón de Huaylas. With time a social club with tennis courts and swimming pool were built for the white-collar and professional staff. Quite in keeping with its geographical and social position, the section was called the *plano alto* (high level).

To carry on the complicated task of construction, large machine shop, electric carpentry shops, and garages were established for the maintenance of the equipment and the fabrication of special parts. Everything from railroad locomotives to exhaust pipes could be repaired here, and the carpentry shops could produce concrete forms or furniture. The range of skills required ran the gamut of the construction and electrical industries. For the first

The hydroelectric complex at Huallanca, situated in the bottom of a great canyon. Amidst the trees to the left is the "plano alto" section where the managers' and engineers' houses were located. In the open area below this, next to the Santa River, were the workers' barracks and apartments. In the distance is the cluster of businesses and houses at the railroad depot. (*Photo by Paul L. Doughty.*)

time most of the workers became subject to the control and benefits specified under the national labor laws. For men who had been farmers, sharecroppers, and peons, wage labor was a novel experience: concepts of vacations, work uniforms, construction safety helmets, and severance pay wrought many changes in their outlook. So too did the labor unions which soon organized them and educated them in matters of legal rights and benefits. Heretofore in this section of the highlands such benefits had had no force of law or champion. The wages paid were the highest in the region at every level and the services and advantages surpassed anything available locally, even in the departmental capital of Huaraz.

Over the years more than 14,000 men were employed at Huallanca, although the maximum number at a given time never surpassed 5,000. Restaurants and secondary services flourished in Huallanca. Regular movies were shown; new schools were built in the *plano alto* and in the *barrio obrero* for their respective clienteles; a church was established, a national civil guard (police) post staffed, a consumers' cooperative founded, and bank and tax offices opened. Within a brief period Huallanca came to enjoy a set of public service and support institutions which placed it on a par with the most advanced city in the department of Ancash (the capital, Huaraz), and surpassed all the other towns and cities of the region, including Huaylas.

Such ascendency resulted in new political needs. Huallanca, which had been a modest "annex" of the district of Huaylas, now wanted and was granted political independence. The change came in 1950, under the Odria dictatorship, when the district of Huallanca was carved out of Huaylas. With the creation of the district came new political authority, officials, and responsibilities. The corporation and its personnel assumed an important role in the life of the new district. This was a change which no one had anticipated at the onset of the project but which over the years to follow came to affect regional politics in important ways. The corporation engineers, for example, strongly supported the political party of one of their former teachers, the architect Fernando Belaúnde, who became president of Peru in 1963. When this occurred the corporation personnel came to have far-reaching informal influence, which led in part to the establishment of the regional office of the new national development program, *Cooperación Popular*, at Huallanca.

Such results of the hydroelectric project in no way reveal, however, the subtle and multiple impact upon the course of events and lives of individuals in the adjacent district of Huaylas itself. In the following pages we shall examine these effects in the areas of technology, social relations, and national integration.

TECHNOLOGY

In the official accounts of the hydroelectric project little if anything is said about the acquisition of skill on the part of the laborers participating in it. Because of the multiple needs of the construction, and later maintenance, it was necessary to develop and train many persons for specific tasks. At first the project was forced to import technicians with special qualifications in electrical work, in mechanics, and in operation of construction machinery. The initial phases of the work also required a vast pool of unskilled labor to perform pick and shovel work. A large number of miners was employed for the blasting and drilling operations, an exceedingly dangerous but important phase of work.

What kinds of skills did Huaylinos learn through participation in the hydro-electric project and how has this affected their lives? Insofar as I can determine, approximately 677 men from Huaylas were employed at some time in this enterprise, or about one half of the able-bodied working men (ages fifteen to sixty-four) in the district at a given time. A sample of workers from Huaylas indicates that they held fifty-one different jobs at Huallanca, ranging from peon to dentist, only twelve of these representing occupational roles previously known to them. This innovative exposure is magnified by the fact that 70 per cent of these men held from two to four different jobs. Most began their employment as peons, the lowest occupational rank, but only 27 per cent of them remained in this position. The majority increased their status and earnings through specialization, allowing them to develop their latent talents.

The high percentage of persons taking advantage of the new alternatives is an indication that the desire for change was only latent and not absent, as some might have assumed of the peasants. The sharpening of technological awareness and skill has therefore left its mark in the district. Huaylinos soon wished to take advantage for themselves of the industrial power generated by the plant which they helped install, maintain, and manage. Intense community pressure was directed at the Santa Corporation to obtain permission to install the new current in Huaylas in 1960. The corporation, despite its hesitancy and general lack of concern for the project, allowed itself to be pushed into acceptance by the Huaylinos it employed, who were the principal instigators of a movement which had the backing of the public at large. Because there were skilled Huaylinos able to oversee the installations, it was possible for the district to achieve the goal with relative facility, utilizing its well-developed traditional system of voluntary public labor for the heavy menial work. As a result, Huaylas became the first district in the region to gain usage of the power from Huallanca.[6] So proud were Huaylinos of their accomplishment and of themselves that they spent some time contemplating how they might best advertise their success. Although they considered erecting a huge electric sign on a mountain that could be seen in the provincial capital, saying "Huaylas, the Electric District," they finally settled for an elaborate and prestigeful inaugural ceremony instead.

The Huaylinos extended the current to as many rural areas as possible.

[6] See Doughty, op. cit.:159–74.

The corporation had not envisioned that the rural people of the district would desire it and was quite unprepared for this expansion. The district government insisted, however, and Huaylas' electricians went ahead with the installations, sometimes utilizing materials " borrowed" from the corporation. Within two years almost 50 per cent of the houses in the district enjoyed the use of electricity, a condition probably unique in the Peruvian highlands.

Taking advantage of their innovation, Huaylinos began to make commercial and industrial use of it. Over the first year four of the five millers in the district had switched from diesel to electrical power for grinding flour, thereby enabling them to lower prices drastically and forcing the remaining old mill out of business. The efficiency of the electrically powered mills was such, however, that by 1969 only two of them were still in regular operation.

A similar course of events took place with regard to the fifty-nine small carpentry shops found in the district. At the onset of electrical power, six men installed modern machine equipment, including routers, lathes, circular and band saws, planers, and drill presses. As a result, Huaylas quickly became an exporter of modest quantities of wooden furniture. Yet by 1969, most of these shops were only partially active and the largest of them had been moved by its owner to the provincial capital, where he might enjoy better access to his purchasing public. In other respects Huaylinos showed similar enthusiasm for the acquisition of additional devices now operable because of their access to electricity. The record here is unclear but it is certain that the use of electrical appliances has become rather commonplace in homes across the district. Radios had already been in appreciable use in the district, powered by converted automobile batteries. Now electric irons have become best sellers in the several Huaylas stores which stock them. Other favorite items are blenders and electric sewing machines. Foot-powered sewing machines had been popular in Huaylas and were widespread household items. These and other items are now commonly purchased in the stores of the district which boast a remarkable array of such merchandise in addition to their customary noodles, bolts of cloth, hand tools, kerosene, and the rest of the typical general store stock.

In 1969 there were also two freezers in Huaylas, utilized for the production of ice cream and popsicles. Several persons had also obtained electric ranges. There seems to be no doubt that these appliances, which had been inoperable or novelty items in the past, were now objects of conspicuous consumption, on the one hand, and income-producing investments on the other. Interestingly, the things gaining greatest attention are primarily associated with the activities of women. Aside from the prestige value accruing to individual and family owners, it can be said that the women of Huaylas have probably benefited most from the electricity. They apparently had no difficulty in supplementing their time-honored manual kitchen skills with mechanical devices, once the opportunity presented itself.

Electricity was not the only technical innovation deriving directly from the hydroelectric plant project. The construction of the *plano alto* in Huallanca created a great deal of interest in Huaylas. It was, of course, the place where the technical elite resided and therefore the subject of much curiosity. The "chalet" style house and building materials employed found their imitators in Huaylas, particularly in the rural areas, where the striving for social mobility was perhaps greatest. Of note particularly was the increased use of windows and various features of room layout and organization.

SOCIAL RELATIONS

It would be an overstatement to say that life in Huaylas was revolutionized as a result of the project, but we note that certain changes indicating shifts in patterns of behavior and social relationships have occurred. One of the observations often made in Huaylas and by outsiders such as the engineering staff is that, surprisingly, many persons had been able to transcend the limitations of their education and background to participate in the development program at several levels. The people who worked at the *hidro*, as the hydroelectric installation came to be called, were typical products of the highland schools; most had only reached the third grade before dropping out of the educational system and were thus semiliterates with a tenuous grasp of arithmetic, Spanish grammar, and patriotism toward the nation state. Intellectually such persons have become convinced of their own inability to become "educated."

This situation is ironic because *Educación* has long been a major concern in Huaylas, as evidenced by the fact that several schools were functioning in the district by the end of the nineteenth century. Today there are fourteen primary schools in the district and, since 1966, a high school. The value of education has been drilled repeatedly into the heads of primary school students over the years by an enthusiastic corps of local teachers whose role has long been held as an ideal objective for the socially ambitious. In 1966, for example, the teachers of Huaylas erected a laudatory monument to their profession (and thus, to themselves) in the plaza of the town. They and most other Huaylinos (as well as the Peruvian public in general) consider *Educación* to be the *sine qua non* of modernization and development and, hence, progress.

For the Andean region Huaylas has a rather high degree of primary schooling, with some 88 per cent of all children enrolled. Review of the school records, however, reveals that the majority of students fail more often than they pass. Thus, of the boys finishing primary school in 1960 only three had never repeated a year, ten had repeated a grade once, and sixteen had failed several times. In the course of a school career most students never finish, but rather, remain in the second or third grade for several years until they eventually become too discouraged to continue. There are several reasons for this, but one of the most significant is that the system does not expect or really encourage all students, despite the rhetoric about *Educación*. Indeed, teachers' attitudes revealed that they anticipated that many of their students, particularly those from rural areas, would often be absent because of working in the fields. It was felt that they were not interested in learning because of their lack of intellectuality. Moreover, the nationally standardized curriculum and class schedule is not of great moment to country children or their needs. An uninspired performance by the children in school is therefore not surprising.

In view of this the aggressive, ambitious behavior of Huaylinos on the hydroelectric project was noteworthy. In Peru the ideal of the "self-made man" is not widely held, for understandable reasons, largely because of the lack of socioeconomic alternatives and the ascriptive nature of the social system. It is not expected that persons who have completed but two grades of school will master complex knowledge or excel in a modern technological context.

The flowering of technical skill among Huaylinos thus resulted in the creation of new social roles which differed considerably from the traditional intellectual models suggested through the schools, which eschew a technical orientation. With the advent of the project, as we have noted, technical skill came to the fore and its chief practitioners became an important reference group.

In Peru, occupational titles are of great importance and are inevitably part of one's public status. The recent President of Peru was called "Mr. Architect," for example, and others are similarly addressed as "Mr. Engineer," "Mr. Doctor," and so forth. The practice of expressing respect for achievements is common in Huaylas, where people have come to bestow the label *engineer* upon strangers as a gratuitously polite gesture. (As a result I was sometimes addressed as "Mr. Engineer Anthropologist.") The titles of mechanic, machinist, driver, and especially electrician are coveted symbols of the new expertise gained through work at the *hidro*, and have been converted into increased social respect, prestige, and stature by those so addressed. As a result of having participated in the project, even those without special attainments gained socially by preferring to think of themselves (with public approval and acceptance) as *obreros* (blue-collar workers) rather than as peons, the lowest of all Peruvian male occupational and social roles. In conducting a census of the district in 1961 I discovered that virtually all of those who had been laborers connected with the hydroelectric plant referred to themselves in these terms. Moreover, they continued to wear the coveralls and hard construction hats which identified them with the project. The hats in particular were of special symbolic importance for Huaylinos, and have become the badge of the *obrero*, replacing completely, in many instances, the high-domed palm hats traditionally worn by most peasants. Thus they become men of "experience and skill," entitled to greater esteem as evidence of increased social worth. This has resulted in a subtle shift in the vocabulary of social class in Huaylas. Whereas it has been common to speak of the "common people," or the "people of *poncho* and sandal," in referring to the "middle" socioeconomic sector of the population, the term *working class* (*clase obrera*) has gained in usage.

Wearing his prestigeful construction worker's hat, Don Carmen Espinosa adjusts the steel point of his traditional plow. Although he once worked in the hydroelectric plant construction, he has returned to farm in the ancient manner. (*Photo by Paul L. Doughty.*)

Finally, the municipal government has confirmed these changes by repeatedly awarding "diplomas of honor" to those citizens who have distinguished themselves in some manner. Thus, individuals earning professional titles and technical ratings are recognized in this manner along with others who have made a gift to the district, built a modern house, made fine furniture, offered new products for sale in a store, or been dedicated practitioners of their profession. Those perfecting skills are therefore constantly promoted as persons worthy of emulation.

THE NEW MEN OF HUAYLAS

In the countryside where Zósimo Chauca was born in 1920 the people farmed their land in small plots and sent their children to the barrio primary school for a few, generally unsuccessful, years. Most did not finish the third year of school; as a result, few were truly literate. The first language Zósimo learned was Quechua, which is the household language of the rural people. He also learned some Spanish and in school he was taught the rudiments of Spanish grammar and some arithmetic, but he dropped out before finishing the third year. Chauca's parents were farmers living in the hamlet of Santo Toribio, a short distance from the town of Huaylas, and Zósimo worked with them in the fields. Just as many other young men from Huaylas, he was conscripted and served in the army on the north coast for two years, returning to Huaylas with a tattoo on his arm as a mark of his adventures. In 1944 he went to Huallanca to work as a mason and apprentice electrician. In the latter field Zósimo found that he had some talent and quickly acquired a reputation as a person who "knew" electricity. Several of the engineers recognized this and encouraged him to study on his own, to borrow their books, and to take correspondence courses. For three years he held a job as an electrician with a company in southern Peru, returning in 1955 to become a foreman in charge of electrical work. From that point he progressed rapidly, his wages rising steadily with his increased knowledge.

Just as his technical skill emerged in a learning situation, so too did his leadership ability as he became foreman and then one of the people controlling the energy output of the plant for the steel mill in Chimbote. He grew in personal prestige in Huaylas, although he now resided most of the time in Huallanca in free company housing. The corporation had provided him originally with an apartmentlike home in the workers' section near the river. Here he had the use of electricity, a public swimming pool, and other recreational facilities open to workers and could purchase most of what he needed in the cooperative or market. Thus, he was able to save a sizable portion of his salary. By 1961 his income was considerably more than that earned by the district inspector of education and more than anyone else at the *hidro* except those of top management rank with university degrees. In 1956 Chauca's official status changed from *obrero* to *empleado* (white-collar worker) and he eventually moved to another residence section of the corporation.

Back home in Huaylas these changes were not unnoticed. Zósimo, in keeping with a common practice of absentee Huaylinos, built a new two-story house in Santo Toribio on a prominent corner. It incorporated such innovations as sash windows complete with glass (a rare item in the traditional highland residence, however well-to-do), tiled and wood floors, a brick fence, covered well, completely plastered rooms, painted trim, and other high-visibility niceties. He was awarded a diploma of honor by the district government for this achievement and was thenceforth praised for his exemplary role. In actuality neither Zósimo nor his family occupied the house, but rather, it was rented at the highest rate in the district, to the director of the boys' school in Santo Toribio.

His role in district affairs assumed similar prominence, for he was now consulted on public matters; he attended and participated actively in town meetings and during the electrification project in Huaylas directed most of the work. His public status and position in the social structure had changed vastly from the time he was the son of poor farmers who descended into the canyon to work as a peon for the corporation. He rose from the lowest social class in Huaylas to equal participation in decision making with the local "upper" class.

Today, despite his achievements, Zósimo acts with quiet confidence rather than with pretense or pompousness, which stereotypically characterizes some who have "made it." His typical dress, like most of the top staff at Huallanca, is an informal sport shirt, wash pants, and "loafers"; his hair is crew-cut and he does not smoke. There is a certain "no-nonsense" air about him, although this does not impair his sense of humor. Family responsibilities weigh upon him and consume much of his income, as he has two children in college, one in high school, and two in grade school.

Chauca has gained the universal respect of his fellow workers and Huaylinos, who consider him an example of "what one can do" if one tries. The engineers comment that Zósimo does not speak "good" Spanish and that he is still somewhat "rustic" in his manners. He still dirties his hands with work and most of his friends continue to come from backgrounds like his own. Whoever speaks of him, however, always ends by saying that he is "very, very skilled. He knows as much as we do even without schooling. He could have been an engineer."

Although Zósimo Chauca accomplished more than most persons, his case illustrates several facets of our discussion. The hydroelectric project gave him the chance to develop technical skills which directly led to his change in living standards and increased respect. This was made permanent by his becoming a key figure on the regular operating staff of the plant. His social mobility was legitimized by his officially becoming a "white-collar worker," a new status symbolized by the new house in Santo Toribio. Especially noteworthy, however, was his demonstration that a man with minimal education was capable of mastering the complex modern technology and that this paid great dividends. Schooling as such was apparently of no importance in his advancement, contradicting widespread views which place so much importance upon it as the first necessity of modernization.

Perhaps the most significant contribution of the project was that it opened ways for Huaylinos to participate more fully in the life of the nation. We have already noted that because of the project, Huallanca changed from an insignificant rail depot to a district capital with a cosmopolitan population. The existence of a new political entity provided opportunity for four Huaylinos to serve as mayor there and several more to act as councilmen. These were in addition, of course, to those who acted in these capacities in their native Huaylas. Two of these men, having first been mayors of Huallanca, became important leaders and mayors of Huaylas in subsequent years, in part because of their connections with the hydroelectric plant. One of them, Fidel Mejía, who was employed as the corporation dentist, utilized his connections with the high-echelon personnel to facilitate the electrification of Huaylas and later to obtain all manner of technical assistance for the district. As a result of his distinguished record as a community leader in Huaylas and his connections with the important people he met as they passed through on official visits to the plant, he was able to launch an interesting political career, culminating in his becoming one of the most powerful regional figures. Fidel Mejía's initiatives, in concert with the engineer who was mayor of Huallanca in 1963, also resulted in Huallanca becoming the center for regional operations of a new development program of the national government. The establishment of this entity in Huallanca resulted in Huaylas being able to take enormous advantage of it. With assistance derived from the development agency then, Huaylinos were able to complete a new 30-kilometer road connecting them more directly to Huallanca and to construct a series of reservoirs in the mountains above the farmland to improve irrigation in the district.

Thus, the political implications of the hydroelectric plant went far beyond anything originally intended or contemplated. It is unlikely that the talented dentist would have settled in his native Huaylas upon completion of his degree if the position as corporation dentist had not been open at the right time. The electricity and other facilities at the plant made it possible for the dentist to use the most modern equipment available, thus giving him a great advantage over the few other dentists in the Callejón de Huaylas. He was able to gain a large clientele, with many people traveling days to see him. Consequently, he became widely known and respected through his profession, as well as for his political role, but both depended upon the original existence of the plant installations. Over the past fourteen years, Mejía therefore became a very important personage at Huallanca in ways extending beyond his dental duties. He filled an important role as a broker between the corporation and the people in an effective but entirely unofficial and unplanned manner. As a dentist he represented a valuable service originally intended only for meeting company personnel needs but one which in fact grew to become a public service for an entire region. Because of his corporation status, on the one hand, and his political role, on the other, Mejía frequently found himself explaining company policy or action to his constituents. By the same token he also played the opposite role of representing the people vis-à-vis the corporation, presenting their complaints, helping them obtain jobs at the plant or in Chimbote, requesting changes in local policy, and soliciting assistance for public projects such as bridge and road building. Clearly he was fulfilling a much-needed community relations role for the Santa Corporation, a position the elitest government had not envisioned as necessary in its dealings with the provincial peasantry.

It can be seen that because the corporation has *no* public policy referent to the area population, this might have been a predictable development. It is instructive to realize that the regional development activities of the corporation came about in great part through the subtle role created by Fidel Mejía. Without him corporation action and impact would certainly have been far less in Huaylas. That he was able to take full advantage of the situation was a function of Mejía's personality, as much as the technological conditions. In the complicated economic and political aspects of corporation activities (the social life in the *plano alto*, management–labor problems, and the interplay of many different and ambitious persons), the abilities of the Huaylas mayor could scarcely be considered as the inevitable products of technological innovations. The key social role of company–community broker was the product of the situation which Mejía, as mayor of Huaylas and as corporation dentist, was able to fill in a unique fashion. What we must emphasize here is that the installation of the hydroelectric complex created a situation that was pregnant with options and opportunities. Huaylinos of many different backgrounds used these options in several ways.

In contrast to the situation in Huaylas, the neighboring districts were not able to make such effective use of the project for their own ends. The mere presence of opportunity does not mean that it will be taken or used in a manner some might prefer. Thus, Huaylas was the first district to obtain actual use of the electric power they helped to create, some four years before the adjacent districts. Indeed, the impact of new technology on these districts was scant.

In the neighboring district of Mato, for example, an interesting comparative case developed. The people of Mato had also participated in the hydroelectric plant construction, but had not profited to the extent that Huaylas had. Mato had never had any electricity, its short access road was poorly kept, and its population was relatively poorer and more rigidly stratified. The economy was dominated by several large haciendas and powerful families. In 1961 the son of one of these families and a native Matino returned from abroad, where he had earned an engineering degree which enabled him to take an important position at Huallanca. Eager to reintegrate himself into provincial affairs and to help his home town, he was instrumental in having a thoroughly modern electrical network installed by the Santa Corporation in Mato in 1964 as the first step in the belated electrification of the rest of the Callejón de Huaylas.

In contrast to the 1960 electrification of Huaylas which had been effected under Mejía's leadership with the volunteer work of the people, the people of Mata contributed virtually nothing to the project, relying entirely upon the corporation. The engineer from Mato found it difficult to stimulate local leadership and involvement and in the end ceased his well-intentioned attempts. Today Mato has electricity, but the people have shown neither the eagerness nor the interest in taking the entrepreneurial advantage of it that occurred in Huaylas. Similarly, there has been no effort or demand to extend the electricity to outlying rural areas in Mato as there was in Huaylas. The mere presence of technological mechanisms, then, is no guarantee that changes will occur or will follow a desired pattern. The existent socioeconomic matrix will determine to an important degree the rules by which the game will be played and who will participate.

Review of the corporation records in this respect indicates that the places which provided the most construction workers were ones whose general social and cultural characteristics resembled those of Huaylas. These places seemed to be those where the people were already looking for social and economic opportunities and where they controlled their own economics. That is, they were not dependents of large haciendas but were independent farmers and in some cases had past experience in the mines or similar heavy construction. In brief, the hydroelectric plant construction selectively affected the area, drawing to it those who already were seeking socioeconomic changes.

For such persons the project hastened their incorporation into the national socioeconomic picture. One of the principal results of the increase in skill among the Huaylinos who worked there was their enhanced ability to migrate successfully to the coastal cities. At the time of the initiation of the project in 1943, the Peruvian government had not envisioned the enormous wave of migrants which was to sweep down from the Andean villages after 1950 to exacerbate urban employment and housing problems on the coast. Thus, there was no policy developed in this respect and workers, upon gaining marketable skills, left the highlands upon their severance from the corporation. In Huaylas, of a sample of 130 men who had been *hidro* workers, only 30 per cent still lived in the district in 1961. Significantly, men of this group held fewer jobs than those who migrated, and only 23 per cent of them held jobs involving new skills, in contrast with 39 per cent of those who migrated. Thus, both the variety and novelty of experience appear to be factors contributing to the propensity to migrate.[7]

Such a migrant was Segundo Callán, a Huaylino who began working for the corporation at Huallanca when he was only twelve years old. Employed initially as a messenger boy and peon, Segundo helped provide an income for his fatherless family in Huaylas. He worked in a variety of light jobs and for a time was a stock boy in one of the warehouses. At twenty years of age he was drafted into the Peruvian army for two years; upon his release he gained employment with a mining company in a place south of Lima. Because of his

---

[7] Portions of this account are taken from a study of Huaylas migrant characteristics conducted by Stillman Bradfield in 1962 (1963:51ff.). Other sections are drawn from my own interviews with the same person, whose name is fictitious.

experience in Huallanca he was able to do some work as an apprentice electrician at the mine where he stayed for a year, leaving to avoid having to marry a policeman's daughter whom he had gotten pregnant. He returned to his home in Huaylas and again found employment at the hydroelectric plant construction. This time he worked as an apprentice electrician and had ample opportunity to perfect his skills in this area, watching others and doing some reading on his own. Just as had been the case with Zósimo Chauca, Segundo was befriended by men who knew their profession and who were willing to teach others. Thus, it was possible for him to "pick up" the knowledge "empirically," as Huaylinos say.

For Segundo this has paid big dividends over the years. With no opportunity for him to practice his trade in Huaylas and coming from a family with little land and with two other brothers, his only recourse was to migrate to the coast at the termination of the construction at Huallanca. In Chimbote he obtained employment at the corporation steel mill as an electrician, largely because he had already had contacts with the engineers and white-collar staff. Thus, he enjoyed a distinct advantage over someone who had not been previously employed by the Santa Corporation. His training in Huallanca as a boy for eight years and later as an apprentice electrician for four more years had provided him with the work habits, knowledge of the workings of bureaucracy, and familiarity with the social structure which permitted him to make the adjustment to living in the expanding city of Chimbote and to work in an industrial setting. It appears that these experiences were just as important to Segundo Callán as the technical skills he acquired. Of the many persons in Huaylas who did not make the successful adjustment to the city, most listed social reasons for returning to their homelands: the inability to take orders and adjust to the time schedule, the lack of kinsmen and close friends, and the lack of opportunity to continue certain village customs. Thus, work at the *hidro* provided a socializing experience which was invaluable in aiding Segundo and many others to adjust to urban, industrial life.

CONCLUSIONS

The hydroelectric project and the steel mill did, of course, achieve the objectives first set forth by the government. Indeed, the plant at Huallanca has been enlarged recently so as to provide sufficient current for the important coastal city of Trujillo, third largest in the country. Energy generated in Huallanca was installed in the major towns of the Callejón de Huaylas in 1967, although the rural areas have yet to benefit as they already had in Huaylas in 1961. In light of its formal goals we conclude that the project was a success: Peru produces steel and the enormous hydroelectric potential of the Andes has begun to be used for regional development outside of Lima.

The impact of industrial electricity on the patterns of life in Huaylas was diverse. Huaylinos had been especially anxious to gain from the anticipated initial step in technological modernization. As people long acquainted through migration with life in the capital city and understanding, in rudimentary ways, the need for industry, they had visions of participating in the technological progress that was expected. Most Huaylinos hoped that their district would come to host new industry.

As we have seen, however, these dreams were not realized. Although native entrepreneurs were quick to take advantage of the new current in 1961 by installing flour mills and woodworking shops, their enterprises did not prosper. Indeed, the net effect of their adventures was to drive some producers out of business, but not to develop any new sources of income or employment. The machines proved to be "unfair" competition in this society where hand crafts like carpentry supplemented a modest farm income. As a result, several of the carpenters were forced to migrate to the cities, and eventually even the most "industrialized" shop which employed nine men in 1963 moved to the larger provincial capital to gain business advantages, leaving most of the employees to return to farming. Thus, paradoxically, the result of "industrial" electrical usage in Huaylas was to reduce the number of persons employed in nonagricultural occupations. This experience showed that even the "natural" course of events could be devastating for the innocent entrepreneur (as the idle electric flour mills testify) and that "development" does not just happen as the casual "ripple effect."

Therefore, the most notable result of the electrification in Huaylas has been to enhance the level of personal convenience by making modern amenities available to many persons. Moreover, greatest interest thus far has been manifested in the acquisition of "women's" appliances for the household. This perhaps represents a key step, if we accept David McClelland's hypothesis that the "emancipation of women" is crucial in breaking restraining traditional norms and accelerating modernization.[8] Although it would be stretching the point to insist too strongly here, it is worth calling attention to the implications of such events even at this modest level. It appears clear that the predilection for such behavior antedated the hydroelectric plant, but the advent of cheap electrical power opened the door to realization.

At a more significant level, however, was the project's effect in accelerating change by rearranging social and economic relationships and increasing the levels of information and skill available in the region and nation. The *hidro* became a regional center for employment and, by the nature of the enterprise, a vast vocational training "school" as well, far larger than any formal technical training institute in the country, and equal to the annual enrollment in vocational schools.[9] This situation opened the opportunity for socially

---

[8] See McClelland, 1961:399–400.

[9] In 1959 there were only 15,962 students enrolled in *all* the technical, industrial schools in the country. That year in Ancash department, there were a total of 728 such students in five vocational schools (*Peru Ministerio de Hacienda y Comercio, Dirección Nacional de Estadística y Censos*, 1961:778). As we noted earlier, over 14,000 men were employed by the project during the construction period.

mobile individuals in the region to achieve certain of their aspirations, principally through the development of technical talents. The construction project provided, in addition, a system whereby these achievements were rewarded and secured. This, of course, was a powerful stimulus to developmental change as it involves individuals. The selective participation of persons from the region leads us to the conclusion that those who migrated to Huallanca had a relatively high achievement orientation and therefore constituted a population which had a high potential for change. Because of the difficulties in predetermining such individuals, the experience suggests that planned modernization efforts should take advantage of opportunities such as this one by consciously directing the learning situation maximizing the workers' motivation change.

The fact that this was not done (or even considered as one of the planned goals of the project) was indicative of the nature of the elitist social system and its assumptions. The traditional Peruvian culture is couched upon the premise that status is essentially static and ascribed. Moreover, the nature of human relationships between social classes is essentially exploitative, with the higher-ranking groups using the lower ones in conspicuous fashion to demonstrate and validate their respective positions. A situation such as that created at Huallanca would seem to have a high potential for conflict, in view of the fact that it juxtaposed top management individuals and the establishment view of social relations with achievement-oriented persons of lower social rank. The fact that talent mobility was permitted, although in essence unplanned, and that financial rewards were forthcoming, probably sublimated interclass resentment and by and large dissolved propensities for conflict of a serious nature, although strikes and labor disputes occasionally occurred. The other outlet for such pressure was migration. Because migration per se has never been considered in a positive light by the ruling groups in Peru, and indeed was often looked upon as a threat to the tranquility of the cities, this predictable result of the project has been especially significant for developmental change. The hydroelectric project served the vital but unplanned function of preparing thousands of peasants with marketable skills which permitted them to migrate successfully to other job centers. By creating alternative social and economic roles and increasing skill and knowledge among the peasantry, encouraging achievement orientation, and stimulating migration, the hydroelectric project played a major role, albeit unplanned, in reshaping the regional society.

6

In many parts of Latin America the *usina* has replaced the old-style, personalistic, labor-intensive *hacienda* in the production and processing of sugar cane. The *usina*, or "factory-in-the-field," represents a modern, mechanized, capital-intensive enterprise whose introduction into rural areas has necessitated far-ranging adaptations by the indigenous populations.

In this chapter Peta Henderson explores the economics of sugar production among Mayan peasants of British Honduras following the establishment of a *usina* and associated large-scale, foreign-owned plantation system in their midst. She shows us that the machines which created the "factory-in-the-field" are not nearly as important as the social and economic effects of the existence of such factories. In a series of detailed descriptions Henderson demonstrates the adaptations of the inhabitants of one village to government directives aimed at increasing sugar production. And we see here, in a classic case of "technology and the farmer," how modern capitalistic enterprise actually favors those who need it least, while disengaging the small peasant farmer from his former status as an independent part of the economy.

A SUGAR *USINA* IN BRITISH HONDURAS

Peta M. Henderson

Peta M. Henderson is a Research Assistant, Department of Anthropology, University of Connecticut. She received her master's degree in anthropology from McGill University, where she had a Ford Foundation Fellowship in the Programme in the Anthropology of Development. She has done field research in British Honduras and the Virgin Islands.

INTRODUCTION

The nature and effects of the plantation as a special form of economic organization have occupied anthropologists working in the Caribbean and elsewhere for many years. Much of the discussion has centered on an attempt to formulate descriptive typologies of the sociocultural adaptations of rural populations to the presence of the plantation in their midst (Wagley and Harris, 1955; Mintz and Wolf, 1957; Mintz, 1959; Wolf, 1959). Old- and new-style plantation systems have been distinguished, based on such economic and social criteria as labor demand, capital investment, ownership type, and degree of personalism in the system of owner-manager and worker relations. Further, it has been suggested that the nature of the crop produced may have important effects on the social structure and residence patterns, as, for example, the requirement of a large and settled labor supply on a seasonal basis in the case of sugar plantations (Manners and Steward, 1953).

The homogenizing influence of the *usina*, or modern factory-in-the-field, has also been emphasized, through the creation of a rural proletariat in an impersonal, large-scale, market-oriented economy. Canamelar in Puerto Rico, described by Mintz (1956), is possibly the extreme type case of such a homogeneous adaptation to the demands of a modern sugar plantation. Moreover, as Wolf (1959) has observed,

> Due to its tendency to amass capital, land and labor, it [the plantation] has frequently brought about the decline and atrophy of semi-independent groups of owners of small property, such as small farmers, or store-keepers, sellers of services to farmers and store-keepers. Through the use of bound labor under conditions of labor scarcity or the employment of cheap labor under conditions of labor surplus, moreover, it has tended to inhibit the rise of small property owners from the ranks of its own labor force. It thus tended to push rival social groups towards the periphery of its sphere of influence, to eke out a marginal existence in Indian pueblo, caboclo village, or Tobacco Road.
>
> [1959:136]

In the same article, however, Wolf recognizes that the social–structural effects of the *usina* may be more complex than a simple owner–wage-laborer polarity. He proposes a series of models of generalized multiple sociocultural adaptations to the new-style plantation. These models take into account the possibility that plantation wage workers may be simultaneously both peasant farmer and/or small property owners, and the models allow for some degree of vertical and horizontal mobility between statuses (Wolf, 1959:145).

The data to be presented here on the recent establishment of a factory–plantation complex in the Orange Walk District of British Honduras represent a special modifying case of the preceding considerations. Three factors must be borne in mind considering this case: first, the relatively important role that the small independent producer has played in the development of the sugar industry in British Honduras (Jones, 1969a); second, the fact that the technical requirements of modern sugar-cane production favor an economy of scale for optimum efficiency; and third, the fact that the *usina*'s plans to mechanize its own plantations as fully as possible in the near future has led to a de-emphasis on the provision of housing and other social services for seasonal wage laborers. To a large extent the plantation's labor needs are filled by the local populace, living in village settlements surrounding the plantation.[1]

---

[1] Figures provided by the Company on employment during 1968 are as follows:

Corozal Area			*Orange Walk Area*	
Agriculture	660		Agriculture	738
Transport	62	During crop	Transport	104
Factory	305		Factory	235
	1,027			1,077
Agriculture	150		Agriculture	327–160 (max–min)
Transport	50	Out-of-crop	Transport	80– 70 (max–min)
Factory	150		Factory	218–150 (max–min)
	350			625–380

Officials of the company claim that plans to mechanize are a response to the irregularity of the resident labor supply. Other complicating factors are the relative ineffectiveness of the

Our investigations of the economic situation in one such village affected by the opening of the new factory indicates that two related processes are at work. These, as Jones (1969b) has suggested, should be viewed as stages in a developmental sequence of sociocultural adaptation, rather than as structural end products of the *usina* system. First, we see the kind of multiple occupational adaptation suggested by Wolf, in a threefold split between wage labor, peasant subsistence (*milpa*) agriculture, and small-scale cane farming. The relative importance of one type of activity over another is determined by the individual's present position in the local economic hierarchy, his command of the resources essential to cane production, and his own calculations of economic advantage.

Underlying this relatively uniform adaptive response to the new factory, however, there are signs of incipient differentiation and stratification at the village level. This may be viewed as the outcome of an economic situation which favors large-scale full-time cane production and which fails to offer adequate security to the small producer. The result, we predict, will be a growing gap between a group of successful cane producers, delivering their cane to the factory but otherwise operating relatively independently of the plantation system, and a group of marginal producers who will become increasingly dependent on wage labor for subsistence.

The present study demonstrates the factors at work which lend support to this projection, through close analysis of the socioeconomic context at the village level. The focus is thus shifted from the plantation social and economic system itself to the struggle of the rural population to maintain its former independence through smallhold cane production. The presence of *la Compania*, however, is pervasive, and the structural and technological conditions imposed by its existence are creating widespread changes in village life in such areas as consumption patterns, material aspirations, cooperative activity, and increased ties with persons and agencies outside the village.

THE DEVELOPMENT OF THE SUGAR INDUSTRY IN BRITISH HONDURAS

The immediate impetus for this study was the construction of a modern sugar factory at Tower Hill in the Orange Walk District of British Honduras.[2] The opening of the factory in January, 1967, has resulted in a widespread shift from intensive swidden agriculture to monocrop sugar-cane production by the Maya Indian inhabitants of the district. Associated with the factory,

---

Northern Can Workers' Union in pressing for improved working conditions for field workers and the predominance in some areas of Mexican workers, whose presence is illegal and who are therefore not protected by national labor laws.

[2] This study is based on research conducted in the village of Douglas in the Orange Walk District of British Honduras from May 20 to July 30, 1968.

View of Tower Hill sugar factory. (*Photo by Peta Henderson.*)

which is owned and operated by the English sugar manufacturers Messrs. Tate and Lyle Ltd., is a large-scale plantation system which depends largely on the Maya for its labor force.[3] This complex, which includes an older factory and associated plantations in the Corozal District, to the north, is of the *usina* type identified by Wagley and Harris (1955) and represents a modern capital-intensive adaptation to world market conditions. Sugar is now the principal export of British Honduras and accounted for 30 per cent of the country's total exports and 54 per cent of its agricultural sales in 1967.

Sugar cane has been grown in the Corozal District since the 1848 *Guerra de Castes* in Yucatan brought a group of Mayan and mestizo refugees southwards across the Río Hondo. During the late nineteenth century there were both haciendas and plantations in the Corozal District. A few haciendas survived the turn of the century and were the principal producers of sugar cane until after the establishment of the Corozal Sugar Factory, Ltd. in 1935. Thereafter, small independent producers began to take production out of the hands of the *hacendados*, selling their cane directly to the factory at Pembroke Hall. Most of these continued, also, to grow food crops on marginal lands. The opening of the new Tower Hill factory at Orange Walk, with a capacity of producing 100,000 tons of sugar per annum, has enormously increased the demand for sugar cane, despite a concomitant expansion of the company's own plantations. At present approximately one third of the

[3] However, the two factories owned and operated by the company (the Libertad factory at Pembroke Hall in the Corozal District, and the Tower Hill factory at Orange Walk) have a more heterogeneous labor force.

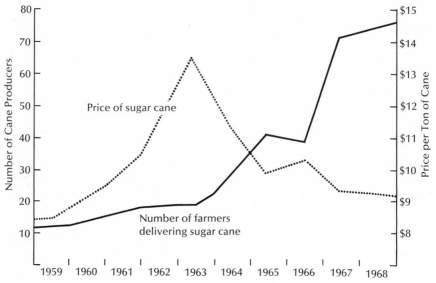

FIGURE 1. Correlation of trends in the price of sugar cane with entry of farmers into cane production, 1959–1968.

sugar cane ground at the Tower Hill factory is produced by smallholders (as against two thirds for company-produced cane), whereas the reverse is true of the Libertad factory in the Corozal District. The stated aim of the Government is a fifty-fifty balance between smallhold and plantation cane, and official policies have been directed toward providing incentives for small-scale cane production in the forms of loans and programs of land distribution.

These policies, following on several years of high cane prices, have led to a rapid increase in the number of smallhold operations in the District. Figure 1, which demonstrates the relationship between trends in the price of sugar cane and the entry of farmers into cane production 1959–1968, illustrates at first glance an almost classic instance of the kind of producer response to high prices predicted by classical economic theory. That is, the table shows that prices had reached a high point of over $13BH[4] in 1963, and immediately the number of cane producers in our sample increased sharply (1964, 1965) in response to this trend. However, at the same time that numbers of new cane producers entered the economy, sugar-cane prices began to decline precipitously. At this point classical economic theory would predict that the number of producers would also begin to level off and eventually decline.[5]

---

[4] $1U.S. is equivalent to $1.65BH.

[5] Grant Jones (personal communication) disagrees that anything resembling the law of supply and demand was at work here. After 1956, he claims, virtually all events in the sugar industry were dictated by government policy; especially after 1959, when the sugar acts were passed. However, the prevailing high prices in the world market for sugar in the early 1960's undoubtedly did influence government policy, which in turn provided loans and increased licenses for small producers.

But the government incentive programs, associated with the opening of the new factory at Orange Walk, account for the further "artificial" rise in the numbers of cane producers in the village in 1966 and 1967. Even though prices of sugar cane continued to fall, those farmers who had entered into the cane economy were by this time involved in complex credit arrangements, reorganization of economic activities, decrease of milpa production, and other accommodations to the new economic situation. These producers, therefore, could not curtail production or get out of cane growing in response to the deteriorating profitability of cane production even if they had wanted to. Their response to the patterning of prices and profits could not be made simply in terms of classical supply and demand theory. The following sections will make clear how this inelasticity in productive decision making has resulted in a tenuous economic situation for the small producer.

RECENT TRENDS IN SOCIAL AND ECONOMIC ORGANIZATION AT THE VILLAGE LEVEL: THE STRUGGLE FOR SCARCE RESOURCES

Land

The village studied is situated in the northwestern section of the Orange Walk District on the Río Hondo, which forms the boundary between British Honduras and Mexico. In 1968 the village had a population of 435, living in seventy-one households. Its location places it squarely in the center of the sugar-growing region, which is restricted to a relatively narrow strip between the Río Hondo and the New River in the northern section of the Orange Walk District and which extends up into the Corozal District to the north. Prior to the opening of the Tower Hill factory at Orange Walk Town in January, 1967, some farmers in the village cultivated cane, which they delivered to the older Libertad factory at Pembroke Hall, but since then they have been required to take it to Orange Walk. The majority of the inhabitants, however, have only recently entered the business of cane production (Figure 1). Traditionally they were milperos, using the technique of shifting "slash and burn" agriculture to plant an area in food crops, notably corn, beans, and various types of squash.

Until 1965 individual milperos generally rented land from the company, or from other private owners, paying 15 cents BH annually per mecate[6] (Romney, ed., 1959:39). The farmers were free to select a suitable piece of land from the available uncultivated bush, and informants state that they used to "make milpa" where they wished. In preparation for the opening of the new factory, however, the government purchased a section of land to

---

[6] 1 acre is equivalent to 8 mecates (approximately).

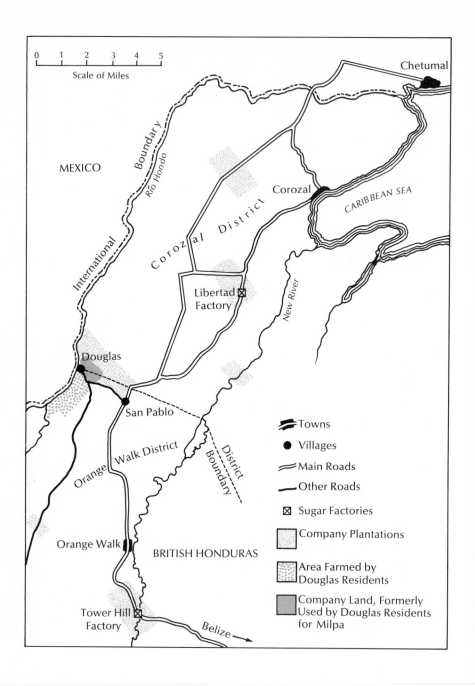

FIGURE 2. Village of Douglas and environs.

the east and south of the village from the company[7] and proceeded to distribute it in blocks of approximately 20 acres (8 × 22 mecates).[8] The only stipulation attached to distribution of these blocks was that the recipient plant some permanent crops on the land in addition to sugar cane. Despite the official policy of one man, one block, various forms of land accumulation are already practiced by the larger farmers, whose own blocks are developed and who want to expand their cane holdings. In addition to the legitimate practice of obtaining blocks in the name of adult family members (wife, grown children), some are entering into informal agreement to harvest part or all of the blocks assigned to others. Government officials are privately expressing concern that this process of land alienation will become institutionalized if, as is presently envisaged, a man becomes eligible to receive title to his block at the end of a five-year period of successful rental.

Of more immediate concern to farmers in the village, however, is the quality of the land assigned to them. When the land was surveyed prior to its distribution, no account was taken of topography, so that some blocks consist partly or wholly of swampy and uncultivatable land, which is particularly unsuitable for growing the milpa crops which still provide a subsistence base for most households. Considerable differentials exist in the quality of blocks distributed to individuals in the village. For the most part the "early" cane producers were allowed to retain the area they had already planted in cane, which tended to be the higher land at some distance from the river. These areas were simply squared off and allocated to the de facto owners. In some cases, though, blocks containing the cane of one individual were allocated to another man, which necessitated short-term sharing arrangements, a situation fraught with potential for factional dispute. Some of the original cane farmers in the village received the equivalent of two or more standard-size blocks, whereas some were unable to obtain a block, or refused the one offered to them because of its poor quality. At the period of research (1968) no further land was available in the vicinity for future distribution to young men in the village.

The net effect of this program of land distribution has been a swift decline in the area planted in milpa crops (Table 1), to the point where most families are at least partly dependent on the local stores even for such staples as

[7] In return, the company was allocated a section of land near the new factory for development of its own plantations.

[8] The situation with respect to payment for land distributed to Douglas farmers was somewhat unclear at the period of research (summer 1968). To date, farmers had paid nothing for blocks distributed in 1965. According to the Inspector of Lands, this was due to a bureaucratic delay in the formation of an *ad hoc* committee to ratify existing land-use arrangements. Blocks are allocated on a lease–purchase ("location ticket") system, with payments by installments over a five-year period after which the farmer gets title, provided that he has developed the land successfully. The amount paid depends on the quality of the land: figures cited were $20 per acre for land beside the road; $17.50 per acre for land 1–2 miles from the road; and $15 per acre for land over 2 miles from the road. (Figures given are in British Honduras currency.) During the period of research, Douglas farmers were uneasily anticipating the imposition of first payments for their plots.

Table 1

Table Showing Decline in Milpa Cultivation to 1968, and (1968) Area
Under Cultivation in Sugar Cane of Seventeen Douglas Informants*

Farmer No.	Mecates in Milpa‡		Percentage Decline	Mecates in Cane (1968)
	Before (Maximum)†	Present (1968)		
1	200	10	95	600
2	150	30	80	50
3	100	25	75	102
4	80	0	100	100
5	50	50	0	5
6	140	24	82.9	207
7	75	40	46.7	20
8	25	25	0	18
9	80	30	62.5	130
10	50	0	100	104
11	64	15	76.6	137
12	125	20	84	181
13	100	15	85	163
14	100	15	85	40
15	250	20	92	15§
16	150	25	83.4	300
17	25	10	60	35

* Sample: 22 per cent of 1968 cane-producing population of Douglas randomly selected.
† Grant Jones believes that these figures are exaggerations. His own earlier sample of Douglas farmers showed smaller milpa holdings immediately prior to the farmers' engagement in cane production. The figures given in the first column of Table 1 were supplied by informants in response to the question, "What is the maximum number of mecates you have ever worked in milpa?" The author is inclined to agree that the responses may be exaggerated, reflecting the farmers' feeling that they were better off in the old days before they entered cane production.
‡ 8 mecates = 1 acre.
§ Estimate, based on informant's cane delivery in 1968, calculated on basis of 3.75 tons sugar cane per mecate.
Mean decline = 83.2 mecates.
Percentage decline (mean) = 71%.

flour, beans, and rice.[9] Reina (1967) has demonstrated some of the cognitive factors involved in selection of suitable land for milpa, as well as the Indian's awareness of different soil types, and some ecological disturbance must be assumed following the government program to settle the farmers in one block. Most farmers still clear a small section of their block for milpa, but their major effort is now devoted to cane production. Thus, the program of

[9] Five stores were operating in the village at the period of research, supplying a population of 435 persons. Bulk purchases, however, were usually made in Orange Walk Town. During the dead season, truck transportation to Orange Walk was available three times weekly.

land distribution has resulted in a considerable reordering of productive allocations, as well as technological adjustment to the requirements of cane production.

Credit

The government's policy of encouragement of smallhold cane production did not stop at land distribution. In preparation for the new factory, loans were made available through the Cane Farmers' Association, repayable at a rate of $1.50BH per ton of cane delivered. The loans were made to farmers wishing to plant cane, the amount depending upon the farmer's adjudged agricultural potential based on his previous production record (if any), his acreage, and so on. Many, spurred by the example of economic success of the long-term cane producers in the village, took advantage of the opportunity (Figure 1). At the period of research the majority of farmers were still repaying the initial loan. Because the pace of repayment is dependent on volume of delivery, only those with already substantial holdings were in a position to liquidate the debt within the first year or two.

Some producers have been able to obtain supplementary personal bank loans, repayable at $2BH per ton delivered, but Orange Walk bank managers were discouraging this practice in the case of the small farmer in the belief that it is no kindness to permit further debt accumulation until the initial loan has been paid off. In general, a man's ability to obtain credit, and its amount, depends on the size of his license to produce cane and his judged "capacity to deliver," which in turns depends upon his acreage under cultivation. From a developmental perspective this becomes a vicious circle for the marginal producer and accounts for the suspicion with which many view the banks. Payments to the farmers for cane delivered to the factory are made by the bank *after* all deductions have been made, a paternalistic practice (albeit justifiable from a financial point of view) which does nothing to lessen the often stated belief that the company and the bank are in collusion against the small farmer.

Cane cutter working in his fields. An area with milpa crops, corn, and banana trees was adjacent. (*Photo by Peta Henderson.*)

The net effect is that, having used the $200BH loan as an initial investment, farmers are now faced with a lack of credit facilities for further expansion, or for the fertilizer and insecticides which would improve their yield. As one bank manager put it, "At present most small cane farmers are just holding on in the hope that the international political situation will change. In the meantime, they are living hand to mouth. Anything extra they put back into the soil or spend in the Clubs." The recent small farmer is faced with little prospect for a reasonable return on his initial investment.

Labor and Time

The traditional unit of production in this region is the household, generally a man and his unmarried sons, because women rarely work in the fields (Hickerson, n.d.:14ff.). The stated norm is payment for help received from persons outside the nuclear family, although some forms of reciprocity are practiced, contravening the norm. The milpero is thus usually restricted to the area that he and available unmarried sons can cultivate themselves, without recourse to outside help. Nonetheless, it appears that substantial amounts of maize were produced by inhabitants of the village, some of whom report up to 250 mecates under cultivation in milpa before they switched to sugar cane (Table 1). Some residents report having acted as entrepreneurs in a regional marketing system, stockpiling corn at the height of the season, and selling it later when it was in scarce supply and prices were high. These same men are now the largest cane farmers in the village, having strategically converted their income from corn into sugar cane at a time when the price of corn was falling and that of cane was rising. The majority of residents, however, continued their traditional milpa activity, supplemented by occasional seasonal wage labor as chicleros.

Having once opted for sugar cane, the decision is relatively irreversible for the small farmer. He has made a reallocation of time and resources in response to changed circumstances (Barth, 1967:667). As we have seen, these circumstances were the establishment of the *usina* in their district coupled with a dual program of incentives to grow cane. Unless a man has a substantial pool of free labor available to him, he is unable simultaneously to maintain his former level of milpa production and expand his cane holdings to the point where profit from the latter, at present price levels, will meet his family's cash needs. In part, this is due to the fact that the cane-cutting season overlaps with the season for felling and burning bush and planting milpa crops (Table 2).

Also competing for the small farmer's time during the *zafra* (cane season) is the opportunity to secure wage labor. Men earn $1.75BH per ton cutting cane for the company, or $1.50BH per ton cutting for other independent farmers on a piece-work basis. Most prefer to work for the company because of the higher pay and the availability of free medical care in case of accident. As a consequence, labor is in short supply among the larger independent

Table 2

Annual Work Circle Associated with Milpa and Sugar Cane
(Orange Walk District)

Month	Milpa*	Sugar Cane
January	Last bean crop harvested Tending and marketing vegetables	
February March	Felling bush	CANE SEASON Cutting Delivering Wage labor
April	Burning bush after full moon Planting corn and squash	
May	Planting corn and rice	
June	Replanting some corn Planting sweet potato, cocoa, yam, watermelon Weeding	"DEAD SEASON" Cleaning Weeding
July	Weeding House building and repairing Planting plantain	
August	Planting plantain and banana Planting corn for December harvest Clearing for bean planting beneath corn	
September	Corn breaking and harvesting Bean planting	Planting
October	Corn and rice harvesting	Cleaning and weeding new cane
November	Main crop red kidney beans planted Corn transported to village for storage	
December	Bean harvest and end of corn harvest Cleaning, weeding	CANE SEASON Begins December 15

* Source: D. H. Romney (ed.), *Land in British Honduras: A Report of the British Honduras Land Use Survey Team* (London: H.M. Stationery Office, 1959), p. 44. Supplemented by information supplied by informants in the village of Douglas, Orange Walk District.

producers, who complain that they must rely on illegal Mexican immigrants to meet their needs. In this respect the large producers and the company are in competition, producing a condition of labor scarcity.

Under present circumstances it appears that the income that can be derived from wage labor exceeds that which can be expected from milpa agriculture, although reliable estimates of the latter are unavailable.[10] Estimates of the weekly income that can be obtained from cane cutting ranged from $15 to $50BH, depending upon the amount of time spent in this activity by the individual. One informant stated that if he and his son worked full time cutting cane for the company, they could average $100BH weekly, or $2,000 BH for a five-month season.[11] The same man delivered 481 tons of sugar cane in 1968 (including his wife's quota), which by a crude estimate of net profit could have earned him $1,500–$2,000BH, assuming low labor and transport expenses and no personal loan repayments. A man with less cane, and lacking unpaid labor and a truck, would find full-time wage employment more profitable. In terms of simple profit maximization, therefore, the present situation favors wage labor over other forms of economic activity, with the exception of the very large independent operations.

In sum, the problem faced by each man is the balance of time he should spend on cane production, milpa, and wage labor. His decision in this regard varies according to the size of his cane holdings, the size of the labor force that he can command, his value priorities, and his taste and capacity for work. There is a clearly stated preference for private enterprise over wage labor, which is viewed as an expedient for meeting immediate cash needs and for saving toward the long "dead season," which extends from June to December in the Orange Walk District. However, only the largest cane farmers can afford to ignore the opportunity to supplement their income from cane by engaging in wage labor.

Transport

Perhaps the single most valuable resource for the cane producer is possession of a truck to haul his cane to the factory, 15 miles away. Not only

[10] Comparative data on income from milpa farming are difficult to obtain because a large proportion of the product is consumed directly, and the remainder is sold locally. Records of such transactions are nonexistent, except in the case of retail shopkeepers. The amount of surplus produced over that consumed would depend on the size of the household unit and the size of the labor force a man can command. In the case of a man engaged in full-time milpa farming, we might assume that the family food expense is virtually eliminated. Estimates of weekly cash expenditures on food ranged from $1 to $5BH per person. Thus in a household consisting of 6 persons, $6 to $30BH would be "earned," plus whatever surplus could be sold. In the case of one household of eight persons, the total cash outlay for a twenty-seven-week period in food, milpa expenses, medical bills, and miscellaneous was $667.83. To meet these expenses the man engaged in wage labor for the company, earning $677.06 over the same period, thus only breaking even. To earn a comparable amount from sale of milpa produced would require a surplus of 60–70 quintals of corn (@ $8 per quintal and deducting for the food expense, by a crude estimate) over the same period. Wage labor appears thus to offer a more secure and possibly less backbreaking way of meeting cash needs, which partly accounts for the decline in milpa production.

[11] Again, these figures may be exaggerations. In order to earn $10 daily, a man would have to cut over 5 tons of cane, a virtually impossible level of sustained activity. Grant Jones suggests that a more reasonable estimate of weekly earnings for a full-time cane cutter is $15–$20. By this estimate the average individual could earn approximately $400 in a five-month season. This supports the contention that the larger cane farmers are unlikely to devote time to wage labor, and pressures on the smaller producers to do so are obvious.

does the truck owner considerably reduce his own transportation expense, but he is in a position to earn additional income through rental of his truck to others at the standard rate of $3.50BH per ton.[12] There were seven trucks in the village at the period of research. Six of these were privately owned, two by the largest producer in the village, two by three brothers; and the remaining two by older men sharing with their married sons. The seventh truck was acquired in early 1968 by a group of twenty, who formed a Cane Transport Cooperative for this purpose. The cooperative venture was beset with factional conflict throughout its brief existence and has since been liquidated (1970). Those who do not have access to a truck often waste valuable time seeking an available vehicle when they are informed that they are scheduled to deliver cane to the factory. At times quotas go unfilled because no transport is available at the appropriate time. Only the private truck owners and their close kin are spared this difficulty. Yet purchase of a truck can require up to $6,500BH (the sum which the cooperative would have paid had it remained in operation), a sum that is beyond the means of the small producer, who lacks access to credit facilities.

THE ECONOMICS OF CANE PRODUCTION

As we have seen in the preceding sections, the economic situation confronting the small cane farmer is characterized by a struggle to acquire the scarce resources which will enable him to maximize his profits while keeping labor and other expenses to a minimum. A closer look at the costs involved in cane production will suggest why small-scale operations are uneconomic at present price levels.

A government official in the sugar industry estimated that a minimum of 250 mecates of cane is required to yield an annual income of $2,000BH,[13] which he considered to be a baseline for the average rural family under present economic conditions. A check of the Register of the Cane Farmers' Association for 1967–1968 showed a mean of 90.4 mecates under cultivation per individual in the case of farmers residing in the village studied. This is a little over one third of the amount necessary to earn an income of $2,000BH. Only one individual registered a total cultivated area in excess of 250 mecate. At present production levels, therefore, it appears that a minimum unit of three license-holding adults is necessary to support the average household. A man working alone is unlikely to attain a level of production sufficiently profitable to permit him to dispense with other types of income-earning activity.

---

[12] However, after a few years of use, maintenance costs are extremely high because of the poor condition of the roads. Truck ownership may, therefore, bring diminishing returns, especially to the smaller producer.

[13] This calculation was made on the basis of a yield of 4 tons per mecate. The figure is probably high in the case of the average small producer.

Support for this assertion may be found in the following estimate of basic costs to the independent cane farmer per ton of sugar cane produced:[14]

Costs of Cane Production	Per Ton Cane
Clearing, planting, weeding	$1.00*
Harvesting	1.50
Loading, transporting to factory	3.50
Repayment of initial loan	1.50
Cane Farmers' Association fee	0.10
Repayment of personal bank loan	2.00
Total costs with personal loan	9.60
Total costs without personal loan	7.60

* If fertilizer and insecticides are used, this estimate should be increased. Few farmers sampled, in fact, used these.

In 1968 the official price per ton of sugar cane paid to the farmer was $9.33BH. Thus, *at present price levels* it is possible to *lose* 27 cents BH per ton if a man is repaying both the initial loan and a subsequent personal bank loan. The small producer must, therefore, reduce his basic costs below the levels indicated. This may be accomplished through one or more of the following expedients:

1. Restricting acreage planted in cane so that a man and his unpaid sons can eliminate all labor costs up to the point of delivery.
2. Eliminating loan repayments by refusing all opportunities for credit.
3. Purchasing a truck, thus reducing the major transportation expense.

It is apparent, though, that although the first and second alternatives may have short-range advantage for the marginal producer, in the long run they restrict his opportunities for expansion and development. The third alternative is feasible only for the producer who has *already* reached a substantial level of production and who has access to credit facilities. In general, it is apparent that present profit margins are so small that a reasonable income may be earned only on volume of cane delivered.

[14] These figures represent a synthesis of information supplied by informants in the village. They represent a maximum estimate which can be reduced if the initial labor costs are eliminated.

Annual income and expense data were generally unavailable. Data supplied by one family showed an income of approximately $1,350 per annum. This family was extremely poor even by village standards and the man was only minimally engaged in cane production. Thus, the $2,000 "baseline" figure cited by the official may represent a reasonable "ideal" for a middle-level cane-producing family.

LEVELS OF ADAPTATION TO THE *USINA:* THREE CASE STUDIES

The foregoing generalizations concerning the economics of small-scale family-based cane production can be clarified through examination of selected individual cases. To illustrate the differential effects of the economic and social processes involved, the three cases presented represent, respectively, a large, a medium, and a small cane farmer (based on the size of their 1968 licenses to produce cane). As will be seen, the nature of the economic forces impinging on these men, and their responses, differ according to their respective command of the resources essential to successful cane production.

Case 1 : The Large Cane Farmer—Jose Ramirez[15]

Ramirez supports a wife, two daughters, and a teenage son. Another son in his early twenties was not present in the village at the period of research. Ramirez had a license to produce 978 tons of sugar cane in 1968, and in actuality he delivered 777 tons. He also worked the block held in his wife's name, delivering 136 tons on her license of 186 tons. The older son, who drives one of his father's trucks during the cane season, had a license of 186

The largest cane farmer in the village converts his truck for passenger runs to Orange Walk Town during the "dead season." (*Photo by Peta Henderson.*)

[15] The names used in the three case studies are pseudonyms.

tons, and 123 tons were delivered on his license. Ramirez also worked cane for his brother, whom he employs as truck driver. This man's license was 234 tons in 1968, with 36 tons delivered. Total deliveries for this productive unit were thus 1,072 tons in 1968. Ramirez, who was formerly a big corn entrepreneur, has been growing sugar cane since 1954. He owns two trucks, which are kept busy delivering his quota of 10 tons daily throughout the *zafra*. He also rents his trucks to others in the village. During the dead season (June–December), one of the trucks is used for regular passenger and freight runs to Orange Walk Town.

Ramirez employs eight to ten men during the cane season, paying them $1.50 per ton of cane cut. Where possible, he employs men from the village, but because of competition from the company, he sometimes has to rely on immigrant Mexican workers.[16] He also employs three or four men for two months during the dead season for planting and weeding, at a rate of $1.25BH per mecate for planting, and $1.50BH for weeding. He pays his brother for his services as truck driver, but not his son. A rough estimate of his expense and income from cane follows:

	Per Ton Cane
Expenses	
Clearing, planting, weeding ($2.50 per mecate @ 4 tons per mecate)	$0.62BH
Harvesting	1.75
Loading, transporting (drivers and overhead)	2.00
Cane Farmers' Association fee	0.10
Total expenses	$4.47
Income	
Profit per ton @ $9.33	4.86
Profit on 1,072 tons cane delivered	$5,209.92

Even allowing for a lower margin of profit (for loan repayments, income tax, fertilizer, and other expenses), it is clear that this man can earn an income well above the minimum baseline on volume of cane production alone. He can therefore dispense with wage labor and milpa farming if he wishes. His major problem is not that of the man who must allocate his time between

[16] Because Mexicans are in the country illegally, their employment by private farmers in the process of cane production is not protected by national labor laws. There is undoubtedly some exploitation by the private cane producer of this source of cheap labor, at the expense of village residents. Ramirez, however, explained his use of Mexicans as an outcome of labor scarcity resulting from competition from the company, which pays cutters more in wages and benefits.

three occupations, and it is clear that he has reached a point of "take-off" in the business of cane production.

Case 2 : The Middle-Level Cane Farmer—David Abascal

Abascal supports a wife and six preadolescent children. He had a license of 186 tons and delivered 87 tons of sugar cane in 1968. For the first time he did not plant any milpa in 1968, although he said that he used to cultivate 70–80 mecates of corn. He first began planting cane four years ago because in those years "cane had some value." Since then, the price has been declining, "but now we can't afford to stop growing cane." Abascal used to cut his own cane, but this year he joined the cooperative and worked on a reciprocal basis with ten other members. He thus saved $1.50 per ton on any labor he might have been obliged to hire. Until 1968 he worked cutting cane for the company for three days each week, devoting the other three days to his own fields. He reported that he could earn up to $22.50 weekly in this manner. He had a personal bank loan which he paid off last year, but he still owes for the Association loan. Abascal believes that the cane farmer has no alternative but to keep planting cane and hoping that the price of sugar cane will rise.

Thatched house of middle-level cane farmer in village. Wealthier cane farmers tend to reside in raised wooden structures. The poorest households lack whitewash, the walls being constructed of planks bound together by vegetable fiber offering poor protection against mosquitoes. (*Photo by Peta Henderson.*)

His major problem, he said, was to obtain an additional loan and more land in order to plant cane.

Abascal represents the case of a man who has opted for full-time cane production, despite awareness of the risks involved. He no longer plants milpa, nor did he work for the company this year. Instead, he joined the cooperative in the hope that by saving money on transportation and labor he might *in the long run* better ensure his future in sugar cane production. He is aware that this decision involves short-term sacrifices, as the following estimates of his costs and profits before and after entry into the cooperative show:

	Per Ton Cane
Expenses Before Entering Cooperative (1967)	
Clearing, planting, weeding	$0.00BH
Harvesting	0.00
Loading, transporting	3.50
Repayment of Cane Farmers' Association loan	1.50
Cane Farmers' Association fee	0.10
Repayment of personal bank loan	2.00
Total expenses (1967)	7.10
Income (1967)	
Profit per ton @ $9.45	2.35
Profit on 138 tons delivered	$324.30
Expenses After Entering Cooperative (1968)	
Clearing, planting, weeding	0.00
Harvesting	0.00
Loading, transporting	3.50
Repayment of Cane Farmers' Association loan	1.50
Cane Farmers' Association fee	0.10
Total expenses (1968)	5.10
Income (1968)	
Profit per ton @ $9.33	4.23
Profit on 87 tons delivered	$368.01

Were it not for the personal bank loan which this man was paying off last year (1967), his estimated profit would have been greater in 1967 than in 1968. In fact, then, participation in the cooperative would have been detrimental because time spent in reciprocal labor with other members of the cooperative eliminated the additional income he received in 1967 from milpa crops and wage labor for the company.

Two factors might help to explain Abascal's decision to join the cooperative despite the risks involved in abandonment of milpa and wage labor. First, he undoubtedly realized that his labor costs would inevitably increase with further expansion of his sugar cane. Second, he looked to the long-term benefit to be derived from reduction of the major transportation expense once the truck had been paid off. Had he continued to work alone, his margin of profit is unlikely to have permitted expansion without a change in the price of sugar cane. Thus, he had opted for full-time cane production through a mechanism of cooperative endeavor. With the recent (1970) failure of the cooperative, his return to the ranks of the part-time wage laborers and part-time milperos appears certain. For only through coopera-tion at a level beyond the household unit, it appears, could a man in his position hope to subsist entirely on income from sugar cane.[17]

Case 3: The Small Cane Farmer—Elijio Gonzalez

Gonzalez supports a wife and three young children. He had a license for 47 tons in 1968 and delivered 47 tons of cane. He has 27 mecates of milpa in his father-in-law's block (which was under water during the summer of 1968, and therefore useless) and 40 mecates of milpa on land loaned to him by another man. He has 18 mecates of sugar cane which he planted two years ago because, he said, the government offered a loan for this purpose. He stated that he would have preferred to use the money to continue growing corn, because sugar cane is "a lot of trouble," and corn prices are high (1968). He usually works alone but sometimes obtains help from the brother of his brother-in-law, whom he pays $1.50BH per ton of cane cut. He does not reciprocate in helping this man cut his cane because he does not have time. Last year he cut cane for the company for about fifteen days, but this year he did not seek wage employment with the company because his own cane and milpa keep him busy. He rents a truck from two different men and pays the standard $3.50 per ton delivered. Calculation of his expenses and profit from cane production are

[17] Of ten cane cooperatives that had been formed, only two remained in operation at the period of research. The Secretary of the Sugar Board was inclined to attribute this high percentage of failure to the "individualistic mentality" of the farmers. A cooperative officer attributes it to their "inability or unwillingness to work together. We are asking them to become businessmen. They do not understand the business and, therefore, cannot trust it. Co-ops complicate their lives and they don't like it, especially because they don't see too many tangible benefits that would make more complications worthwhile," he said. However, he added that he feels that cooperatives are the only feasible alternative to ineffi-cient, subsistence-level farming.

	Per Ton Cane
Expenses	
Clearing, planting, weeding	$0.00BH
Harvesting	0.40
Loading, transporting	3.50
Repayment of Cane Farmers' Association loan	1.50
Cane Farmers' Association fee	0.10
	5.50
Income	
Profit per ton @ $9.33	3.97
Profit on 47 tons delivered	$184.71

Gonzalez can expect to feed his family and earn a little cash income through sale of cane if he keeps his labor costs to a minimum and if he husbands his own time carefully. His economic calculations appear to be based on minimum risk rather than maximum profit. He is too close to the margin of subsistence to relinquish traditional reliance on milpa agriculture in favor of cash cropping and wage labor. So long as this is true, the prospects for improvement of his standard of living are poor. It is unlikely that he would be considered eligible for a personal bank loan with his present small license. Cane production on this scale is obviously inefficient and places heavy demands on a man's time. The question may be raised whether in due course he will face the alternative of abandoning his efforts in this direction and of relying on a combination of milpa and wage labor for a living. It may be justifiable to extrapolate from his case to that of many other recent entrants into the cane economy in the district.

SOCIOECONOMIC PROFILE OF A CANE-PRODUCING VILLAGE

The preceding analysis of the economic context confronting the village cane farmer, and of the range of adaptations to this situation, suggests a widening gap between a group of large producers able to subsist on volume of cane production alone, and a more marginal group, for whom continued cane production will become increasingly uneconomic and time-consuming. In the middle ranges of the continuum from large to small cane farmer, men like David Abascal are struggling to maintain a level of cane production which will preclude the necessity of relying on wage labor for the major portion of their income. To achieve this, new and unfamiliar modes of

economic organization are being tried, involving an extension of the productive unit beyond the household. To date, these efforts have met with
little success because of a combination of factors, including low profit
margins, factionalism, and a cultural preference for working alone. Until
profits from cooperative endeavor, as well as resources, are shared, it appears
unlikely that these attempts to make a living in cane production will succeed.

Although the precise cut-off point between success and failure cannot be
predicted on the basis of available data, other variables may be important
indicators of success, permitting cautious generalization and prediction.
A consideration of these variables follows. The projections made here are
based on current conditions in the sugar industry; a sudden favorable or
unfavorable trend in the world market for sugar could radically alter the
picture at the village level.

Table 3 presents a matrix of socioeconomic variables associated with cane
production. The twenty-five informants[18] are rank-ordered by volume of
cane deliveries during the 1968 season.[19] The variables selected for comparison
and correlation with this rank-ordering are of two types:

1. Ordinal data: socioeconomic information, including length of time
   the informant has been delivering cane, his age, size of household,
   number of unmarried sons in household, land under cultivation in
   sugar cane and milpa crops, previous milpa production (maximum),
   license quota, and percentage of quota delivered in 1968.
2. Nominal data: material indicators of economic status, ownership
   of or access to a truck, wood house, other sources of income earned
   by members of the household, men employed, wage labor performed
   for others.

From inspection of the data presented in Table 3 it is apparent that there
is a strong positive correlation between an individual's volume of delivery
and the length of time he has been delivering cane.[20] The men who began

---

[18] The sample of twenty-five cane farmers in Table 3 approximates a stratified random
sample. An effort was made to include representatives of all levels of cane production,
based on volume of delivery in 1968.

[19] Cane delivery figures and license quotas for 1968 given in Table 3 include all cane-
producing members of a household, assuming this to be the basic productive unit. In most
cases this includes a wife and/or unmarried adult sons. In a few cases involving joint
households, the delivery record and license quotas of married sons is also included. Figures
given for "mecates under cultivation in cane" also include all cane-producing members of
the household. In many cases licenses are taken out by the household head on behalf of
spouses and unmarried sons in order to qualify for additional blocks of land and larger
delivery quotas.

[20] The rank correlation coefficient, using the Kendall tau formula (Siegel, 1956), is tau =
0.46, which, converted to a z score, is significant at the 0.001 level. A more perfect correlation would have been obtained, were it not for informant numbers 22 and 24, who have been
delivering cane for nine and eight years respectively. These men rank low on volume of
cane delivery. Both men have full-time employment with the Company, relying on kinsmen
to cultivate and harvest their cane. Clearly their major income-earning effort lies elsewhere
than in cane production.

Table 3
Socioeconomic Variables Associated with Cane Production

Informant	Cane Delivery 1968* Tons	License Quota 1968* Tons	Percentage of Quota Del.	No. Yrs. Del. Cane†	Age	Number in Household	Number of Adult Sons Unmarried	Mec. u/c Cane 1968*	Mec. u/c Milpa 1968*	Mec. u/c Milpa Before*	Percentage Decline Milpa	Truck—Owns or Access to	Wood House	Other Source of Income	Performs Wage Work for Company	Employs Wage Laborers
1	1072	1568	68	10+	50	9	2	600	10	200	95	Owns	Yes	Store	No	Yes
2	603	494	82	10+	43	13	0	272	25	?	?	Owns	Yes	No	No	Yes
3	481	378	78	10+	47	10	1	350	25	150	83	Owns	Yes	No	No	Yes
4	269	448	60	9	60	9	2	355	0	150	100	Owns	Yes	Store	No	No
5	213	258	82	5	42	12	2	180	30	80	62	No	No	Teacher	No	Yes
6	180	214	84	10+	65	3	(1)	100	0	?	100	No	Yes	Store	No	Yes
7	166	282	59	10+	36	9	0	228	15	100	85	Father-in-law	No	No	No‡	Yes
8	133	460	29	4	58	9	4	253	10	?	?	Coop.	No	No	No‡	No
9	130	258	50	4	55	5	1	125	10	25	60	Coop.	No	No	No‡	Yes
10	116	214	54	10+	45	2	0	184	20	125	84	Coop.	No	No	Yes‡	No

				10+												
11	104	186	56	4	59	4	0	102	25	100	75	No	Yes	Teacher	No	Yes
12	104	219	47	8	60	10	2	200	20	250	92	Coop.	No	No	No‡	No
13	103	186	55	8	37	8	1	104	0	50	100	Coop.	No	No	No‡	No
14	96	186	51	4	41	10	0	?	?	?	?	No	No	No	Yes	No
15	91	112	81	4	37	7	0	69	30	30	0	No	No	No	Yes	No
16	90	186	48	5	28	7	0	137	15	64	76	No	No	No	No	No
17	87	186	46	5	42	8	1	100	0	80	100	Coop.	No	No	No‡	No
18	86	86	100	2	41	9	1	?	24	140	83	Coop.	No	Store	Yes‡	No
19	78	144	54	2	37	12	0	90	15	100	85	Coop.	No	No	Yes‡	No
20	73	72	100	2	36	6	2	50	30	150	80	No	No	No	Yes	No
21	62	144	43	2	42	11	0	?	0	75	100	Coop.	No	No	Yes‡	No
22	58	186	31	9	28	7	0	119	10	?	?	No	No	Driver	Driver	Yes
23	47	47	100	4	28	5	0	18	67	67	0	No	Yes	No	Yes	No
24	38	108	35	8	55	7	0	50	37	100	37	No	Yes	Company	Captain	Yes
25	6	60	10	2	39	9	0	20	40	75	46	No	No	No	Yes	No

Key

* = Includes all members of household who hold license to deliver sugar cane.

† = Where two or more members of household included, figure given is for individual with longest delivery record.

‡ = Members of cooperative, 1968. Worked for company previously. Delivery record.

Del. = Delivered, delivering.

Mec. = Mecates. 8 mecates = 1 acre (approximately).

u/c = Under cultivation.

? = Information not available.

producing eight to ten years ago or more were in a position to profit from the era of high cane prices, and to expand their cane holdings before the program of land distribution restricted individual holdings to one block. The number of years a man has been producing cane is, for obvious reasons, also related to his age. Long-term cane producers tend to be ten or fifteen years older than more recent producers. However, among the top 50 per cent of the sample there are five producers under fifty years of age, all but one of whom have been delivering cane for ten years or more. Some of these began delivering cane in their thirties or late twenties, which accords with the pattern among the lower 50 per cent of the sample.[21] At the time when they entered the cane economy, however, the norm was still milpa agriculture, and their decision to experiment with cane production indicates a more entrepreneurial spirit than is true of those recent producers who have responded blindly to government incentives.

The availability of adult unmarried sons as a source of unpaid labor has some bearing on a man's productive capacity, for reasons discussed earlier. Whether, in fact, this advantage is directly reflected in the cane delivery figures or whether it is better calculated in terms of additional income from wage labor and milpa cultivation is impossible to estimate. However, statistical correlation of rank order on cane deliveries in 1968 and number of adult sons in household[22] suggests that this factor may be of some importance in determining a man's production in a given year. This situation favors the older producers over the younger men who are supporting a household of preadolescent children.[23]

Few persons at any level in the rank ordering fulfilled their license quota in 1968, reflecting a general response to adverse growing conditions resulting from insect (froghopper) attack. Nonetheless, those who are high on the rank-ordering delivered a significantly greater percentage of their quota than did the middle-level and small producers, with some exceptions.[24] It appears, then, that the large-scale producer, through greater productive efficiency, has an advantage over the small farmer in terms of the proportion of his cultivated cane that he can harvest and deliver, even in a poor season.

On inspection, the decline in milpa production has been uniform at all levels. Several informants, who ranked low in cane production in 1968, claim to have had fairly substantial holdings of corn in the past. One can deduce, therefore, that the present disparities in level of cane production are

[21] Younger, unmarried men in the village do take out cane licenses, but their cane deliveries are included in the figure given for their father's household for the purpose of this study. Hence, the sample does not adequately represent the younger cane producers in the village.

[22] Correlation of the rank ordering on cane deliveries in 1968 and number of adult sons in the household results in a tau of 0.23, which, converted to a z score, is significant at the 0.05 level.

[23] The mean household size in 1968 was six persons (seventy-one households).

[24] The rank correlation coefficient of 1968 deliveries and percentage of quota delivered is significant at the 0.01 level. This result is surprising in view of the fact that the three individuals who delivered 100 per cent of their license quota in 1968 are ranked low in terms of gross deliveries in 1968.

a function of the time at which the individual decided to switch from corn to cane. In other words, the data suggest that the size of a man's milpa operation in the past is *not* a reliable predictor of the scale of his present operation in sugar cane.

With respect to size of household[25] there is little systematic variation along our rank ordering of large to small cane producers. The hypothesis that larger households would tend to maintain larger milpas is not supported by the evidence either. There is a slight tendency for the small cane producers to maintain larger milpas, indicating greater dependence on subsistence production, but the difference is not significant. It is clear from the evidence (1) that many households are now relying on retail stores for food supplies and (2) that in earlier times substantial surpluses of food crops were being produced and presumably sold for cash profit.

MATERIAL INDICATORS OF ECONOMIC STATUS

The data shown in the right-hand columns of Table 3 suggest some obvious correlates of success in cane production. Only the large producers own trucks. However, access to a truck through membership in the cooperative (now defunct) or through close ties of kinship extends to the middle-level cane producer. The small producer must rent where he can.

Residence in a wood house is another indicator of economic status. The norm for the village is mud and wattle with thatched roof. Although wood houses are not exclusively concentrated in the upper levels of the cane producers, inspection of the column headed "other sources of income" helps to explain the deviations. For example, number 11 has two daughters who are school teachers in the village and a son in the U.S. Air Force. Number 24 is employed full time by the company and earns $25BH weekly.

The larger cane farmers do not engage in wage labor for the company, although frequently their unmarried sons do. Smaller producers depend more on the additional cash income derived from wage labor. Several members of the cooperative reported that they used to cut cane for the company but that they did not in 1968 because they were engaged in reciprocal labor with other members. This accounts for the small number reporting wage labor for the company in 1968. Since the demise of the cooperative, it is reasonable to assume that this number will have increased.

Table 3 also demonstrates the fact that only the large cane farmers employ men on a regular basis during the *zafra*. The two exceptions, numbers 22

[25] Grant Jones (personal communication) questions the usefulness of the household as a conceptual unit of production. In the case of the rural Maya, he suggests that a more meaningful unit is the kin-based corporate group of variable composition—single nuclear families, extended families, complexes of patrilocally extended nuclear family households with separate kitchen areas, and so on. Both Jones (1969a) and the author based their analysis on single households, but we are in agreement that this may be misleading.

and 24, are employed full time by the company and employ kinsmen to work their cane.

In summary, an examination of selected socioeconomic variables in relation to volume of cane production suggests that the long-term cane farmers of middle-age or older men are most likely to be the large producers. The large producer is more likely to have the assistance of adult sons and to employ men on a regular basis. He will probably own a truck if his license quota and cane delivery exceeds 200 tons of sugar cane. He may live in a wood house, although access to other sources of income is a determining factor in some of the instances recorded of this type of status symbol. Because of his greater command of the essential resources and because of the higher level of productive efficiency which results, the large producer is able to harvest a higher percentage of his cultivated cane than the small farmer (by the criterion of percentage of license quota delivered in a poor season). The marginal cane producers, at the bottom of the rank-ordering by cane deliveries, tend to maintain proportionately larger milpas as security, although there has been a general decline in the production of food crops following the widespread switch to cane farming in the village. The large cane farmer is unlikely to engage in wage labor for the company, whereas the small producer is impelled to do so if he aspires to more than the barest subsistence livelihood (see Case Study 3).

CONCLUSIONS

The situation in the Orange Walk District of British Honduras provides an interesting case study of the early stages of socioeconomic adaptation to a *usina* system. Although the data presented are based on a single community and are hence incomplete, some tentative conclusions may be drawn from the analysis which have implications for the future of the inhabitants of this region.

It is clear that the structural situation confronting the small village cane farmer is not encouraging insofar as the prospects for general economic development are concerned. We do not predict a total disappearance of independent cane production in this area. Rather, it appears that present circumstances favor a widening gap between large and smallhold operations, as has been the case in the Corozal District to the north (Jones, 1969a). Avenues for expansion and technological improvement are virtually blocked to all but those who entered the business of cane production early, at a time of high prices and favorable world market conditions. The demands of modern cane production favor large-scale operations and capital resources which only those who have *already* reached a substantial level of production seem likely to achieve under present conditions. The production of sugar cane is both time-consuming and exhausting unless the owner can command a steady labor force at certain times of the year. However, the peak periods of activity in cane, milpa, and wage labor coincide, a situation which does not permit rational allocation of work time by the small farmer. Because wage labor offers better prospects for attaining an acceptable cash income than does milpa agriculture, and because, in any case, the majority of farmers have drastically reduced their level of milpa production, it is predicted that the situation will be characterized by a growing dependence on wage employment. As Jones has put it in the case of the older cane-producing Corozal District to the north,

> An original positive indigenous ecological response to sugar cane by Maya swidden cultivators has reached a progressive stage of what might be called "ecological inviability," as the greater economic power and spread of the plantation system appears to indicate the progressive disappearance of all forms of peasant agriculture.
>
> [1969:12]

Substantiation of this prediction in the case of the Orange Walk District must await future research and may depend on external factors, such as United States policy toward Cuba and trends in the world market for sugar.

It is scarcely reassuring that at a time when many Caribbean nations are phasing out their sugar-cane production and are encouraging agricultural diversification, the government of British Honduras has chosen to take an opposite course, toward intensive monocrop sugar-cane production. Despite a decline in prices the policies which, through specific programs of financial incentive and land distribution, have encouraged the Maya milpero to concentrate his efforts in sugar-cane production have not provided adequate protection against the risks involved. A policy which makes credit for expansion and improvement contingent on the scale of an individual's *present* operation is hardly calculated to produce rapid development among small producers. The monopolistic position of the *usina* within the British Honduras sugar industry, a poorly developed union organization, and an almost total lack of effective agricultural extension programs further contribute to the noncompetitive position of the small cane farmer. The company's mechanization policies, when fully implemented, are a further threat to those who are coming to rely on wage labor to supplement their precarious income from sugar cane.

A final stage in the developmental sequence of sociocultural adaptation to the *usina* may yet be the ultimate reversion of a rural proletariat to subsistence agriculture, or widespread migration from the area.

7

The spread of snowmobiles among the peoples of the North American and European arctic provides us with a particularly striking instance of rapid change in microtechnology. The conversion from traditional dog sled to gasoline-driven vehicles took place in a single year in some Eskimo communities ; in other areas the change has been somewhat more gradual but nonetheless dramatic.

If we compare the "snowmobile revolution" with the coming of the automobile into Euro-American cultural life, we can suggest that the social consequences of the technological development will be complicated and far-reaching. The parallels between the two cases are indeed instructive. During the first few years of the "Snowmobile Age" there have been instances of violent crime committed from snowmobiles (reminiscent of the role of fast getaway cars in the heyday of the Chicago gangsters) ; death and serious injury from snowmobile accidents, which remind us of holiday traffic tolls ; and interest in snowmobile races in northern towns, which sounds like a re-enactment of the Indianapolis 500. On the other hand, the snowmobile, like the automobile, appears to extend the range of social contact ; emergency medical services and other life-preserving actions are speeded up ; and the added speed of travel increases the range of economic choices for many people—at a high cost, of course.

These developments on the arctic scene are all very new, and the data provided by Pelto and Müller-Wille are but a prologue to the study of this technological and social transformation.

SNOWMOBILES:
Technological Revolution in the Arctic[1]
Pertti J. Pelto and Ludger Müller-Wille

Pertti J. Pelto is Professor of Anthropology, University of Connecticut. He did graduate study at the University of Finland and received his Ph.D. from the University of California. He has done field research in Finland and is interested in Lappish culture. His many publications include a recent book, Anthropological Research: The Structure of Inquiry.

Ludger Müller-Wille is at the Seminar für Völkerkunde at the University of Münster in West Germany. Born in Göttingen, he has studied at the University of Helsinki and has done extensive field research in Utsjoki, Finland, which was the basis for his Ph.D. dissertation.

Few technological developments have had more far-reaching consequences for sociocultural change than have innovations in methods of transportation. Developments in sailing technology brought on the Age of Exploration during which Europeans "discovered" and conquered the rest of the world, the railroads were a major factor in the transformation of the western United States, and the automobile is generally considered a primary element in the moral and cultural revolution in Euro-American culture that took place earlier in this century. The transformations taking place during the present jet and rocket age are strongly influenced by technological breakthroughs in air transportation.

[1] A large part of the materials for this paper, particularly those dealing with Eskimo use of snowmobiles in arctic Canada, are from tape-recorded interviews with a number of anthropologists and geographers who have carried out field work in the Canadian Far North. In the fall of 1967 (at the annual meeting of the American Anthropological Association in Washington, D.C.), we had a lengthy interview with David Stevenson of Dalhousie

The technology of transportation has always been of special importance in arctic and subarctic areas, where snow and ice make travel extremely difficult for two-legged, heavy-footed man. Since at least Iron Age times, men in northern Europe made use of skis to facilitate their travel, and snowshoes played a similar role in the forests of northern North America. In northern Europe there is archaeological evidence of sleds from Mesolithic times. At first the sleds were pulled by men themselves, but long ago, arctic peoples discovered ways to harness animals to pull their sleds. The development of dog sleds in about A.D. 800–1000 appears to be associated with a time of significant cultural change across the arctic. Until very recently reindeer-powered sleds were a major means of transport for the native peoples of arctic Europe and Asia, whereas dog sleds were man's best answer to the problem of getting across the snowfields of the North American arctic.

During the past few decades various gasoline-powered vehicles have come into widespread use in arctic economies, but they did not replace dog sleds and reindeer sleds because they could not operate in the rough and roadless terrain in which arctic peoples make their living. Thus airplanes, automobiles, and various tractors and caterpillars have been used extensively in the arctic only by governmental agencies (postal department, transportation department, military units, and so on) and by some private commercial enterprises. For the ordinary citizen, hauling supplies and traveling from place to place depended to a large extent on animal-drawn sleds until the beginning of the 1960's.

Small, one-man snowmobiles, or "ski-doos" as they are frequently called, began to make their appearance in the arctic in the early 1960's. The invention of these machines is largely due to the efforts of two men—Carl Eliason of Wisconsin and Joseph-Armand Bombardier of Quebec (cf. Schiller, 1968). Both men had struggled for a number of years to perfect machines for driving in snowy terrain, and both had succeeded in developing snow vehicles which were operating in arctic areas before 1960. In the 1950's Bombardier was successfully manufacturing a seven-passenger "snow bus" (selling for $7,500) that operated on half-tracks with a front steering mechanism on

University. We obtained a rich series of interviews with arctic ethnographers at the Conference on Intermediate Adaptation in St. Johns, Newfoundland, in the winter of 1968. Persons who contributed information on snowmobiles at that time included David Damas, Richard Hill, Lee Guemple, Milton Freeman, and Peter Usher.

Further data were obtained in interviews at the Northeastern Anthropological Association conferences in Ottawa in May, 1970. The ethnographers interviewed included David Moyer, Derek Smith, Lorne Smith, and Peter Usher.

Research on snowmobiles in Finnish Lapland was carried out by Martti Linkola, Pekka Sammallahti, and Pertti Pelto in the spring and summer of 1967, particular in the Sevetti-järvi region. This research was supported with funds from the Wenner-Gren Foundation for Anthropological Research, whose aid in this study is gratefully acknowledged. Mr. Ludger Müller-Wille, of the University of Münster, spent a number of months in field research in the northernmost district of Finnish Lapland in 1969 and 1970. His research was focused in Utsjoki, which was the first community in Finnish Lapland to experiment with mechanized reindeer herding.

Lapps driving to trading post with reindeer sleds in presnowmobile days. (*Photo by P. J. Pelto.*)

metal skis. Eliason patented a motor toboggan in 1927, which operated with a 2.5-horsepower engine. Eliason toboggans found their way into the Far North in small numbers, but they were not durable and had little impact on arctic transportation systems. It appears that the major design feature that delayed the development of one-man snow machines was the problem of finding a really reliable, lightweight, inexpensive engine. In 1958 Bombardier found an extremely effective two-stroke, single-cylinder engine in Austria which weighed less than 30 pounds. Within two years he had gone into production of the Ski-doo, the first successful one-man snow vehicle. This machine held a near monopoly in the first years of the "snowmobile revolution"—hence the name ski-doo has come to be the accepted generic label among arctic peoples in both Europe and North America. By the late 1960's a large number of other manufacturers had entered the field with vehicles that ranged in price from $700 to over $1,000. It is estimated that by 1970 there were a million snowmobiles in use in North America.

The inventors Bombardier and Eliason were both concerned with the practical, utilitarian functions of their projected snow vehicles (in 1934 Bombardier's son had died on the way to the hospital as his horse sled floundered in snow drifts), but the manufacturers of snowmobiles quickly found that their vehicles tapped a pleasure and recreation market of phenomenal proportions. The "snowmobile revolution" in the northern tier of the United States, throughout southern Canada, and in many areas of Europe, means primarily a rapid and large-scale restructuring of winter sports and recreation. Snowmobile races, "snowfaris," weekend visits to cabins that were previously inaccessible in the winter, and many other activities have

Lapps reindeer herder starting up his snowmobile (Utsjoki, Finland). (*Photo by L. Müller-Wille.*)

brought about a sharp growth of winter revenues in some resort areas and have necessitated the rapid enactment of legislative measures to curb the harmful ecological side effects of this new intrusion into winter environments.

In the Far North, few people can afford to spend sums of $700 or more for recreation; however, Eskimos, Lapps, and other northerners quickly found that snowmobiles have a wide variety of very practical uses, varying with local environmental economic conditions. Also, governmental agents, teachers, medical personnel, forest rangers, and other people with jobs that require extensive travel discovered that snowmobiles are usually more efficient than dog sleds or reindeer sleds for getting around the roadless backlands.

This paper reviews some aspects of the "snowmobile revolution" as it developed in a number of communities in Lapland and northern Canada. The information thus far available indicates that the economic utility of snowmobiles depends to a great extent on local ecological factors which vary considerably in different parts of the arctic. In places where the snowmobile has been integrated into major parts of the economic system, significant changes are occurring in practically all aspects of culture. These changes appeared to be occurring very rapidly in the period 1965–1970, justifying our use of the term *snowmobile revolution*, and some of the reverberations from this technological change will continue for a number of years to come.

In the following sampling of data, special attention will be given to

1. Identification of the first "acceptors" of the innovation.
2. Review of the uses to which the snowmobile is adapted.
3. Examination of "cost accounting" of snowmobile ownership.
4. Projection of ecological effects in different areas.

SNOWMOBILES IN FINNISH LAPLAND

The first Bombardier Ski-doo reached Finland from Canada approximately at the end of 1961 or the beginning of 1962 (Pelto et al., 1968). This first machine was on display in the market square of Rovaniemi, the capital of Finnish Lapland. The vehicle attracted considerable attention, and one of the first display models was purchased by a schoolteacher in the little settlement of Partakko in northeastern Finland. The schoolteacher said that he was immediately impressed with the snowmobile's obvious possibilities for fishing trips and other recreational travel. His readiness to try the new machine is explained, in part, by the fact that he is an excellent mechanic. As a bachelor schoolteacher he had more available cash than most for investment in something whose economic usefulness was unknown. In addition to the schoolteacher, a nurse, a postman, and a forest ranger were among the first people to acquire the new vehicles and try them out in the backlands.

The first significant acceptance of the snowmobile by Lapps for use in connection with reindeer herding took place in the northernmost parishes of Finnish Lapland, especially in Utsjoki and Inari. This fact is very important to note, for these reindeer-herding areas are among the most isolated and traditional regions of Finnish Lapland. Utsjoki, in particular, has a higher proportion of Lappish-speaking population than any other parish in Finland, and the economy is more dependent on reindeer herding than are the regions to the south, closer to the capital, Rovaniemi (see Figure 1).

Before outlining the story of the spread of snowmobiles, we need to turn our attention to some critical features of the physical and social environment. For the most part, Finnish Lapland is sparsely populated boreal forest, dotted with many small lakes and streams. There are no truly mountainous areas, though the relief is more impressive in the northwest corner, near the Swedish border. Because of poor drainage, many of the low-lying areas have extensive bogs and marshes. In southern Lapland there are large stands of firs; but the pine forests become more predominant as one goes north, until we reach a point, near Inari in the north, where the pine forest, too, becomes quite sparse.

FIGURE 1. Some of the communities using snowmobiles in Finnish Lapland.

Birch trees are found in abundance throughout Lapland, but beyond the last stragglers of coniferous forest, the birch takes over entirely, although northern (tundra) birches are small and twisted dwarfs compared to the species farther to the south. Unlike the high arctic in North America, Finnish Lapland has no true tundra areas in which trees disappear altogether, and the comparative mildness of climate (by arctic standards) is vividly exemplified by the fact that in most regions sedentary agriculture with milk cows is possible through some heroic efforts on the part of both animals and men.

Because small-scale sedentary farming has been possible in many areas of northern Finland, the Lapps have taken on a sedentary or, at most, a half-nomadic way of life, often keeping a few cows in addition to their herds of reindeer. Many have given up herding altogether in favor of farming or sedentary occupations in the small hamlets that dot the main roads of the area. In the southern portions of Lapland there are lumbering operations and some mining, although wage-labor occupations are few and low paid throughout Lapland. Only in the population center of Rovaniemi (about 29,000 people in 1970) are there significant numbers of service occupations, but Rovaniemi is 200 miles south of the herding areas of Utsjoki and Inari. The northernmost areas of Finnish Lapland, close to the Norwegian border, have more open tundralike landscape than do the districts to the south; and the differences in the physical landscape have important effects on the habits of both the reindeer and reindeer herdsmen. They also have powerful effects on the utilization of snowmobiles for reindeer herding.

The first ski-doo arrived in Utsjoki in December, 1962, in the winter following the "demonstration" by the Partakko schoolteacher. During the period December, 1962–January, 1963, four of the leading Lapp reindeer herders of the local reindeer association bought snowmobiles. All four were wealthy by local standards, and all except one were less than fifty years of age. These men quickly began experimenting with mechanized reindeer herding. Because major aspects of reindeer herding are controlled by the cooperatively organized district associations, it is doubtful that experimentation with snowmobiles in connection with the herds could have taken place if these first owners of machines had not been leading figures in the association.

During the next winter season (1963–1964), almost all the Utsjoki herders purchased snowmobiles and sold their previously indispensable sled reindeer to Finns, who wanted these sought-after animals for reindeer racing. The last Lapp in Utsjoki to travel by reindeer sled was a seventy-year-old herder who held out until the winter of 1965–1966 before buying a machine. He still traveled by reindeer sled in 1966–1967 (Müller-Wille, 1970).

Curiously, in Utsjoki parish the people (mostly Finns) of the central village did not begin to acquire snowmobiles until 1966. These people, several of whom could be expected to have larger cash incomes than many of the reindeer men, evidently saw the ski-doos as reindeer-herding machines, which they did not need in their more sedentary occupations. However, by 1969, six of the nineteen snowmobiles in the Utsjoki village area were used exclusively for recreation (four owned by Finns, two by Lapps) (Müller-Wille, 1970).

The men of Utsjoki have extensive contacts with the reindeer herders in Inari parish, just to the south. One of the first major reindeer roundups of the year occurs at the border between the two reindeer associations, and all later roundups in both areas are attended by herders from both districts. In January, 1963, the herders of the Muddusjärvi reindeer association (Inari) experienced great difficulties in bringing a large herd of reindeer from their grazing grounds to the roundup corral. As an experiment the association hired Uula Lansman, one of the Utsjoki ski-doo owners, along with two ski-doo-owning local herders, to drive the reluctant animals 70 kilometers to the waiting reindeer men. The experiment proved a success, the animals came to the corral, and the leaders of the Muddusjärvi association were quickly convinced that snowmobiles were practical in herding operations. The snowmobile revolution was on.

Although we do not have specific data concerning the adoption of snowmobiles for most of the other districts in Finnish Lapland, it appears that their experimentation with snowmobiles came later, and many reindeer herders in the more southerly districts found that the vehicles were not practical for direct herd contact, although nearly all of them report that snowmobiles are used in hauling supplies and personnel to herding sites. The case of the Paatsjoki association is instructive. In March, 1963, a large herd of reindeer had taken up a position in a relatively inaccessible area of the district, so the herders asked the Finnish forest ranger (who is a member of the association) to help round up the animals with his snowmobile. This operation was described as a success, yet the Paatsjoki men have since made only limited use of snowmobiles in reindeer herding.

To understand the differential acceptance of snowmobiles for reindeer herding in Finnish Lapland, we must take careful note of the physical landscape. Utsjoki parish is characterized by open tundra conditions; the rolling hills are interspersed with broad areas of muskeg swamp and small lakes. The sparse vegetation consists of dwarf birch, willows, and a variety of bushes, grasses, reeds, and other arctic plant life. Wind-blown snow makes the region bleak and featureless in winter, and the repeated snowfalls harden into a compact surface that provides a wide-open highway for snow vehicles. When the weather is good there are few obstacles to visibility—thus there are few places for recalcitrant reindeer to hide from their owners. South from Utsjoki the landscape is increasingly forest-covered. There the snow does not become hard-packed and snowmobiles often find it tough going through the soft drifts. The often dense vegetation provides further advantage for the reindeer over the snowmobile (cf. Müller-Wille and Pelto, 1971).

Snowmobiles were adopted very quickly by the Lapps of northeastern Finnish Lapland, in part because there is such a variety of transportation needs to be filled. The machines immediately proved their utility for hauling firewood from the forests, and water from the lakes and streams. Hunters and fishermen carry food and other supplies out to backland cabins on their ski-doo sleds. Expeditions to the stores or trading posts that in earlier years required a two-day round trip can now be made in a few hours. Very few residents of Lapland, whether Lapps or Finns, doubt the utility of these machines in accomplishing the transport tasks of their households. However, it is in reindeer herding that controversy has arisen over the use of the machines, and it is in connection with reindeer herding that we can see how environmental features affect the relationships among men, machines, and animals.

Before the advent of snowmobiles, the hired herders of each reindeer association went out in the late fall on skis and reindeer sleds to gather the herds for the winter roundup (cf. Pelto, 1962). Often it required weeks of work for the men to comb the backlands, gradually accumulating the small groups of animals into larger and larger herds. Finally, when most of the animals were in the control of the herdsmen, the several herds would be driven to the roundup corrals. At the corrals the individual owners captured and claimed their personal reindeer, killed some animals for food and for trading purposes, paid debts, earmarked their calves, and then took charge of their personal herds for the balance of the winter. These roundups also permitted the association to count each man's herds, in order to assess "head" taxes.

In most reindeer districts at least two roundups were required in order to gain control of the herds. In the wide-open areas of Utsjoki parish the herdsmen were often able to gain relatively full control of their animals early in the winter, but in districts with heavily wooded areas, the last roundups were often in March and April. Even then it was usual that numbers of animals remained "wild" throughout the winter. (It is common practice for the reindeer men to leave portions of the herds "wild," in order to avoid paying taxes on them and to "leave something in the bank" toward future needs.)

Using snowmobiles in place of the slow-paced reindeer sleds and men on skis, rounding up the reindeer can now take place much more rapidly. In the Utsjoki area the herds are allowed to roam in freedom until it is time for a roundup. Then about ten herdsmen speed into the backlands on their machines to comb the area for herds. Operating in twos and threes they bring the captured herds to an agreed-on point at the end of the day and return home for the night. For the next several days the operation is repeated until enough animals have been gathered to make a roundup. Then the drive to the corral begins.

A large herd can travel about 20 to 25 kilometers per day. Snowmobiles drive slowly along the flanks and the rear of the herd, keeping up a steady pressure. "Lead" reindeer keep the herd moving forward in an orderly fashion. The earlier practice of leading the herd with a bell reindeer (led by a herdsman on skis) is not necessary when snowmobiles are used. The final part of the drive—luring and forcing the animals into the corral itself—is still quite difficult, even with snowmobiles, for the animals may scatter wildly if they panic at the sight of the enclosure.

All of these herding operations proceed fairly smoothly in the Utsjoki reindeer area, and so little time is required to arrange a roundup that the association may hold a number of them throughout the winter. The men have found that they can successfully control the reindeer and keep track of herds. Their machines can easily outrun the animals, and a small number of herdsmen can effectively comb the district in a short period of time.

After the Utsjoki men demonstrated the effectiveness of snowmobiles to their Inari neighbors, they too adopted a mechanized herding system. However, it appears that the ski-doo is not an unqualified success in this area. In the open, tundralike areas of the northern half of the district there are no problems in herding operations, but nearly half of the district is wooded, especially the rocky hills in the west and the irregular coastlines of Lake Inari. Here the herdsmen often leave snowmobiles behind and follow the elusive reindeer on their skis. Many people have complained that since snowmobile herding came in, they have been unable to control the animals that hide in the wooded areas. Some of the seasoned veterans believe that more and more of their northern herds are seeking sanctuary in the forests and thickets, where snowmobile herding is ineffective.

Problems of herding reindeer in forested, rocky regions are especially acute in the Paatsjoki district, immediately to the southeast of the Inari area. In spite of their close contacts with mechanized herding, the Paatsjoki men have, for the most part, continued to gather and control their herds on skis, though they use ski-doos for hauling men and equipment to the roundups and for practically all transportation purposes other than direct contact with the reindeer.[2]

In the spring of 1967 these woodland herders began to make cautious use of snowmobiles in driving their herds, once the ski men had them gathered and under control. A bell reindeer in front of the herd is still considered essential, and the motorized herders keep well to the rear and on the flanks. (A reindeer herd on the march is a very thin, long column, for they usually maintain no more than a double or triple file of animals. Because the snowmobile leaves a semisolid track through the snow, this narrow path made by a lead vehicle is an aid in keeping order in the herd.)

Although the Paatsjoki herdsmen have cautiously moved toward more mechanization of herding operations, it appears that they cannot employ the "blitz" tactics that work so successfully in the wide-open Utsjoki landscape. Farther south, many reindeer associations, particularly in heavily forested areas, make no use of snowmobiles in direct herding operations, although most of them have numbers of ski-doo owners among their memberships.

Several other factors should be noted in connection with these ecological differences. The northernmost reindeer districts are strongly Lapp-dominated, whereas most of the people in the other districts are Finnish. Roughly coterminous with the Lapp-Finnish ratios, we also find that the farther north one goes in Lapland, the greater the percentage dependence on reindeer herding. Only in the northernmost parishes is reindeer herding a major economic mainstay of the people. Also, the northern tier of reindeer districts has the largest numbers of "big reindeer men." That is, the tendency in the southerly districts is for the holdings of individual owners to be relatively small—a minor secondary occupation supplementing their farming and lumbering activities. Finally, it is important to note that the more southerly districts of Lapland have more complete road networks, and road-operated motor vehicles are in widespread use. Certainly the fact that many of the people in southern Lapland own trucks or automobiles has had an influence on their attitude toward snowmobile use.

---

[2] Since 1967 the former Paatsjoki Association has been officially designated Vätsäri Association. Recent reports (1971) indicate that they have greatly increased their use of snowmobiles in herding.

COSTS OF SNOWMOBILE TRANSPORTATION IN FINNISH LAPLAND

In 1968–1969 the prices for snowmobiles rose, following the devaluation of the Finnish mark. By 1969 the machines cost from 3,800 to 5,000 Finnmarks when purchased from the local dealers. This is about $1,000 in U.S. currency (1 Finnmark equals 24 cents U.S.), and reflects freight costs as well as import duties. However, snowmobiles made in Scandinavia and Finland do not appear to be significantly cheaper. We compiled the following cost-accounting figures in 1969, converting cash costs into equivalent units of reindeer (also see Sammallahti, 1969).

Table 1

Cost of Operating Snowmobile:* Utsjoki

	Finnmarks	Reindeer
Initial cost of vehicle	3,800	20–25
Gasoline (one year)	1,000	6
Repairs (one year) (replace rubber tracks, fan belts, and so on)	600	3–4
Total first-year cost	5,400	29–35

* Cost is for operation of snowmobile in heavy reindeer herding for entire season.

We were given estimates of about 2,000 Finnmarks, or twelve reindeer, as the second-year costs (not counting depreciation of the vehicle). To be able to afford these depletions in his reindeer stock, a herder would need to be operating with a herd of at least 260 to 300 animals. Few reindeer herders in Finnish Lapland actually have herds of that size, although we should note that the men in Utsjoki who so quickly turned to mechanized herding were precisely the ones whose herds could absorb these costs. In the Inari area many reindeer men are reputed to have sold most of their animals in order to buy ski-doos.

Because the cost estimates above are actually quite conservative, we must be somewhat mystified by the fact that large numbers of reindeer-herding families in poorer communities such as Sevettijärvi (see Pelto et al., 1968) have bought machines. Where does the money come from, granted that once it is purchased the snowmobile has a wide range of uses? The following points are pertinent:

1. The machines can usually be bought on a time-payment plan, but most such contracts must be paid up within twelve months. Initial

Utsjoki Lapps stop off at gas station. (*Photo by L. Müller-Wille.*)

costs thus cannot usually be carried over through two reindeer seasons.

2. Because the machines replace draft reindeer, which bring good prices as either meat or racing reindeer, a man with a fairly good "fleet" of sled reindeer was able to pay up to half of his initial costs on the "trade-in" from animal power to gasoline power. Only the top 15 to 20 per cent of reindeer herdsmen would be counted in this category, however.

3. Throughout the northern districts of Lapland, snowmobile men are now paid wages of up to 50 Mks per day while working for the association. (In contrast, the daily wage for a man on skis is 10 to 15 Mks.) The snowmobile herder must pay his own expenses from these wages, but it appears that steady employment for the association is one source of revenue that can be used to offset some of the high costs of snowmobile operation. In effect, the reindeer associations are subsidizing the snowmobile owners. In the Paistunturi district (southwest of Utsjoki) the snowmobile men aggregated a total of 801 working days for the association during the season of 1967–1968, whereas ski men worked a total of only 285 days (Müller-Wille, 1970).

4. The sale of transportation services is an important secondary economic pursuit for reindeer men. Among the Skolt Lapps of Sevettijärvi, for example, hiring transportation is ubiquitous. Families without snowmobiles regularly hire the ski-doo men for their freight trips to Norway and to take children to school, sick persons to the clinic,

and so on. Because no one nowadays drives to reindeer roundups by reindeer sled, nonowners of ski-doos often must pay to get to the backlands corrals. Tourists are another source of freight-and passenger-hauling revenue.

The poorer families who pay the snowmobilers for transportation services often are using old-age pension checks and other relatively new sources of cash, thereby spreading the costs of snowmobile operation to a large segment of the population. In a very real sense the snowmobile men have shifted their operating costs to the entire population.

5. The snowmobile makes it possible to exploit hitherto underutilized resources of the area, particularly the fishing in more distant lakes. Thus the snowmobilers can increase their noncash food resources in order to funnel available cash reserves into gasoline, spare parts, and other machine outlays.

In spite of these several ways in which the costs of snowmobile ownership have been managed in northeastern Lapland, it seems clear that numbers of families cannot afford to own the machines, and some of the people who now have them will ultimately be forced to give them up unless the economic picture changes. The comment is frequently made, by owners and nonowners alike, that "those machines are eating the reindeer."

The ways of making a living in the Finnish arctic have always been many-sided, combining reindeer husbandry with fishing, hunting, trapping, and other pursuits. Nowadays there are some wage-labor opportunities, small-scale (very small-scale) agriculture, and relatively considerable sums of money coming into families as old-age pensions, family bonuses, and other "transfer payments." The ways in which the high costs of snowmobile ownership fit into this economic picture are still being worked out, partly through rather extensive changes in the entire reindeer organization.

SKI-DOOS IN THE NORTH AMERICAN ARCTIC (CANADA)

The arctic areas of northern Canada are very different from Lapland in many respects. Regions inhabited by Canadian Eskimos are much greater in area and are much more remote from populated centers than are the portions of Lapland described previously. Agriculture is unheard of and even the boreal forest is far to the south. Most Eskimo populations are oriented, at least in part, to a maritime economy, with considerable dependence on seals, walruses, and other sea mammals. Vegetation is much sparser than in Lapland, distances are greater, and the arctic winter is much more severe in most Eskimo areas than it is in Lapland. Game is still abundant in a number of Eskimo areas, whereas hunting and trapping are relatively insignificant throughout most of Lapland.

Most Eskimo populations operate at least in part in terms of a cash economy, but their dependence on a monetized economy is much less than that of the Lapps. Moreover, in many areas the Eskimos have much less interaction with non-Eskimo populations than do Lapps with the neighboring Finns, Swedes, and Norwegians.

Aside from these generalizations, it must be recognized that important differences exist in the various environments of Canadian Eskimos, and these seem to be very important for understanding differences in the impact of the snowmobile on their ecological adaptations.

The ski-doo has now become a commonplace in most portions of the Canadian arctic, and in many areas sled dogs have been eliminated altogether, just as draft reindeer have become anachronisms in much of Lapland. It is interesting that in both cases the now superfluous draft animals have often been purchased by a more moneyed class of people for recreational racing. In both cases, also, the investment in a gasoline-driven machine has made possible a reduction in the amount of time and energy needed to maintain the complex arctic household transportation systems.

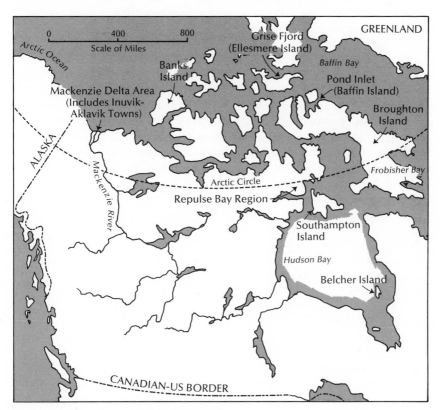

FIGURE 2. Use of snowmobiles in Canada.

The following "case histories" are an attempt to provide a preliminary inventory of the ways in which snowmobiles have come into use in different Eskimo communities. Most of these data are from interviews with ethnographers who had extensive research experience in the affected communities, and much more research needs to be done to examine some of the ecological and other questions suggested by these data.

Broughton Island*

Dr. Stevenson was last in contact with the Broughton Island people in the summer of 1965, and prior to that time he spent a number of years in the area carrying out anthropological research. He reports that in early 1963 only one man in the Broughton Island community had a ski-doo. This man worked for the DEW Line, so he not only had a cash income but he was also familiar with complex machinery; and therefore he had the wherewithal to experiment with ski-doo ownership and maintenance. In 1963 a rabies epidemic killed off about 95 per cent of the dog population. After that the Eskimos all purchased snowmobiles and did not replace their dogs. Of twenty hunters in the community, only one still uses dogs regularly, and when Stevenson was last in contact with them, there were only about thirty-seven dogs left in the entire community.

The people of Broughton Island have had greater contact with complicated machinery than have most Eskimos because many of them were employed by the DEW Line and worked with snowmobiles, caterpillar tractors, loading machines, and other equipment. Their acquaintance with machinery, plus possibilities of cash incomes, may have facilitated rapid acceptance of the ski-doos in the community. Apparently one of the first effects of mechanized transportation was that the population, which had been strung out along the coast for a number of miles, has nucleated into two main, kinship-based camps. Use of the snowmobile makes it possible for these people to live in more compact settlements and still reach their hunting grounds in daily trips. Hunting trips that used to take three days can now be made in twelve hours.

Regarding hunting, Stevenson reports that, "You can get just as close to the seals with a ski-doo as you can with dogs . . . if they're driving along with a ski-doo and they don't change the pitch (of the motor) the seal doesn't panic. . . . You can get so close that they don't use the traditional shield. They simply stay on the ski-doo. And when you are close enough, the one with the rifle jumps off and sits down and shoots."

In addition to hunting trips, the men from Broughton Island have made visiting trips to other communities, including Clyde River and Clanetok, traveling round trips of 600 to 700 miles and more.

Stevenson noted that there are many situations in which the ski-doo has

* Data from Professor David Stevenson, Dalhousie University.

disadvantages. Much of the area utilized by Broughton Islanders is rough sea ice, with crevices that are quite difficult to negotiate by snowmobile. In times past the Eskimos were able to cross fairly serious crevices because their long sleds could span the cracks in the ice. Also, when ice is breaking up dog teams can jump from ice block to ice block, maintaining the safety of sled and driver; the snowmobile in a similar situation would quickly disappear into the sea.

In summary, new patterns of hunting and travel have developed because of the snowmobile, and there appear to be considerable changes in social behavior (e.g., visiting), settlement patterns, and other characteristics among the Broughton Island people since the coming of gasoline-powered winter transportation.

MacKenzie Delta Area (Inuvik and Aklavik)*

Dr. Hill resides in Inuvik, one of the main population centers in the northern Canadian arctic. In connection with his research and administrative duties he travels widely in the Inuvik region. He states that the figures given in this report are approximations and should be taken with a certain amount of caution.

By 1968 there were between 150 and 250 snowmobiles in the Inuvik region, most of them owned by "urban types" or town dwellers. However, quite a number of machines are used in the trapping economy. Dr. Hill suggests that some individuals travel as much as 200 miles in their hunting activities with snowmobiles, but traveling such distances is not common. It is more usual for individuals to go out about 50 miles with the machine and return to the settlement after a day's hunting. The snowmobiles are also used a good deal in general transportation and recreation.

The first people to get snow machines in this area were employees of the Canadian Wildlife Service, the Department of Indian Affairs and Northern Development, and other government agencies. The first machines arrived in the area perhaps as early as 1959, although the men who are dependent on the land for subsistence (mainly Eskimos) relied on dogs until the winter of 1966–1967. Since that time there has been a rapid transition to snowmobiles, and the dog population, estimated at 1,000 ten years ago, is now down to about 200. Very few of these dogs are in the settlement of Inuvik itself.

Dr. Hill notes that the snow vehicles are most useful and most widely accepted in the northern part of the Inuvik district, where there is wide-open tundra, no trees, and a considerable cash economy among the people. In that area the snow is always hard-packed, making snowmobile travel easier and safer than is the case in the deeper snows of forested areas.

Derek Smith described the situation at Aklavik as one in which a small wage-earning local elite (approximately the top 10 per cent in terms of

* Data from Professor Derek Smith and Dr. Richard Hill, Department of Indian Affairs and Northern Development.

income) has been able to take advantage of the snowmobile in order to increase their economic well-being through hunting. Use of the snowmobile thus allows the wage earners, "to have a foot in two ways of life" and also to keep in contact with kinsmen and friends who remain in "the bush" in their hunting camps.

Banks Island*

Dr. Usher has carried out several months of geographical field work among the Eskimo fox trappers of Banks Island, and last returned to the area in 1970. He reports that the first snow vehicles in the area arrived in 1962–1963. These were three Eliason Autoboggans. The first experiments by Eskimos with the machines were not happy experiences. They did not trust the machines and went out in pairs—a snowmobile man plus a man with dogs, hence they did not gain any speed by use of the machines because travel was geared to the speed of dog teams.

The earliest use of snowmobiles was to haul ice from a lake some distance from camp. Dr. Usher observed that it might have been economical for the men to pool their money to pay for one snowmobile to use for ice hauling, but it is not at all usual for the Eskimos in this area to pool their resources in this fashion. The three men who purchased snowmobiles in that early time were very innovative people and successful trappers. They had a fairly sober approach to spending their money, so Dr. Usher felt that they were making a serious attempt to innovate with snowmobiles, but the experience was negative. There were some mechanical troubles with the machines and in 1965 none of them was in use any longer.

It should be noted that the Eskimos of Banks Island experimented with new technical devices particularly when they have had unusually productive trapping years. With extra cash available from good sales they purchase new machinery, replace old equipment, and try out a few new things. This must have been the case when the first snowmobiles were purchased back in 1962–1963. After that time there were several years of economic stagnation brought on by low productivity in fox trapping. Then, in 1965–1966, they had another fairly good year in fox trapping and two or three men bought Bombardier Ski-doos. Two of the persons who brought these machines were nontrappers. One was a wage earner, a maintenance man at the Department of Transport weather station; the other was a Royal Canadian Mounted Police special assistant. Both of the men had regular incomes, and probably also had more than average access to information about snowmobiles and maintenance of machinery. They also ran trap lines during the winter of 1966–1967. The maintenance man at the weather station trapped over a hundred foxes; he was able to go out at night after work, and his fox catch

---

* Report by Dr. Peter Usher of the Department of Indian Affairs and Northern Development.

for the winter was quite large, considering the small amount of time that he invested in it. Without the enhanced mobility provided by snowmobiles it would have been practically impossible for the two wage earners to carry out trapping activities.

It is of considerable importance to the history of snowmobile adoption on Banks Island that 1966–1967 turned out to be a "fantastically" good year for foxes. All the trappers did exceedingly well, including the two men who were trapping part time. At the end of this season everyone was ready to buy snowmobiles, particularly because the two men with machines had done so well during the season. The trappers on Banks Island order all their supplies and equipment for the coming year in the spring for shipment later in the year. In the spring of 1967 the supplies that were ordered for the following year included ski-doos for nearly everyone in the community.

Returning to the matter of the innovators of the year before, it should be noted that they not only were taking fewer financial risks in the purchase of snowmobiles, but they also were taking fewer physical risks because their use of snowmobiles was restricted to relatively short trips near "home base." If the original innovators had been full-time trappers risking death from cold, as well as loss of productivity in the event of breakdown in the hinterlands, the attempted innnovations might not have turned out so well. One of the machines that was in use during the winter of 1966–1967 was a Polaris Colt, which had no breakdowns during the winter, and several Polaris machines were ordered in response to this successful "demonstration."

The trappers now prefer to travel in pairs. With two snowmobiles traveling together, the men have insurance against breakdown, while achieving speed and mobility. Faster traveling allows the men to increase their productivity greatly and also reduces trap-line losses. In earlier years they lost 10 to 15 per cent of the catch on the trap line because of predation by other foxes and occasional wolves, as well as escapes from the traps. Thus, the speed of the snowmobiles along the trap lines has a twofold advantage. It remains to be seen how seriously the men of Banks Island may overtrap their area with their new-found mobility. Because the men on Banks Island can now reduce the number of dogs, they may be able to reduce a number of capital expenditures for boats, rifles, and other equipment which have been largely devoted to hunting food for the dogs.

Cambridge Bay and Repulse Bay*

Dr. Damas reports that he first encountered snowmobiles at Cambridge Bay in 1963, when there were three or four machines in the area. He returned briefly in 1965 and there were two additional machines.

In 1965 snowmobiles were just beginning to be used on the trap lines. Before that they had been used in localized hunting, fishing, and hauling.

* Report by Professor David Damas, arctic ethnologist at the National Museum of Canada.

Extension of the use of the snowmobiles to the trap lines would represent a major attempt to broaden the effectiveness of the snowmobile in economic activities.

Up to the winter of 1967–1968 the only ski-doos in use at the community of Repulse Bay were the two owned by the Catholic mission. At Spence Bay in the spring of 1965 one of the Eskimos employed by the Department of Northern Affairs bought a snowmobile. He used it for hunting and fishing and other short trips, especially in the evening after his job was over.

Dr. Damas notes that the areas he visited in the courses of his field work are among the most isolated communities in the Canadian arctic, and he would expect that they have been among the last to experience contact with the new snow vehicles. Also these areas are relatively low in cash incomes, so that very few people could afford to purchase snowmobiles even if they wanted them.

Belcher Island*

The Belcher Island economy consists of hunting, trapping, and carving, as well as welfare payments. Most food is from hunting. Dr. Guemple estimates the population of Belcher Island at about 185, with an adult male population of about forty-five.

Snowmobiles did not reach Belcher Island until the fall of 1966. At that time three men (Charlie Kaigulaki, Sam Crow, and Lukasi Nuktaluk) all purchased snowmobiles. The three innovators are apparently men of some stature and importance in the community. Sam Crow was the Hudson Bay's trader from 1955 to 1964. Charlie Kaigulaki is a camp leader and "has managed to get himself into a position of leadership . . . he is the best hunter in the camp. . . ." He is the only remaining child of a formerly large, extended family. Nuktaluk is the son-in-law of Sam Crow. He is a good hunter, becoming relatively powerful, rather adroit politically, and he is quite westernized. In 1967, he was gaining more informal power because he had the only ski-doo in the south camp, and hence was in a strategic position concerning the periodic supply trips to the north camp, 60 miles away.

The three machines at Belcher Island were used occasionally in fox trapping, but without much success because the terrain is too rough. The Eskimos feel the machines are most effective on the sea ice, but in this situation their usefulness is limited to a very few months of the year. Until about the 15th of January, the machines can be used for hunting out at the edge of the sea ice, about 20 miles away. After that, the ice is frozen all the way to the mainland, so hunting possibilities at the edge of the sea ice cease.

At Belcher Island, as in many other areas of arctic Canada, supplies of gasoline are quite irregular. By spring, they are usually out of gasoline and throughout much of the summer there is no gasoline available for the motorboats.

* Report by Professor Lee Guemple of the University of Western Ontario.

Guemple made a cost analysis of snowmobile use compared with dog sleds (including estimates of the cost of supplying the dogs with food, the value of time saved because of the speed of the snowmobile, cost of repairs and maintenance, and other relevant data). He estimated a figure of about $3 a day for operating costs of snowmobiles and a cost for dog-sled maintenance of approximately the same figure. However, he points out that dog sleds are useful for a longer period throughout the year, so the snow vehicles would appear to be less economical. He also notes the importance of the dogs for a number of other purposes. The dogs are the Eskimos DEW Line. They constitute an "early warning system." When traveling, the dogs will stop at the edge of dangerous ice or crevices, whereas a snowmobile has no such sensitivity. Dr. Guemple notes that dogs have always been considered to be intermediate between man and the other animals, for the dog has a special place in the mythology and social world of the Eskimos. The goddess of the sea has a dog standing guard outside her domicile, and dogs are thought to attract and maintain evil that otherwise would attach itself to humans.

At Belcher Island the men have had a number of breakdowns with their snowmobiles, some of which may have been due to freeze-ups caused by water in the gasoline. Thus a number of factors seem to have been working against the ecological utility of ski-doos in that area, as contrasted with the situation on Banks Island and in northern Lapland.

Grise Fiord on Ellesmere Island*

Grise Fiord is one of the most northerly human communities in the world (76° latitude), and the Eskimo inhabitants are quite isolated from the rest of Canada. They are highly dependent on hunting, but the area has plenty of game so people do not have to go far from home base to gain their livelihood. There are fifteen households in the community and when Freeman was there (for the two-year period from 1965–1967) one snowmobile was brought in during the summer of 1966. There are three Eskimos in the area who are employed for wages, and the man who bought the snowmobile was one of these—a Royal Canadian Mounted Police constable. The machine was a Bombardier Ski-doo. This man is a very active hunter who, in addition to his wage work, supports his own household with his hunting and also contributes to the support of his mother's household. Because he works a regular eight-hour day, he can go out to hunt only after work. For these relatively short hunting trips, a snowmobile is ideal. There is a scarcity of fresh water in the area (scarcity of salt-free ice) and he makes frequent trips out to the icebergs to chip pieces for his immediate family as well as for the families of two of his siblings. Thus he has certain constant hauling responsibilities for the family of his brother and the family of his brother-in-law while these two are out hunting.

* Report from Dr. Milton Freeman of the Memorial University of Newfoundland.

This first snowmobile owner on Ellesmere Island had the financial means to purchase a ski-doo, hence he did not have to go into debt. Also, because he works for the government he has been able to keep his machine in a heated garage so he does not have to struggle with cold-weather starting. In a letter dated May 3, 1971, Freeman informs us that "... Grise Fiord hunters all have ski-doos now, though most men still have dog teams ... they get little use it seems."

Southampton Island*

Southampton Island, in the northwestern corner of Hudson Bay, appears to be another case in which the snowmobile is of only marginal usefulness in the local ecological setting. Moyer found that the really successful full-time hunter-trappers continued to use dogs exclusively, and by informal agreement snowmobiles are not used in their portion of the island. On the other hand, at least thirty ski-doos have been purchased by the local inhabitants, principally by persons who have substantial cash incomes. Thus, on Southampton Island the snowmobile appears to provide a means by which full-time wage workers can go out hunting and trapping evenings, weekends, and other off-hours. Use of snowmobiles eliminates the necessity to keep dogs, so a rather serious problem in logistics has been solved by the advent of the machines.

Moyer notes that full-time wage workers (various government construction projects, plus Hudson Bay Company's clerks) need to hunt for their own food supplies, because meat sharing is important in the social system, and meat and fish are not bought and sold by the people. The wage workers are the most "pro-white" in social attitudes, hence they are particularly likely to experiment with technological and other innovations. However, a significant further factor in the differential purchasing of ski-doos is brought about by the *timing* of available cash. The ski-doos arrive and are available for sale in the late summer and fall, when the wage workers have extra cash, but the hunter-trappers do not.

The Southampton Island situation may be a case in which the differential utility of snowmobiles has served to heighten already existing factional differences between the full-time hunter-trappers and the pro-White wage-earning population. The division is partly generational, but it appears to be based on kin groupings as well. It remains to be seen whether there are other factors in the situation that might work to reduce the psychological and attitudinal differences between the snowmobilers and the dog men.

Pond Inlet †

At Pond Inlet in the northern part of Baffin Island the first snow vehicle was an Eliason Autoboggan, brought in on special order for one of the

* Data from Professor David S. Moyer, Memorial University of Newfoundland.
† Data from Mr. Lorne Smith, University of Manitoba.

police officers in the fall of 1962. As in other cases mentioned earlier, the vehicle was not a success and was junked after two years of unsatisfactory performance. The first Bombardier Ski-doo arrived in 1964, and by 1968 there were twenty-two Eskimo-owned ski-doos at Pond Inlet. "At other settlements on Baffin Island, ski-doo use has expanded similarly. For example, at Arctic Bay there was one Eskimo-owned ski-doo in 1964, two in 1965 and by spring 1969, there were approximately twenty ski-doos in use. Cape Dorset had over sixty ski-doos in use by spring 1968, and a growing pile of wrecked Ski-doo and Polaris machines on the garbage dump." (Smith, 1970:2)

Smith notes that the new motor vehicle owners of the Far North show some habits reminiscent of suburbia in the States. ". . . (Like) car owners, ski-doo owners often waste ten minutes starting a frozen ski-doo motor rather than take five minutes to walk to the store. . . . At noon, ski-doos race down the hill from the Government garage as Eskimo employees go to lunch. On Sunday ski-doos loaded with two, three or four people roar down the street to the church, passing the less fortunate who have to walk . . ." (Smith, 1970:3). The Pond Inlet snowmobile owners are mostly wage earners, much as is the case on Southampton Island. Smith found that of fourteen dog-team owners in the community, only four were wage earners, while fifteen of eighteen ski-doo owners (in his informant sample) were employed.

"For an employed Eskimo, ski-doo ownership makes good sense, because he is able to enjoy the best of two worlds. He is assured of a steady wage from his employment, and at the same time because of the mobility afforded by the ski-doo he does not have to depend on expensive store bought food; he can still obtain a major portion of his food through traditional methods" (Smith, p. 7).

The full-time hunter, on the other hand, appears to gain very little advantage by purchasing a snowmobile. The cash outlay is high, and he cannot easily increase his sealskin catch sufficiently to pay for the increased costs. In fact, a full-time trapper-hunter with ski-doo may be wasting meat, because he no longer feeds the seal carcasses to his dogs.

THE COSTS OF SNOWMOBILE USE IN ARCTIC CANADA

The price tag on a ski-doo delivered at Pond Inlet is approximately $850, including freight costs. In most areas purchasers must be able to pay at least $500 to $600 in cash, for the trading post credit policies have been rather strict with regard to the new machines.

Lorne Smith circulated a questionnaire among the ski-doo owners at Pond Inlet and derived the following average operating costs:

Table 2

Average Costs of Snowmobile Operation (Canada)
(from Smith, 1970)

Gasoline (65 gallons @ $1.10)	$71.60
Oil (mixed with gasoline at 1 quart per 5 gallons)	37.80
Repairs (not counting labor)	25.00
Total costs per month	$134.40

Costs of snowmobile operation are for heavy use in hunting and recreation.

In the Southampton Island area Moyer estimated the operating costs to be about $3 per day. The Pond Inlet estimates may be slightly high, but there is no denying the fact that it costs a lot to operate the ski-doo.

Traction belts are one of the more costly items which must be replaced frequently, especially in areas where salt water causes deterioration of the material. The belts cost $80 to $100. Sparkplugs, fan belts, suspension springs, and oil seals are also items that require frequent replacement.

The maintenance costs of snowmobiles would be even greater if the Lapps and Eskimos were not exceptionally capable as mechanics. Most snowmobilers in the arctic have learned to take care of minor repairs themselves, and some highly innovative emergency repairs have occurred, including whittling new axles out of birchwood. One Lapp even constructed an entire snowmobile from spare parts.

Milton Freeman described a bear-hunting expedition on Ellesmere Island during which the snowmobile-driving hunter had motor trouble far from home. In order to work on his machine in the subzero cold, he built an igloo over the snowmobile and then completely dismantled the motor. After some twenty-four hours of tinkering, he was able to get it going again, and returned safely home. Many similar stories from various parts of the arctic attest to the ingenuity of these arctic mechanics. On the other hand, some men are more capable as repairmen than others. In Utsjoki the one full-time repair shop has trade from a far-flung Lapland clientele, and the proprietor's reputation as a repairman has even reached people on the Norwegian side of the border.

THE SPEED AND CONVENIENCE OF SNOWMOBILES

From the warmth and comfort of centrally heated homes, we Americans often romanticize about the Eskimos' trusty dog teams or the Lapps' reindeer sleds. We have a wistful belief that the patient people of the arctic hunt, trap, and herd their animals in unhurried calm. It comes as something of a shock to our romanticism to learn that these people have been relatively quick to kill or sell their dogs and reindeer in order to buy snowmobiles. Why are they so eager to purchase these noisy and expensive machines?

In earlier field work Pelto was impressed with the emphasis on mobility among Lappish reindeer herders (Pelto, 1962). We were also impressed with the difficulty and tediousness of travel by reindeer sled. We have observed instances in which herdsmen had to pursue their draught reindeer for several hours before they were able to harness the animals for travel.

If draught reindeer are tethered (as they must be during travel stops) they must be fed. A familiar sight at a travel stop or roundup site is that of the herdsmen one by one excusing themselves from the evening card game and drinking party to go out into the night to move their reindeer to fresh grazing. Getting the draught reindeer and harnessing them up for travel often required an hour or more.

Traveling along by reindeer sled at a pace of perhaps 20 to 25 miles a day is a peaceful and rewarding experience, but when a blizzard threatens, or someone is ill and in need of medical attention, the most patient Lapp reindeer man becomes impatient with the slowness of progress and anxiously prods his reindeer to quicken their pace.

With dog teams among the Eskimos the situation must be much the same. Apparently dog teams can manage 40 miles in a day in good travel conditions, but distances are greater in the North American arctic and the blizzards more dangerous than in Lapland. If the dogs do not tangle up the harness a man can get his team in shape in about half an hour, and the dogs are not out grazing in the backlands a mile or more from home, as is usually the case with the Laplanders' reindeer. But the Eskimo has the additional burden of hunting for food for his dogs, and this requires a very large outlay of time. Surely it must be painful, in situations of food shortage, to be forced to give good red meat to dogs when there is not enough food for the family.

Because means of transportation are of such crucial importance in the arctic, we may hypothesize that northern hunters and herders frequently experience psychological tensions concerning the problems of travel. "If only we could reach home before the storm breaks. . . ." Many arctic people have also had personal experience with the kind of situation that Joseph Armand Bombardier suffered in trying to transport his son to a doctor through the snowdrifts. We are reminded also of John Honigmann's observations about northern Indians hanging around the trading post, using one and another excuse to delay the inevitable departure for the loneliness of their backland trap lines, from which contacts with other persons would be so difficult and time-consuming.

Compared to the slowness of dog sled and reindeer travel, the snowmobile presented the people of the arctic with truly astonishing new mobility. In northeastern Finnish Lapland the market trips to Norway that once required three days can now be completed in six hours. What had been a two-day journey from the Tsiuttijoki roundup site to Sevettijärvi village is now an easy four hours. In the Canadian far north the day's dog-sled trek of forty miles can be accomplished in three hours by snowmobile. The trip to the edge of the sea ice to hunt seals used to be a four- or five-day round trip for Broughton Islanders, with a total of nearly three days spent in traveling. Now the total travel time is twelve hours, and they frequently go out and return on the same day. Pond Inlet snowmobilers can go out on the weekend for hunting and in two hours they reach the caribou herds. After killing a couple of animals they can still return the same day, avoiding the necessity of making camp out in the backlands. This new mobility is a "great leap forward," in spite of the fact that the machines are very expensive. It is quite significant that in many areas the recreational uses of the snowmobile came *after* they had been put to economically important uses.

The quick adoption of snowmobiles in the arctic is not simply a reflection of the arctic peoples' love of technical gadgetry. It is especially in the realm of personal mobility that a new technological breakthrough would be most attractive to Eskimos and Lapps. The snowmobile revolution *is* a revolution because of a quantum leap in mobility. Human history suggests that people have always devised ways to pay for quantum leaps of this magnitude, no matter how expensive they are.

ADAPTATIONAL FEATURES OF SNOWMOBILES

The two most outstanding features of snowmobiles are their relatively high cash costs and their powerful contribution to speedy travel. The high cost is, of course, a very serious disadvantage; on the other hand, the speed and convenience of travel is of great economic, social, and psychological importance. Apparently some arctic people are willing to risk serious depletion of capital reserves in order to acquire a snow vehicle. This is especially marked among the Lapps, where some individuals have sold off most of their available reindeer in order to make the payments on their ski-doos.

The high monetary cost of snowmobile ownership is certainly evident in the data on differential acquisition of machines. In both Lapland and arctic Canada the first people to acquire snowmobiles have been individuals with steady wage work or other relatively solid economic means. In Sevettijärvi and Utsjoki (Lapland), most of the people with snowmobiles are above the median in "material style of life" (cf. Pelto et al., 1968; Müller-Wille, 1970), and in arctic Canada the first people to get ski-doos were overwhelmingly wage earners with sufficient margins of economic security to afford experimentation (cf. L. Smith, 1970; Moyer, 1970; Usher, 1966).

For those who could afford the snowmobiles (especially if they were among the early adopters), there were also some economic gains. In Lapland those first innovators were the ones to be hired by the reindeer associations for herding activities; they appear to have gained important decision-making power in herding operations; and they were able to profit by selling transportation services to other people. Among the Utsjoki herders the first snowmobilers already were the local decision-makers but they further consolidated their leadership through the new technology. Among the Eskimo communities, it appears that the first snowmobiles were of great economic importance to wage earners, who had already gotten rid of their dogs or were maintaining dogs at great personal expense and effort. The coming of the snowmobile suddenly got these wage workers out of a serious adaptational bind, for they could get rid of their dogs and still maintain hunting activities. In some cases they were able to engage in sizable trapping operations as well. As Lorne Smith put it concerning the Pond Inlet situation, they became "weekend hunters."

At Broughton Island the snowmobiles apparently came as something like an "adaptational rescue," because their dog population had been so seriously decimated by disease. At some of the other locations—for example, Belcher Island—it is not clear whether any economic advantages accrued to the first adoptors.

However much the *first* snowmobile owners might have gained in at least short-run adaptational advantages, the people who were next in line to acquire machines are in a more dubious adaptive position. In Lapland, for example, there are not herding jobs for nearly all the snowmobile owners, and the spread of ownership automatically depletes the client population of people who hire transportation services. Thus, at first the cost of snowmobile acquisition was spread to most of the rest of the population. Now this is no longer true, and each purchaser must in some way make the payments himself. Because these later purchasers are poorer in reindeer herds, material goods, wage incomes, and nearly every other economic index, they would appear to be in further economic jeopardy now than they were before the snowmobile revolution.

As the snowmobile has come to dominate reindeer herding and related activities in Finnish Lapland, machine ownership has become more and more necessary for successful economic activity. Because of the speed and efficiency of the snowmobile, reindeer roundups are now held on very short notice. Where roundups in presnowmobile days were usually announced at least two weeks ahead of time (and there were only two main roundups in each district), roundups are now held on twenty-four-hour or forty-eight-hour notice, the word being spread by telephone and snowmobile to all the people of the district. Very often the motorized herdsman goes to a roundup and returns on the same day. Many of the reindeer men grumble that it is now impossible to keep track of their animals (at the roundups) unless one travels by snowmobile.

Economic activities have become enormously speeded up in Lapland, especially in reindeer herding, and each individual is locked into a very complex association system in which he does not have the possibility of

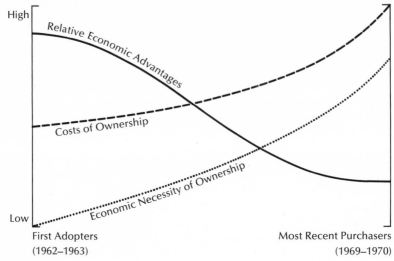

FIGURE 3. Economic advantages of snowmobile ownership relative to costs in Finnish Lapland.

setting his own work pace. This lesson was brought home when we inter-viewed the most traditional herdsman of the Skolt Lapp community in Sevettijärvi. He told us that he dislikes the snowmobiles, but next year (1968) he must purchase one in order to get around to all the roundups and other important herding events. Those men who cannot buy snowmobiles appear to be at a serious disadvantage under present conditions.

Summing up the situation in Lapland, it appears that as the direct costs of snowmobile ownership have increased, there has, at the same time, been a concomitant decrease in the relative economic advantage of ownership. Nonetheless, each individual reindeer herder is practically forced to acquire a machine, just to keep up. Figure 3 illustrates these relationships.

In the Eskimo communities the pattern of declining economic advantage and rising costs does not appear to develop. The costs seem to have remained relatively constant, because there was little or no initial "cost-sharing" through hired use of the vehicles. The machines have, from the start, been used mainly by individuals for their own transportation purposes, and nonowners have neither the cash nor the need to hire the services of the snowmobilers, except in unusual cases. Moreover, the economic "necessity" for ski-doo ownership has not apparently increased, because there are very few organized group activities in connection with the dominant hunting and trapping economy. To be sure, the "demonstration effects" of highly successful hunting and trapping may in some instances put competitive pressure on men to emulate the snowmobilers, but as the data now stand, they are not left out of economically important events because of their slower dog-powered transportation.

In some areas of the Canadian arctic it appears that portions of the Eskimo population have derived clear economic advantage from the use of snow-mobiles in hunting and trapping. The examples from the Mackenzie Delta and from Banks Island are especially striking. In the Banks Island case the snowmobilers were already successful trappers before the coming of the machines. Now that they can eliminate the large outlays of energy (and equipment) formerly required to maintain their dog teams, they can concentrate more fully on their trapping activities. Dr. Usher believes that they are increasing their "harvest efficiency."[3]

In the Mackenzie Delta region, Derek Smith reports that the top wage earners who were able to acquire snowmobiles have been able to engage in extensive hunting activities, thus further enhancing their already secure economic situations.

In at least one area where snowmobiles have speeded up hunting and trapping activities, the typical response is to shorten work hours and work days. Whereas checking trap lines may have been a full-time activity earlier, with the faster travel using the ski-doo, the trapper checks his traps more frequently (thus cutting down on losses), yet he has more leisure time to spend at home. Rather than increase his economic earnings, the trapper hunter holds economic gain constant and takes his "profits" in the form of free time (Moyer, 1970).

SNOWMOBILES AND SOCIAL INTERACTION

In many areas it appears that the snowmobile has increased the amount of both intracommunity and between-community contacts. In Lapland it is now possible to assemble groups of people quite quickly for social events such as dances, movies, and other recreational activities. Since the coming of the snowmobile, one enterprising Lapp family has instituted twice-monthly movie sessions at their house, and the movies are usually followed with dancing. Such social gatherings were not economically feasible until rapid transportation came to the area.

We recall the "old days" of 1958–1959, when the young men in Sevettijärvi village would spend hours trying to collect enough girls for a dance, frequently without success. Now the effective radius for gathering an impromptu dance group is tripled, automatically enhancing the likelihood of success.

In Utsjoki, we found that the snowmobile repairman at the village has a large and growing clientele, including some herdsmen from Norway. The logistics problems of snowmobile maintenance thus add to the increased social interaction. In addition to these factors, it is interesting to note that Lapp reindeer herdsmen now seldom spend nights out in the open backlands. Even though it costs some extra gasoline, the herdsmen often drive to the nearest house to spend the night.

---

[3] More recently Dr. Usher has found that most of the gains in trapping efficiency have been converted into increased leisure time, rather than into expanded trapping. Thus, the overall impact of the snowmobile on the Banks Island economy appears to be rather small at this time.

In the Canadian arctic there are many examples of long-range visiting by snowmobile. On Broughton Island, for example, the families have found it possible to move closer to one another into nucleated settlements, because they can still get out to their hunting areas effectively with the ski-doos. On Belcher Island there appear to be growing contacts between the "north camp" and the "south camp" because the snowmobile journey between the two is so much easier than the same trip by dog team. In the past, Eskimos have been quite eager to visit in distant communities whenever possible, but now their visiting expeditions to points 300 to 400 miles away (and further) are much easier and more frequent. For example, the Broughton Islanders now visit Clyde River (about 350 miles), carrying 45-gallon gasoline drums for refueling along the way (Stevenson, personal communication).

In the Mackenzie Delta area, Derek Smith notes that the Aklavik snowmobilers are able to have increased contacts with their friends and relatives out in the bush. On Southampton Island, Moyer found that ski-doos increased the full-time wage earners' possibilities of engaging in highly valued meat exchanges. Because reciprocal meat giving is such an important social intercourse, the wage workers, lacking the time to hunt, were in danger of becoming increasingly isolated from the more traditional Eskimos. The snowmobile changed that—possibly even helping to conserve certain traditional social patterns by putting the wage workers back into traditional hunting action.

Many other examples of the intensification of social interactions could be cited; in general, the pattern is quite clear. Snowmobile travel approximately triples a man's effective "socioeconomic speed." Compared to the pre-snowmobile era, he can get to three times as many places, and that frequently implies greatly increased social contacts.

Another, related, social effect of snowmobiles should be mentioned. In many areas a new social event—snowmobile racing—has been developed, contributing still more opportunities for the intensification of the social network. In Lapland there were snowmobile races in Inari, Partakko, and many other locations during the spring of 1967. The first snowmobile races were held in Utsjoki in 1969. The race at Utsjoki village on March 30 of that year drew a crowd of about 800 people, the largest gathering there since the road between Finland and Norway was opened in 1958.

SOCIAL DIFFERENTIATION AND SNOWMOBILES

Data on the relationship of snowmobile ownership to economic position in Lapland suggest that social differentiation between the "haves" and the "have-nots" is likely to be intensified by the economic effects of snowmobiles. A number of the middle-range reindeer herders told us that the mechanization of herding is forcing all except the wealthiest owners out of the reindeer business. There were already some clear differentiations between the "rich" and the "poor," but until now the poorer Lapps were not significantly handicapped in their participation in herding activities. Every man had sufficient sled reindeer to travel to the roundups, to his herds, and to carry out his other hauling and transporting. The less well-off families had to fish more and their sons frequently sought out wage-labor opportunities, but the structure of action at the reindeer roundups and other important events showed a striking egalitarianism. In fact the active hired herdsmen of the association included some of the poorest, as well as the richest, men in the area.

Now the picture is different. The wealthier half of the population can afford snowmobiles, while many of their kinsmen and neighbors cannot. Because of the far-reaching significance of snowmobiles for economic activity, the relative disadvantages of the poorer people have been increased, making it very likely that there will be a push toward greater socioeconomic stratification.

Among the Canadian Eskimos snowmobiles seem to contribute to increased social stratification in some areas, but not necessarily in all the different ecological zones. In Aklavik Derek Smith notes an increased social separation between the Eskimo elite (wage workers with snowmobiles) and the "bush people." In spite of the fact that the snowmobiles make it possible for the wage workers to have more social contacts with their relatives and friends out in the hunting areas, the economic gap between rich and poor is worsening. Smith says that, "The snowmobile has introduced a polarization, a differentiation within the community . . . which (worsens) . . . by relative deprivation, the position of bush-oriented, relatively traditional Eskimo families . . . and this, of course, has given rise to friction between the segments, to dissatisfaction because the highly acculturated snowmobile owners . . . are . . . considered to be stingy and mean because they don't involve themselves in the traditional sharing practices" (D. Smith, taped interview, May, 1970).

The same tendencies to stratification appear to be developing at Pond Inlet as well. Lorne Smith said the wage-earning half of the population, who are the snowmobile owners, appear to be developing into a higher prestige stratum, and the machines themselves are seen as a status symbol. The people who use dog teams "seem to be on the defensive."

On the other hand, Moyer argues that, at least on Southampton Island, the differentiation of snowmobilers from nonsnowmobilers is not one of social stratification. He points out that the full-time hunter-trappers are *not* economically handicapped, and they could afford to buy snowmobiles if they wanted to. On Southampton Island, then, the ski-doos appear to contribute to a social cleavage in which the nonowners do not see themselves as economically or socially handicapped. The snowmobile owners are wage workers (part- or full-time); they are more acculturated and more socially involved with white men; and they frequent the recreational activities at the Department of Transport base. Moyer argues that the snowmobiles are in some respects a "leveling mechanism" with regard to socioeconomic stratification, because the machines absorb a large proportion of the wage workers' cash advantage, which might be otherwise spent on material goods that have greater status symbolism. It is possible, then, that in some parts of the arctic the separation between snowmobile men and dog men will develop into a nonstratified differentiation involving two equally successful ecological niches.

In areas such as Banks Island and Broughton Island practically every able-bodied male owns a snowmobile. In these situations the presnowmobile ecological context did not set up one group of persons (the early adopters) in a favored economic position. Everyone has been able to afford a machine, and a stratification between "haves" and "have-nots" did not develop.

In this paper we have not included information concerning the impact of the snowmobile in Alaska, but the data that have reached us (cf. Francis, 1969) indicate that developments in arctic Alaska have been broadly similar to those among Canadian Eskimo communities. Concerning the effects of the snowmobile on social stratification, Francis notes that, "A certain minimum cash income is essential to hunting and fishing, which is the major occupation of the villagers of arctic Alaska. Because of increasing mechanization of an effective hunting system, the minimum cash income is continually rising. Unless wage opportunities increase accordingly, there is reason to suspect that the gap will grow between the properly equipped and the ineffective hunter. . . . Once again the ante is being raised . . ." (Francis, 1969:78).

As we survey this range of variation in the social impact of snowmobiles, we are struck with two important facts:

1. The advent of an expensive new machine does not by itself automatically cause an aggravation of social stratification.
2. The social effects of the new technology can be quite different from one ecological setting to another, depending on the details of local technoenvironmental adaptations.

ECOLOGICAL PROBLEMS

It took Americans forty years to realize that the mobility breakthrough provided by the automobile exacted a high cost in environmental degradation. With the snowmobile the possible detrimental effects to the precarious balances of nature were made apparent very quickly. For example, in Finland snowmobile-borne hunters wiped out most of the bear population in a single season. Laws were quickly passed. They were quickly passed as well in the northern tier of states—Minnesota, Wisconsin, Michigan, and so on—as hunters found that the snowmobile gave them overwhelming advantages over almost all snowbound game animals.

In the arctic north there are not ever-expandable numbers of citizens who will go out and kill for recreation. The populations there kill caribou, seal, walrus, and other game in order to maintain a precarious arctic diet. They do not have admiring families to the south who will applaud as acts of honor their expanded capacity to kill.

The ecological impact of the snowmobile involves the increased decimation of game, noise pollution of the backlands, junkyard effects of retired machines, air pollution from combustion engines, and many other effects. But we must quickly note that the overkill effect of snowmobile use in Finland and other regions is partially offset in the high arctic of Canada by the decreased necessity to feed hungry carnivorous dogs, the former mainstays of the transportation system.

In northern Finland the snowmobile makes exploitation of distant fishing lakes easy for even the busy reindeer herder. Our informants mentioned a number of well-known isolated lakes (from which the catches of fish are supposed to reach legendary proportions) that are now regularly visited by snowmobile-equipped fishermen. Hunting of arctic ptarmigan and willow grouse in Lapland may also reach more ecologically significant levels through use of the snowmobile.

Compared to the Canadian and Alaskan arctic, Lapland is a densely populated environment. One additional factor—for example, the snowmobile —can bring about serious environmental problems comparable to the decimation of the beaver, loss of reindeer herding grounds, and other sweeping environmental effects of the northward push of "civilization." Fortunately, the Finnish, Swedish, and Norwegian governments are more attuned to the preservation of environments than are their counterparts in the Western Hemisphere.

To people used to the impressive silences of arctic backlands, the sharp roar of the snowmobile can be perceived as serious noise pollution. Both Eskimos and Lapps comment on the possibility that the machines will frighten game animals as well as the domestic reindeer (cf. Müller-Wille, 1970; Moyer, 1970).

Among the Lappish herders there are some men who feel that the snowmobile will eventually frighten the reindeer so badly that the herds will dwindle and the entire industry will terminate. On the other hand, it is surprising to find that many animals show little fear of the machines, and Stevenson reports that Eskimos at Broughton Island can approach quite close to seals on their machines, because the animals have no instinctive fear of machine-caused sounds. In any case some sensitive species are likely to suffer from this new noise, and all arctic animals will undoubtedly change their habits at least to some extent in response to this modification of the environment. Meanwhile, perhaps the manufacturers will be forced by conservation-minded people to develop silent motors.

At this time it is not feasible to predict the main lines of ecological impact of the snowmobiles. It is best to be quite suspicious. After all, the usefulness of automobiles—so benign and progress-inducing—for long masked the threats they posed to the environment. In many parts of the arctic the snow-mobile may yet bring about serious imbalance of the fauna on which native life depends.

But the positive features of snowmobiles should not be denied, any more than we deny the usefulness of food-producing innovations such as the domestication of barley, wheat, cattle, pigs, and sheep. For many arctic peoples the snowmobile provides a straight-out increase in food-getting capability. In the race to feed families, the machine has once again aided people to fulfill their basic needs.

René Dubos said that "mere survival is not enough for man." Enhanced food-getting is not enough, if the environment becomes increasingly degraded through decimation of game, noise pollution, and the other exhausts of a combustion-engine way of life. But with regard to the snowmobile, the effects on the high arctic way of life are not at all clear as yet.

SUMMARY AND CONCLUSIONS

If we looked at the data from only one geographical area we could easily come to some wrong conclusions about the effects of the snowmobile on the social and economic systems of arctic peoples. The tremendous importance of ecological setting on the impact of snowmobiles is evident in the very different reactions of ethnographers to the snow vehicles. In Lapland our fellow ethnographers have seen the impact of the snowmobile as something close to a social and ecological disaster. In the Utsjoki region, however, Müller-Wille views the snowmobile revolution in mildly optimistic terms. Some researchers among the Eskimo pronounced emphatically that "the Eskimos will never give up the dogs," but this prediction appears to have arisen in ecological settings where the speed of the snowmobiles provided no important economic advantages to offset the very real costs. An observer of the Banks Island situation, on the other hand, could easily be led to conclude that the snowmobile is a major technological advantage for all Eskimo groups, because the cost accounting of ski-doo use seems so favorable in a situation of excellent trapping and hunting.

Of course, all the data reviewed here should be taken with caution, for the long-range effects of snowmobile ownership and use have not yet been played out. On-going research throughout the next few years—in several different locations—is essential for an evaluation of the full impact of snowmobiles on arctic populations. Our preliminary survey provides some of the main outlines in terms of which future studies can be carried out. Comparative studies of the snowmobile revolution should consider the following:

1. Variations in the relative strengths of the hunting and trapping sector versus the wage-earning sector in different regions should be considered.

2. The presnowmobile state of social differentiation in various communities should be an important dimension for selection of cases for study.
3. Comparative studies should include careful assessment of physical facts of terrain, weather, vegetation, and other environmental factors affecting the technical utility of snowmobiles.
4. The cost-accounting of snowmobile use should include more rigorously defined quantitative data than has been the case in our studies thus far.
5. *Intra*community variations in ecological adaptations are extremely important to consider in assessing the differential effects of snowmobile use.

The effects of the snowmobile will be profound in practically all areas of the arctic. The elimination of dog populations, speed-up of rates of social interaction, increased social differentiation, plus possible long-range ecological disturbances, are bound to bring about striking new patterns of ecological adaptation in many areas. Of course, the effects of the snowmobile cannot be taken in isolation, but must be viewed in relation to other agents and factors of sociocultural change. Nonetheless, studies focusing on this singular technological development can do much to increase our understanding of how technological innovation brings about sequential transformations in economic, social, and other aspects of culture.

8

As indicated in the preceding chapter, there is an important distinction to be made between macro- and microtechnology. Doctors Robbins and Kilbride have made the distinction absolutely clear. They are not dealing with the ramifications of a river dam or with the consequences for social change of a new city. They asked instead, "What are the effects of the little technological things on people's lives?" They examine the results on some people of rural Uganda of the introduction of radios, wrist watches, bicycles, and other easily acquired accouterments of civilization. In the case of the bicycle they point out that it has increased mobility and the sheer volume of social contacts among people. Pelto indicated similar results in his study of the snowmobile. It may be that one of the most important general effects of technology is its role in bringing more people face to face more often. Another important and general effect seems to be a change in the traditional roles of women. Robbins and Kilbride's comment that "men would probably have their women without the mobility the bicycle affords" is an invitation to research of the role of technology in intersex social relations.

MICROTECHNOLOGY IN RURAL BUGANDA[1]

Michael C. Robbins and Philip L. Kilbride

Michael C. Robbins is Associate Professor of Anthropology, University of Missouri. He received his Ph.D. from the University of Minnesota and then taught at Pennsylvania State University. He has done field work and research in Tanzania and Uganda and has published widely on the Baganda.

Philip L. Kilbride is Assistant Professor of Anthropology, Bryn Mawr College, and Research Associate at Markerere University College, Uganda. He received his Ph.D. from the University of Missouri. He has done field work in Uganda and has published materials on psychological characteristics of the Baganda.

There have been several investigations of the impact of large-scale technological innovations and material changes on the social structure and culture

[1] We would like to take this opportunity to acknowledge and express our gratitude for the generous support and assistance of several persons and institutions. In particular, we would like to thank the Makerere Institute of Social Research, Makerere University College, Kampala, Uganda, for their help during our tenure there as Research Associates in 1967 and 1969. Our fieldwork in 1967 was supported by a grant from the Agricultural Development Council and a National Science Foundation Institutional grant administered by the Pennsylvania State University. Our field work in 1969 and the data analysis for both periods have been supported by the Wenner-Gren Foundation for Anthropological Research, a grant from the Graduate School Research Support Fund at the University of Missouri, and by Biomedical Sciences Support Grant Fr–07053 from the General Research Support Branch, Division of Research Resources, Bureau of Health Professions, Education, and Manpower Training, National Institutes of Health. Most importantly, we would like to thank our Baganda colleagues Constantine Banabakintu, John M. Bukenya, Margaret Dambya, Mere Kisekka, Vicent Matovu, and Acquilino Ssenyondo for their patience, wisdom, hospitality, and untiring labor on our behalf. Nona Paguio and Patricia Robbins provided considerable help in the analysis of the data and the preparation of the manuscript.

of many of the world's populations. Somewhat neglected in the increasing number of these studies, however, has been the investigation of the consequences of the introduction and use of small-scale or "microtechnological" innovations.[2] Microtechnology nominally refers to such technological processes and material items as radios, bicycles, flashlights, sewing machines, baby bottles, toothbrushes, timepieces, culinary practices, contraceptives, cosmetic arts, and so on. Most of these are relatively inexpensive and small in size and can be individually owned, used, and operated. These characteristics should not imply, however, that they are either insignificant to local populations or to the study of the processes of technocultural change in general. In fact, a main purpose of the present article is to call attention to the manner in which their diminutive appearance often belies their great importance and salience to the individual members of a local community. In our view, these are often "the things" people work for, save for, and spend a great deal of time planning to acquire.

In this chapter we intend to disclose some of the economic, social, and ideational consequences of the acquisition, ownership, and use of microtechnology in a small region of rural Uganda. Our aim is to present a descriptive integration of our field observations and informants' statements of four basic ways in which microtechnological items and processes have affected the individual and the community:

1. They have affected the economy of the household and community by both increasing the efficiency of productive and distributive processes and by constituting major consumption aspirations.
2. They have increased the quantity of social organization in the local community. That is, they have increased the length and number of events and activities in the community and facilitated their coordination and predictability (cf. Wallace, 1958, 1961).
3. They have contributed to a revision in the content of the individual's personal and social identities.
4. They have modified the individual's information level and his degree of certainty and security.

We shall begin by first providing a brief description of the local peasant population and community where the research was conducted. Second, we shall describe the procedures we employed to collect our information. We will then take up a consideration of the role some of these items have played. Finally, we will attempt to discuss, by way of summary, what we interpret to be the major changes and modifications brought about by their ownership and use.

[2] The radio is perhaps a notable exception. See Clark (1969), Miller (1969), Kerr (1969), and the entire issue of *Rural Africana* (No. 5, 1968) devoted to rural communication in Africa, for comprehensive reviews and bibliographies of research concerning the impact of the radio and other communications media in Africa.

RESEARCH SITE AND POPULATION

Our research was undertaken in a rural parish (*muluka*) we shall call "Lusozi," in the southwestern portion of the former kingdom of Buganda in southern Uganda. Lusozi is located 76 miles southwest of Kampala city and eight miles northeast of Masaka, a town of about 2,500 persons.[3] Lusozi is an officially recognized territorial and political administrative unit with a chief who is primarily responsible for collecting taxes and resolving minor conflicts. Lusozi includes six villages (*byalo*), each of which also has a chief who is responsible to the parish chief. Each village contains approximately twenty farms. Several parishes comprise a subcounty (*gombolola*), which in turn is a territorial subunit of the county (*saza*). These territorial-administrative units are not, however, cohesive social groups and, indeed, subcounty and county chiefs are often distinct from most peasant farmers. Frequently, they are highly educated, urbane, and in several cases, non-Baganda, though this is a recent pattern, starting with the abolition of the kingdoms in Uganda in 1966. The parish chief of Lusozi and the village chiefs are local people and maintain a kind of insider–outsider role while representing both government and constituents (cf. Follers, 1955). In Lusozi there are about 2,000 Baganda and a lesser number of immigrant farm laborers or porters. These non-Baganda (mostly Banyaruanda and Bachiga) from Ruanda, Burundi, and Western Uganda, care for cattle and work as porters and farm laborers for the Baganda. Most Baganda in Lusozi practice a small-scale agriculture of plantains, sweet potatoes, and cassava for subsistence and raise coffee and tea for cash. There are also two large Mailo land-estate holdings in the area (cf. Mafeje, 1969). Subsistence farming is primarily a female activity supplemented by the porters, whereas both Baganda men and the outside porters are mainly involved in the growth and sale of cash crops. Several men also earn additional cash by engaging in full- or part-time occupations in either Lusozi, a nearby trade center, or in Masaka. Many of these jobs are skilled and semiskilled, for example, taxi drivers, medical assistants, clerks, tailors, barmaids, and teachers, at both the primary and secondary school levels. Households and farms are dispersed and constitute the basic socioeconomic unit in Lusozi. Most farms are 3 to 5 acres in size. The homes themselves are frequently strung out along roads or paths and positioned in among the family gardens and banana groves. The mean household size in Lusozi is 4.5 persons per dwelling. In a social survey conducted in 1967, we found that 30 per cent of the households were nuclear in composition, 33 per cent were expanded (nuclear plus additional relatives), and 37 per cent

[3] There are many excellent summary accounts of the sociocultural system of the Baganda (e.g., Southwold, 1965; Fallers, 1960). Roscoe (1911) contains particularly valuable and relevant information on traditional Kiganda technology and industries. For additional information on Lusozi and our general research aims and procedures, see Robbins et al., 1969, and other articles cited under our names in the references.

atomistic, that is, lacking a co-residential spouse-pair.[4] Joint or extended families are rare. Although there are still a few polygynous unions, the marriage pattern is almost exclusively monogamous.

At least 50 per cent of the population has received some education. The mean is about 3.5 years.

The pattern of social life at the village and household level tends to conform to most models of the peasant society. People in Lusozi are quite individualistic and rarely enter into long-term permanent relationships. Instead they seek the short-run advantages of more profitable dyadic relationships. Traditionally, there was considerable residential and social mobility and Baganda frequently moved about attaching themselves to chiefs, wealthy landowners, and kinsmen (cf. Perlman, 1970). Today most important activities are transacted with neighbors and friends. Some group or corporate cohesiveness, however, is still evident in Lusozi. For example, individuals belong to exogamous clans and lineages which occasionally gather to decide on matters of inheritance, marriage, and residence. Christianity is the predominant religion and most people in Lusozi belong to a formal church. About 15 per cent of the population is Muslim, and a lesser number either claim no religion or adhere entirely to traditional Kiganda religious beliefs. Finally, clubs or voluntary associations are sponsored by the subcounty headquarters to assist villagers in developing certain skills needed for participation in the "modern world." A literacy club, craft guild, and community center, for example, were recently established for adults. The manufacture and sale of traditional crafts (mats and baskets in particular) provide some additional cash income for women.

Differences in occupation, cash income, land ownership, and formal education have all contributed to the social stratification of Lusozi. The social structure of Lusozi could be conceptualized as consisting of four broad strata or categories of people. First, there is the *rural elite*, a relatively modern group, including the older landed gentry who have considerable wealth and access to modern culture, material and otherwise. Many members of the rural elite (e.g., a doctor, religious cleric, and two large Mailoland-owners) speak English and manifest a modern material style of life in their homes, cars, and television sets. They also maintain residences in the urban area of Kampala and are involved in social networks that transcend the rural parish. In most cases their children are acquiring or have obtained university educations, often abroad, and occupy important professional, commercial, and governmental positions in the urban areas. Few of the children of this group, in fact, have stayed in Lusozi. Our observations suggest that this group is beginning to form a "status-culture" (cf. Fallers, 1959). A second important group in Lusozi could be called the *young moderns*. These are the younger, relatively less affluent individuals who have had a

---

[4] For clarification of the specific definitions used in this conceptualization of household composition, see Rodgers (1967).

good deal of formal education and possess a modern outlook in attitudes and dress. These people would be represented by schoolteachers, medical assistants, clerks, and some shopkeepers and small businessmen. They differ significantly from the rural elite, however, in not having the land or wealth to acquire an elaborate modern material life or participate as intensively in modern sociocultural activities. Another conspicuous group of individuals are the older, traditional residents who have relatively little land, wealth, or education. These we would call the *peasant farmers*. Most speak only Luganda, the local language, live in traditional homes, and adhere the most to traditional Kiganda culture. Often, however, they aspire to a modern material style of life and desire a modern formal education for their children. In many cases they make considerable sacrifices to obtain the requisite cash for school fees. Finally, Lusozi has a number of individuals who are somewhat *marginal* to both traditional and modern groupings. They include in most cases, Baganda vagrants, "school-leavers," the landless and unemployed and occasionally the prodigal sons of the rural elite. This group also includes many porters and non-Baganda from other areas. Individuals in this group often associate with each other and exhibit deviant behavior in the form of crimes against property and persons and excessive alcohol use.[5]

From this description it is evident that the people of Lusozi conform quite well to models of peasant social life. They are primarily subsistence agricultural farmers who are involved in a limited-cash economy. They are individualistic yet articulated to the larger community and nation-state. Modernity is also reflected in their material culture and technology. The domestic group is the predominant social unit and one meets the individualistic, competitive, interpersonal environment through dyadic relations.

METHODS OF DATA COLLECTION

The data presented in this chapter were collected over a two-year period (in 1967 for six months, and again in 1969 for three months). During these periods the authors lived in Lusozi. In general, our field research has been concerned with the psychological and social consequences of the modernization process as it has been occurring in this rural area. In 1967 we randomly selected and investigated, through structured-interview schedules, 109 households. The interview schedules were designed to collect basic demographic and socioeconomic information which we could use both to describe the area and to investigate the modernization process. During our research in 1967, several kinds of data concerning modern technological items and their uses were collected. In addition to these formal procedures, we also used techniques of participant observation to collect qualitative data on

[5] For additional information on alcohol use in Lusozi see Robbins and Pollnac (1969), and for additional information on the delineation of these sociocultural subgroupings see Robbins et al. (1969).

behavioral events, activities, and settings in the parish. During the summer of 1969 a more limited social survey schedule was administered to thirty-four individuals, selected as representatives of positions along a hypothetical modernization continuum. This continuum was largely determined from our previous knowledge of the area. This instrument included several questions specifically designed to produce data on the present ownership of several microtechnological items, their date and place of purchase, and information of an evaluative nature (e.g., "What is the most important item you own and why?" "How has owning a radio changed your life?"). The interviews were conducted in Luganda with the aid of local research assistants. In addition, several semistructured interviews were conducted with "key informants"—individuals whom we felt were experts on the consumption habits and aspirations of the local population. One of our best informants, for example, was a local village shopkeeper with twelve years of education, who was himself directly interested in these things from the perspective of personal profit. Through visiting homes and participating in local events, we were also able to observe their daily use. For example, during our fieldwork in 1969 we were able to witness the reaction to the radio news of several major international and national events: the American lunar landing, the assassination of Tom Mboya of Kenya, and the Pope's visit to Uganda, in whose honor several village ceremonial parties were held. We were able to attend one of them and observe the use of the radio news to coordinate party activities in the village with the events taking place in another part of the nation.

In presenting these materials, our aim for the most part has been to let our respondents' eyes be our own. That is, we have tried to describe the consequences of the use of microtechnology as recognized by the people themselves. Only occasionally have we allowed ourselves to comment on what we feel may be latent effects. Part of our reasoning is that in this relatively unexplored area, it is wise to use an inductive-empirical approach. Although a larger and more carefully selected sample and a more extensive survey instrument would have been desirable, our time and resources prohibited this. Our results, therefore, should be evaluated as exploratory, tentative, and from the perspective of the obvious limitations of the procedures we used.

MICROTECHNOLOGY IN LUSOZI

Although several observations were made of a wide variety of microtechnological innovations, this discussion is mainly concerned with bicycles, radios, kerosene lanterns, torches (flashlights), timepieces, coiffure-processing and visual technology and media (cameras, photographs, and so on). The frequency and per cent distribution of the ownership of some of these items is shown in Figure 1. Figure 1 indicates that the only universally owned

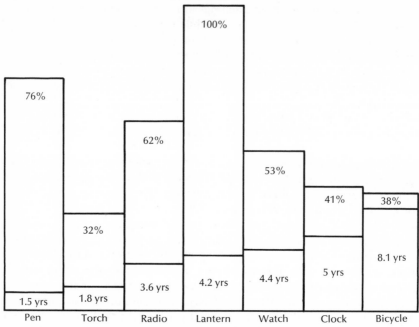

FIGURE 1. Relation of mean length of time and per cent of sample owning items.

item are the lantern, followed by pens, radios, wrist watches, clocks, bicycles, and torches, respectively.

The bicycle has been owned the longest, followed by the clock, watch, lantern, radio, torch, and pen. Of particular interest is the apparent lack of relationship between the extent and the length of ownership. This suggests that one cannot necessarily infer the length of time or age a material item has been present from the extent of its distribution (a common assumption of the age-area hypothesis in anthropology; cf. Graves et al., 1969). A good example of this can be observed in the case of the fountain and ball-point pen, which are owned by 76 per cent of the sample but only for a mean length of time of 1.5 years (mode = 1 year). These data suggest, therefore, that *rate* of adoption can vary dramatically item by item. To illustrate this more vividly, we present in Figure 2 a cumulative graph of the adoption-rate curves of several items. Along the vertical axis we represent the cumulative per cent of owners, and along the horizontal axis, the time of adoption (when the item was acquired). Research on the diffusion of innovations has demonstrated that the adoption of an innovation is usually normally distributed when plotted over time. That is, it displays a "bell-shaped" curve. This distribution will be essentially "S-shaped" when plotted on a cumulative basis (Rogers, 1962:152–92). The normal S-curve represents the "usual pattern of adoption"; that is, an innovation will initially be received by a small percentage of

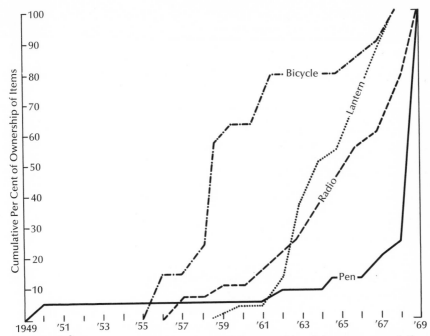

FIGURE 2. Relation of cumulative per cent of ownership of items to cumulative per cent of time.

people and later be adopted by most of the people, leaving a small percentage of late adoptors or "resistors." Figure 2 shows that to a degree the rates of adoption of the lantern and, more clearly, the bicycle have tended to follow the normal adoption process. The radio and pen, on the other hand, have been more recently adopted and at a more rapid rate. Evidence for the more rapid adoption of the radio can also be observed by comparing the results of our ownership survey in 1967 (39 per cent) with our survey results from 1969 (62 per cent). Generally speaking, these differential adoption rates undoubtedly reflect both an item's current popularity and its *perceived* utility. An investigation of the specific factors involved, although beyond the scope of this paper, would constitute an important goal for future research.

Of all the items considered in our survey, our respondents selected the radio and bicycle as the most important item they either presently owned or desired. An interesting way of observing the perceived use of items is to examine the percentage distribution of items that are owned and still operate, that is, those that are being maintained in working order. In Table 1 it can be seen that most items are kept in working order, but timepieces less than others. One interpretation suggested by our respondents themselves is that timepieces are largely ornamental. That is, a large component of the perceived usefulness of a wrist watch is as an overt symbol of a modern cultural

Table 1

Per Cent of Items Owned in Working Condition

Items	Per Cent of Those Owned That Are Working (%) (n)		Per Cent of Those Owned That Are Not Working (%) (n)		No Response (%) (n)	
Radio	95	(21)	5	(1)	0	
Watch	78	(14)	22	(4)	0	
Clock	69	(11)	12	(2)	19	(3)
Torch	91	(10)	9	(1)	0	
Pen	100	(26)	0		0	
Bicycle	100	(13)	0		0	
Lantern	97	(33)	3	(1)	0	
Total	91	(128)	7	(9)	2	(3)

identity. This function can be performed simply by ownership and display, irrespective of its use in time estimation.

Table 2 shows the location and distance from Lusozi of the place of purchase of several of these items. These data reveal that most microtechnological items are easily available and have been acquired either within Lusozi itself or only a short distance away. With these comparative data in mind, we turn now to a discussion of each item separately.

Bicycles

The bicycle is an extremely important item in Lusozi. This is in large part due to its primary economic value as both a potential source of income and a capital investment. One informant, with whom we were discussing the relative importance of the bicycle to the villagers, said, "The bicycle comes first. It is used for transport to and from work and for making money by trade . . . coffee, fish, bread and milk traders all use bicycles." He also noted that few women today ride bicycles, although girls will occasionally use them for pleasure. Part of the resistance to the use of the bicycle by women is undoubtedly due to the nature of women's clothing and to the fact that only "men bikes" (with a bar between the seat and steering post) are currently available. Mature Baganda women are expected to wear the *busuuti*, an ankle-length dress. Younger girls, however, can wear either shorter-skirted school uniforms or pants. It is likely that if the bicycle "boom" continues, either women's clothing will be modified or bicycles with a drop frame (the "girl's bike") will be adopted. In fact, it is surprising that this type of bike has not yet been widely adopted. A considerable amount of attitude change, however, will probably also be necessary on the part of both sexes because most people

Table 2

Place of Purchase of Microtechnological Items

Location	Distance (miles)	Radio (%)	Watch (%)	Clock (%)	Torch (%)	Pen (%)	Bicycle (%)	Lantern (%)	Per Cent of All Items Purchased in Each Location
Parish		0	0	0	9	31	0	12	9.28
Trade center	5	0	0	0	9	0	0	3	1.43
Masaka-town	8	82	61	81	73	31	100	79	70.00
Kampala and/or other districts	More than 80	9	17	0	0	0	0	3	4.28
No data: no response (or) gifts		9	22	19	9	38	0	3	15.71
Totals		100	100	100	100	100	100	100	100.00

feel that women look rather undignified mounting and pedaling a bicycle. Moreover, men would probably rather have their women without the mobility the bicycle affords. All of this is not to suggest that women are not given rides as passengers. In fact, a common sight in Buganda is a man pedaling his bicycle to church or on a visit with his wife riding sideways holding a child and some of their belongings. The essence of these remarks is that the bicycle is mainly of instrumental value to males and predominantly a masculine technological item.[6]

In Lusozi 38 per cent of the individuals surveyed in 1969 had bicycles and considered them their most important item.[7] The most frequently mentioned uses of the bicycles are personal transportation and the movement of goods in distributive economic activities. The economic activities people say bicycles facilitate are traveling to work and getting out to the fields; transporting goods (particularly coffee and fish); renting them to other individuals and hiring them as taxis for public transportation. Individuals with bicycles, for example, can collect and purchase coffee from their neighbors and then transport this coffee to a nearby (3 miles) coffee-processing plant, earning 5 shillings each trip (1 shilling = 14 cents). Normally, one large sack of coffee is carried on a bicycle. Owning a bicycle can also save the individual 2 or 3 shillings, the cost of a round-trip taxicab ride to Masaka.

In addition to enhancing the efficiency of these economic activities, people in Lusozi have also recognized several less obvious consequences of bicycle ownership and use. For one thing, the quantity of social interaction and communication within and beyond Lusozi has been greatly augmented. Friends, and particularly relatives, who often live at a considerable distance from one another, can now be contacted and visited more frequently. People on personal visits usually return with information and gifts (often food) for their friends and neighbors. By offering the use of the bicycle, which children enjoy riding for pleasure, it is also easier to induce a child to

[6] For an enterprising article on the impact of the "bicycle boom" in the United States, see Aronson (1952). His material is particularly relevant to the relationship of the bicycle to cultural definitions of sex roles. Gerlach (1963) provides important information on the role of bicycle traders on the East African Coast. Several observers, both African and other, have been impressed by the variety of uses Baganda make of their bicycles. Kariuki (1963), a Kenyan, who spent several years in Buganda, observes that "Most people seem to own bicycles in that country and they use them in remarkable ways: it is common to see live goats strapped on the carriers on the way to market and some bicycles carry enormous loads. One day in a village near Budo I was surprised to see a cyclist with a stove fixed to his carrier; he was cycling along peeling potatoes, cooking them, and eating them without dismounting at all."

[7] In 1967 our household survey revealed that 50 per cent of the homes had bicycles. The discrepancy may relate to the difference between using households as the units of analysis for some comparisons and individuals as the units of analysis for others. A person responding to the 1967 survey, for example, reported a bicycle present if anyone belonging to that house possessed one. In 1969 our survey was concerned with individual ownership. This same note of caution also applies to making comparisons between the two time periods for the other items. The difference between these periods, therefore, should also be viewed from the perspective of the adoption *rates* as well as the differential proportion of ownership.

transport messages and goods. This is an important and longstanding socio-economic role for children. Usually they receive a penny for running errands within the parish.

For another thing, bicycles have promoted and solidified other social relationships. For example, the bicycle can be used to transport neighbors, friends, and/or their goods as favors. Several informants stated that they felt more socially desirable because they possessed a scarce commodity. The temporary loaning of bicycles is also a sign of warm friendship and considerable trust. One informant, for example, when discussing the rights and duties of ritualized drinking friendships (*abekinywi*), said of his friend, "He is such a good friend he can even come to my house to take the bicycle without asking."

Conversely, conflict among neighbors and friends can be provoked by the refusal of a ride or the loan of a bicycle. Also on the negative side is the fact that bicycles are easily and frequently stolen. A great deal of concern is expressed about thieves and one must spend a considerable amount of time in locking and keeping track of one's bicycle. This is, of course, true of several items we will be discussing. Some people in the village also mentioned that robbery and burglary have increased since microtechnological items have become more commonly available.

Auxiliary equipment (e.g., locks) and continuing maintenance costs (e.g., tires) often require the individual to increase his economic endeavors. One individual whom we know quite well told us he was going to have to manufacture *waragi* (local "illegally" distilled gin) the next day in order to acquire 24 shillings needed to purchase a used tire for his bicycle so that he could transport his and his neighbors' coffee to the processing plant. Bicycles and several of the other technological items we have mentioned have provided additional economic activities for mechanical experts, and many persons are now becoming part-time specialists in bicycle repair. One rather interesting response to the question concerning how owning a bicycle had changed his life was made by an eighteen-year-old boy who worked at the coffee market. He indicated that he had chest pains when riding his bicycle. Research potential lies in the areas of motor skills, physical health, accident rates, and other disabilities resulting from or related to the use of bicycles. Although we lack firm statistical evidence, we think that a great number of the automobile–automobile and automobile–pedestrian road accidents involve bicycles.[8]

[8] The Uganda police department reported in the *Uganda Statistical Abstract, 1969* (Table U.E. 10) that in the years 1963–1968 pedal cycles were primarily responsible for more than 1,500 traffic accidents each year, ranking third among all other vehicles. During the same period the following number of pedal cyclists were killed or injured. The figures in parentheses denote the number killed:

1963	1964	1965	1966	1967	1968
991 (84)	1157 (98)	1017 (104)	993 (96)	1050 (81)	1048 (128)

In sum, the bicycle has had obvious and important impacts on both the behavior and culture of the people of Lusozi. It has increased the ease of transport of both persons and goods in the area. It constitutes an important capital investment and has served to increase the personal income of owners. It has facilitated communication and visiting by extending social networks through space. It has become a vehicle for personal pleasure and an outlet for recreation. Additionally, bicycle ownership is a symbol of prestige and success. On the negative side are the continuing maintenance costs, and health and property losses. Future research should be directed at more precisely identifying the social and economic inputs and outputs of bicycle ownership.

Radios

The modern national culture is largely perceived by the people of Lusozi through their exposure to several visual and auditory mass media. This, of course, is true in many parts of the world and has been the focus of several recent studies.[9] The transistor radio in particular is considered extremely valuable by people in Lusozi. The majority of the population (62 per cent) either owns a radio or is saving and aspiring to acquire one. When asked what they considered to be the most important item they owned or desired, the people of Lusozi overwhelmingly chose the radio along with bicycles. Only one of the twenty-two owners in our sample has a radio that is not in working condition, an impressive point when one considers the continuing maintenance costs for batteries. A battery costs about 1 shilling and most radios require six. The radios themselves cost between $14 and $50. It is extremely difficult to acquire a radio for less than $20 near the parish. Manufactured items in general are very expensive in Uganda because few are made locally. Figure 2 shows the rapid radio adoption rate, as do the comparative figures from our 1967 (30 per cent) and 1969 (62 per cent) surveys of ownership.

Several people commented on why they so strongly desire a radio.

> We buy radios for news and announcements. When a person dies in a certain family, and a person is going to hold a succession ceremony, a twin ceremony, or a wedding party, he passes this to his relatives through the radio, so it is very helpful to householders or people who manage a house.
>
> It keeps visitors busy when one is away trying to get beer or preparing food. Also it shows that the person is rich, particularly if he owns a big radio.
>
> It makes a person get more friends than before and the neighbors come for news and announcements. When they don't, they don't because there is no music for young people.
>
> To those that are not married, the radio makes women to love the men.

Another informant commented at length on the changes that have occurred among the people as a result of the radio.

[9] See footnote 2.

Government puts on programs explaining why and encouraging customs to be changed. Many people have in fact changed. Women have been encouraged, and many now do, to eat chicken, pork, eggs, lung fish and corn. Traditionally men prevented women from eating chicken and these types of things although women liked it. The men feared there would not be enough for everyone. . . . In the old days, men did not respect their wives. They could beat them. The radio has made men change. The radio has given knowledge as to how to care for children and to prevent diseases such as coughing, polio, kwashiorkor, measles. . . . "Bring the children to be vaccinated" is announced on the radio. . . . The radio also informs people to follow the government policy.

In our view a primary role of the radio has been to allow the individual to gather information about and participate in activity sequences far removed in time and space. Through the radio, events of international significance become topics of discussion and interest on the local scene. During the summer of 1969, Pope Paul visited Uganda. Although the Buganda region of Uganda is predominantly Catholic, his visit was a nondenominational nationwide event. At least six months prior to his arrival, there had been several preparations made by the Uganda National Government and the Council of Churches to inform the population and prepare the city and its facilities for his visit. Many announcements concerning his trip were broadcast daily and several other forms of advertising on shirts, dresses, buttons, and signs were visible. The major celebrations were held in Kampala, where hundreds of thousands of people went to see the Pope in person. We observed what was taking place in the rural parish.

The first activity we noted in Lusozi was that approximately three days before the Pope's arrival many people began arranging local ceremonial house parties to be held concurrently and in honor of the visit. Some parties became two-day affairs, although most lasted only one day. For the majority of persons the radio was the only way to keep in touch with what was taking place. The two people in the area who owned television sets were deluged with visitors. A Peace Corps friend of ours reported that he had approximately thirty people crowded into his living room to watch the events on his television. Most of these were schoolboys and their friends who knew him, as he was teaching at the nearby secondary school. Others went to Masaka, eight miles away, to see the Pope on the television sets in the restaurants and hotels. One of the wealthy members of the rural elite in Lusozi who owns a television also had a private party. But for the average farmer the radio was the only way to follow the events.

The party we attended began at 11 A.M., with soft drinks, pineapple beer, and dinner served to a small group of close friends and relatives at noon. A special outside enclosure was constructed with mats, chairs, and tables, including one table for the radio. The householder also played the record player. The main party began with a series of prayers and the serving of pineapple and banana beer at 3 P.M. Of special interest was the synchronization of traditional Kiganda cultural activities with this modern national one which was taking place. For example, a traditional Kiganda song sung in Luganda was extemporaneously modified for the Pope by a farmer who was a noted singer and expert on traditional music. Four hymn books which had been borrowed from the local primary school for the day were used at the party; there was a good deal of group singing and praying synchronized with the events taking place in Kampala and broadcast over the radio. Present at the party were old and young adults, children, Europeans, Muslims, Catholics, and Protestants. An analysis of the composition of the group revealed that 50 per cent of the people attending were relatives neither of the householder nor of his wife. During the party, which ended at about 9:30 that evening, after the drinks were gone, there was a mixture of traditional singing and dancing. Occasionally, someone would stop to make a short speech or prayer or a toast to the Pope and then continue singing and dancing. The radio was going all the time.

On the day of this great national event, the people of Lusozi felt, and were in fact, integrated into the modern national culture through the radio and, in fewer cases, the television.

The radio is normally given a prominent and visible place in the home. It is often decorated and proudly displayed. On occasion, people may carry their radios from house to house and radio ownership enhances one's social identity and desirability. One informant mentioned that "owning a radio makes one become civilized." Another stated that after owning a radio, "I became modern and no longer feel lonely." Still another individual, expressing his desire for a radio, said that if he had it, it would make him proud and "decrease my problem." Others emphasized the advantages of radio ownership in "keeping up to date," "reducing ignorance," "getting new friends," "being modern by having new ideas," "learning new languages," "improving English," and "being considered a high and rich person." For some the radio may be of considerable economic importance. For example, small shopkeepers or hairdressers who want to improve their business can do so by installing a radio to attract people; those who come to stand around and listen may purchase a few items. For bars, it is a necessity to have some kind of music or entertainment available. The radio, therefore, is also an important capital investment and improvement for those in business.

Although the radio has been of primary importance in extending the range of activities and events that one can learn about and participate in, it has also provided economic well-being and comfort, and increased the amount of social interaction and friends that one can obtain. Most of these consequences are largely of an overt behavioral nature. On the cultural side, new goals and aspirations have also arisen as a result of radio broadcasts. New goals for child rearing, new foods, and an interest in other products have all been stimulated by advertising on the radio. Accordingly, the radio has created new frustrations, wants, and aspirations. Information and education programs have also set standards for people's behavior.

Of considerable importance, too, is relief from boredom and fatigue.

Many rural villagers have had some education and spent some time outside their present environment. This has stimulated their appetite for the complex and novel stimuli of the city and places beyond. Many of the traditional tribal activities and events are either extinct or unimportant in the parish today, resulting in expressions of boredom. As social groups and events have declined in number and importance, and individualism has increased, people have spent considerably more time alone, particularly in the evenings. The radio partially fills this gap with talk shows and music.

In sum, the radio is an important source of information about family affairs, ceremonies, and announcements concerning different relatives. One informant, for example, stated that he no longer worries about his relatives because he can now hear announcements concerning their well-being. It provides general news and information about the world outside. It has helped people establish new friendships and provides occasions for people to get together. It has added to individual identity and self-conceptualization as a modern person. Finally, radio ownership has made life more comfortable by relieving boredom through music and news.

Timepieces

Traditionally, the Kiganda day was segmented into rather large and under-differentiated time segments (relative to a Western conceptualization of time). Several investigators, however, have noted that as people become more modern, they are more likely to become more conscious of, and proficient in, estimating the passage of relatively short, objective time intervals (Doob, 1960; Gay and Cole, 1967).[10] As people have moved into the modern world, their involvement in jobs and activities that are relatively more precisely scheduled and regulated has been reflected in their growing concern with the passage of short time intervals. Concomitantly, there has been a growing dependence on the use of technology to aid them in their estimations. This is clearly reflected in Lusozi, where a large number of people now possess both wrist watches and clocks. Our 1967 survey revealed that 27 per cent of the persons in our sample owned clocks and 29 per cent had watches. Two years later our survey revealed that these values were 47 per cent and 53 per cent, respectively.

The advantages of possessing and using timepieces is manifest in our informants' responses to our question concerning how owning them had changed their lives. The most frequent response was that watches helped regulate one's activities, particularly going to work. One informant stated, "I do not have a bad record at my place of employment because I am always on time." Other individuals mention they "no longer are overworking themselves" because their activities can be scheduled in a more relaxed fashion. One male who performs a variety of jobs and has had six years of

[10] See Mumford (1934) for a useful discussion of the intimate relationship of the clock to other technological developments in the Western world.

education has owned his watch for two years and claims that he can "walk confidently knowing the time I have to get to work and to other places. As a result I rarely move quickly." The regulation and scheduling of activities has, therefore, in the eyes of several informants, made life easier. Of interest too is the fact that watches in particular are considered valuable because they can be used to keep track of time no matter where one is, and at night and on cloudy days. The clock, on the other hand, is normally kept in one place. Other individuals also mention that watches and clocks help them learn "regular time," a recognizably valuable skill. Women indicated the importance of having a clock or watch for their household duties, particularly preparing food. One, a thirty-two-year-old married woman with five children and five years of education, mentioned that she can "always be regular at things, particularly in preparing my food." Other women emphasized the importance of a clock as an interior house decoration.

Of considerable importance also is the role of a timepiece as a symbol of modern self and social identity. Several of our respondents remarked that owning timepieces made them "feel more pride and decorate their person." With a watch, one informant stated, "I am considered an educated person because of being on time wherever I go." Another stated, "I feel happy when it is on my hand. . . . It is an important decoration and because of it I am considered a modern person." Others said, "It shows that I am rich." And with a watch, "I am considered European."

During our field work in Lusozi, we were frequently asked by watch owners to compare our time with theirs, and a great deal of pride was evident when their watches closely approximated our own. The symbolic ornamental value of watches and clocks compared to the other microtechnological items we have been considering is also shown in Table 1 by the per cent of inoperative timepieces that are owned.

In general, timepieces have been extremely important for scheduling, regulating, and coordinating individual and group behavior. They have increased interpersonal predictability because persons can now precisely indicate when and where they will be someplace. Also of importance is the relationship of possession to identity. Watches and clocks provide a means by which individuals can symbolically indicate their relative social, cultural, and economic positions.

Lanterns and Torches

Two other very important technological items widely found in Lusozi are lanterns and torches (flashlights). These have been of utmost importance in making possible the extension of behavioral events and sequences in time. Many activities in the past were carried out primarily during daylight hours or relatively near an individual's home because of the problem of traveling or working after dark. Travel at night *is* in fact hazardous because of real and imagined thieves, assassins, and supernaturals. There is a notable fear of the night, and people who walk about the village beyond nine in the evening are often subject not only to assault, but to accusations.

The torch or flashlight, in addition to providing light, is also useful as a defensive weapon and for identifying strangers and other objects along the road.

In 1969 our survey showed 32 per cent of the people questioned owned torches and everyone in the sample possessed a lantern. One of our informants, when asked, "Has the torch or lantern brought changes into the lives of the people of your community?" answered,

> *Yes, they have. They have made a person not fear the night. Owning a torch saves money because a person without one will burn many matches while walking about after dark. Also at night in the house one will always know he has light so that if someone comes, he will just flash his torch. It gives the feeling of security.*

Most of his remarks are related to the flashlight. The lantern, he felt, had not caused any changes and functions simply as a source of light inside the home. We observed, however, that people with lanterns conversed and continued their activities late into the night, and many school students were seen using the lantern in order to study in the evenings. The importance of these two devices, then, seems to lie primarily in the extension of activity sequences through time and space—allowing increased travel, because people need not worry about returning home after dark and the extension of activities into the late evening.

Of the many interesting responses concerning lanterns and torches, no one replied that the torch was his most important item, and of the twenty-three not possessing a torch, only one indicated that it was his most desired item. For the thirty-four lantern owners, however, 25 per cent mentioned that this was their most important item, emphasizing the impossibility of activity at night without one. None of our informants mentioned that torches and lanterns contribute to a modern identity. Rather they seemed to perceive these items in terms of their practical advantages.

Hair Straightening

The Baganda have long been known for their concern with their personal appearance and their ability to look attractive in modern, Western clothing. Fallers (1961:682) notes that

> *One of the striking characteristics of Baganda is their ability to wear Western clothing with a real feeling for style. Over much of Africa, Western clothing is worn like an uncomfortable, ill-fitting uniform, but Baganda men and women have penetrated sufficiently into the inner recesses of Western style that many of them can wear Western clothes with real taste.*

Of particular importance in Lusozi, and elsewhere in southern Uganda, has been the impact of technological processes associated with hair care. In 1969, 75 per cent of the women we interviewed reported they "burned" (or straightened) their hair. None of the men, however, reported doing so. In 1967, 42 per cent of our respondents (mainly women) reported that they liked to straighten their hair.

Hair straightening usually involves the simple application of a heated iron comb to the hair, although sometimes curlers are used. Before straightening, the hair is washed and oil is applied (coconut oil, petroleum jelly, or East Indian oils). Most combs and oils are made in Kampala and Nairobi, and particularly durable combs are imported from Europe, especially Germany. Because hair straightening by specialists is sometimes expensive (1 shilling in Lusozi, 3 shillings in Masaka), many women do their own hair or have their friends help them. Combs are also in fairly short supply in Lusozi, so that a person owning a comb is frequently asked to lend it to friends and relatives. Homes with a female secondary school student are particularly likely to have such a comb. Beauty salons (*abooki be'nviri*), however, are widespread not only in the towns and trade centers, but also in Lusozi. Here several women earn additional cash working as part-time specialists in beauty care. One woman, for example, not only manufactures and sells several alcoholic beverages in her home, but also employs several village women to help her manage a "hair-burning" operation. She maintains one special room which she devotes entirely to this. Hair straightening also provides an opportunity for women to come together. During such sessions in the home of a specialist, women are seen sitting and drinking together, exchanging news and gossip. The beauty parlor is becoming an important behavioral setting for information exchange and visiting as it is for women in the West.

The "modern, urban image" is the model for hair styling. In preparing their hair, women often follow suggestions heard on the radio or emulate styles displayed in magazines. This, of course, is also true of their apparel, including jewelry, watches, clothes, head scarves, and the increasingly widespread use of wigs and hair pieces. Hair straightening is becoming an important preparation for social events. When women attend dances or ceremonies, they first go to towns and visit salons, where they spend a considerable amount of time preparing their personal appearance. Those women whose hair has not been straightened recently will normally wear either a head scarf or a wig.

Over-all, it is the younger, educated, and cosmopolitan women who find it important to straighten their hair, and hair straightening is a symbol of a woman's identification with modern culture. Using data collected in 1967, we compared people's subjective self-identifications as a "modern European-type person," "a traditional Muganda," or "mixture" with their responses as to whether or not they straightened their hair. The results indicated that those who considered themselves either a "mixture" or a "modern European-type person" tended to be most likely to straighten their hair.

In our survey in 1969 we inquired what advantages there were in hair straightening and how hair straightening changes a person's life. Five of the twelve women who did, responded that it improved their marital relations because it made them look more beautiful, younger, or modern. For example, one thirty-year-old housewife, with four years of education and three children, responded, "I have kept a little bit the husband from running after many women." Another woman, age twenty-seven, with seven years of education and two children, said, "Since straightening and looking more beautiful, I am loved more by my husband." Another, aged thirty-two, with five years of education and five children, stated, "After straightening, I always feel fit to stay with young and modern women."

Hair straightening, then, has had an important impact on the ideational culture by revising the content of individual cultural identities, particularly those of women. It has also provided a visible symbol of the growing generation gap.

Visual Technology and Media

Like many other African societies, communication in Buganda, particularly in the rural areas, is still primarily dependent on verbal–auditory channels, with a proliferation of folklore and proverbs, elaborate speech-making, and a cultural focus on music (cf. Kilbride, 1968: Kilbride and Robbins, 1969). Over the last several decades, however, there has been an influx of visual technology in the form of cameras, cinemas, photographs, magazines, newspapers, and so on. The use of many of these items has either been learned through formal institutions such as education and government training programs or through voluntary contact and accumulation. Photographs, in particular, have for some time been popular and most people strongly desire representative visual materials. Many homes, for example, contain large numbers of photographs and illustrations on the walls, and people take great pleasure in owning and displaying them.

Table 3 presents some data from our surveys showing the distribution of several of these items in Lusozi. Of particular interest is the large proportion

Table 3

Per Cent of Sample Using Visual Technology and Media

	1967	1969
Movie attendance	54	34
Magazine reading	47	51
Cameras owned	5	5
Photographs on inside wall of house	68	76
Magazines and/or paintings on the wall	47	

of homes which contain photographs and magazine illustrations on their inside walls. In most cases they are used for decoration and as symbolic representations of people and things to be emulated and acquired. As an example the following inventory of pictorial materials was made in the home of a middle-aged peasant farmer.

Photographs on the wall (colored and black and white)
1. The informant as a young man.
2. Informant with friends.
3. Family friends from Europe.

Calendar Pictures or Magazine "Cutouts"
1. Pope Paul.
2. A Catholic saint.
3. Gina Lollobrigida.
4. Betty Grable.
5. An African girl.
6. A civet cat.
7. The British royal family.

In his home there was also a painting, made in school by the informant's child, portraying several people in a work scene. This informant also expressed interest in obtaining a picture of a relative who was expected to die. He also wanted to have pictures taken of several other people he knew well. He was aware that with pictorial materials, he could store information for the future. Photographs and other visual materials are also used to entertain visitors and break down communication barriers in order to facilitate social interaction.

The use of visual materials has also had a great impact on perceptual skills and habits. As we have tried to demonstrate elsewhere (e.g., Kilbride and Robbins, 1968 and 1969; Kilbride, 1968; Kilbride, Robbins, and Freeman, 1968), many older, less-educated traditional residents of Lusozi have difficulty processing information presented through this new modality. In the course of our research on visual perception we administered a number of tests designed to assess the degree to which individuals possess skills necessary to identify objects in pictures correctly and to perceive depth in pictorial representations. Successful performance depended for the most part on the ability to use cues to depth, for example, object size, perspective, and superimposition. We found that these visual skills were most developed among those who had been more continually exposed to modern settings such as schools, businesses, and urban areas, where visual media are extensively used. The proliferation of visual media, which continues to accelerate at a rapid pace, has provided new codes for information storage and recall. Printed and illustrated materials have increased the individual's awareness and knowledge of distant things and events. The spread of modern visual technology has also had a considerable impact on cognitive and perceptual skills. Over-all, this suggests that new visual sensory–perceptual modalities are being emphasized, in addition to the more traditional verbal–auditory channels, and it is reasonable to predict that they may eventually supersede them.

DISCUSSION AND CONCLUSION

In our view microtechnology has had an important impact on at least four dimensions of the fabric of individual and social life in Lusozi.

1. It has significantly affected the economy of the household and community by increasing the efficiency of productive and distributive processes and constituting major consumption aspirations. The bicycle, as we have seen, has been of considerable economic advantage in the transportation of persons and goods. At the same time the desire to own and maintain a bicycle, as well as other microtechnological items, has stimulated cash-producing activities and the emergence of several occupational specialties. Radios, and the music and news they provide, are also important for attracting persons to small business operations such as shops and bars. We would anticipate that construction, distribution, and maintenance of other small-scale technologies will soon provide additional economic and occupational opportunities (e.g., beauty salons, commercial photography, watch repair).

2. Microtechnology plays an important role in increasing the quantity of social organization in the local community. Microtechnology often extends and augments the length and number of events and activities in time and space and the probability that they will take place. The radio, for example, is often the focal point for people to come together to share music, news, and announcements of relatives and friends in other areas. Kerosene lanterns, by producing the requisite lighting, obviate the restriction of important activities, ceremonies, and visiting to the daylight hours. Timepieces and radio announcements facilitate the planning, coordination, and predictability of numerous family and community events. Bicycles extend the spatial limits of social involvements.

3. The use of microtechnology has profoundly revised the content of personal and social identities. Owning a fountain pen for the purposes of displaying to others a symbol that one is an educated modern person is recognized by respondents themselves as being as important to self and others as using it for writing. Similar generalizations about the uses of other innovations as badges of modern identities, of course, would apply to wrist watches, radios, hair straightening, and so on.

4. Finally and perhaps less obviously, microtechnology has contributed to a modification in the information levels of the individual and the community. Knowledge, certainty, security, and freedom from boredom have all been enhanced through its use. Radios, for example, have provided entertainment, as well as news of relatives, friends, and the outside world. This has served to

reduce anxieties. Information concerning health, baby care, and so on, has also been enhanced. The coordination of events by timepieces has further served to reduce the stresses associated with waiting (cf. Pelto, 1966). Flashlights have mitigated the fear of "things of the night." The opportunity to "manipulate," "explore," and "model" with novel objects (itself an intrinsically rewarding experience; cf. Harlow, 1953; White, 1959; Hunt, 1965) augments curiosity and information about other technological processes. As one informant observed, "Children learn about electricity while playing with flashlights and batteries."

Most of our discussion up to now has been slanted toward the relatively more positive consequences of microtechnology for the individual and the community. In fact, certain negative effects are visible. Among these are the problems of the "have-nots," who do not possess the means to acquire many of these increasingly desirable items. There has been a demonstrable rise in frustration levels, envy, and the use of illegitimate and harmful means of acquisition, such as robbery, burglary, and murder. Correspondingly, there has been an increase in fear, suspicion, and mistrust in interpersonal relationships. There are also cases of seemingly irrational priorities, with the expenditure of quite limited household incomes to provide the funds for original purchase and continuing costs of these items.

We have relied largely on our informants and their interpretations of the "meaning" and "consequences" of the acquisition of microtechnology as the primary basis for our interpretations. In so doing, we have neglected the "seamy side" of modernization to the extent to which our informants have. Furthermore, we believe that anthropologists have been overly concerned in the past with spreading "cautionary tales" about the ill effects of technological change. In so doing, we feel they have ignored the fact that many of these "things" constitute important ingredients of the content of contemporary cultural values, and that they occupy an integral role in the social organization of the Little Tradition at the community level.

Finally, we hope that our emphasis on Euro-American technology in this paper has not implied that the modernization process as it is occurring in Uganda today is either entirely technological or necessarily "Western" or "European." In fact, many indicators of non-Western modernization can be observed, particularly in the areas of expressive culture. Many of the styles in music, dance, and dress currently in vogue, for example, can be shown to be ultimately derived from West Africa and the Congo.

In the foregoing discussion we have indicated some of the important, yet often overlooked, changes taking place in a rural region of Uganda as the result of the ownership and use of relatively small-scale technology. Although there are undoubtedly some striking differences, these trends are probably similar to situations in other societies undergoing modernization. They deserve attention in future research.

A sample of potential questions for consideration in future research might be as follows:

1. What factors account for the variance in the differential rate and extent of adoption of microtechnological items and processes? That is, what characteristics of individual modernization offer the best prediction of adoption patterns? Rogers (1969), in a recent monograph, provided a comprehensive introduction to the problem and some exciting leads for future research.
2. What is the nature of the relationship (if any) between the ownership and use of traditional microtechnology and the receptivity to, and patterning of, the adoption of modern microtechnology (cf. Spier, 1968)?
3. What is the nature of the relationship between the acquisition and use of microtechnology and individual health, disabilities, accidents, and perceptual, cognitive, and motor skills? Provins et al. (1968) present a useful introductory review of research in this area and some important research guidelines.
4. What is the nature of the relationship (if any) between early (or late) experience with microtechnology and the adoption and use of other technological innovations? Is there a transfer of technical skills? For example, do children who have had the opportunity to play and learn to use microtechnology display relatively more rapid learning rates in related technical skills later on?
5. What is the nature of the relationship (if any) between the adoption of modern material culture and technology and the adoption of modern cultural concepts, attitudes, and behavioral styles (cf. Robbins and Pollnae, ms.)?

Researching these questions could, it would seem, have important implications for those developing countries interested in technoeconomic development and in enhancing the technical and vocational aptitudes and abilities of their populations.

9

To say that technology affects peoples' lives is so true it is almost banal. But when we think of "technology" in this context we usually have visions of machines, or products of those machines, putting men out of work. Or we think of massive projects such as the hydroelectric power plant in in the high Andes described by Doughty. Or we may think of such consumer items as snowmobiles or transistor radios. But we rarely pause to consider the effects of really basic inventions, such as the wheel or the plow, possibly because we take them so much for granted.

In this chapter Professor Honigmann considers some of the social and economic effects of two of man's most basic inventions: the settled community and the permanent dwelling. For some of the people of Inuvik and for even more in Frobisher Bay the permanent houses there were the first such dwellings they had ever used. However, in keeping with the complex bureaucratic society in which houses were introduced to town-dwelling native people, access to them has not been a simple matter of construction and moving in, as may have been the case earlier in human history. As Professor Honigmann shows, the adaptation to houses in these communities has had marked effects on intragroup social relations as well as on behavior between arctic ethnic groups.

HOUSING FOR NEW ARCTIC TOWNS[1]

John J. Honigmann

John J. Honigmann is Professor and Chairman, Department of Anthropology at University of North Carolina. He received his Ph.D. from Yale University and has been a frequent contributor to the literature, including The World of Man, Understanding Culture, *and* Personality in Culture *and* Arctic Townsmen (*both with Irma Honigmann*).

INTRODUCTION

Houses are artifacts. In fact, they have been called machines for controlling the environment, or as Dubos (1965:269–70) puts it, for shutting out "insults" from the outside world and regulating the nature and intensity of the stimuli that individuals receive. Although houses may be regarded in the category of other artifacts—plows, metal axes, and guns, for example—it would be highly unrealistic to treat modern dwellings among modern arctic people primarily as things, for the social organization accompanying their introduction has been more conspicuously eventful. Because of the scarcity of modern dwellings in far northern communities, their cost (especially if they are to meet legal standards), the distances involved in transporting materials needed in construction, and the lack of substantial private capital,

[1] Field work in Frobisher Bay was financed for Irma Honigmann and myself by the Northern Co-ordination and Research Centre of what is now called the Department of Indian Affairs and Northern Development. The same source supported Irma Honigmann's research in Inuvik (on which I have drawn), whereas my work there was funded by the National Science Foundation (Grant No. GS 939).

housing in the Canadian arctic to a considerable extent involves government. For example, the government as landlord sets rules for acquiring and retaining a house and thereby influences the behavior of people who want to live in modern dwellings. For these reasons the social dimensions accompanying housing in the Far North will receive more attention in this paper than the house as artifact. First, I take up the way housing in its social dimensions has confronted people in two new Canadian arctic towns with new challenges and problems, and how those people have adapted to the challenges. I use the term *adaptation* in a somewhat special sense to designate overt behavior directed toward overcoming some kind of limitation, meeting a demand or opportunity, or solving a problem confronting or presented to specific actors. Adaptation does not necessarily imply that the actors manage to achieve or avoid what they are adapting to; hence adaptive strategies may be further examined to evaluate their long- and short-term success or failure. Second, in the pages that follow I look at some of the concomitants of housing, particularly at how in one town housing has contributed to social stratification, affected marriage, become involved in hostility, and helped to regulate social behavior.

ADVENT OF THE TOWNS

At the end of World War II not 1 per cent of the Eskimo population in Canada lived in a house that conformed to minimum standards set by the housing laws of the Northwest Territories (Phillips, 1967:157). Then in the early 1950's, as the public conscience of Canada slowly awakened to its responsibilities for the arctic and subarctic people and a new northern service began to operate in the federal government, ambitious plans were laid for social development in the North, including the amelioration of poor housing conditions (Robertson, 1967). The plans also included construction of two new administrative centers, Frobisher Bay in southern Baffin Island and Inuvik above the Arctic Circle in the Mackenzie River Delta, towns that quickly drew native populations attracted by construction jobs and by subsequent prospects of employment. In fact, employment for native people, who were being driven out of trapping by its uneconomical character, constituted one of the aims in town building. Plans for the towns, therefore, had to pay some attention to housing both for the native population and for people arriving from the south to take jobs calling for specialized skills and training. The next several paragraphs mention the origins of the towns and briefly sketch their layout and housing types as I observed them at the time of field work in 1963 and 1967.[2]

[2] For more details on Frobisher Bay see Honigmann and Honigmann, 1965, and for an earlier period, Yatsushiro, 1963; for Inuvik, Ervin, 1968, presents styles of life, and publication based on my field work is forthcoming (Honigmann and Honigmann, in press).

This view shows Apex Hill, a portion of Frobisher Bay town, looking toward the ice-locked harbor. (*Photo by John Honigmann.*)

The commonest type of housing in Inuvik and Frobisher is the 512. These were photographed in Inuvik. (*Photo by John Honigmann.*)

Frobisher Bay

As a government-planned administrative center, Frobisher Bay began in 1955, the year when the neighborhood called Apex Hill was built. In 1963 Apex Hill, located 3 to 4 miles from the government offices and the U.S. Air Squadron, contained 362 Eskimos, ninety-five of whom lived in the Rehabilitation Centre, a short-lived experiment in providing former hunters with new productive skills. Housing for families containing Eskimo workers generally differs from that assigned to rehabilitants, the former mostly living in three-room frame dwellings (called "512's" in the Canadian North) and the latter in simpler one-room houses said to be appropriate for persons who had just come off the land, where they lived in tents and snowhouses. Fifteen Eskimo families own three-bedroom dwellings that they cooperatively erected as members of a housing co-op. The town contains two other neighborhoods. One is the so-called Air Base, inhabited mostly by transient workers from southern Canada and by forty-seven Eskimos supported through government employment. The other neighborhood is Ikhaluit, where nearly 500 Eskimos and one nonnative live. In the Air Base, nonnative and native families reside in one-story corrugated-steel apartment buildings. In Ikhaluit, where steady employment is less prevalent than in the other two neighborhoods, housing also varies considerably. Some families rent one-room, 370-type "welfare houses," a few of which are privately owned, and many live in privately owned, unelectrified, self-made cabins (called shacks by whites), built of odds and ends but often quite attractively furnished and containing more than one room.[3] Nobody in Frobisher Bay owns the land on which his

[3] In 1967 Ikhaluit received a large number of new houses provided under a new Eskimo housing program (McElroy, 1968:27).

Self-made cabins in Ikhaluit, Frobisher Bay in 1963.

dwelling stands. Housing density scarcely differs between the three neighbor-hoods; it is 5.9 in the Air Base and 5.6 in the other two places. Although men outnumber women in the Eskimo population, Frobisher Bay is not a town dominated by single Eskimo men who have migrated there in search of work; rather, it is a community of families, and this is reflected in the pattern of housing. All the houses in Frobisher Bay, as well as in Inuvik, are designed to accommodate single families, and the great majority of households in the two towns contain independent nuclear families with perhaps the addition of a visitor or a boarder. The prevailing family type is not a consequence of the kind of houses available to native people but represents a pretown pattern that has been adequately documented by ethnographers working in the Far North.

Inuvik

Construction of Inuvik also began in 1955. Much more compact than Frobisher Bay, this western arctic town in 1967 contained two neighborhoods, an East and a West End. In the East End are private houses and small apartment buildings occupied with few exceptions by government-employed transient workers from southern Canada and their families. Other workers live in single-staff quarters, the nurse's residence, and two hostels. Consider-ably more varied housing in the West End accommodates mainly Eskimos, Indians, and Indian Metis families, who are mostly supported through govern-ment jobs held by persons of both sexes. Whereas East End housing is serviced with running water, piped heat, and piped sewage, the 1,025 native people living in the West End, including those in sixteen cooperatively built homes, live under far less modern conditions, though practically all West End houses are electrified. Generally, native West Enders live in three-bedroom frame houses (including a large number of 512's) which they own or rent. The homeowners had a chance to buy 512-type houses cheaply (after they had served the construction companies that built the town) and to pay for them in small installments. A number of homeowners also own the lot on which their dwelling stands. Some families received their houses and lots in full or partial compensation for dwellings they abandoned in Aklavik, the settlement that Inuvik was originally supposed to replace. Scattered throughout the West End are one- and two-bedroom welfare houses, as well as a few cabins and tent frames. The latter two types of dwellings are all that remain from a notorious "tent town" that coincided with the building phase of Inuvik's history and persisted for some years afterward (cf. Lotz, 1962). Houses not on privately owned ground are also subject to being moved by the government. Thus, several welfare dwellings that formerly stood in the former Rehabilita-tion Center's area have been shifted to other parts of the West End. Around 1962 tent frames used by men who did not yet have houses were forcibly moved from the river terrace where the main town stands to lower ground; the move provoked anger.

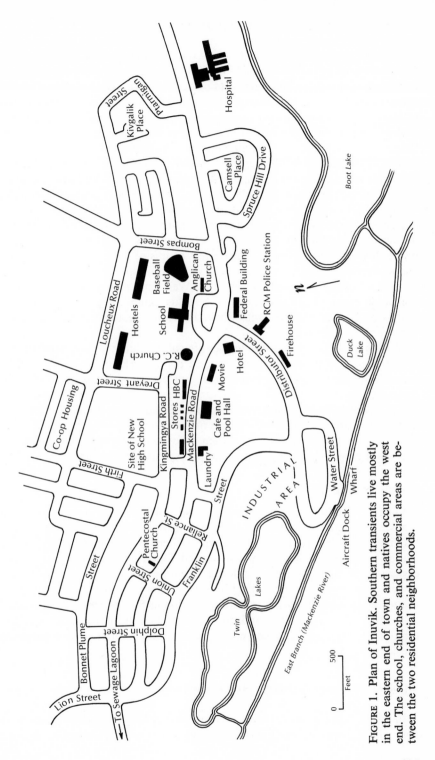

FIGURE 1. Plan of Inuvik. Southern transients live mostly in the eastern end of town and natives occupy the west end. The school, churches, and commercial areas are between the two residential neighborhoods.

233

In 1967 rumor spread that welfare and rental houses located in an attractive grove overlooking two lakes would be shifted to make way for the trailers of a construction camp, but quiet protests by nonnatives and a change in administrators may have led to a change in plans. The majority of renters pay the government which owns their homes; but a half-dozen houses belong to two nonnative landlords, one of whom resides in the East End. (We rented our house from an Eskimo who had taken a job upriver and moved with his family.) Families living in government homes who get behind in their rent or payments are not dunned or dispossessed, and it is doubtful if back payments of rent will ever be made up fully. Average house density is about 5.3 in the West End (Housing Survey, 1966). But average density is deceiving; I calculate about 800 native persons living in dwellings with two bedrooms or less, the densities of which run from six to seventeen persons per house. Some 200 people live in houses with 512 square feet or less of floor space that contain ten or more persons. According to a 1966 federally sponsored housing study, 10 per cent of the occupied houses in the West End (including those used by nonnative families) are substandard, but this figure compares well to conditions in the small settlements which many native townspeople have left upon moving to Inuvik.

In Aklavik 40 per cent of the houses are substandard; in Fort McPherson, 36 per cent; and in Arctic Red River, 22 per cent (Housing Survey, 1966). Inuvik contains a larger proportion of unmarried native persons of both sexes than Frobisher Bay. For those unmarried persons without families or young people who wish to live independently adequate housing is hard to find. People are of course fully aware of their housing difficulties; they perceive that the houses available to them differ in quality, and in many cases they want a better dwelling than the one they currently occupy.

Levels of Acculturation

Inuvik's English-speaking native townspeople have for some time been familiar with modern housing and other amenities. Many lived in well-built trapline cabins before moving to Inuvik. Others worked in Aklavik, a large nearby settlement, where they also owned frame houses. By contrast, the eastern arctic Eskimos are much less acculturated and rarely lived in houses or held jobs before coming to Frobisher Bay. However, extended hospitalization (often for tuberculosis) in southern Canada familiarized Eskimo of all ages with modern buildings and appliances, but it did not provide any significant facility with English, which even schoolchildren are reluctant to speak.

ADAPTING TO TOWN HOUSING

In this section I propose to discuss how native people in the two towns have gone about acquiring dwellings (noting as well what they might do but do not) and how they have proceeded to maintain their homes. It should be kept in mind that these adaptations have been made by people who voluntarily elected to move into town. Jobs are not the only reason they did so. For example, some parents with school-age children chose to move into town because by doing so they avoided sending the youngsters off to residential school for the greater part of the year, and elderly or sickly people find that town life provides greater security than a small settlement.

How Dwellings Are Acquired

Probably the commonest way in which a native family acquires a dwelling in town is by accepting employment with the federal or territorial government, thereby becoming eligible to rent a government-owned home. (In the case of single workers who lack other residence, employment usually brings accommodation in single-staff quarters, a room in the hostel, and so on.) Dwelling space is generally limited, and so some time may elapse before adequate housing becomes available for a native employee. When it is available the living space tends to be assigned rather than chosen, with the result that what the family gets is not fully suited to its size and needs for space.

Northern towns are small enough for officials to know individual workers and their families by name, but in finding adequate housing it nevertheless helps if the employee has a patron in the administrative branch of the government or if his immediate nonnative supervisor is willing to press for a house or a house larger than the one he now occupies. Sometimes a man or his wife repeatedly visit or phone a responsible official or the social worker to emphasize their need for housing. Thus, renting a house requires an individual to become economically integrated into the larger society and to enter personal relationships with nonnatives. These actions run contrary to the autonomy previously enjoyed by native persons vis-à-vis the larger society (Wilson and Wilson, 1945:108–16).

A second way of getting a home in the North is to buy one, nowadays usually a prefabricated dwelling; a one-room Eskimo low-cost home[4] ordered through the government costs about $600 to $1,000 delivered, or a larger house may be secured through a housing cooperative. Prospective Eskimo homeowners are eligible for a subsidy of up to $1,000, which, together with the owner's labor in erecting his house, substantially reduces the cost of a dwelling. Indians in Canada, when it comes to home ownerships, are not without government assistance, including loan funds, but in Inuvik they have hitherto lacked the advantages that accrue to Eskimos through the Northern Administration branch of the federal government.[5] Metis, being legally equivalent to nonnatives, have none of the special facilities available to

[4] For floor plans and other details of these and other homes commonly available in the North see Thompson, 1969.
[5] See "Social Benefit Programs for Residents of the Northwest Territories," 1967, Vol. III:203–207.

native people. Only responsible, steadily employed workers are welcomed as members of the housing co-op by the association's president or by the co-operative officer attached to the government. These men make catalogs available to a new cohort of members, explain the somewhat intricate process of applying for mortgage loans, assist in preparing papers and orders, and arrange for shipment from the south. The members take delivery the following spring, probably receiving the free services of government equipment in moving the heavy materials to the housing site. Co-op houses tend to be concentrated in one part of town.

The help of native co-op members and other neighbors with special skills in electrical work or carpentry is especially valuable in erecting the homes. Private and co-op house building, like rental housing, requires substantial economic and social integration into society. A job is a guarantee that the owner can pay the mortgage. Co-ops themselves are relatively complex groups for far-northern people, the meetings, the need to work with comparative strangers to build cooperatively, and the long line of communication to the southern supplier involve the prospective homeowner in an intricate, unfamiliar social system. A system so complex would probably never have begun or survived without the leadership of nonnatives or of sophisticated Eskimos who were trained by nonnatives and have expert advice and assistance readily available in the administrative offices of the government.

History may show a decline in private building beginning about 1966; this is due in part to a vastly expanded rental program for natives. Under this program the government has constructed a large number of multiroom houses across the arctic that rent for no more than 20 per cent of a family income or that can be purchased by people who have been paying on an older house (Caverhill, 1969). Word that construction would soon begin in Inuvik was no doubt partly responsible for the fact that a new cohort of co-op members forming in 1967 included mainly nonnatives and one Metis, but no Eskimo and Indians. The decline in private building in Inuvik may also be due to the fact that the demand for home ownership has been pretty well met. Currently, possession of a new house in town only appeals to a restricted segment of the native population, namely to families that contain a nonnative or Metis spouse and are imbued with middle-class values and to all-native families similarly motivated to acquire possessions and expand their standard of living. Such values will continue to be generated in Inuvik, but most existing families with those orientations appear to have been satisfied with regard to home ownership.

In the past, more than today, a third way of acquiring a house was simply to build a cabin or tent frame on some convenient vacant piece of ground. Migrants to town in search of jobs, and professional trappers desiring a place to put up, built such tar-paper-, sod- and canvas-roofed shelters. Their dwellings still exist, being concentrated in peripheral parts of Frobisher Bay and Inuvik, but they are generally regarded as aberrant and policy calls for their destruction as soon as possible. By contrast, to build a cabin in the settlement or bush, where most native townspeople formerly lived, required mainly the will to cut logs and the ability to scrounge a little lumber, plywood, and glass. A mission or trading company might object to building on its property, but otherwise nobody cared where the frontier-type home went up. Today in Inuvik even if a man owns a lot, he must legally have his housing plans approved before starting to build, and there are minimum standards that his dwelling must meet. Summer visitors are allowed to erect tents only in specially reserved areas lying along the riverfront. It is such restrictions on previous autonomy that natives and nonnative northerners in the Mackenzie Delta condemn when they assert that their "freedom" has been curtailed by the "southern invasion" of the North. Local regulations concerning housing also serve the function of restricting the flow of migrants to Frobisher Bay and Inuvik, migration being dependent on having relatives or friends with whom newcomers can stay until they find a job and receive a dwelling. Single-family occupancy of most homes indicates that not many families are being accommodated in this fashion in either of the two northern communities.

In a fourth means of acquiring a dwelling, old people and others in need of social assistance secure housing as part of the social welfare program. The major adaptation involved is for such persons to make their needs known to the social welfare officer, who has a certain number of dwellings at his or her disposal and assigns them to clients. Generally speaking, housing allocated to welfare clients is less comfortable or attractive than government-owned rental houses, and it is definitely less modern than new co-op homes. Small families, elderly couples, or unwed mothers with a single child are especially likely to be assigned only a modest dwelling. However, in Apex Hill several rehabilitants and families on welfare live in 512-type houses like those that government workers occupy.[6]

Three of the four adaptations for getting a dwelling are mainly personally initiated rather than being matters of group enterprise. The co-op, on the other hand, represents individuals who have pooled their resources to get a house. Although it is government policy to ameliorate housing conditions in the North, the policy has obviously been carried out within a set of priorities that, consistent with Western civilization's social structure, prevents all persons from being treated equally. For example, in Inuvik the best housing located in the East End goes overwhelmingly to highly skilled nonnative workers recruited from southern Canada. In both towns the government, the major source of rental housing, rents homes only to persons who accept government jobs or who are eligible to receive social assistance. Private enterprise in home building is also restricted to regularly employed persons, who alone are eligible for mortgage loans and subsidies to buy the prefabricated structures meeting acceptable standards. Local regulations forbid families without jobs from using their ingenuity to build self-made frontier-style dwellings in which to live while sojourning in town. The rules surrounding

---

[6] I have heard that under the new rental program described above, native welfare clients will receive the same housing as other people.

town housing most severely block people who want to live in town but do not want to take jobs and young people, especially young men. Government jobs are largely held by older workers. Young men find it difficult to get or hold jobs. They also do not wish to live at home, or they have moved to town without their family. Yet their jobless status makes it practically impossible to find a place to live independently.

The great extent to which most people are willing to take a job as a condition for securing town housing no doubt explains in part why in neither town has the native community as a whole or any component ethnic group organized politically for more or better housing or to alter the rules by which housing is assigned. Nevertheless, people are not satisfied with the houses they occupy; some renters complain of overcrowding; others point to gaps in the walls of welfare housing that makes the buildings cold. There are people who do not like the location they have been assigned to live, and families in self-made cabins and rental or welfare housing often face the unwelcome possibility that the government will move their dwelling or condemn it as unfit for habitation without something better being offered. Apathy is the reason, especially in Inuvik, why such people do not organize in behalf of new housing policies. The political action that does exist has mostly originated with nonnative publicists who are concerned with furthering native interests and improving the community in general. Among those activists is the newspaper editor in Inuvik and the Inuvik Village Council, a body which in 1967 contained no native member (but it did include two nonnative men and one woman married to natives). The council urged that some of the services piped into East End homes be extended to the West End, at least to the co-op houses, and it even secured a commitment from the government to finance an experimental extension of piped water and central heating to the co-op housing area.

Maintaining a Home

Adaptation to housing also takes place when a family tries to improve the place where it lives to make it more attractive and comfortable or seeks to retain its rights and possession. Motives to maintain a home generally do not extend to maintaining the appearance of a house or its surroundings. The strongest efforts go into (1) paying rent or installments to keep possessions and (2) ensuring that the house is warm and comfortable by securing oil, electricity, and water and furnishing it at least minimally with whatever necessities are not supplied, such as bedding and utensils. Privately owned homes require more appliances, including one or more stoves, a water tank, and a commode. Even for western arctic people who lived in houses before moving to Inuvik, many of these are new goals; formerly they hauled water from the river, cut wood for fuel, and did not have to worry about paying rent or electric bills. Even today the goals are distributed unevenly in the town population, one reason being that welfare clients have their supplies delivered regularly and, like most renters, can look to the government landlord to provide basic appliances. To the extent that the goals apply to a family, achieving them demands a job in order to earn money.

Economic analysis would probably reveal that a relatively small proportion of earned income is spent annually on household maintenance by most families. Rents are low and only a small proportion of people are motivated to accumulate furniture, paint, and do repairs, nor do they often desire to plant a flower garden and lawn (as one Indian woman does in the Inuvik co-op area).[7] As in the past, homes can still be partly furnished through minimum expenditure of money by a man making his own furniture with wood scrounged from dumps or, like borrowed tools, from the shops where they work. Native townspeople in Inuvik make less use of self-made furniture or things salvaged from the dump than Eskimos living in Ikhaluit, and that is, of course, compatible with the former group's higher level of acculturation.

In both towns the house complex is "incomplete" for many people, especially when appraised by middle- and working-class standards current in western Europe and America, though in Inuvik incompleteness is rarer than in Frobisher Bay. By incompleteness in housing I mean that the dwellings are unaccompanied by all the traits and values that ideally accompany them in the society whence they have diffused. Their incompleteness is reflected in bare furnishings, in the unconventional mode of furnishing, and in signs of hard use. Where such characteristics do not show up, it is not necessarily an indication that values making for completeness prevail. Relative completeness may be due to the fact that modern furnishings and necessary services are supplied by the government owner. As a consequence of incompleteness, housing for most people is not only relatively cheap but unfraught with competitive strivings, identity and other psychological needs, and anxiety, factors that make a house the single most important source of change in the United States (Gans, 1967:277, 292). Native children in the North also gain through the incompleteness because their spontaneity at home is not surpressed for the sake of protecting the home. Unsurprisingly, incompleteness brings misunderstanding and even disparagement from nonnatives and visitors, who deplore native "carelessness" with possessions and call the West End a slum. Incomplete social change, we are once more reminded, invites contempt and ridicule (Mead, 1956:448).

PERSONAL AND SOCIAL REPERCUSSIONS OF HOUSING

Now I will examine housing in Frobisher Bay and Inuvik as it is related to social stratification, marriage, and expression of hostility, together with the role of housing in regulating behavior.

[7] See, for example, the housekeeping standards observed at two small settlements, Cape Dorset and Baker Lake (Thompson, 1969:Ch. 2).

Implications for Stratification

I have observed little tendency in the two new northern towns for social relations among natives to follow social class lines. In Inuvik informants themselves insist that the "native" community constitutes an egalitarian social system and they condemn signs of social exclusiveness. Nevertheless, in both towns differences in housing can be used by an observer to mark off social categories. For example, among Frobisher Bay Eskimos, some people own co-op houses whereas others live in multiroom rental houses, one- or two-room welfare homes, and unelectrified self-made cabins. A former highly egalitarian people has become more differentiated by virtue of housing, coupled with unequal motivation to acquire dwellings of certain quality and secure economic integration into the larger society. Inuvik reveals a similar pattern of differentiation, but one made more complex by three factors: first, the town's bifurcation into two neighborhoods with very unequal housing (see Figure 1); second, greater variety in the means of securing dwellings; and third, three native ethnic groups which, as we shall see, tend to participate unequally in available housing. It might be thought that the priority system which reserves high-quality East End homes for nonnative transient workers, in effect restricting 93 per cent of the native population to less modern West End homes, would inspire competition among natives for the better homes. However, with rare exceptions, native people with whom we spoke did not express resentment against their segregation. Although many strongly want better housing than that to which they are assigned, and individually communicate their wants to government officials, both they and their nonnative spokesmen in the Village Council accept tacitly the rule that gives highest priority for good housing to transients, whose technical or professional superiority the native population therefore tacitly acknowledges. The council seeks mostly to upgrade West End housing, and as such upgrading occurs (for example, through rental housing programs mentioned previously), it may continue to avoid conflict in the politically unself-conscious native community.

The manner in which housing expresses social stratification is most evident in Inuvik with its several ethnic groups. (It is least evident in Apex Hill, Frobisher Bay, where housing of the same quality is assigned to many families, and it may become less evident in Inuvik as a result of the new housing program.) In the following analysis of Inuvik I will focus on 193 native and part-native families. One third of those families are attached to the community through owning some kind of frame house. The rest rent, live in welfare houses, or—mostly in the case of trappers—have no dwelling in town. Both the extent of home ownership and access to quality homes varies from one ethnic group to another. Table 1 arranges housing in order of quality, with East End rental housing being the highest grade and a tent frame or cabin the lowest. The table shows that part-native families with a nonnative head stand in the best position with regard to their access to East End, fully serviced

dwellings. The large group of families headed by an Eskimo relatively frequently own quality housing through membership in the housing co-op,
but when it comes to ownership of any kind of frame house other than a
tent frame or cabin (whether in the co-op or elsewhere in the West End),
they are exceeded by Metis family heads, 40 per cent of whom rate as homeowners. This compares to 39 per cent of the nonnatives married to native
spouses and 32 per cent of the Eskimo heads. Families headed by an Indian
are in nearly all respects in the poorest position with respect to housing.
None lives in East End rental housing, none owns a co-op house, 21 per cent
own nonco-op frame dwellings, and a large proportion rent a frame house or
are welfare clients living in such a building.

Table 1

Housing and Ethnic Status in Inuvik: Native and Part-Native Family Heads

| Type of Home in West End | Ethnicity of Male or Female Family Head | | | | All |
	Indian %	Eskimo %	Metis %	Nonnative %	Families %
Total number of families (= 100%)	(34)	(86)	(45)	(28)	(193)
Rents in East End	0	2	4	39	8
West End:					
Owns frame co-op house	0	15	2	4	8
Owns nonco-op frame house:	21	17	38	36	25
Owns any kind of frame house	21	32	40	39	33
Rents frame house or lives in frame welfare house	47	45	33	21	39
Owns tent frame or cabin	9	0	4	0	3
No house in town*	18	20	13	0	15
Housing unknown	6	0	4	0	2

*Many of these families live by trapping and spend only limited periods in town, during
which they live with kin or friends.

Additional information revealing the inferior quality of Indian housing is
brought out in the Housing Survey (1966), which reports that out of sixteen
overcrowded and otherwise unacceptable homes, nine are occupied by
Indians, three by Eskimos, and four by "others." Average density, however,
is somewhat greater in Eskimo than in Indian homes (5.7 to 5.4, respectively).
Stratification with respect to housing, like most kinds of stratification,
reflects unequal power; first, unequal power that comes from occupying
economically unequal positions in the community. Nonnatives hold the
most highly skilled jobs. Together with the Metis they have also been most

often steadily or fairly steadily employed in the period of time surveyed. Nonnatives, Metis, and Eskimos are better able than Indians to work effectively with white supervisors and more often possess the social skills needed to get and hold jobs. For example, they use alcohol more responsibly, though not necessarily to a lesser extent than Indians. Second, power in Inuvik derives from the degree to which a native family incorporates middle-class norms of the dominant society, the society that controls jobs on which housing closely depends. Obviously a part-native family, one headed by a nonnative, will be more likely to incorporate such norms than all-native families. Among the latter, Metis family heads (having been reared in a family with a white parent or white grandfather) embody dominant social norms more often than Eskimo family heads or Indian family heads. Power also comes from the degree to which a native group is favored administratively; the Eskimo's favored position in the Northwest Territories, compared to the position of Indians and Metis, is revealed by the comparatively large proportion of Eskimo families that have managed to buy a co-op house.

Implications for Marriage

Marriage and the establishment of a family mark the individual's entry into adult status. Evidence from Frobisher Bay (McElroy, 1968:17), Inuvik, and elsewhere in northern Canada (Graburn, 1969:192) demonstrates that marriage tends to be deferred beyond what it was in the period immediately preceding the present. In Inuvik young men especially delay marriage; among Indians none below twenty-four has been wed, and only 13 per cent of the Eskimo young men below that age have been. Reasons for postponement vary, but in both Frobisher Bay and Inuvik a combination of two complex, closely related factors appears to be highly influential: first, the scarcity of jobs for young men, combined with young men's difficulty in holding jobs; second, the manner in which acquiring a house depends closely on occupation and income. The dependence of housing on a job has been sufficiently stressed. It remains to point out that an enterprising couple who wish to live in town and cannot find a house will not be allowed to build a cabin, nor is the welfare officer likely to assign a house to young newlyweds, especially if, as frequently happens, the marriage is consensual rather than legal.

Another alternative is to live with parents, and in some cases this happens, especially in Frobisher Bay; but the low incidence of this arrangement indicates that it is not a realistic one in contemporary arctic culture. Of course, a couple could marry and live by trapping in the bush, building a house there to suit themselves, but few young men and women are likely to be attracted by such a career. Thus, the close ties between housing and a job in town (which places young men especially at a disadvantage) leave few alternatives for a couple when it comes to finding a dwelling and effectively act to postpone marriage.

Involvement of the House in Hostility

Frobisher Bay and Inuvik are both familiar with interpersonal aggression, which, especially in the latter town, occasionally takes the form of anger working itself out through the medium of houses and their furnishings. For example, a man locked out by his wife, to warn him to control his drinking, attacks the door; a woman rips telephone lines from a building; a youth in drunken rage smashes windows and furniture in a new house; and a woman, angered by her husband spending money he was supposed to use in paying on a house, sells that dwelling. According to a news item in the Inuvik *Drum* (1969), the government spent $11,531 in one year repairing rental houses damaged by drunken persons. Just as aggression mostly occurs between close kin and friends, so anger is frequently worked off against a person's own home.

Using the house as a target of aggression suggests that people, especially when drunk, see the house or its contents as something possessing objective value and therefore as a medium through which to hurt other people and sometimes even themselves. Unfortunately, we do not know whether in the past, particularly in the western arctic, where there has long been a pattern of heavy drinking and use of cabins, people also worked off aggression against their dwellings.

Housing and the Regulation of Behavior

One of the most interesting discoveries made in Inuvik is the extent to which quality of housing (in association with ethnicity) correlates with lawabiding-ness. The following discussion refers not only to family heads, but to 204 native men over twenty-one. (Comparable data are also available for twenty-eight nonnative men married to native spouses, but they have been excluded in order to control somewhat for cultural background.) In a community where 55 per cent of all native men over twenty-one were convicted in court at least once in the eighteen months prior to July, 1967, mostly for offenses against the liquor laws, very large proportions of native men owning a co-op house (87 per cent) or living in the East End rental housing (100 per cent) remained lawabiding, as Table 2 reflects.

A smaller proportion of native men dwelling in West End nonco-op houses that they own, rent, or secure by virtue of being welfare clients, re-mained lawabiding, and the proportion is still smaller among those who possess no house in town. Contrary to our expectations, the proportion of lawabidingness is higher for men renting a West End frame house than it is for men who own such unassuming frame houses (55 and 44 per cent, respectively). But without any kind of frame house, whether rented or owned, lawabidingness drops to 32 per cent. Cause may not be inferred from these figures, and we are content to conclude that having a stake in society, as indicated by a quality home and a job (for quality homes depend on income

Table 2

Housing and Lawabidingness in Inuvik: Native Men Age Twenty-One
and Over

Type of Housing	Never Convicted in Sample Period %	Convicted in Sample Period %	Total Number (=100%)
Rents in East End	100	0	4
West End:			
Owns frame co-op house	87	13	15
Owns nonco-op frame house	44	56	32
Rents frame house or lives in frame welfare house	55	45	56
Neither owns nor rents frame house in town*	32	68	95
Housing unknown	—	—	2
All men	45	55	204

* Comprises men living with family of orientation who are not responsible for their own housing, as well as men with tent frames and cabins and those lacking any house in town.

from employment), relates directly to the way a man regulates his conduct by avoiding conviction.

SUMMARY

Housing in two new far-northern Canadian towns has presented Indians, Eskimos, and Metis with new goals that many individuals and families have found to be worth striving for, even though the cost includes subordinating their previous autonomy in social relations entered into with the larger society. Housing, with its attendant rules or priorities, has brought out stratification in these hitherto largely undifferentiated societies, stratification appears most clearly in Inuvik, where the situation is complicated by the presence of several ethnic groups. Families established through marriage between a native woman and nonnative (white) man own and occupy the best housing, and families headed by an Eskimo or Metis are also favored when it comes to owning a house. Indians are in a relatively poor position with regard to housing, which reflects their comparatively low standing in the town's economic system. Housing is also a factor in the postponement of marriage and has become a target of drunken aggression. At the same time, owning or living in quality housing correlates with lawabidingness and therefore appears to act as a regulator of conduct.

10

After World War II the government of Mauritius took steps to eradicate malaria. Quite predictably, population skyrocketed. When Professor Benedict went to Mauritius the problem was already acute and the government was taking measures to combat it. In this paper Benedict recounts the historical circumstances which caused overpopulation through the use of technology and the lack of social planning needed to accompany its use. But Benedict does not dwell here on the primary effects of technology (the use of pesticides or birth-control devices). Instead he takes us on a step-by-step tour of the social structure and demonstrates how this structure aided in creating the problem of over-population in the first place and how it has stood in the way of solutions designed to reverse the growth rate. We see that "technology" by itself is irrelevant to our understanding of culture change. Instead we see the intricate web of relationships between technology, social structure, human problems, and efforts at solving them.

Reflecting on the problem of the anthropologist's role in bringing about change, Professor Benedict candidly discusses his personal involvement with government family-planning programs. And this, of course, leads us to ask whether the anthropologist might not be one more piece of Western technology in the lives of countless non-Western peoples.

CONTROLLING POPULATION GROWTH IN MAURITIUS

Burton Benedict

Burton Benedict received his Ph. D. in social anthropology from the University of London. He taught at London School of Economics before becoming Professor of Anthropology at the University of California. Dr. Benedict has done extensive field work, most recently in Mauritius, Seychelles, and Malawi. He has written widely, including several books, and is the editor of Problems in Small Territories.

Overpopulation, like sin, is quite safe to be against. Scientists, politicians, preachers, and protesters of all sorts warn us daily of the disastrous future which awaits mankind because of his propensity to breed. Yet, at the same time that we are desperately attempting to find ways of controlling population growth, we are increasing our efforts in combating disease and improving world health, thus creating conditions which greatly accelerate population growth. Our general failure to connect these two desiderata and to make intelligent plans so that we do not control death without controlling birth is nowhere better demonstrated than in the small island of Mauritius. Here the humanitarian efforts of the government to control malaria after World War II have led to a disastrous population explosion in which the population has nearly doubled, unemployment has risen, and the costs of government services—particularly education, relief payments, and health—have soared. This outcome was entirely predictable, yet there were no plans to deal with the problem. It was not until it was already too late to avert disaster that attempts to limit population growth were made. Will Mauritius be a pattern for other parts of the world? One hopes not, but the overpopulation of Mauritius and the attempts to deal with it deserve close attention. In this paper I

246

shall attempt to show how the situation arose, how it exacerbated, and what the difficulties were in attempting to introduce birth control. The emphasis will be on the social structure, for social factors were instrumental in accelerating population growth and in obstructing plans to decelerate it. The social factors were neither uniform nor static. I shall examine the ways in which they changed over time so that, for example, some form of birth control became acceptable to some people.

Between 1955 and 1957 I spent twenty-one months in Mauritius doing anthropological field work[1] (Benedict, 1961a). Toward the end of my stay my wife and I were involved in setting up the first family-planning clinic on the island.

THE SETTING

The island nation of Mauritius lies in the Indian Ocean some 500 miles east of Madagascar and 20 degrees south of the equator. On its 720 square miles, an area about one tenth the size of New Jersey or Wales, are crammed

[1] Research was carried out under a grant from the Colonial Social Science Research Council, to whom grateful acknowledgment is made. Opinions expressed in this article are those of the author and not of any government authority.

Carrying cane through the fields. (*Photo by Burton Benedict.*)

nearly 800,000 people, and the population is increasing at a rate approaching 3 per cent per annum. Three geographical factors inhibit the development of Mauritius: its small size, its isolation from world markets, and its lack of natural resources. The island is entirely dependent on agriculture, and one crop, sugar, accounts for more than 97 per cent of all exports. The arable land of the island, comprising about one half of its area, is 92.6 per cent planted in sugar cane, 3 per cent in tea, and only about 4 per cent in food crops (figures derived from Mauritius, 1966:44, 51). Mauritius must import most of its food. Rice constitutes the largest import, both in quantity and value. Flour, grain, meat, edible oils, and fats constitute major imports. Fresh vegetables are grown in small gardens or between the maturing rows of sugar cane. A variety of tropical fruits grows throughout the island and some fresh fish may be had from the lagoons, but by and large the inhabitants must buy imported food. Mauritius is agricultural but it produces cash, not subsistence crops.

Most sugar cane is grown on large plantations, which produce over 60 per cent of the sugar in twenty-three factories. The remaining sugar comes from some 26,000 small holders, cultivating plots from under one quarter of an acre to about 100 acres. Many of these have grouped themselves into cooperatives for consigning their crop to the company-owned factories. As one would expect, the sugar industry is the highest employer of labor on the island. Sugar even divides the year into crop and intercrop seasons. Sugar is the source of prosperity, indeed the economic *raison d'être* of Mauritius, but it also lies at the root of many of the social problems affecting the island.

THE PEOPLING OF MAURITIUS

When the Portuguese discovered Mauritius early in the sixteenth century, they found a richly forested island with no human inhabitants, virtually no mammals apart from large fruit-eating bats, and several species of large flightless birds, the most famous of which was the dodo. The Portuguese made no attempts to settle the island, merely using it to provision their ships on the voyage to India. They did, however, greatly alter its ecology by releasing pigs, goats, monkeys, and, inadvertantly, rats. In 1598 the Dutch took possession of the island, naming it after Prince Maurice of Nassau. The Dutch imported slaves from Africa and exploited the ebony forests of Mauritius, but they never had a large enough labor force or sufficient support from Holland to colonize the island successfully. They abandoned Mauritius in 1710. In 1715 the French formally took possession of Mauritius, renaming it Île de France. The French successfully colonized the island with settlers from the neighboring island of Bourbon (now Réunion), which had been occupied by France since 1654, with slaves from Africa and Madagascar and with artisans from Pondicherry in south India. The plantation system was established and coffee, sugar cane, cotton, indigo, cloves, and other spices were introduced. Thus from the earliest times the emphasis was on cash crops, though manioc was introduced from Brazil as a food for the slaves.

Mauritius is subject to fierce tropical cyclones, and planters soon discovered that the tough, flexible sugar cane was better able to withstand these storms than coffee, cotton, and spices. More and more planters turned to sugar. More and more slaves were imported to work the sugar. They came from many tribes and spoke many different languages. On their arrival in Mauritius men were separated from women and small children to be sold separately (St. Pierre, 1800:112ff.). The African cultures of the slaves did not survive such treatment and gradually slaves and their descendents developed a variant of French culture. The situation was complicated by the emergence of a class of free blacks and coloreds. The former were freed slaves; the latter were the products of miscegenation between white men and black women. Until 1803 free blacks and coloreds were legally equal to whites, but after this date the French governor, Dacaen, promulgated laws intended to separate free coloreds from whites. They were kept on separate registers, attended separate schools, served in different sections of the National Guard, and were forbidden to intermarry without the express authorization of the Governor (Prentout, 1901:142). Thus legal sanction was given to a social color bar that already existed. Today the legal sanction has disappeared, but the social color bar remains. The coloreds and blacks, known today as Creoles, have French language, manners, and culture. They have established a social hierarchy based on color, education, and ancestry.

The Île de France was a thorn in the British flank during much of the eighteenth century. As early as 1746 an expedition from the Île de France had captured Madras from the British, though the French later sold it back to them. Privateers operated from the island, capturing British East Indiamen and often selling the cargoes to Yankee traders from Salem, Boston, Philadelphia, and New York (Toussaint, 1954:9). Finally, in November 1810, the British captured the island with a force of sixty ships and 10,000 men. The capitulation signed by French Governor Dacaen on December 3, 1810, provided that the inhabitants be permitted to retain their religion, laws, and customs. Thus the Roman Catholic Church, the French civil code, and the French language and culture were given official sanction and to this day have remained prominent cultural features of Mauritius.

The British restored the name Mauritius to the island. They set up the machinery of colonial government, but very few Britons settled in the island. The plantation owners, much of the commerce, and many government positions remained in the hands of the Franco-Mauritians. In the 1820's the combination of the introduction of steam engines in the sugar mills and the reduction of duties leveled on Mauritian sugar imported into the United Kingdom greatly increased sugar production. The colony became virtually a single-crop plantation. More and more slaves were required for this increased production and British attempts to stop the slave trade were systematically evaded by Mauritian planters (Mauritius Slave Trade, 1826). In 1835 slavery was abolished throughout the British Empire. The population of Mauritius at that time totaled 101,469, of whom 76,774 were slaves. The planters received a little over 2 million pounds sterling compensation. Ex-slaves were supposed to remain with their former masters for a period of four years as apprentices. They were to be paid wages and learn a trade. In fact, little was done to help them find new modes of livelihood or attract them to the estates. They left as soon as they were able. In 1839 perhaps 30,000 left the estates (Barnwell and Toussaint, 1949:153) and went into the towns or formed settlements in uninhabited parts of the island. Laboring on the estates was associated with their former despised status as slaves. The planters were faced with a serious labor shortage. They turned to India.

Indians were brought to Mauritius under a system of indentured labor that was in many respects little better than slavery (Benedict, 1961a:22–23). They were engaged in India by agents of the planters on five-year contracts. In the early years of immigration, between 1834 and 1839, there was virtually no government regulation of immigration. Deception as to the location of Mauritius and the conditions of work, overcrowding on ships leading to death and disease, and other abuses led the government of India to suspend emigration from 1839 to 1842. In 1842 the government of Mauritius appointed a Protector of Immigrants in Mauritius and emigration agents in India and guaranteed return passages to India. In the years that followed, however, most of these safeguards were withdrawn or evaded by the planters. In 1847 the "double cut" was introduced, which provided that no month in which an engaged laborer was absent for more than six days should be reckoned as part of his service. Between 1853 and 1857 free return passages were withdrawn and great pressure was put on immigrants to reindenture. One method of doing this was the introduction of the pass system in 1867, which restricted the movement of Indians who had completed a period of indenture. The courts and the police were used to maintain a controlled cheap labor market. The abuses of the indenture system have left a legacy of distrust between Mauritians of Indian and European descent.

The influx of Indians radically changed the size and composition of the population of Mauritius. In 1835 Indians constituted only a minute proportion of a population of 100,000. Ten years later they made up one third of a population of 158,000, and fifteen years after that, in 1861, they made up two thirds of a population of 310,000, a proportion they have maintained to the present. Between 1834 and 1910, when regular immigration ceased, more than 450,000 Indians were brought to Mauritius and only about 160,000 were repatriated (Kuczynski, 1949:791).[2] They were shipped to Mauritius from the ports of Calcutta, Madras, and Bombay. They included both Muslims and Hindus of many castes and even a few Christians (Benedict, 1967). The majority came from Bihar, the United Provinces, Orissa, and Bengal and

[2] In 1923–1924 another 1,400 immigrants arrived, but subsequently most of these returned to India.

spoke dialects of Hindi. The second largest category were the Tamil and Telegu speakers of south India. Third, with many fewer immigrants, were the Marathi speakers of the Bombay area. In the early years of immigration only males were brought in, but disorders on estates led government officials to fix the percentage of females to males. Later whole families were brought in together.

Another group of Indians reached Mauritius between 1829 and 1865. These were traders from the Gujerati-speaking areas of west India and Bombay. Most were Muslims from the states of Kutch and Surat. They settled in Port Louis and their numbers greatly increased after World War I (Beejadhur, 1935:66–67). They became dealers in rice and cloth. Today nearly all trade in these commodities is in their hands. Unlike the indentured, they were able to maintain contact with India, where they often returned to marry.

The final ingredient in the ethnic *pot pourri* of Mauritian society is the Chinese. A few Chinese were to be found in the island in French times (Milbert, 1812, Vol II:186–91; Billiard, 1822:42) and a few came during the early nineteenth century. In the latter part of the nineteenth century and in the first half of the twentieth century their numbers increased, so that by 1962 they numbered 23,000 and constituted nearly $3\frac{1}{2}$ per cent of the population. They came as traders and shopkeepers. Today nearly every Mauritian settlement has one or more Chinese shops in it. Like the Gujerati traders, the Chinese have maintained contact with their mother country, though in recent years this has been Hong Kong rather than mainland China. Relatively few Chinese women came to Mauritius and the Chinese have intermarried with the Creoles (Benedict, 1965:20–21).

THE PLURAL SOCIETY

Mauritius is a plural society. Her immigrants have amalgamated into a single people but have maintained a separateness in varying degrees in varying social contexts. The plural nature of Mauritian society is an important factor in the introduction of any change, including the attempt to regulate population growth. It is easy to remark cultural differences among Mauritians: the clothes they wear, the languages they speak, the religion they practice, differences in kinship structure, in traditions, and in customs of many kinds. Physiological clues are less certain. Physiognomy is a poor guide for distinguishing an Englishman from a Frenchman, a Muslim from a Hindu, or a Hindu speaker from a Marathi speaker. The Creole population contains individuals who look Indian, African, European, and Chinese. The nature and extent of pluralism in Mauritius can be better appreciated if one looks at the whole economic and political structure of the island. To what extent are ethnic, cultural, linguistic, or religious differences reflected in the economic structure? To what degree do they play a part in the political and legal structure?

There are correlations between occupation and ethnic groups. Most sugar estate owners are Franco-Mauritians; most agricultural laborers are Indians; most retail shopkeepers are Chinese; most artisans and fishermen are Creoles; most importers of rice and cloth are Gujerati Muslims.[3] However, these categories are not exclusive. There is no legal backing to them as there is in South Africa. There are some Indians who have large sugar-cane holdings or interests in large estates. There are Creole laborers, and Indian shopkeepers, artisans, and fisherman. There are Chinese, non-Gujerati Indian, and European importers. After the sugar industry, government is the largest employer in Mauritius, and one finds members of all communities in government service, often furiously competing with one another. The professions, too, contain members of all ethnic groups. Occupational mobility appears to be increasing in Mauritius, aided by a widespread educational system, the availability of scholarships and such devices as a public service commission for government posts. The occupations which require the most capital, such as the sugar estates and the trading and commercial concerns, are most restricted of access.

Though occupational mobility and differential economic status may tend to diminish pluralism, they do not necessarily abolish it. They can create economic and social classes within each ethnic section of the population rather than a single class cutting across all sections. This has occurred to a certain extent in Mauritius and it is here that cultural features, including language, religion, traditions, and customs, play a part attaching an individual to his ethnic section rather than his economic class. To say that Franco-Mauritians control the sugar industry is not to say that all of them do, but only that certain individuals and families do. Many Franco-Mauritians lead lives of precarious gentility close to the poverty line. Economic mobility does mean, however, that there are opportunities for class loyalties to override ethnic ones. Muslim, Chinese, and Franco-Mauritian businessmen have more economic interests in common than they do with poorer members of their own communities. Muslim, Hindu, and Creole dock workers join the same labor union. Small planters of various ethnic categories have formed cooperative credit societies. Economically Mauritius shows signs of diminishing pluralism (Benedict, 1962), but economics are intimately linked with politics, and in Mauritius both are about to be engulfed in the flood of population increase.

POLITICAL STRUCTURE

Politically, ethnic considerations have always played a part in the island's history (Benedict, 1970a). In French times slaves, of course, could not vote. The island quickly turned its back on the French Revolution when it was

[3] For a more complete listing see Benedict, 1965:26.

proposed to emancipate the slaves. Under British rule, even after an elected element was introduced into the legislature in 1886, the property qualifications placed upon the franchise effectively disenfranchised virtually all Indians and the overwhelming majority of the Creoles. This restriction persisted until 1948, when the franchise was extended to both sexes with a simple literacy *or* property-holding qualification. The electorate increased from 12,000 out of an estimated population of 428,000 in 1946 to nearly 72,000 out of an estimated population of 447,000 in 1948. For the first time Indo-Mauritians, who composed two thirds of the population, controlled a majority of seats in the Legislative Council.

Prior to 1948 ethnic politics had taken the form of a struggle between the Franco-Mauritians and the Creoles, who as early as 1843 had petitioned Queen Victoria for greater representation in the Legislative Council. With the constitution of 1948 both Creoles and Franco-Mauritians as well as other minority ethnic communities, such as the Chinese and Muslims, began to fear that they would be overwhelmed by the Hindu majority. Ethnic, cultural, linguistic, and religious affiliations became symbols of political solidarity, especially at times of election (Benedict, 1965:60ff.). Various schemes were introduced, including to date, three new constitutions to try to solve the Mauritian dilemma of giving minority ethnic groups adequate representation while at the same time playing down communalism in politics.

The latest constitution, under which Mauritius achieved independence in March, 1968, provides for a Legislative Assembly of seventy seats. The island is divided in twenty three-member constituencies and every voter casts three votes. The hope is that even if the first and second votes are cast along ethnic lines, the third will be cast along lines of political conviction. After these sixty members are elected, eight "specially elected" members are chosen. The first four of these go to losing candidates who received the largest number of votes in the election and who come from ethnic categories of the population that are underrepresented in the legislature. The second four specially elected members are chosen from losing candidates with the most votes on the basis of both ethnic category and political party. The final two members are elected from the small island dependency of Rodriques, some 350 miles east of Mauritius. These provisions are designed to ensure that the legislature contains members of various ethnic categories proportionate to their numbers in the population while at the same time enabling party politics to operate on other than ethnic lines. The specially elected members can preserve the ethnic composition of the legislature but cannot be used to frustrate the will of the electorate. The single election held so far under this constitution appeared to go smoothly (Mauritius General Election, 1967), but it is clear that communal conflict is an ever-present danger in the island. Many issues and factions are apt to assume a communal cast (Benedict, 1957). In 1967 unrest in Port Louis apparently caused by the recent laying off of large numbers of workers from public works projects took the form of gang wars between Creole and Muslim youths. During elections politicians appeal to voters along ethnic, religious, or linguistic lines. Indeed, cultural characteristics previously not much emphasized may be appealed to. In the elections of 1963 appeals were made to Tamil voters against Hindi voters and to low-caste voters against high-caste voters. The multiethnicity of Mauritius makes it possible to structure any program of social and political change in terms of ethnic conflict. Attempts to control population growth have not escaped this difficulty.

POPULATION GROWTH

In the eighteenth and nineteenth centuries the population of Mauritius grew by immigration, first of Europeans and Africans and then of Indians. It did not grow very much by natural increase. This was due to very high mortality rates. Although the slave population increased from 15,027 in 1767 to 65,367 in 1807, "deaths probably exceeded births" (Kuczynski, 1949, Vol. II:762). Smallpox, cholera, influenza, plague, and malaria periodically decimated the population. The first reported smallpox epidemic was in 1742 and further epidemics occurred in 1754, 1756, 1758, 1770–1772, 1782–1783, and 1792–1793. The epidemic of 1756 was said to have killed half the slaves belonging to the planters; that of 1770–1772, one fifth to one quarter of all slaves; and that of 1792–1793, 4,000 people in three months out of a total population of 58,000 (Kuczynski, 1949:873). Vaccine was introduced in 1802, but there were still small outbreaks throughout the nineteenth century. Cholera first struck Mauritius in 1775, and there were epidemics in 1819–1820, 1854, 1856, 1859, and 1862. It seems to have been imported from India on each occasion and to have struck most severely in Port Louis, where it was estimated that one in eight died (Anderson, 1918:111). Influenza first broke out in epidemic proportions in 1851. A second epidemic in 1893 caused 3,441 deaths, but the greatest devastation was during the post-World War I pandemic, which reached Mauritius in April, 1919, and killed 12,860 by the end of the year (Kuczynski, 1949:875). The plague was a fairly steady killer from 1899 until its eradication in 1927, though it rarely killed as many as 1,000 in a year (Kuczynski, 1949:875). Dysentery, typhoid, and enteric fever were endemic, as was malnutrition, and no doubt contributed to the low rate of natural increase.

Except for a few cases of people who had contracted the disease outside the colony, malaria was unknown in Mauritius until 1865. In that year there was an outbreak of the fever which quickly spread to reach epidemic proportions by 1867. Between January, 1867, and June, 1869, it is probable that 40,000 to 45,000 people died of malaria, representing one ninth to one eighth of the population (Kuczynski, 1949:877). Colonel Nicholas Pike, the American Consul at Mauritius at the time, describes the scene as follows:

It was distressing to pass through the streets; in every corner was some poor creature, suddenly struck down, and crouching on the ground to die. In the out-

skirts of the city and country roads the victims were so numerous, that the police and sanitary committees were insufficient to succour half the poor wretches and many died by the roadsides before help could be brought to them. Near Roche Bois I have seen them lying in groups, dying and dead. Not a house within a radius of half a mile from the one I then occupied had a living person in it, except at a shop belonging to three Chinamen, two of whom died later. In many cases as soon as a Malabar got the fever, he would hasten to his house and shut himself in to die; for such was the fear of it, to be attacked was the tocsin of death to him.

[*Pike, 1873:105–106*]

The disease altered the population distribution of the island. Port Louis, where one twelfth of the population died in April, 1867, alone and where the death rate for the year reached 247 per 1,000, became an anathema. All who could moved toward the uplands, for it was found that there were few cases of malaria above 600 feet. By 1869, malaria had encircled the island and became endemic on the coast, with a regular summer rise in incidence. By 1906 it was invading the higher areas of the island (Brookfield, 1959:7–9). Malaria became the principal cause of death. Population growth in Mauritius was controlled by malaria. Between 1881 and 1944, the average annual rate of increase was less than one half of 1 per cent (Titmuss, 1961:45).

As early as 1907, Sir Ronald Ross had identified *Anopheles gambiae* as the vector responsible for transmission of malaria on Mauritius. He recommended filling and clearing, combined with the distribution of quinine, but very little was done. In 1922, a second vector, *A. funestus*, was identified, but little progress was made in eliminating breeding places. Finally, in 1948, a new scheme consisting of house spraying with DDT was introduced. By 1952 both *A. gambiae* and *A. funestus* had been eradicated (Dowling, 1953). The effect on population growth was dramatic. In one year the death rate fell by 32 per cent (Titmuss, 1961:47). The birth rate rose, though it is not clear how closely this is associated with the eradication of malaria. Between 1948 and 1958 population increased at the rate of 3 per cent per annum. The final report of the officer in charge of malaria eradication warns of the dangers of population increase (Dowling, 1953:32).

GOVERNMENT ACTION

In April, 1953, the Governor appointed an investigating committee of twelve members "To consider the problem presented by the present trend of increase of population of the Colony in relation to its economic resources and potential productivity; and to investigate and report on the practicability of any methods of resolving the problem" (Mauritius, 1955:i). The committee did not present its report until February, 1955. It is clear that it had had great difficulties. One member had resigned and was replaced; two members were added. Only eleven members signed the report. Four members added statements to the end of the report, two of them being notes of reservation and dissent. The report analyzed demographic trends and examined the impact of rapid population growth on employment and the social services, including schools, old-age pensions, and housing. It faced the problems of control of population growth by emigration and birth control, comparing Mauritius to India, China, Hong Kong, Japan, Malaya, Singapore, and Barbados. Finally the report recommended (1) the highest priority to increasing productivity on the island; (2) the promotion of family planning; (3) the opening of negotiations with other countries for emigration of Mauritians and the setting up of a fund which would allow families rather than individuals to emigrate; (4) a reorganization of the building industry in Mauritius so that houses could be more cheaply built, as a recent report had indicated that Mauritius would require over 10,000 new houses annually. The dissenting statements added to the report came from Franco-Mauritian and Creole members of the committee who opposed birth control in varying degrees. The Report of the Committee on Population did not result in any governmental action, but it did lead to a discussion of the problem in the press and in the Legislative Council.

Late in 1957 an extensive survey into employment, unemployment, and underemployment was begun under the direction of R. W. Luce. This report, published in 1958, estimated that there were 25,000 able-bodied unemployed and 3,000 underemployed persons in Mauritius at the end of March, 1958 (Luce, 1958: 30). Moreover, the rate of unemployment among school dropouts was increasing and would probably double within the following decade. All this was due, of course, to the rapid growth of the population. The report recommended emigration, though it provided no indication as to what countries would be willing to receive Mauritians. It also recommended increased production of food crops, particularly the potato (Luce, 1958:31–32). Government reaction to this report took the form of a statement issued by the Legislative Council entitled "The Luce Report: A Time for Decision." The major emphasis of this statement was on increased production, both industrial and agricultural. The government piously hoped, "To slow down, and if possible arrest, the increase in population" (p. 4), but at the same time timorously stated; "It is not for the Government to advocate methods of birth control which are offensive to important sections of the population, as in any case such methods are only of contributory importance and are usually confined to those social strata where the problem of population increase is least acute. The main activity is required in the masses of the people, who suffer most from excessively large families and there are many methods of family limitations which can be advocated without offence to any section" (p. 6). There was no indication as to what these methods might be. The statement also exhibited a kind of upper-class ethnocentrism, assuming that birth control was only needed among the "masses," which is demographically quite untrue for Mauritius. One might also make the point that elites, by definition, are not as numerous as nonelites.

The major point, however, was that the colonial government was afraid of the political consequences of the birth-control issue. At this time the

Roman Catholic Church was very much opposed to birth control. The Bishop of Port Louis had declared he would oppose its introduction anywhere in the island, not just among Roman Catholics. Nearly all Franco-Mauritians and Creoles are Catholic; they make up over 28 per cent of the population. Whatever they might do in private, Roman Catholic leaders would not support birth control publicly. Many Muslim leaders were also opposed to birth control. The specter of ideological conflict was real enough to intimidate the government. The government statement concluded by asking for a technical mission to advise the government.

Accordingly, in November, 1959, a commission was appointed under the leadership of Professor J. E. Meade, an economist from Cambridge. Another commission under the leadership of Professor R. M. Titmuss of the London School of Economics had been appointed earlier in 1959, to consider the "whole field of social security, health and welfare in Mauritius" (Titmuss, 1961:xi). These two commissions worked very closely together and their reports were published in 1960. I have criticized them in some detail elsewhere (Benedict, 1961b). Both reports faced the population problem squarely and maintained that if steps were not taken to stem population growth, no other form of development could succeed. Both reports agreed that emigration could not solve the population problem. It was not under Mauritian control, but depended on the willingness of other countries to accept Mauritians. Few countries had shown such willingness, and those that did could not pay for the immigration of Mauritians. This cost would have to be borne by the Mauritian government, which was clearly beyond its means. The Meade report investigated very thoroughly the prospects for agricultural and industrial expansion, including modifications that would have to be made in government and in the educational system. Both reports noted that pluralism was wasteful of the economic and social resources of the island. This is evident in the inhibition of social and economic mobility, where criteria of ethnicity can override criteria of ability. It is also clear in the educational system, where, for example, a large part of the curriculum had to be devoted to language (v. Benedict, 1958). The Meade report stressed, however, that without population control even its 129 recommendations could not avert disaster (p. 230).

The Titmuss report dealt more directly with the population problem by proposing a series of disincentives for large families which they hoped would keep population growth within manageable limits. At the same time that the Titmuss Commission was trying to limit population growth, it was also trying to reform the system of public assistance which, in effect, subsidized large families by basing relief payments on the number of children an applicant had. By 1963 public assistance had become the most costly element of government expenditure, surpassing education for the first time (Mauritius, 1963:25). The commission was faced with the dilemma of trying to give real force to a program of birth control, and at the same time trying to help the poorest families, which were often the largest. They opted for the three-child family and attempted to encourage it by proposing to pay a cash benefit to all families with three or more children under the age of fourteen, provided that the mother was over twenty-one and that the household head had not been liable to income tax in the previous year. The subsidy was thus only to go to the poor. No payments would be given to families with fewer than three children, nor would there be additional payments for more than three children. Families which had fewer than three children would be rewarded with higher old-age pensions. To encourage the spacing of children, a cash maternity payment would be made to a woman who had not borne children in the previous two years, again provided she was over twenty-one and had fewer than three living children. As an incentive to delay marriage, a cash payment would be made to the father of the bride provided the bride and her husband were twenty-one or older at the time of marriage and that the girl had not previously borne children and the father was a nontaxpayer. Essential to the plan was the wide dissemination of information about birth control. Clinics were to be established throughout the island.

I had been consulted about this plan and had expressed serious misgivings as to whether it would work, because it was based on assumptions that were not those of Mauritians. It assumed a degree of planning among more Mauritians, which they could not afford. Mauritians live in a cash economy; nearly all necessities can be bought only with cash. The demand for cash, particularly among the poor, is overwhelming (v. Benedict, 1958b). In these circumstances I predicted that large numbers of couples would attempt to secure the cash benefit, which is paid only on the birth of the third child, by having three children as quickly as possible. Even if a woman delayed marriage and childbearing until she was twenty-one (thereby allowing her father to receive a payment) and spaced her children at two-year intervals (thereby qualifying for the maternity benefit), she could still have three children by the age of twenty-five, leaving a considerable period of fertility before her. In my view, however, few women would do this.

The incentives to qualify for the three-child cash benefit would probably outweigh the incentives for the spacing of children, for the maternity benefit was not worth nearly so much as the three-child one. At the low economic levels at which most laborers live, a family which was receiving a cash benefit on the birth of the third child would probably not consider itself to be much worse off, and probably would not be much worse off on the birth of a fourth child. The fourth and possibly subsequent children were unlikely to be seen as diminishing opportunities for those who already exist. They might be the very ones who would succeed. Certainly the promise of a higher old-age pension, which one might not live long enough to collect, was exceedingly unlikely to inhibit procreation. Such long-term planning is a luxury that is not available to the very poor.

Both Hinduism and Islam place a very high value on the production of children, particularly male children. Wives can be and are returned to their parents if they fail to produce children. A woman does not gain fully adult status until she is a mother, not just a wife. Her future depends not on an old-age pension, but having sons. They are her social security. They win the respect of her husband and her mother-in-law. They assure her that she will be a mother-in-law herself. A man, too, must have sons to carry on his lineage, to help him in this work, to bring him honor and status in the community. The pressures to marry early and to produce children early (especially sons) are very strong. They operate against provisions for spacing children and for postponing marriage.

Postponing a girl's marriage until she is twenty-one runs counter to a whole range of Indian (both Hindu and Muslim) religious and social values. Moreover, from an economic point of view, no poor Indo-Mauritian family could afford it. It is well known that Indians favor early marriage for girls. A girl must be a virgin when she marries, but she has natural sexual desires and it is not only unkind to frustrate these by keeping her from marrying but it becomes increasingly difficult to control her and keep her away from men as she gets older. Among Indo-Mauritians marriages are still arranged by the parents and it is a major religious duty for a man to marry off his daughters. The longer marriage is postponed, the more difficult it becomes to arrange, for doubts are cast on the girl's character and that of her family. An unmarried girl must be protected and her reputation carefully guarded. She cannot be allowed to wander about or to go to work alone, but must be kept in the house. Poor Indo-Mauritians cannot afford to keep a girl in relative idleness until she is twenty-one. A further difficulty arises from the fact that patrilocality is the rule among Indo-Mauritians, at least in the early years of marriage. A girl in her late teens or early twenties is not apt to get along very well with her brothers' wives. They resent her interference, particularly if she is not working as hard as they are. They have enough trouble with their husband's mother without having to deal with an adult unmarried sister's claims on their husbands. The newly married man is put in a difficult position. Does he side with his wife or his sister when they quarrel?

A curious aspect of the Titmuss proposal was that the marriage benefit was to be paid to the father of the girl, not to the girl herself.[4] This could hardly be an inducement for the girl to wait patiently at home for four or five years after the normal age of marriage in Mauritius. It also assumes that the father would be able to control his daughter. Even in Indo-Mauritian families girls grow more independent as they grow older. Few fathers in Mauritius, particularly in poor families, could exercise such control. Few mothers would support the attempt. The whole notion is based on an idea of a very autocratic patriarchal family which hardly exists in Mauritius, particularly among the poor. Only the wealthy can be effectively autocratic; only the wealthy can afford late marriage for their daughters, but wealthy fathers would not be eligible to receive the marriage benefit. It is clear that

[4] Another curiosity about this proposal, coming as it does from leading socialist intellectuals, is that it runs counter to efforts to raise the status of women as it supports arranged marriages and patriarchal authority.

the small marriage benefit could not outweigh the factors conducive to early marriage among Indo-Mauritians. Among Creoles, who tend to marry later, the marriage benefit might be more frequently paid, but there would be even less excuse for paying it to the girl's father. Many of the poorer Creoles live in consensual unions of varying duration. Illegitimacy is common. The husband/father is often a peripheral role, as has been described for the West Indies. To pay a benefit to a girl's father under such circumstances could hardly affect the decision of a girl to postpone marriage to the age of twenty-one.

A final difficulty with the Titmuss and Meade proposals was a political one. Both reports stressed the need for determined government action. Both demanded their acceptance or rejection *in toto*. Mauritius was moving rapidly toward independence. The British government wanted to help solve the population problem, but it also wanted political stability. Many politicians wanted power. The problems of pluralism were ever present. The temptations to pluck the roses, such as the payment of family cash benefits, and avoid the thorns, such as a vigorous birth-control program, were very strong. Yet attempts were made. In April, 1960, the Financial Secretary, a British civil servant, announced in the legislature that the government had decided to implement a policy of planned parenthood based on the Titmuss proposals, backed up with birth-control clinics and a massive publicity campaign. These proposals met a storm of opposition from the Catholic Church, from leading Franco-Mauritian politicians, from some Hindu and Muslim leaders, and even from some supporters of the government. The opposition was so strong that the government, fearing defeat, adjourned debate for a year. In April, 1961, the debate resumed. By this time the Catholic opposition had agreed that the rhythm or safe-period method of contraception could be used. This, of course, is a very inefficient method of birth control. The Legislative Council failed to set up an effective birth-control program, but it passed a family allowance scheme granting Rs. 15 per month to nontax-paying families with three children under fourteen years of age. In 1964 the Roman Catholic Church informed the Minister of Health that it would have no objection to government funds being used to subsidize voluntary family-planning agencies, even where their methods differed from those approved of by the Church. Aid was solicited from overseas organizations and publicity campaigns were mounted in 1965–1966.

THE ANTHROPOLOGIST AND FAMILY PLANNING IN MAURITIUS

A combination of fortuitous circumstances and my own actions and wishes enabled me to play some part in establishing birth control in Mauritius. I reached Mauritius in 1955, shortly after the publication of the "Report of the Committee on Population, 1953–54," referred to previously. I was, of course, aware of the population problem and had discussed the matter with officials in the Colonial Office in London before going out to Mauritius, and with Government officers in Mauritius shortly after my arrival, but I did not see the investigation of population problems as one of the main aims of my field work. I was in Mauritius to carry out a study of the social structure of the Indo-Mauritian community. I settled into a village in the north of the island and began my work. This work included the collection of data on marriage and the family, the domestic economy, and the political, economic, and religious organization of the community.

As already mentioned, the population problem was discussed in the press and by politicians. As one would expect, awareness of the problem was differentially distributed throughout the population. The more educated, who were usually those in the higher income groups living in urban areas, were more aware of the problem than rural agricultural laborers. Discussion of family planning extended from the town to the village elite, but to the laborer, feeding his family was a much more immediate problem than limiting it. "That can wait till later," said a Hindu laborer to me in 1956; "the important thing is to have more work and better pay for the poor laborers." Statistics about the size of the population, the island's resources, and the rates of population growth had little meaning to those not trained to think in such terms. The reasons for birth control had to be seen in immediate personal terms by the people involved, not in long-range statistical trends demonstrated by outsiders.[5] The villagers of Mauritius did not see their own lack of employment in terms of overpopulation. Yet some understood the problem in personal terms; some women wanted respite from childbearing; some newly married men wanted to know how they could postpone having children for a year or two. Men in the village in which I was working began to ask me about birth-control methods. I had also received inquiries from a demographer who had worked in Mauritius in 1954 (Brookfield, 1957, Appendix 1:120–21). Finally, in February, 1957, I had been asked by the International Planned Parenthood Federation whether in the course of my research I had been led "to formulate any ideas how, taking into account local sentiment, diversity of races and religion, the recommendations of the Committee on Population in Mauritius could be implemented." By this time I had already completed more than a year's field work in the island.[6] In April, 1957, I submitted a short report on family planning in rural areas of Mauritius to the International Planned Parenthood Federation in London, the Colonial Office, the government of Mauritius, and Professor Raymond

---

[5] This tendency is not confined to poverty-stricken Mauritian villagers. A recent survey carried out among 1,059 faculty, graduate students, and undergraduates at Cornell University showed that although 84 per cent favored family limitation as a way of solving the population crisis, 65 per cent wanted three children or more. Only 30 per cent favored two children and a mere 5 per cent wanted one or none (Eisner et al., 1970:337).

[6] I had returned to England between August, 1956, and March, 1957.

Firth at the London School of Economics, who had been one of the major academic sponsors of my trip to Mauritius.

FACTORS AFFECTING FERTILITY

Three sets of factors can affect fertility and fecundity within a population:

1. The first set involves such physiological factors as diet, disease, or length of fertile period in women. These clearly operate in Mauritius. As we have seen it was a radical change in the disease pattern which was almost entirely responsible for the meteoric growth in population.

2. A second set of factors might be called indirect social factors, in the sense that they consist of customs or practices which affect both fertility and fecundity but which people themselves do not primarily think of as such. These practices include age at marriage, incidence of separation or divorce, absence of spouse, incidence of celibacy, periods of sexual abstinence associated with religious or other ceremonies, postpartum sexual abstinence, widowhood and incidence of widow remarriage, and polygamy. Evidence from other societies, though of very poor quality, would seem to indicate that most of these factors do not affect fecundity significantly (Nag, 1962). Only a late age at marriage, a high rate of separation and divorce, widespread polygyny, and along period of postpartum abstinence would appear to be significant in reducing fecundity (Benedict, 1970b). In Mauritius there was some evidence that Indians were marrying a little later than in former generations, but this mainly has meant a diminution of child marriages, when brides are unlikely to be fertile in any event. Age at marriage differs for different sectors of the population. The Indo-Mauritian women marry earliest, the Sino-Mauritians next, and the general population (a category including Creoles and Franco-Mauritians) marries latest, as Table 1 shows. It also shows that a greater proportion of Indo-Mauritians and Chinese women marry than do members of the general population. Since 1881 the fertility of the Indian population has been from 20 to 25 per cent higher than that of the general population. In 1952 it was 45 per cent higher. The fertility of the Chinese has been even higher (Mauritius, 1956:29).

Divorce and separation rates are low in Mauritius, particularly for Indo-Mauritians. As mentioned previously, a major cause of separation would be the failure of a woman to produce a child. Among Creoles of the lower economic class, consensual unions are common and may be limited in duration. Roberts (1954) has shown that this type of union is correlated with lower fertility rates in Jamaica. The same may hold true for Mauritius. Polygyny barely exists in Mauritius, nor are there significant periods of postpartum sexual abstinence. It appears unlikely that any of these indirect social factors has much effect in reducing fertility. They certainly do not counteract the enormous rate of population growth now occurring.

3. A third set of factors involves conscious efforts to limit population and

Table 1*

Proportion of Mated† to Total Women in Each Age Group 1911–1952‡

Population

Age Group	General					Indo-Mauritian					Chinese				
	1911 %	1921 %	1931 %	1944 %	1951 %	1911 %	1921 %	1931 %	1944 %	1952 %	1911 %	1921 %	1931 %	1944 %	1952 %
15–19	10.2	12.2	10.0	10.1	12.0	57.2	58.2	40.6	49.9	54.7	32.0	30.7	28.7	16.3	11.8
20–24	45.3	44.0	42.1	39.0	48.6	83.8	80.4	71.7	79.3	84.3	80.0	64.0	78.8	72.6	71.3
25–29	48.0	62.9	64.1	58.9	70.8	80.1	84.5	79.5	83.3	88.7	90.0	81.9	87.5	81.5	86.4
30–34	64.3	68.5	69.8	65.8	74.6	86.4	83.8	79.1	82.1	88.0	92.0	91.9	85.0	83.2	89.7
35–39	66.1	66.1	68.8	66.2	74.9	83.5	80.0	78.1	78.8	85.1	90.0	89.0	82.8	83.6	88.0
40–44	64.0	61.1	63.5	63.1	71.3	85.6	72.3	70.2	70.5	78.6	80.0	70.1	80.4	82.0	88.9
45–49	58.9	52.5	56.9	58.4	65.9	60.7	62.3	66.7	63.2	70.0	80.0	52.3	83.3	80.9	79.5
Total	47.6	50.4	49.7	47.2	56.3	76.4	74.7	67.7	71.3	78.1	81.0	73.1	76.6	69.1	67.0

* From Mauritius, 1956, p. 44.

† The term *mated* here comprises women who are civilly and/or religiously married and who live in "de facto" or "consensual" unions. It leaves out widows, separated, and divorced women.

‡ The census of 1962 does not distinguish ethnic categories in the tables of marital condition. But the percentages for the ages and marital condition for the whole population appear consonant with patterns for previous censuses (v. 1962 Census Vol. I, Table 6, p. 13).

includes voluntary sexual abstinence, all contraceptive practices, abortion, and infanticide. Infanticide appears to be rare. At least it is rarely reported in crime statistics. Abortion is certainly practiced, but because of its illegality, it is very difficult to estimate its incidence. One Mauritian doctor has reported that he turned away 176 women requesting termination of pregnancy in a period of ten months. Fifty-eight of these were Muslims, fifty were Hindus, and sixty-eight were Catholics. The ten most recent of these were all married, were mostly poor, and had had among them fifty pregnancies and five abortions already (Mansoor, 1965: 34). My own impression is that abortion is common, particularly for illegitimate children. The cost at the time of my field work was reputed to be Rs. 50,[7] and many of the practitioners were reputed to be nurses and midwives. There are also plenty of home remedies in use, ranging from jumping off tables, to drinking infusions, to insertion of foreign objects into the uterus.

At the time of my field work contraceptives were rarely used in the villages. Where they were, the initiative invariably came from men who had frequent contacts with the town, for contraceptives could be purchased only from a very few pharmacies in town. The contraceptive used was the condom. It was not used regularly, was more apt to be used outside marriage than within it, was disliked as interfering with sexual pleasure, and was very expensive for the average village budget. Other contraceptives, such as the diaphragm, foaming tablets, and spermicidal jellies were virtually unknown. Neither the oral contraceptives nor the intrauterine device were available in 1955–1957. A very few men attempted to practice the rhythm, or safe-period, method, but coitus interruptus seemed to be more regularly used. It is noteworthy that both the use of condoms and the practice of withdrawal depend on male initiative. The woman has no control over these contraceptive techniques.

Despite the readiness of people to say they wanted family planning without really considering the problem, I believed that there really was a demand for birth-control techniques among the more educated villagers and that the possibility existed for the spread of this demand to other villagers. The attempts at birth control, however sporadic and inefficient, indicated some demand. The factors militating against this demand were religious and political and were intertwined. There were also economic problems and problems of where and with whom to begin a family-planning campaign.

THE RELIGIOUS FACTOR

Hindu objections to birth control centered around the idea that it destroys life, or as one informant put it, "What is planted must be allowed to grow." This view was not a deep-seated belief among most Hindus. Like most of the

---

[7] The Mauritian rupee is linked to sterling. At the time of my field work 1 rupee equaled 1s., 6d., or 21 U.S. cents. At present it equals 18 U.S. cents.

Muslim Ghoon festival, Port Louis. (*Photo by Burton Benedict.*)

ethnic groups of Mauritius, Hindus look outside the island to their country of ancestral origin for a charter for many aspects of their beliefs and behavior. The fact that India officially supported birth control convinced most Indo-Mauritian Hindus that there could be no major religious grounds for opposing it. By language and sect Hindus can be divided into at least a dozen categories, but such sects are not organized on an islandwide basis comparable to a church which can pronounce dogma. This militates against organized objections to birth control on religious grounds.

Islam is a more rigidly defined creed than Hinduism. The Muslims of Mauritius have a more closely knit religious organization than the Hindus (Benedict, 1965: 37–39). A number of Muslim leaders opposed birth control as un-Islamic. This position was countered by some younger Muslim professionals and intellectuals who discovered *hadiths,* or traditions of the Prophet whereby he was said to have sanctioned coitus interruptus in certain cases. They also cited a 1937 *fatwa,* or religious ruling, issued in Cairo which sanctioned birth control. Nevertheless, religion was more often cited by Muslims than by Hindus as an objection to birth control. They wanted to know what the position of Islam was on the matter. Hindus would not phrase it in this manner.

In the middle 1950's the Roman Catholic Church was adamantly opposed to any form of birth control except the rhythm, or safe-period, method, and even this was permissible only in certain cases, such as if childbearing were a danger to the mother's health. Despite this stand, some Catholics did practice birth control, though they would not support it openly. The Church of England and the other Christian religions in the island did not oppose birth control. In 1962 these only constituted about 1.5 per cent of the population.

The official opposition of Muslim leaders and the Roman Catholic Church constituted a political deterrent to the spread of birth control but in my view would have little to do with whether the adherents of these religions actually practiced contraception. In general, it would appear that birth control is not inhibited by religious belief *on an individual level*. Denunciation by the Bishop of Port Louis would have little effect on whether the individual Creole fishermen used contraceptives, but it would inhibit legislation on family planning or even the formation of voluntary family-planning associations.

THE POLITICAL FACTOR

Mauritius in the 1950's was also a colony approaching independence. The British government, for economic and political reasons, was eager to grant this independence, but it wanted to turn over power to a stable community with a reasonable chance of forming a viable nation. The colonial government was exceedingly reluctant to encourage any program which might foster communal conflict. In the middle 1950's birth control seemed to be such a program. There was the strong official opposition of the Roman Catholics, which included the Franco-Mauritians, who were the most economically (and, until 1948, politically) powerful section of the population. There was also Muslim opposition, and some Hindu leaders were claiming that birth control was a governmental device for limiting the Hindu population so that Christians might increase. Though many colonial officials were personally sympathetic to birth control, they were reluctant to give it official sanction.

Approaching independence also meant an intense power struggle was underway among Mauritian politicians. Birth control could be a factor in that struggle. It could be used to rally Roman Catholics behind certain politicians or parties. Rival factions among the Hindu population could also use the issue. At this period one of the daily papers frequently warned against the "Hindu menace." Certain Franco-Mauritian politicians maintained that it was Hindu policy to increase their numbers in order to swamp other ethnic groups. They appealed not only to the Roman Catholic Creoles, but to the Muslims.

THE ECONOMIC FACTORS

The poverty of the vast majority of Mauritians meant that they were unlikely to buy diaphragms, condoms, and spermicidal jellies. Without some form of government subsidy, even foaming tablets, the cheapest contraceptive available in 1957, were unlikely to be bought by many. Yet at this time government subsidies were out of the question. The whole concept of economic planning (of which family planning is an instance) is based on notions of economic and social mobility held by middle-class Westerners, not by poverty-stricken Mauritians. The poorest Mauritians do not conceive of upward social mobility in terms of having fewer children. On the contrary, children are a source of support and social security in an economic system with low employment and inadequate pensions. It seemed likely that the very poorest Mauritians would neither be able to afford nor be much interested in practicing birth control.

PROBLEMS OF APPROACH

Family planning seeks to control human fertility. It is therefore concerned with relations between the sexes. These differ not only from society to society, but, leaving individual variations aside, between various groups and classes within the same society. In Mauritius different patterns obtained among Franco-Mauritians, Creoles, Hindus, Muslims, and Chinese. In addition, there were considerable differences associated with class and to some extent with sect within each of these broad ethnic categories. In studying relations between the sexes two fundamental questions need to be asked: "With whom do sexual relations take place?" "With whom are sexual matters discussed?" These rarely coincide. In very many societies one can discuss sexual matters with people with whom it would be unthinkable to have sexual relations, and it is very often considered highly improper to discuss sexual matters with one's sexual partner, particularly if that partner is the spouse. This pattern prevailed among Indo-Mauritian villagers. Men discussed sexual matters with other men of their own age, but generally not with kinsmen and not with older men. A man could discuss sexual matters with a mistress or a prostitute, but not with a fiancée or wife. Indo-Mauritian boys often get their first heterosexual experiences from prostitutes, older married women, or widows, often from the Creole population. They enter into marriage with strangers. As related previously, young Indo-Mauritian girls are carefully supervised. Marriages are arranged by parents. There is no dating or period of sexual experimentation and no discussion of sexual matters with any member of the opposite sex. Girls gain sexual information from their mothers or older women. Before and after marriage both men and women seek companions of their own sex. It is often only in old age that men make close confidants of their wives. The stringent segregation of the sexes is marked in such places as the cinema and weddings or other religious ceremonies, where men and women are seated separately and do not converse with each other. Within the household an Indian woman should speak only to her husband, sons, father-in-law, and husband's younger brothers. Traditionally, a woman should avoid her husband's older brothers. Women do not appear when male guests are entertained, and female guests are taken into the women's quarters. Some of the wealthier Muslim families still keep their women in purdah. A woman interacts chiefly with other women who are members of her household, neighbors, and relatives.

A fundamental question in introducing family planning was whether initial approaches should be made through men, women, or both together. The latter alternative was clearly out of the question. Men and women had to be approached separately. Although the ultimate success of family planning in Mauritius depended on women, because it was female contraceptives which were to be used, to approach women without first approaching the men would be almost certain to lead to failure. Though many women have considerable informal authority within the family, all formal decisions are made by men. To approach women without first consulting their husbands would, if possible at all, be likely to engender suspicion on the part of women and opposition on the part of men. Moreover, there existed in Mauritian village various associations in which family planning could be discussed by men.

A second fundamental question was where to begin, in the town or in the rural areas. The towns of Mauritius—Port Louis, Beau Bassin/Rose Hill, Quatre Bornes, Phoenix/Vacoas, and Curepipe—have less sense of community than the villages. There are fewer face-to-face contacts, greater differentiation in economic and social status, greater political diversity, and few associations which bring large numbers of the population together. The social organization of the village is more compact, and social relations exist among all or most villagers.

The politics of the town are to a large extent the politics of the island. Thus, a new program, particularly a controversial one, quickly becomes a national issue. Anyone important enough to direct such a program in town is important enough to have important enemies. Village leaders, on the other hand, are less involved in national politics and have only to contend with local rivalries. In villages where these are not too strong, I believed there would be a good chance of the acceptance of a family-planning association. There was also the rather negative point that failure in the town might represent a major setback to family planning in the island, whereas failure in a village would not be so devastating.

The report I submitted to the International Planned Parenthood Federation in April, 1957, concluded as follows:

> (a) Demand for family planning exists in rural areas among a small but influential section of the population. There is a possibility that demand may spread to other sections of the population.
> (b) There is no serious religious objection to family planning among Hindus.
> (c) Family planning should be carried out by a voluntary organization and not through government.
> (d) The greatest possible use should be made of existing village organizations such as village councils, socioreligious associations, sewing classes, etc. The cooperation of village leaders should be sought.

(e) *Family planning should be introduced quietly on an individual basis, at least to begin with, but final decisions in this matter should be taken with the advice of village leaders. Some villagers may prefer group discussions.*

(f) *A pilot program of family planning might be undertaken in one or two villages which would serve as a guide in planning a larger program.*

SETTING UP A FAMILY-PLANNING ASSOCIATION

The I.P.P.F. responded favorably to my report and agreed to help by sending literature and a supply of foaming tablets. Government officials informed me that they would do nothing to hinder the setting up of a family-planning association but reaffirmed that they would give no help or recognition to such efforts. The most serious immediate consequences of this stance were difficulties in importing the foaming tablets, as at that time there were restrictions on the importation of contraceptives; in addition, the association was denied use of government facilities. The ideal way of distributing foaming tablets would have been through government dispensaries, which are located throughout the island and which women are used to attending. A woman could pick up foaming tablets at a dispensary without advertising the fact that she was practicing birth control, as she would if she went to a special family-planning clinic. The restriction also meant that we could get no official assistance from government doctors, nurses, or midwives. In a country as small as Mauritius one cannot proceed very far up any ladder without running into government. Virtually every social service is a government service and nearly all trained women are employed by government.

Despite these handicaps, leading members of the village in which I worked were determined to go ahead. We had been receiving more and more inquiries about birth control from villagers and from leaders and acquaintances in neighboring villages. Planning the first meeting was a political operation of some delicacy. It was necessary to assure a wide base of support taking into account the various alignments in the village: territorial, linguistic, religious, ethnic, associational, kinship, and economic (v. Benedict, 1957; 1965).

The village was bisected into unequal portions by about 300 yards of sugar-cane land belonging to a neighboring estate. The lower section is the more populous and also differs in ethnic composition from the upper section. Leaders from the two sections have often been opponents in village council elections, and disputes as to the allocation of village services or improvements have frequently been structured in terms of opposition of the two sections. Territorial alignments often override alignments by kinship, ethnic, religious, or linguistic affiliation. Therefore it was important to have leaders from both sections at the inaugural meeting. Of the twenty-four village leaders invited to the inaugural meeting, five came from the upper section and nineteen from the lower section of the village. The meeting itself was held in the lower section.

The village population of 2,853 was 62 per cent northern Hindu, 13 per cent Telegu Hindu, 9 per cent Tamil Hindu, 10 per cent Muslim, 4 per cent

Roman Catholic Creole, and 2 per cent Chinese. Members of the last two categories took little part in village political affairs. Eighteen of those invited were northern Hindu, two were Tamil, two Telegu, and two Muslim.

Every village in Mauritius has one or more Indian socioreligious associations. These are usually known under the generic term *baitka* (from the Hindi verb *baitna*, "to sit"), though Muslims term their association *jammat* and some Hindu sects and linguistic groups prefer the term *subha* ("society"). The *baitka* is chiefly devoted to religious ritual and mutual aid of its members. Before the advent of village councils (the first village council was not formed until 1946), the *baitka* was the principal village organization, settling disputes among its members and protecting them from the alien society in which they lived. Membership in a *baitka* is acquired by the payment of a small entrance fee (usually 1 rupee) and maintained by the payment of monthly dues (usually 25 cents of a rupee). The active members are men, but they represent their wives and children. A boy must become a member in his right on reaching a certain age (usually eighteen) or upon marriage. A member is entitled to use the *baitka* premises, which is usually a small hut of thatch or galvanized sheet iron, for recreation and ritual. It is a general meeting place for members. Women may use it on special occasions when there are religious ceremonies or special classes for their benefit. *Baitkas* often sponsor schools for the children of their members where an Indian language (Hindi, Tamil, Telugu, Marathi, Urdu) is taught and religious instruction is given. A member may borrow *baitka* property, such as benches, mats, tarpaulins, lamps, and large cooking vessels, for a marriage or other ceremony at his house. If a death occurs it is the duty of members of the *baitka* to notify the relatives of the dead person throughout the island. Members must assist the deceased's relatives with mourning and funeral rites. Failure to attend is punishable by fine. The family of the deceased receives cash compensation from *baitka* funds, the amount of which varies with the age and sex of the deceased. Each *baitka* has a president, who may be the founder of the *baitka* and is usually a man prominent in the village. There are other officers, such as vice president, secretary, and treasurer.

There were eleven *baitkas* in the village. Representatives from nine of them were invited to the meeting, including northern Hindu, Tamil, Telugu, Muslim, and both the orthodox (*Sanatani*) and reformist (*Arya Samaji*) sects of Hinduism. The presidents of the five largest and most influential *baitkas* were invited. A federation of five northern Hindu *baitkas* had been formed under the leadership of a popular priest (*pandit*) who was president of one of the *baitkas*. We approached him and he agreed to allow the inaugural meeting to take place in his *baitka*. Thus we were assured a familiar setting in which villagers would feel at ease.

Broadly speaking, there are two types of village leaders, the traditional and the "modern." The traditional leader derives his position through his connections with the sugar estates. Often he is a job contractor who brings laborers onto estates to perform set tasks (Benedict, 1961a: 24, 70, 149–50;

Meade, 1961:62–65). He will often make loans to laborers during the inter-crop season to keep them tied to him for the crop season, when labor is short. He has good relations with the estates and can often obtain such privileges as the use of uneconomical land for planting vegetables or permission to gather fodder for himself and his clients. Job contractors frequently found *baitkas* or become their presidents. There were nine job contractors invited, three of whom were also *baitka* presidents. Another type of traditional leader is the middleman who makes loans to small planters to help them harvest their sugar cane. Two of these were invited. Traditional leaders tend to be older men who stress traditional Indian religions, languages, and cultures.

The "modern" leader tends to be younger and to have some Western education. Instead of relying exclusively on an Indian language or the Creole *patois*, which is the *lingua franca* of the island, he knows some English and French. His connections are not with the sugar estates but with the government hierarchy. Typically he is a civil servant, such as a schoolteacher or welfare officer. He is often active in the local youth club (football—i.e., soccer—is wildly popular in Mauritius) and draws support from the younger people. Older people may also go to him to receive help and advice in dealing with the government. Both traditional and "modern" leaders may have connections with national politicians. Five of these invited were "modern" leaders. Both types of leaders were to be found on the village council, which at the time of my field work was composed of eight elected and four nominated members. Nine of the twelve members had been invited to the inaugural meeting.

The president of the village council was a young Western-educated leader employed in the government youth service. He was an astute politician who had won the largest number of votes in a recent village council election. He had also been elected to the district council which comprised representatives from the villages in the north of the island. He worked at district headquarters and through his job as youth officer visited all the villages in the north. He was the first person I approached about family planning. He quickly became an enthusiastic supporter of the idea. It was he, in consultation with other village leaders, who drew up the list of people to be invited. It was a measure of his political astuteness that he predicted correctly four out of the five officers who were subsequently elected at the meeting.

The inaugural meeting of the Mauritius Family Planning Association was held on the evening of October 2, 1957, in a thatched hut which served as the *baitka* premises. About fifty men attended, including twenty-three of the twenty-four invited leaders. Through my interest in family planning I had contacted a Muslim doctor from Port Louis and his wife, who was also a doctor, and they attended to explain contraception to the villagers. The president of the village council explained the purpose of the meeting and the two doctors gave brief talks on birth control and displayed various contraceptives. There was general agreement to establish the association formally, and villagers then proceeded to found it exactly as if they had been founding a *baitka*. A president, vice president, secretary, and treasurer were elected, taking into account the power structure of the village. In order to make matters equitable on this score, an assistant treasurer, two auditors, and an executive committee were chosen. Thus twelve village leaders were incorporated into the association, representing all the alignments mentioned previously. From the more populous lower village came eight of the twelve committee members, including the president, vice president, treasurer, assistant treasurer, and one of the auditors. The other four, including the secretary, who was the president of the village council, came from the upper village. One Telugu (the president), one Tamil (the assistant treasurer), one Muslim (a committee member), and nine northern Hindus reflected the main cultural categories in the village. Among the twelve were eight traditional leaders, including the president, vice president, and treasurer, and four "modern" leaders, including the secretary, assistant treasurer, and both auditors. Leaders of five *baitkas* were on the committee, including both Sanatani (orthodox) and Arya Samaji (reformist) sects. Three of the wealthiest men in the village were also included.

Still following the *baitka* model, members agreed to charge an entrance fee of one rupee and a monthly subscription of 25 cents of a rupee. This had an added advantage in that contraceptives would not be issued to non-members, thus possibly evading Catholic objections. Membership would be open to anyone, regardless of religion, on payment of the entrance fee. Contraceptives were to be purchased by members at cost and the proceeds used to buy more supplies.

The following week, on October 9, 1957, members met again to raise money to launch the association. Again proceedings were traditional, following the same pattern that would have been used to raise money for a religious festival or the building of a temple. The amount given by a village leader was to be matched by other leaders. Those lower in the hierarchy give proportionally. The contributions are made in public at the meeting but are often the subject of informal negotiations beforehand, so that the over-all scale of contributions can be fixed. A man who is consistently and publicly generous rises in prestige and influence. The system allows for a certain mobility and jockeying for position and there is interest and excitement at this display. By the end of the meeting 250 rupees had been raised.

Shortly after the founding of the Mauritius Family Planning Association the woman doctor and my wife addressed the women of the village in the *baitka*. There were no men present and discussion was fairly frank and open. Contraceptives were displayed. Yet it was clear that much more intensive efforts would have to be made. The greatest need was for trained women, preferably from the village itself, who could explain birth control to the women.

My wife and I left Mauritius on October 20, 1957, so that my firsthand knowledge of family planning in Mauritius ends on this date, yet I kept in contact to some extent. The president of the village council remained an enthusiastic proponent of family planning. Moreover, he began to see his own career as bound up with family planning. He has attended conferences in London and a special training course in the United States and has become a major figure in the family-planning movement on the island.

SUBSEQUENT DEVELOPMENTS IN FAMILY PLANNING

The association itself suffered a number of vicissitudes, though it has survived them all to date. For a considerable period it was successful as an association but not very successful in promoting family planning. Branches sprang up in other villages. By July, 1958, twenty-two villages had family-planning associations. Yet in all of this activity Mauritians demonstrated their ability to set up associations rather than practice birth control. The association lacked steady supplies of contraceptives; it had no trained personnel to give instruction; it failed to keep adequate records of supplies distributed or women contacted. Yet it did help keep the idea of family planning before the public. It was a channel of communication between Mauritius and the I.P.P.F. and other overseas organizations which were interested in helping Mauritius check its population growth. It was there with some knowledge and expertise when the climate of opinion became favorable to birth control. It contributed to bringing about this change of climate and its history reflects this change (v. Brouard, 1965).

The association was officially registered in February, 1958, and a national politician who was also a doctor became president. In May, 1958, the first clinic was opened in the original village in the presence of the Minister of Health, an indication that birth control was gaining importance as a national issue. This clinic, however, was forced to close within a year, mainly because of personnel difficulties. The association remained in existence. It was recognized by the I.P.P.F., sent delegates to International I.P.P.F. conferences, and received visits and advice from I.P.P.F. personnel. In January, 1960, it changed its name to the Family Welfare Association in an attempt to mollify antibirth-control sentiment and win some support from the sugar industry. Then the Titmuss and Meade reports appeared and caused the furor reported earlier in the paper.

With funds from the I.P.P.F. and other foundations, a clinic was built in Port Louis, which now became the headquarters of the association. By 1963 oral contraceptives began to be issued and shortly replaced all other contraceptives. In 1965 the association changed its name back to Mauritius Family Planning Association. There were still many difficulties because of inadequate finances, government indecision and vacillation on birth control, and inauguration of a Catholic-sponsored family-planning movement called Action Familiale, which advocated only the safe-period method (Guy, 1968). Finally, in 1966, a government campaign for family planning was launched with assistance from a number of overseas bodies. At the end of 1967, 5,695 women were registered with the Action Familiale and 10,732 with the Mauritius Family Planning Association. Also there was a slight drop in the crude birth rate and the rate of natural increase (Mauritius, 1967:7). It is not clear what the causes of this drop are or whether it marks the beginning of a trend. Family planning no longer rests entirely on the efforts of unofficial voluntary associations, but has become government policy, a move which must appear inevitable if Mauritius is to make a serious attempt to stem population growth.

THE ANTHROPOLOGIST AS AN AGENT OF CHANGE

My own position as an agent of change was in many ways peculiar. I was a source of information. Some men wished to practice birth control, but the only means they knew were abstinence, coitus interruptus, or the condom. A few had heard that there were other methods but did not know what these were. I was able to tell them about female contraceptives and to explain, at least in a rudimentary fashion, how they worked. Thus I helped to create or at least focus a demand. When I began to receive information from I.P.P.F., this communication function was greatly expanded. Birth-control pamphlets were translated into French and later into Hindi. I also had useful contacts in the town, such as that with the Muslim doctor and his wife.

More important was my position in the village. Villagers assumed that I was working for government. Many thought I was some sort of spy. I told people that I intended to write about them and that I hoped what I wrote would benefit them. Many people befriended me and suspicion diminished as the months went by. Even those who distrusted me disliked my getting only one side of the story, especially if it were not their side. Many assumed I had some vast unspecified power which derived from the British government in London and could be exercised over the governor if necessary. I remained an outsider, but a friendly one with some sort of power. This status assisted me in helping to found the Family Planning Association.

From the government's point of view I was also an outsider. I was in Mauritius under a special fellowship. I did not belong to the overseas colonial service and was not even a British subject. I could give no orders. I had no specified duties. I was attached to no government department. If I chose to involve myself in family planning and it was a failure or drew indignant protests from religious or political leaders, the government was not responsible. It was only the irresponsible activity of an ill-advised American. On the other hand, such a failure would not make much difference to me, as I had no permanent stake in Mauritius or the colonial service and was about to leave the island. Nevertheless, what I was doing was of interest to the government, for if it could be shown that there was a real demand for birth control, this might move the government to implement a family-planning program.

In other words, government officials could credit or discredit my activities as they saw fit without harming the government or me. Thus my position as an outsider was of considerable use to both villagers and government. It allowed me to move within the village social structure and between the village and the wider social structure of the island, a mobility denied to those more heavily committed to that social structure. Paradoxically, villagers paid attention to me because they thought I was connected to government. Government paid attention to me because they knew I was not.

In a small multistranded community like Mauritius the outsider can be used to considerable advantage. The overseas expert is a common phenomenon nowadays, but he rarely spends enough time in a country to effect real change, and often his advice, particularly on questions of social policy, is inappropriately based on his experience in another country. The anthropologist who spends a year or two in a country can help to effect changes. One way he can do this is by his interstitial position in the local power structure. He must make his own moral decisions. I had no doubts about family planning, but the real decisions were taken and the real changes were made by Mauritians and not by me.

CONCLUSION

In many ways Mauritius can be viewed as a microcosm of the earth's population problem. The eradication of disease and improved health services have led to an unprecedented increase in population, which continues to grow at a dangerous rate. This population growth has outstripped the country's ability to support itself. Unemployment is rife and increasing, and this is leading to political unrest. Divisions within the population are such that concerted action by government cannot be taken. Political leaders feared conflict or sought the advantage of one community over another. By this vacillation and political infighting, valuable years were lost, for the population explosion was clearly predictable. The analogy can be pushed too far. Mauritius is a tiny, isolated, agricultural country with a one-crop economy and few possibilities of diversification. The rest of the world has more opportunities than this.

Yet, with the possible exception of Japan, the rest of the world has not been noticeably more successful than Mauritius in foreseeing or controlling its population growth. It is probably too late to avoid a demographic disaster in Mauritius, and the rest of the world may have to rescue this island people from the consequences of their overbreeding. A somber question remains. Even if birth control had been introduced in the 1940's, would enough people have practiced it to slow or halt population growth? One cannot be easy about the answer. Most Mauritians are too poor to plan their families. It is difficult to imagine what would have persuaded them to do so. Yet attitudes change. In the 1950's most people in Mauritius were ignorant, misinformed, and/or hostile to birth control. These attitudes have changed. Mauritians can now choose whether or not to practice birth control. Some are practicing it. The experience in Mauritius shows that birth control depends on a great many more factors than the availability of easily used contraceptives. On the one hand, there must be an understanding of the social structure of the community. If family planning concerns intimate relations between men and women, it also concerns political and economic relations within the whole community. On the other hand, it must be recognized that family planning succeeds or fails insofar as people see *their own individual life chances* in terms of more or fewer children. These estimates not only vary between groups and individuals but can change for a given individual over the course of his life. Governments can influence these attitudes and estimates. There can be tax disincentives for large families such as those proposed by Professor Titmuss or even sterner measures which would actually tax children. More drastic would be to put contraceptive chemicals in the water supply. Such "solutions" clearly raise grave moral and political questions which go beyond the scope of this paper.

But by whatever means planners attempt to limit population, they should at least avoid the mistakes of failing to look ahead. Those who fought disease did not consider the population problem they were engendering. Let those who are fighting population increase be aware of the future economic, political, and demographic consequences of their own campaigns.

11

As in the case of overpopulation on Mauritius discussed by Burton Benedict, the major technological impact was a fait accompli by the time Dr. Bernand arrived on Kalymnos. The synthetic sponge had already taken its toll of the natural-sponge markets, and Kalymnians were well into the process of adapting to the new situation. In this essay Bernard deals with the history of sponge fishing, the role of technology in the industry, and the social effects on a "monocrop" island when synthetics threatened its primary economic base. The case is interesting as an example of a widespread phenomenon. It is not a government program; it is not a new city or dam or other major project; it is not the sort of thing Robbins and Kilbride describe where people have access to microtechnology that they perceive as beneficial to their lives. Instead, 8,000 miles from Kalymnos a synthetic substitute was invented which threatened the livelihoods of people who worked with the natural counterpart. Here the product is sponge. It might have been nylon and its effect on the silkworm industry, or plastic buttons and their effect on the mother-of-pearl industry, or nuclear power and its effect on the Appalachian coal industry. On Kalymnos the fight to stay in the world's markets has led to a strategy which may prove effective in other areas: technology is being rolled back, and ancient, less expensive modes of production are being reinstated. The same thing may well happen to snowmobiles if it turns out that they cost more than their fun value is worth.

KALYMNOS, ISLAND OF THE SPONGE FISHERMEN[1]

H. Russell Bernard

H. Russell Bernard is Associate Professor of Anthropology at Washington State University and was recently a Fulbright Lecturer and Research Fellow, University of Athens. He received his Ph.D. from the University of Illinois and has done a great deal of field work in Hidalgo, Mexico. He lived in Tarpon Springs, a Greek-American sponge-fishing community, and on the island of Kalymnos, Greece. He has published widely on this topic and on linguistics and has helped to make a documentary film, Aegean Sponge Divers: Matadors of the Deep.

INTRODUCTION

The most striking thing about Kalymnos has for a long time been its sponge-fishing industry. The most striking thing about this island today is the apparent strength of its economy and the survival of the sponge industry against massive competition from synthetics.

This chapter discusses what happened on Kalymnos. Briefly, historical, political, cultural, technological, and economic factors combined in the period from 1800 to 1960 to make Kalymnos the undisputed world center of sponge fishing. Beginning around 1960, the threats of synthetic sponge

[1] Field work was carried out on Kalymnos for one year, 1964–1965, two weeks of December, 1966, and on several field trips during the year 1969–1970. Field work at Tarpon Springs consisted of several months during the summers of 1963 and 1964. Research has been supported at various times by the National Defense Education Act, Social Science Research Council, University of Illinois, Wenner Gren Foundation, and Fulbright Foundation; these institutions' support is gratefully acknowledged. Thanks to Dr. Robert Littlewood and Dr. Henry Irwin of Washington State University for criticisms of earlier drafts.

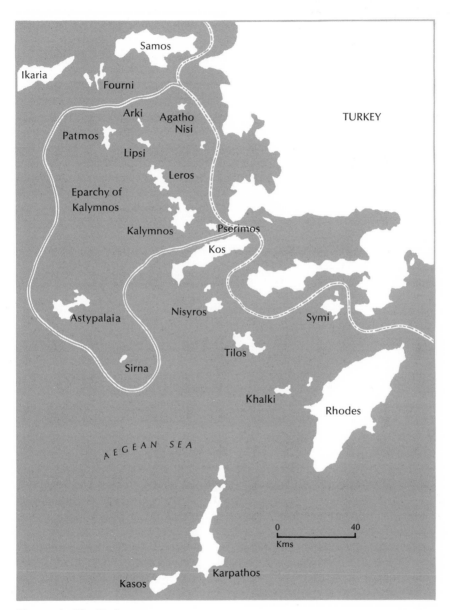

FIGURE 1. The Dodecanese.

competition caused a major labor migration. This led to a decline of importance of the sponge industry in the Kalymnian economy. The causative fears of this migration were not realized, however, as demand for marine sponges remained high. The industry thus nearly destroyed itself. In recent years sponge fishing has made a dramatic comeback by changing its technology. For a while it appeared that sophisticated new diving equipment such as Scuba gear and portable decompression chambers would provide the answer to the industry's difficulties. Surprisingly, just the opposite is the case: the sponge industry is vigorous again because its technology was "primitivized." The Kalymnian economy today seems quite healthy and sponge fishing remains the single most important part of it. Though 85 per cent of all cultivable land in the Dodecanese is on Kos and Rhodes (Figure 1), Kalymnian sponge continues to account for 90 per cent of all foreign exports from the island group.

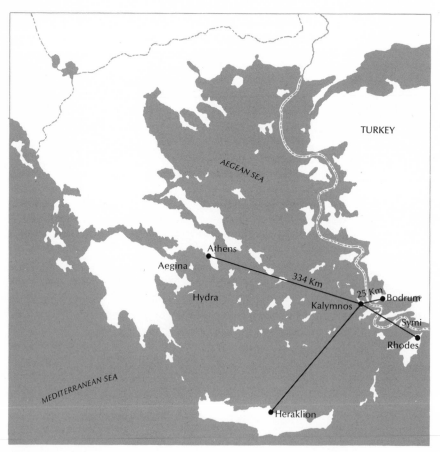

FIGURE 2. Greece.

SETTING AND HISTORY

Kalymnos is 110 square kilometers of mostly rocky land, located 332 kilometers southeast of Athens, 145 kilometers northwest of Rhodes, and 25 kilometers west of Bodrum, Turkey (Figure 2). Only 18 per cent of the island is arable and most of the good land is too steep to be really productive. Still, slightly over 13,000 people inhabit Kalymnos, making it the most densely populated island in Greece.

The coastline is jagged and steep, and the island is cut lengthwise by three mountain ranges and two valleys. The port city of Pothea has nearly 10,000 inhabitants, making it an "urban area" according to the National Statistical Service of Greece. Xora, a short kilometer and a half from Pothea, has another 2,000 people. Perhaps 100 families (3 per cent of the total population) are engaged in agriculture; a like number make their primary income from shepherding. There are around 10,000 sheep and goats in the villages of Vathy, Dassos, Bothinous, Arginonda, Skalia, Emborios, Palionisi, Argos, and the islets of Telendos and Pserimos (Figure 3).

Most men in Pothea are engaged in commerce, trade, professions, or services (Table 1). But the principal adaptation of Kalymnos is to the sea which surrounds it. In ancient times Kalymnos sent her best youth for training in the Rhodian navy. The neighboring island of Kos, with its lush, flat lands, provided Kalymnos with most of its summer fruits and vegetables. It still does, and Kalymnians call the people of Kos *Kotes*, or chickens, to show their disdain for people who are tied to the land. One informant told me, "The ancients said that the three most terrible things in the world are fire, woman, and the sea. Man must do battle with all three to be strong. We have." The prowess of *Kotes* as firefighters was never established during my stay on Kalymnos. Needless to say, however, Kalymnians do not rate *Kotes* very high as mariners or lovers.

The impact of the sea on Kalymnos is profound. In 1965 I estimated at least 1,000 adult males were engaged locally in octopus fishing, commercial deep-sea fishing, and sponge fishing. Roughly 300 more were abroad in the Greek merchant marine. Another 50 to 100 men, depending on the season, worked in drydock and repair facilities. In all, about one third of the male work force, ages twenty to sixty-four, was active in sea trades. The most important of these was sponge fishing.

The exact date when Kalymnians began fishing for sponges is lost in antiquity, but there can be no doubt that it has been the mark of the island for centuries. When Suleiman II captured the Dodecanese in 1521, the Kalymnian surrender was marked by the sending of sponges and loaves of fine white bread. The symbolism of this gift, it is said, was not lost on the Sultan: Kalymnians neither grow grain, nor are they poor; they fish for sponges and buy only the best flour (Myres, 1944). The Sultan was obviously impressed; he granted Kalymnians unlimited use of the mainland for the

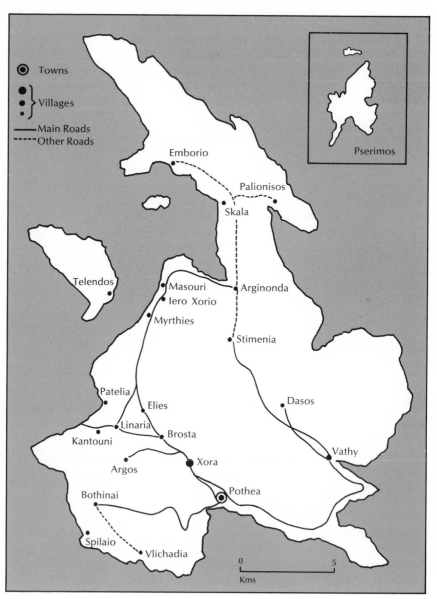

FIGURE 3. Kalymnos.

Table 1

Surveys of Artisans and Shops on Kalymnos*

Coffee grinders	2	
Knitting shops	3	
Furniture makers	8	
Cobblers	25	
Machine shops	8	
Contractors	4	
Mosaic works	1	
Electrical repair	3	
Sweet shops	9	
Tailors	8	
Woodworkers	13	
Bakeries	11	
Metal-working shops	7	
Soap makers	1	
Appliance sales	3	
Lamp makers	2	
Distillers	9	(including tavern owners)
Paint shops	3	
Paint makers	1	
Salt grinder	3	
Tanners	5	(including one chamois factory)
Blanket makers	1	
Meat shops	9	(including three frozen-meat stores)
Floor makers	4	
Weavers	2	
Ships ways	2	
Jewelry shops	5	
Goldsmiths	3	
Ice makers	1	
Wine shops	2	
Auto repair	2	
Auto rental	1	
Motorcycle sales	2	
Watchmakers	4	
Barbers	15	
Sugar refineries	1	
Rug makers	1	
Dry cleaners	2	
Kerchief makers	1	
Spice packaging	1	
Restaurants	14	
Movie theaters	4	(two summer and two winter)
Hotels	6	(accommodating 350 persons, excluding rooms for tourists and traveling salesmen)
Sponge merchants	50	

* Source: Chamber of Commerce, Kalymnos (1964).

Dolphins and other hazards mean constant repair of fishing nets.

collection of firewood, gave them almost complete autonomy in the regulation of internal affairs, and collected very little tribute aside from sponges. At that time sponges were as valued as silks, perfumes, and spices, and many islands in the area (Kastellorizo, Symi, Khalki) were active in production. In 1830 the tribute collected from the Dodecanese was about $10,000, barely enough to maintain the mosques on Kos and Rhodes. So long as the Ottomans did not interfere with their religion or customs, the Dodecanesians coexisted well with their rulers, as they had with the knights of St. John, the Genoese, the Venetians, the Byzantines, and the Romans before them.

The industrial revolution created great demands for sponges. By 1840 the major sponge islands of the Aegean (including Aegina and other non-Dodecanese islands) had fished out the Greek and Turkish waters. In that year Kalymnians and Symians simultaneously discovered vast resources off the coast of Derna, Libya. The discovery prompted further searches. In 1860 great new beds of sponges were found off the coast of Benghazi, and in the next twenty years they were found extending all the way west to Tunis. Between 1840 and 1890 the sponge-fishing islands really began to prosper. There were markets for sponges and people with a long tradition of sponge fishing to supply those markets. The populations of the sponge islands began to climb (Table 2).

Table 2

Population of the Dodecanese, 1821–1947*

Island	Area in Km²	1821–1828	1850	1900	1910	1912	1917	1922	1931	1936	1941	1947	Inhabitants per Km² 1910	1947
Rhodes	1412.0	31,500	33,000	43,000	54,000	54,000	36,560	45,000	54,800	59,933	61,567	55,181	31.8	39.0
Karpathos	306.0	7,500	8,000	8,500	9,500	8,527	6,930	7,500	6,580	7,861	7,231	7,416	31.0	25.9
Kos	288.7	11,000	12,500	15,700	16,500	14,570	15,070	16,000	21,170	19,845	18,231	18,545	57.1	62.6
Kalymnos	128.2	5,000	7,600	19,400	20,000	23,200	14,950	15,500	16,500	15,439	14,872	12,227	162.2	95.3
Astypalia	113.6	3,000	3,000	2,500	2,000	1,780	1,380	1,370	11,610	1,754	1,771	1,800	17.6	15.8
Leros	71.5	4,500	4,600	6,400	6,000	6,000	4,880	4,000	5,500	7,159	10,979	6,161	96.5	86.1
Kasos	69.4	5,250	5,600	6,500	6,700	5,700	1,850	1,760	1,920	1,904	1,367	1,336	96.5	19.2
Tilos	64.3	2,000	1,950	1,900	1,850	1,300	2,100	1,160	1,230	1,226	1,131	1,085	28.7	16.8
Symi	63.6	6,250	8,000	18,000	19,500	2,450	7,300	7,000	9,460	8,182	4,147	4,090	306.6	64.3
Patmos	57.1	4,500	4,000	4,000	3,700	2,720	2,660	2,550	2,990	3,208	2,665	2,736	64.7	47.9
Nisyros	48.0	3,300	3,500	4,700	5,000	5,000	4,300	3,160	3,430	3,404	2,592	2,499	104.1	52.0
Khalki	30.3	1,200	1,500	2,900	3,000	3,215	2,200	1,300	1,790	1,470	754	731	99.0	24.1
Lipsi	17.4							560	960	981	817	873	—	50.1
Kastellorizo	11.5	2,500	3,500	8,500	9,000	4,020	2,000	2,700	2,230	2,269	1,111	663	782.6	57.6
Total	2,681.6	85,000	96,750	142,000	149,530	143,82	102,180	109,560	130,830	132,638	129,285	115,343	55.7	43.0

* Source: Agapitedes, 1946, p. 417.

285

During the seven months of good weather from April through October, the sponge fleet sailed south to North Africa and fished what they could, using the primitive methods of breath-hold diving. To operate at great depths a man would plummet to the bottom, holding a flat, elliptical 15-kilogram marble slab before him. The slab had a hole in one rounded end where a line was attached from the boat. The man had time to pick up one or two sponges before he had to tug on the line, signaling that he had to be pulled back up rapidly for air. The system was crude, but it worked. In spite of the fact that all divers suffered broken ear and nasal membranes, as well as impaired vision, they continued to work at depths of 30 to 70 meters in search of what was referred to as the "golden fleece of the sea." Aprocryphal stories of breath-holding dives to 90 meters are still part of coffeehouse folklore. The market price for sponges was very high. Profits were limited only by the size of the harvest and this was limited only by technology.

In 1885, the *skafandra*, or deep-sea diving suit, was introduced from France. The men were afraid of the contraption (the story has it that it took a woman to try it first in order to shame the men into using it), but they tested it and the results were, as might be expected, phenomenal. Sponge production rose dramatically and new elements of danger were introduced into diving: the bends and embolisms.[2] But this did not deter the Dodecanesians. In what must have been one of the most striking cases of all time of the effects of new technology, Symi and Kalymnos swelled with migrants from other islands and the nearby Turkish mainland, where large Greek colonies existed until 1922. Between 1850 and 1912, the populations of Kalymnos rose from 7,600 to over 23,000; Symi's rose from 8,000 to over 22,000.

The Pothea–Xora area grew into an urban center. Until 1804 the small Kalymnian population had lived in Kastro, a small mountain fortress which protected the citizens from recurrent pirate attacks during the Middle Ages. Then Xora became the capital and a few people cautiously built homes around the perfect harbor of Pothea. By 1900 land prices in Pothea were equal to those of major European cities (Myres, 1944). Sponge markets flourished. Processing plants proliferated as people took advantage of the boom by investing their capital in sponge stocks for resale in England, Germany, and France. Boats were built as rapidly as artisans could turn them out. Sponge fishing became a way of life, and money flowed into Kalymnos as sponges flowed out.

The continuous input of foreign capital encouraged the growth of merchan-

---

[2] For a full discussion of Kalymnian casualties from diving, see Bernard, 1967. Briefly, bends are caused by supersaturation of the blood with nitrogen inhaled in normal air under pressure. When the pressure is released rapidly, as when a diver ascends rapidly, the nitrogen "boils" and escapes in bubbles. The bubbles may damage nerve tissue, causing death or paralysis. The phenomenon is akin to what happens when a bottle of warm beer is opened quickly. Air embolisms are caused by the diver's failure to exhale when ascending. Under reduced pressure the volume of air in the lungs expands, causing rupture damage.

dising and the opening of shops. Kalymnos became the second largest trading center in the Dodecanese, the first being Rhodes. It was already the administrative center of all the islands north of Kos (Figure 1), as well as the center of a diocese and the seat of the Metropolitan (Bishop) of the northern Dodecanese. In addition, sponge fishermen placed a high value on education. Kasperson has shown that Kalymnos and Symi both produced an inordinate number of poets, artists, sculptors, statesmen, teachers, doctors, dentists, and lawyers. It was the Golden Age of sponge fishing (Kasperson, 1966).

The first crisis of the twentieth century for Dodecanesian sponge fishing occurred in 1912, when the Italians captured the Dodecanese from the Ottomans. They were greeted as liberators and brothers in Christianity (Shear, 1943), and they proclaimed the islands would shortly be given free choice of political association. Three years later, in 1915, Italy suspended all sponge fishing off the coast of Libya (which they had also taken from the Turks), ostensibly for military reasons. Italian boats were encouraged to take up sponge production. In the secret Treaty of London (April, 1915), Italy was promised full sovereignty over the Dodecanese in return for her support of the Allies in the war (Wambaugh, 1943).

These events had dramatic effects. The population of Symi fell by 67 per cent in five years (Table 2). The largest sponge production flotilla in the world (over 200 vessels) vanished from Symi. There are no sponge boats there today, and the population is about 2,500 persons.

The sponge islands of Greece fared better than the Italian Dodecanese. In time, though, with the coming of synthetics, they too dropped from the picture. In 1930 Aegina (Figure 2) had an estimated fifty boats in operation, most of which fished the North African sponge grounds after 1920, when wartime restrictions were lifted. In 1965 only three boats registered at Aegina; in 1970 there were none. Hydra (Figure 2) had its own sponge fleet. In 1950 fourteen vessels registered for sponge fishing out of that island. In 1954 there were only four. By 1960 not a single boat remained.

In the Dodecanese several islands came through World War I with relatively less population decline than Symi. In 1925 there were an estimated thirty-five boats in operation on Khalki. World War II initiated an exodus. By 1947 there were only 731 people on the island. In 1950 only two sponge boats remained.

Kalymnos fared best. The flexible and diversified trading economy developed during the second half of the nineteenth century helped prevent a mass exodus between 1912 and 1917. In addition to trade and professionalism, Kalymnians developed a small, first-class citrus industry and several good-sized olive groves. Some men, of course, went into the merchant marine, a perennial source of employment throughout the Aegean. From about 1900 to 1940 there was a cigarette-rolling industry employing 800 women. Thirty-five per cent of the population left when the Italians closed the North African sponge grounds, but around 15,000 stayed right up to the present day. Sponge fishing continued in Aegean waters until after World War I, when North

Africa was reopened. In 1922 a new diving system was introduced, called *fernez*, after the man who invented it. It employed a face mask and an attached air hose, but no dry suit. The diver went down nude with the marble slab,

Table 3

Output, Number of Vessels and Persons Employed in Greek Sponge Fishing, 1948–1964*

Year	Sponge Output (kg)	Vessels	Divers and Crew	Yield/Man(kg)
1948	117,760	216	1,951	60
1949	161,280	229	2,706	60
1950	168,960	224	2,607	65
1951	143,360	194	1,970	73
1952	128,266	186	1,780	72
1953	63,836	120	1,108	58
1954	126,592	143	1,710	74
1955	135,484	159	1,614	84
1956	120,696	149	1,484	81
1957	120,184	169	1,634	74
1958	108,250	158	1,488	73
1959	100,000	105	1,186	84
1960	85,913	83	844	102
1961	70,645	87	739	96
1962	89,948	110	1,047	86
1963	97,011	113	1,125	86
1964	97,970	117	900	109

* National Statistical Service of Greece.

but could stay down for long periods. The system has remained unchanged except for the adaptation of modern wetsuits against the cold. In 1928 the marine engine came to Kalymnos. Hundreds of oarsmen were put out of work, but production was increased with the new mobility.

Between 1910 and 1940 Kalymnians produced more than 80 metric tons of sponge a year. A 5.5 per cent municipal tax on sponge sales produced revenues of more than $45,000 a year for payment of teachers and sanitation workers, for dock maintenance, and for local government (Zirounis, n.d.). The sponge merchants grew very wealthy. The richest of them all, a Mr. Boubalis, became a legend in his own time, building an old-age sanitarium, a hospital, two high schools, a grade school, and an orphanage.

The affluence of Kalymnos was unchallenged—until the cellulose sponge appeared in the United States soon after World War II. Housewives turned immediately to the synthetics, which were cheaper than marine sponges and which came in convenient sizes, shapes, and colors. Sponge fishing went into world-wide decline. Production in Greece fell from 168,960 kilograms in 1950 to 97,970 kilograms in 1964 (Table 3). But Kalymnos alone produced 56,102 kilograms, or 57 per cent of the national output in 1964, and during the general world slump in sponge fishing of the 1960's, the island maintained both production and export of sponges, and actually increased the dollar value of its exports (Table 4). Disparate events combined to make this possible.

Table 4

Kalymnian Exports, 1958–1969

Year	Kilograms Exported	Value in Dollars	Average Price/Kg
1958	53,499	1,081,698	20.22
1961	67,845	1,335,307	19.38
1962	65,768	1,267,923	19.27
1963	68,653	1,498,904	21.83
1964	62,288	1,337,763	20.51
1968	61,167	1,846,012	30.18
1969	53,143	1,510,503	28.42

In 1906, six years before the Italian occupation of the Dodecanese, two sponge-diving brothers from Aegina discovered 9,000 square miles of unexploited sponge beds in accessible waters out to 25 fathoms off the west coast of Florida. They founded the Greek colony of Tarpon Springs, 26 miles from Tampa. As the repression of the Italian occupation grew in the Dodecanese, many of the sponge fishermen from Kalymnos, Symi, and Khalki migrated to Tarpon Springs. By the beginning of World War I more than 2,000 Greeks (almost all men) had established themselves in the colony. In the twenty years prior to the end of World War II Tarpon Springs became the world's largest producer (Bernard, 1965).

In 1939 a blight, known as the red tide, made its appearance in the Caribbean. The disease, whose cause is as yet unknown, was recorded several times during the nineteenth and early twentieth centuries. There is no effective control of the tide, which kills all marine life in its path. In 1939 it destroyed dozens of small shrimping, clamming, crab-fishing, and sponge-harvesting operations in the Bahamas. The outbreak lasted a year. It swept up past Cuba and dissipated just south of the United States, leaving Florida's shores untouched.

It was precisely at this time that a method was found of converting the pulp of wood wastes into the synthetic cellulose sponge. Great industrial resources were mobilized for the development of this new product and for the improvement of its then poor absorption and lasting qualities.

Soon thereafter, World War II began in Europe, and Mediterranean sponge production (along with all international shipping) was again restricted. The demand for sponge for industrial uses was at an all-time high in the United States. American involvement in the world conflict turned the research and production efforts of the major chemical companies to war materials. Thus the Caribbean industry had been wiped out by the red tide, the Mediterranean was cut off, and the development of the synthetic sponge was stalled by war: Tarpon Springs was left with a virtual monopoly on the American sponge markets.

In 1946, 200 vessels were in operation, and nearly $3 million changed hands on the Tarpon Springs Exchange. Greek coffeehouses and nightclubs featuring bouzouki music and dancing girls flourished in the free-spending maritime atmosphere. Greek culture in general enjoyed a renaissance in its American setting. Because immigration from Greece was cut off during those years, the boom went on with no substantial increase in population, and per capita income skyrocketed.

The prosperity was short-lived. In 1947 the red tide struck again, this time off the west coast of Florida. Tons of dead marine life were washed ashore on the beaches of St. Petersburg, according to local newspapers. The largest and most lucrative sponge grounds in the world were decimated. The disease came from the tip of Florida and worked its way north. Sponge boats tried

Washing and bleaching of sponges provides work for older men on the island.

to work ahead of the tide, but without success. Sponges crumbled to dust in the divers' hands as they pulled them off the host rock. In 1948 only $1 million changed hands on the Tarpon Springs Sponge Exchange, by 1953 less than $250,000.

Almost overnight the course of world sponge fishing was altered. Demands for natural sponges for industry remained high in the United States. Greek sponge merchants in Tarpon Springs, New York, Chicago, St. Louis, and other cities turned once again to the Mediterranean. Many of the American merchants had relatives on Kalymnos, and direct family ties became rapid channels of communication for market demands. Postwar political events in Greece helped Kalymnos meet these new market demands from the United States.

In 1948 the Dodecanese islands, after 700 years of foreign rule, were awarded to Greece by the United Nations. The Agricultural Bank of Greece immediately subsidized farming and fishing there with the infusion of capital development funds and loans, and Kalymnians were repatriated from Gaza where they had been wartime refugees. Thus capital, labor resources, waiting export markets and tradition set the stage for a resurgence of the sponge industry which had been curtailed by war. While the cellulose sponge priced most islands out of the market (see page 289), Kalymnian sponge fishing survived again.

In 1950, 23 per cent of the estimated male labor force was engaged in sponge production; another 15 per cent worked in processing and distribution. Jobs such as bleaching and trimming were a source of employment for older seamen who could no longer stand the rigors of six months a year at sea.

In 1958 it appeared that the demand for natural sponges had stabilized. The housewife markets had been lost, but synthetics still had not been perfected for use in many industries. The washing trades (automobiles, windows, factories), the ceramic and leather-tanning industries, and hospitals continued to use natural sponges for their absorptive, textural, and natural hygienic properties. Kalymnos had a partial monopoly on sponge production and prospects looked good for the future.

It was false hope. Everything depended on the absence of mass synthetic production in Europe. In 1950 cellulose sponges were manufactured in limited quantities in Sweden. By 1958 Germany, France, and Belgium had developed fresh patents of their own. The industrial producers of synthetics possessed almost unlimited capital for advertising and merchandising, as well as for research and development. Markets for marine sponge began to shrink again, boats lay in dry dock, and on Kalymnos divers, captains, and buyers alike were faced with decisions for the future.

The sponge buyers were able to liquidate some of their holdings in order to obtain capital for reinvestment. The favorite form of investment became, and continues to be, the building of hotels on beachfront property. An organization of merchants and professional men, including doctors and lawyers, joined with the wealthiest of the sponge buyers to form an organization

During the winter the sponge boats are hauled out of the water and fixed for the following summer's trip. However, many boats have recently remained in drydock year round as the industry has declined.

for the promotion of tourism. They published maps and brochures. Some of the buyers had warehouses and distribution facilities in France, Spain, Germany, or England. They were able to supply these warehouses with sponges bought in Bodrum, Turkey, only a few hours away by small craft. As the industry languished in Kalymnos, the obscure sponge business in Bodrum began to flourish. In 1965, 9 metric tons of sponge worth over $77,000 was bought by Kalymnian buyers. Other buyers decided to liquidate their business and retire. One man, who is today among the most successful of the Kalymnian sponge merchants, converted his island warehouse into a factory for the manufacture of synthetic sponge, cut from foam blocks he imported from Belgium and resold in France. The irony of his success is lost on no one in Kalymnos.

The buyers were able to implement their decisions easily, but the captains were not so fortunate. Their capital was tied up in hardware such as boats, diving equipment, and the like, and no one wanted to buy a used sponge boat. Their cash reserves were no match for those of the buyers, so some of the captains retired. Others managed to convert their boats into small cargo vessels for interisland transport of fruits and vegetables. Like the buyers, those that could stand the pressure remained in the business.

They complained they could no longer make decent profits from sponges. In fact, most captains and buyers could do better with their capital in bonds or banks. But, like many farmers in the United States who earn less than 4 per cent on their yearly investment, they consider their work a way of life not to be abandoned lightly.

This was not the case with divers. They had no liquid capital to manipulate, nor were they tied down by ownership of land, warehouses, or boats. They are usually quite young and have shallower roots and fewer ties to break than entrepreneurs like captains and buyers; they deserted Kalymnos in droves. The traditional maternal pressures against leaving the natal home were lacking. Kalymnian mothers of absent sons expressed open relief that their boys were not in the dangerous business of diving. The industrial opportunities in Australia and West Germany in the 1960's were practically inexhaustible, and the Greek merchant marine was becoming the largest in the world (Tables 5 and 6). For the young men there was absolutely nothing to lose. Many of the older divers remained, but even they were attracted overseas when, in the early 1960's, Tarpon Springs began a comeback by importing Kalymnian divers. On Kalymnos a shortage of diving labor replaced the

Table 5

Permanent Migrants from Greece, 1958–1964*†

Year	Number of Migrants (Approximate)
1958	25,000
1959	22,000
1960	47,000
1961	58,000
1962	84,000
1963	100,000
1964	107,000

* Source: National Statistical Service of Greece.

† Does not include "temporary" migrants, most of whom are on merchant ships. In 1964 there were 47,616 such migrants, of whom only 1,179 were women and 40,470 were males, 15–45 years of age.

Table 6

Greek Merchant Ships by Category, 1932–1964*

Year	(000 GRT) Total Tonnage	Total Number	Tanker and Cargo†	Passenger	Misc.‡
1932	1,430	558	429	115	14
1939	1,837	557	500	56	21
1946	502	138	122	14	2
1952	1,270	489	421	38	30
1957	1,563	549	463	46	40
1958	1,905	616	519	49	48
1959	3,344	827	695	65	67
1960	5,384	1,043	907	65	71
1961	6,393	1,165	1,006	68	91
1962	6,774	1,232	1,047	74	111
1963	6,938	1,314	1,110	79	125
1964	7,249	1,422	1,196	97	149

* Source: National Statistical Service of Greece.

† The National Statistical Service of Greece lists only Greek flag vessels. Greek ships flying convenience flags (Panama, Liberia) account for more than twice the tonnage shown here.

‡ Including tugs, cable ships, international water fishing boats, and so on.

synthetics as the primary enemy of sponge fishing and, ironically, Kalymnians and Kalymnian-Americans were set against one another in a battle for economic survival. On Kalymnos the traditional relationship between divers and captains was almost reversed and the switch nearly destroyed sponge fishing entirely.

PLATIKA

Until 1937 the sponge operations were run on shares. Each diver got a unit share of the profits; the deck crew a half share each; the captain two shares, one for himself and one for his boat. After a sponge sale the captain took the costs of the trip off the gross profits before shares were divided. He alone determined the operation costs. The net profits to be divided were what the captain said they were. Apparently, the system was badly abused.

A contract system was instituted (Dodecanese law 560/1937, Koundouris, 21) to protect the interests of the divers. Deck crew members received a fixed sum under the new law as their total salary for the sponge-fishing season. They got part of their wages in advance to pay for separate maintenance of families while they were at sea. Divers got a percentage of their production rather than a fixed sum, based on experience, capability, and bargaining skill. They, too, would be given a part of their earnings in advance. At the end of the trip, when the sponges were sold by the captains, each diver would then receive his share, depending on the size of the contract he had with the captain and how much he had taken in advance.

Ideally, an average diver of five years' experience might negotiate a 42 per cent contract with a captain. He would expect to catch 165 kilos of dry sponge and would take 26,000 drachmas in advance, as established by the Agricultural Bank and by law (Table 7). At sea, the diver would keep his

Table 7

Legally Established Limits for Advanced Payment to Divers*†

Type of Equipment	Class of Diver	Platika Limit
Foreign Waters		
Skafandra and	A′	26,000 dx.
fernez	B′	22,000
	C′	18,000
Narghile and nude divers and bottle		
divers	A′	34,200
	B′	19,800
	C′	16,200
Greek Waters—All Types of Equipment		
	A′	17,100
	B′	15,300
	C′	13,500

* Source: Agricultural Bank of Greece.

† In depths up to 18 fathoms the diver must contract for a minimum of 26 per cent of his own catch. In depths beyond 18 fathoms the minimum allowable contract is 28 per cent. The actual mean contract in 1964 was 35 per cent, with variations ranging from 30 per cent to 50 per cent for a few divers. The maximum percentage of a contract allowed by the Agricultural Bank for loan purposes is 43 per cent. This was exceeded in numerous cases.

sponge on strings marked with his personal symbol—a coin, a swatch of cloth, a piece of leather—so the captain could keep track of his production. If the captain should sell the sponge catch of all his men at an average of 700 drachmas per kilo, then the above diver would receive 22,510 drachmas

$(165 \times 700 \times 0.42 - 26,000)$ at the end of the sponge market, usually around mid-December.

The new system created its own problems. Kalymnian folklore is filled with grizzly stories of death at sea in the old days when there was supposedly no limit to the captain's power over his men. The captains ruled their boats absolutely and forced their men to dive into dangerously deep waters. Among men who dived with deep-sea gear, casualty rates are said to have been astronomical. The greed of the buyers, who demanded sponge for their lucrative foreign markets, was transferred to the captains who overworked their men to the point of death. This is the way the picture is usually painted on Kalymnos about life in the sponge business "in the old days."

The nature of the industry and its socioeconomic structure ring true, for there is nothing so intimately "Greek" as the game of mutual social and economic exploitation. The most vivid explanation of this game was what one informant called the "drowning-man theory of Greek life." "Picture, if you will," he said, "humanity drowning shoulder to shoulder in the sea—such that to save oneself the only way is to put your right hand on the shoulder of the man to your right and your left hand on the shoulder of the man to your left and push, thereby keeping yourself above water."

Many writers have noticed this behavior (Friedl, Campbell, Vasiliou, and so on), and Campbell (1968:339–40) has aptly shown its basis in the values and child-rearing practices of Greece.[3] He says,

> The members of a family are united in the face of a hostile world. . . . The mother who in her person is the moral and expressive center of family life, continues . . . throughout her life to pour an almost unconditional affection and admiration upon her children; especially her sons, in contrast (and perhaps in compensation for) the often pragmatic relations with her husband. But, as a means to control her children, a mother also resorts to stratagems of deceit and promised rewards which are rarely delivered. Although the transparent dishonesty is soon comprehended by an intelligent child, his dependence forces him to accept the terms and idiom of this behavior. Thus, attitudes of suspicion and cunning which in later life are to be so appropriate in dealings with unrelated persons are in part learned within the context of the relationship that stands for the quintessence of love and confidence.

In fact, it is not only common for a man to find these qualities appropriate, but the nature of family life in Greece makes a virtue of exploitation of everyone but godparents and close friends, close neighbors, and "poor people." Aside from the people in one's "in-group," as George Vasiliou calls it,

---

[3] Vasiliou has also addressed himself to this issue, saying that Greeks have "in-groups" composed of family, ritual kin, and close friends who are not to be exploited; everyone else is part of the "out-group" and is fair game. He also gives great weight to the Turkish occupation of Greece and the successful use of cunning to prevent de-Hellenization during those 375 years of Ottoman rule. Campbell does not emphasize male–female role conflict as much as I have (Bernard, 1967) in this development of the mutually exploitative behavior exhibited by adult Greek men and women. But both the historical and sex-role-conflict explanations are still open to serious question and testing, so I have left them out of this discussion.

everyone else is a *ksenos*, or stranger,[4] and fair game. Thus it did not take the captains long to find ways of exploiting divers within the framework of the new law.[5] The tactics were not one-sided, however. If the new law did not stop captains from cheating their divers, it at least gave the divers equal opportunity to cheat the captains. *Platika* was this opportunity.

The proper Greek word for prepayment is *prokatavoli*. It carries the connotation that the advance is a downpayment and that the balance of the wages will be paid at the end of the sponge trip. On Kalymnos this is not the case; divers receive *all* their year's earnings, or *platika*, in advance.

The system works in this manner: A typical sponge-fishing expedition comprises two diving boats and a mother ship on which food supplies and processed sponges are stored during the six months' voyage. The total crew averages between thirty-five and forty men. Excluding the cost of this basic hardware and its depreciation, the cost of running such an expedition is roughly 850,000 drachmas or $28,000.

Ideally, the crew and divers are signed on by March. In April the boats are provisioned with food and fuel for the half-year voyage ahead. By Easter the boats have left for North Africa, where they remain until fall weather drives them home. When the expedition returns in October or November, the sponge market begins. By January the sponges have changed hands from the captains to the buyers; the divers have begun six months of ostentatious leisure; the captains have paid off their debts to the bank and to the private financiers, banked their profits, and resumed their search for capital to finance the next trip.

The captains begin early in January to negotiate loans from the Agricultural Bank for the cost of the trip. The bank is only licensed to lend the captains a part of the total cost, because as we have seen, the law stipulates that only part of a man's wages may be paid in advance (compare Table 8, line 1, with Table 9, total). Captains are forced to borrow the balance from the buyers at 20 to 40 per cent annual interest.

In 1965 the largest *platika* received was 90,000 dx. On a 50 per cent contract a man would have to catch 257 kilos of sponge selling at 700 drachmas a kilo just to come out even ($257 \times 700 \times 0.50$). This is more than any man could produce. The captain who paid this *platika* took a theoretical "loss" in order to make some actual gain. A novice diver might receive only 20,000

---

[4] This word is one of the most difficult I have found to translate into English. Its use varies, depending on the nature of the "threat" one feels. To the people of a village, when they stand together against another village, the outsiders are all *ksenoi*. To the people of a neighborhood, those of adjacent neighborhoods or parishes are *ksenoi*. If a close family friend or godparent betrays the trust of his in-group by exploiting his friend, it may be said, "Well, he was a ksenos anyway; we should have known better than to trust him."

[5] In an effort to establish bonds which prevent exploitation, divers may ask captains to baptize their children, or captains may ask buyers. It is very rare for divers to ask buyers; and in fact, there seem to be fewer cases of captains asking buyers than divers asking captains. These differences appear related to social distance and a rather intuitive approach to the "appropriateness" of asking someone very much out of one's social class.

Table 8

Agricultural Bank Loan Schedule for a Captain Employing Ten Divers*

Expense	Amount
1. Divers' advance pay. For ten divers. Four first-class divers, three each second and third class (see Table 7).	224,000 dx.
2. Crew's wages.	104,265 dx.
3. Food for sponge boat crew and divers and for mother ship crew for six months.	92,820 dx.
4. Fuel, oil, and grease for mother ship and sponge boat.	20,160 dx.
5. Licenses, port pilot fees, etc.	41,000 dx.
6. Insurance for vessels and sponge catch.	13,000 dx.
7. Maintenance and ship's provisions (compass, maps, lines, pulleys, hardware, etc.).	45,000 dx.
8. Mother ship (rental, crew salaries).	105,000 dx.
9. Miscellaneous unforeseen expenses.	6,755 dx.
10. Emergency fund held in abeyance at the bank.	16,000 dx.
Total	668,000 dx.

* Source: Agricultural Bank of Greece, Kalymnos Branch, 1965.

Table 9

Typical *Platika* Payments to Ten Divers on a Sponge Boat

Diver	Experience	Platika (advance)
1	Novice	30,000 dx.
2	Novice	25,000 dx.
3	Three years	37,500 dx.
4	Four years	40,000 dx.
5	Four years	42,000 dx.
6	Seventeen years	45,000 dx.
7	Twenty-two years	47,500 dx.
8	Seven years	65,000 dx.
9	Eight years	70,000 dx.
10	Twelve years	55,000 dx.
Total		457,000 dx.

drachmas in *platika*; with a minimum 35 per cent contract, and with sponges selling at 700 drachmas per kilo, he would have to harvest 86 kilos (86 × 700 × 0.35) to come out even. A novice might not make up even that small quota. Even if he does, the most the captain can expect in profits is 39,135 dx. (86 × 700 × 0.65). A master diver can expect to catch around 205 kilos in a good year. If the man receiving 90,000 drachmas makes this quota, the captain's actual profit is 53,500 drachmas (205 × 700 − 90,000), even though the *platika* is actually 63 per cent of the catch (205 × 700 × 0.63 × 90,405), and thus is an illegal contract. In a sense, of course, the captain is cheated. By law the diver is responsible only for fulfilling the *prokatavoli*, or 26,000 drachmas. If he failed to make the expected gain, the captain could lower the *platika* offer the next year and spread the word among other captains to do likewise. But this was a rarely used sanction, for *platika* was a debt of honor. If a diver did not fulfill the debt, it was usually not because he slacked off. In this actual case the diver died partway through the trip. He had already made enough to fulfill the *prokatavoli*. Theoretically, the money beyond the *prokatavoli* had never been paid. The captain had no recourse but to write off a portion of the *platika* at a huge loss.

Each diver naturally demands as much *platika* as he can get, the amount being a linear measure of his virility. It is computed according to the following formula: the current market price of sponge per kilo, plus about 5 per cent inflation on next year's price. This is multiplied by the number of kilos a man expects to produce based on his previous record plus a small yearly increase during the first six or eight years of his career as he reaches a maximum production plateau. And finally, this is in turn multiplied by the maximum percentage contract a diver feels he can negotiate with a captain. A few thousand drachmas are added as a bargaining cushion.

Whereas deck crews and nondiving personnel tend to remain fairly stable from year to year, the diving population is fickle, shifting among the various captains every season. When a diver is approached by a captain to sign on, he demands his prereckoned earnings in advance. He asserts his right to the *platika* by pointing to the continuing high casualty rates (Table 10).

When the boats are at sea, they work all day some miles from the mother ship. When they return at night for food, they hand over the day's catch to a special crew which processes it and reports the dry weight to the captain. Every three or four weeks the divers are given a tally of their progress by the captain. But there is no way to check the captain's figures. If a high-*platika* diver is producing poorly or if a novice diver turns out to be a prodigy, the captain shuffles the sponge around to cover his risks. This way he is owed no *platika*, nor does he owe extra wages at the end of the trip.

Divers rationalize their scheming to gain *platika* by saying, "Everything you get in advance is everything you're going to get." In spite of this, there is normally more sponge produced than the cost of the *platika*, so captains usually wind up owing their men money.[6] The captain's "bonus wage" debt is reduced through collusion with the buyers against the divers.

[6] Consider a diver who negotiates a 40 per cent contract and 54,000 drachmas in *platika*, based on the assumption that he will catch 192 kilos of sponge selling at 700 drachmas per kilo. He catches 211. Thirteen kilos are secretly juggled to make up the *platika* debt of a similarly contracted man who produced only 179. Ideally, the captain still owes the first diver 40 per cent of 6 kilos times 700 drachmas, or 1,680 drachmas.

Table 10

Casualty Rates for Kalymnian Divers*

Year	Divers	No. of Boats	Avg. No. Divers per Boat	Paralyses	Deaths	Casualty Rate (%)
1950	513	56	9.16	15	0	2.92
1951	429	48	8.94	12	3	3.50
1952	409	42	9.74	12	8	4.89
1953	305	34	8.97	7	1	2.62
1954	386	41	9.41	9	2	2.85
1955	409	44	9.30	10	2	2.93
1956	342	41	8.35	10	1	2.92
1957	386	44	8.77	11	6	4.40
1958	384	43	8.93	12	2	3.65
1959	351	36	9.75	8	0	2.28
1960	279	29	9.62	11	1	4.30
1961	247	28	8.82	7	1	3.24
1962	240	25	9.60	7	1	3.33
1963	257	39	6.60	7	3	3.89
1964	235	36	6.53	1	8	3.83
1965	197	27	7.30	9	6	7.61
1966	94	15	6.27	3	0	3.19
1967	229	39	5.87	6	1	3.05
1968	199	38	5.23	7	1	4.02
1969	250	44	5.68	3	1	1.60

* Sources: Harbor Master's office, Kalymnos, and Agricultural Bank of Greece for 1967 1968, and 1969.

In a typical sponge sale there is a direct conflict of interest. The captain demands a price and the buyer counters with a lower one. When negotiations reach an impasse, the captain agrees to accept the buyer's "final offer" of, say, 700 drachmas per kilo. He insists he is capitulating and that he really should be getting 710. The buyer lets the record state that only 670 drachmas were paid. The captain does not account to his divers for the 30 drachmas difference, and this puts money into the captain's pockets when payments beyond *platika* are computed.

In the end it seemed that everyone came out fairly even. In the Kalymnian world it appeared almost heresy to replace this system with one less taxing on the wits. Some men (divers as well as captains) went so far as to say that life otherwise would be dull. They were proud of the Kalymnian tradition and their genuine fame throughout the Dodecanese as slick businessmen (the inhabitants of Kos were especially vocal on this point), and they seemed to relish the idea that non-Kalymnians could not operate successfully with a *platika* system such as theirs.

Platika was more than an economic plan, of course. It was a total social experience for the sponge men and for other Kalymnians who extended credit to the divers and to their wives while the men were at sea. A complex of myths, values, social norms, and physical realities justified it. People battled one another like chess players, to be sure. But the system contained its own set of brakes that kept the actual extortion behavior within fairly well-understood limits. Buyers held captains in debt at usurious rates; captains distributed the wealth of the buyers and the Agricultural Bank to their crews, chandlers, merchants, machinists, and divers whom they held in debt with *platika*. Buyers were aristocrats, powerful in local politics. Captains were intermediaries playing both ends against the middle and rewarded with substantial wealth, if not prestige. Divers were rewarded with wealth and a strange kind of homage.

The average diver earns twice in six months what a similarly educated day laborer earns in a year. In addition, he used to enjoy a social license for antisocial behavior, freedom to spend his money hedonistically, and a spurious adulation from society in general as a folk hero. The lower socioeconomic levels of Kalymnos really did admire divers. Small boys listened eagerly to divers' tales of heroics at sea; for them it was an honor to serve a really virile, high-*platika* diver his coffee. On the other hand, the genteel levels of society, the landlubbers, have always had great disdain for the divers as a class. They gossip about the divers' wives, saying that divers are regularly cuckolded during their absence at sea. In fact, there is little justification for the gossip, but it persists. The same landlubbers give the divers a great send-off each year, and a "banquet of love," but in reality they despise them as a

Table 11

Diving Statistics for Fernez Divers, 1965

Depth (Meters)	Average Time on Bottom (Minutes)	Extreme Bottom Time (Minutes)	Average Ascent (Minutes)	Recommended Ascent†
33	31	45	7.9	20
37	31	50	4.8	25
40	29	40	4.2	25
43	22	29	4.6	20
46	21	38	7.1	30
49	16	28	6.1	25
52	14	19	5.2	15
55	12	16	5.1	20

* Source: Observation.

† Recommended ascent time (in minutes) is for the average dive, not the extreme. Staying down for 38 minutes at 46 meters, for example, necessitates a 65-minute ascent for safety. Also, these figures are for single dives. Ascent time rises radically when three dives are made in eight or ten hours.

low, uneducated, rowdy class. One merchant said, " The divers are the shame of Kalymnos. How can we ask tourists to come here? What can we show them, a bunch of drunks?" Still, until recently, the colorful antics of divers were more than tolerated, even venerated. In the final analysis they did risk their lives for the economic well-being of Kalymnos. Their casualty rates proved that (Table 10).

As it turns out, the reality of death and paralysis from bends, and its mythological underpinning of Kalymnian landlubber–seafarer social relations, are all tied to *platika*. By taking 60,000 drachmas in advance, a man needs 215 kilos of sponge to fulfill his debt. It is impossible to do this without making at least three dives a day. A boat working in waters of 35 to 40 meters (intermediary depths by Kalymnian standards) would have seven divers, all with similar obligations. Twenty-one dives a day requires each man to spend maximum time on the bottom and surface rapidly. According to the diving statistics I collected at sea in 1965, it is surprising that the casualty rates are not higher (Table 11). They are terrifying enough, however, and they give meaning to the demand for *platika* and all that goes with it.

During the last decade the Greek government has tried to reduce the casualty rates of Kalymnian divers through educational programs,[7] and has failed. It was assumed that the problem of the Kalymnian divers was technological and that proper equipment and training would solve it. Kalymnians *knew* they were risking their lives. They even knew how to lower the risk. There was simply no way of stopping *platika* and the social edifice built on it.

PLATIKA AND SOCIAL CHANGE

The system was overly complex, adjusted to an insulated socioeconomic climate, and so specialized that it was incapable of change. As divers left and sponge production fell, the power in Kalymnian society reassessed the role of the industry and men in it. Tourism was envisioned enthusiastically, and remittances were on the increase. The mothers of boys who might have died 20 fathoms down were not the only ones glad to see their sons go abroad. The merchants who did not want "drunken bums" around were delighted, especially because it mean an increase in the flow of hard, foreign exchange on Kalymnos with which more overseas consumer goods could be ordered. The divers' license for antisocial behavior was revoked.

In 1960 a law was passed requiring divers to place one half of their legal advance (still only one third or less of the actual *platika*) in a bank under

---

[7] The only diving school in Greece was opened; today it is inoperative from lack of interest and funds. In 1969 the government formally requested an American naval vessel to call on Kalymnos so the frogmen could instruct the local divers on techniques for avoiding the bends. In 1965 La Spirotechnique, a company which markets diving gear designed by M. Jacques Cousteau, attempted a similar venture.

their wives' names before they could ship out. In 1964 female entertainment was banned in Pothea during the winter months when the sponge fishermen are at home. This has since been relaxed somewhat by allowing nightclubs in outlying villages to open with live entertainment. But at the time the law was passed it was clearly designed to protect the Kalymnian women. The women, in fact, had gone in a group to the mayor's office demanding that something be done. Response to such demands would have been unthinkable ten or fifteen years before.

The overt antagonism and ambivalence between townspeople and sponge fishermen erupted openly. The Kalymnian Tourist Union began propagandizing the "banquet of love" and the departure of the sponge fleet as major tourist attractions. Athenian dignitaries and a few tourists had always been drawn to the affair, but now Kalymnians were systematically exploiting the "sponge festival" along the same lines as the famous yearly "wine festival" at Daphne. In 1965 the authorities on Kalymnos arranged elaborate programs of native dancing and dramatic productions. Great banners were hung over the main quay proclaiming slogans such as, "Come Back Safely, Our Heroes." Hundreds of people crowded the yacht club to attend the banquet and it was a matter of social prestige to be invited. No divers were invited, except for a few officers of the Divers' Union. The same was true in 1970, when the island turned out an elaborate program to honor the visit of the Greek Foreign

The sailing of the sponge fleet is a major ceremony on Kalymnos; recently it has become a tourist attraction. Here Kalymnians sincerely wish their divers "Bon voyage and come back safely."

The exodus of the sponge fleet is a religious and public affair. Dignitaries, priests, and official naval personnel all take part.

Minister on the occasion. The sponge festival has become an ever more important tourist attraction, even as the old-time sponge fishermen have faded from the scene.

Redefinition of the divers' role was the beginning of a reaction that sent ripples through the Kalymnian social structure. *Platika* was a perfect vehicle for increasing the monetary rewards of diving in lieu of the nonmonetary ones which had been taken away. Where 60,000 drachmas in *platika* was astronomical in 1960, by 1965 it had become a common figure. The man who got 90,000 in 1965 was considered a superman. In 1970 many diving contracts were reportedly negotiated between 70,000 and 100,000 drachmas.

Divers started taking small advances from several captains, telling each that he would go to sea with him. Captains retaliated by taking the divers' sea papers as insurance when the first advance was made. Divers continued to negotiate contracts with more than one captain. The second would have to buy the sea papers from the first, the third from the second, and so on. This set the captains against one another in the fight for scarce labor.

Captains made expeditions to other islands and even to Piraeus to recruit divers. One put ads in the Athenian and Piraeus newspapers offering *platika* to men who would become divers. Kos and other nearby agricultural islands, where disenchanted youths did not want to continue in their fathers' steps as farmers, provided a temporary respite to the shortage. In 1965 more than 40 per cent of the diving population in the sponge fleet was non-Kalymnian.

Traditional relationships between captains and buyers and among buyers changed. Buyers used to control the market and the bargaining behavior of captains because captains were in debt to them. Production scarcities tended to reverse this situation. When the market began in October, the captains would wait to be approached by the buyer or his representative. Once the initial haggling had been accomplished and the two parties had agreed to negotiate a price for the captain's sponge, it was a matter of honor that negotiations would continue until the buyer had bought the sponge or negotiations had been broken off by mutual agreement. Buyers were restrained by custom from approaching a captain with a bid once a captain had opened official negotiations with one of their confrères. Captains were similarly restrained from seeking out new offers after bargaining began with a particular merchant. It was incumbent upon the captain to make sure, during the initial dickering, that the buyer was the one with whom he wanted to continue to deal, before the parties reached an agreement to go to the bargaining table. Now captains pit buyers against one another, initiating negotiations with one, while secretively seeking out counteroffers by others. The buyers respond eagerly and have become more suspicious and exploitative of one another as they compete for scarcer and ever more expensive sponges.[8]

Still further difficulties arose, beginning in 1963, and continuing to the present, when a sponge buyer from Japan came to Kalymnos during the winter market season. Acting through an English–Japanese interpreter, he bought silk sponges (particularly the variety known as *fino-mantapas*) for use in the cosmetic industry as applicators. Because his markets are for piece goods, whereas those of the Kalymnian buyers are generally for bulk weight, the Japanese merchant was able to outbid every Kalymnian by as much as 200 drachmas per kilogram. In 1963 this was 20 per cent more than the established market price.

The intrusion of a non-Kalymnian (not to mention non-Western) buyer into the system created mild havoc. In the traditional market system the buyers always approached the captains. For the Japanese this rule was

[8] A common practice among the buyers is to trade off parts of sponge catches. This may be a cash transaction or a direct barter or a combination of the two. A sponge catch consists of six grades in three species, and buyers negotiate for all grades in a single species at a time. If a buyer acquires several hundred kilograms of a grade of sponge for which he has no market, then another buyer may take them in trade or for cash, or both. One buyer purchased some silk sponge in 1965 from another merchant who had acquired them on consignment from a wholesale customer in Europe who had failed to resell them. The first buyer offered his colleague a direct cash payment to take over the consignment. Prior to this a third buyer had made the second an offer and an agreement had been reached on price. The agreement was broken when the first buyer offered the same price, plus an option on some sponges that the second needed for his own markets. This failure to live up to an agreement would have been an unlikely occurrence a decade ago.

306 TECHNOLOGY AND SOCIAL CHANGE

suspended, and captains sought him out to take advantage of his high offer. By the time the local buyers capitulated, it was too late. The outsider had cornered the market on silks. The Kalymnians felt betrayed by their own people; the captains had not given them a chance to make a competitive offer. The captains, however, observing the etiquette of Kalymnos with other Kalymnians, could not approach the buyers first. Because the Japanese buyer did not know any of these rules, there was no loss of ethics in approaching him. This practice has added measurably to the breakdown in buyer–captain relations.

During all of this, sponge economics went out of control. Divers imported from other islands just to work on the sponge boats held no loyalty to Kalymnos or its inhabitants, or its unspoken limits on the mutually exploitative system they called *platika*. And as the landlubbers redefined the social role of divers, and the noneconomic fringe benefits of being a diver disappeared, even local Kalymnians were relieved of the responsibility of maintaining those limits. A tremendous strain was placed on the men, for in spite of the pressure to demand all they could get from the captains, and more, the pressure of *filotimo*, that concept of personal and family honor that is central to all Greekness, remained strong. So the more *platika* they got, the more sponges they needed to fulfill the honor debt and the harder they worked at sea. The casualties of 1965, when the inevitable market crisis came, are the results of the *platika* system run wild and traditional values that have remained constant.

Higher *platika*, high casualty rates among men with *filotimo*, and progressively worse shirking and malingering among men without it, sent captains into increasing debt. Sponge prices skyrocketed. The buyers could not raise their resale price because synthetics were getting better and cheaper. They cut profit margins to meet the captains' prices. In mid-January of 1965, when negotiations for the next trip should have begun, only 30 per cent of the sponge catch had been sold. The buyers had formed a group and had decided not to give in, just to show the captains that they could not get away with yet another price increase. The captains said they could not sell for less because of the inflation of *platika*. The deadlock brought the Undersecretary of Industry (himself a Kalymnian) to the island for a meeting of captains and buyers. He heard both sides and ordered the captains to make some concessions to the buyers. He further ordered the buyers to send their representatives around to the captains' warehouses to search out individually suitable catches and to offer the captains a fair price (slightly below what the captains demanded). The prestige and authority of the Minister got the negotiations started and, with one exception, all catches were sold within a few months. But the resolution of the 1965 crisis did not solve the basic problem of labor shortage, competition from synthetics, runaway *platika*, a breakdown in interpersonal relations among members of the industry, and so on.

In April, 1970, after five more years of near-crisis each market season, another deadlock was reached. Boats that should have been preparing to leave remained in dry dock, and $1.3 million in sponge lay unsold and baled in the captains' warehouses. The buyers were down to where there was really no room for bargaining. They could still sell every sponge they could get, they claimed, but they could simply not afford to acquire sponges at the current prices demanded by the captains. The latter could not afford to lower their prices any more. Their margins had been genuinely exhausted by *platika* increases. If they could not sell their sponges, they could not pay off their debts; nor could they negotiate further loans to go to sea. The situation was both critical and ludicrous, and everyone knew it. There were sellers with a product to sell and buyers in the market to buy; and no one could afford to do business.

To make matters worse, Egypt and Libya began to think of exploiting the sponge industry themselves. Although these countries have not yet been able to develop a large native industry, they have tried to protect their resources for future development by restricting the number of licenses for fishing by boats under Greek registry in their waters. Since the Arab–Israeli conflict of 1967, Egypt has restricted its waters entirely. In recent years Kalymnians have fished off the Tunisian coast. The prices of the licenses there included the training of native Tunisians aboard Kalymnian vessels, a stipulation acceded to only grudgingly. Cyprus has opened its waters to Kalymnian vessels on occasion, but the political situation there is precarious, so licenses are only issued irregularly. Besides, Cyprus has its own sponge industry to protect. For the most part, the Kalymnians have been forced to fish in local Greek waters where diving is more difficult (because of the mountainous configuration of the ocean floor) and where sponge quality is generally poorer than in North Africa.

ECONOMIC AND SOCIAL ADJUSTMENT OF KALYMNOS AND THE SPONGE INDUSTRY

In the last twenty years two economically curious things have occurred on Kalymnos. First, there was a decline in marine sponge production that was more rapid than the decline in demand. And second, in spite of the economic and social strains this placed on Kalymnos and its sponge men, the island and sponge fishing continue to thrive, ever better than previously.

The prosperity is reflected, for example, by the fact that in 1970 Kalymnos had at least 200 per cent more telephones than a decade before. There are twice as many users consuming nearly three times the electrical power of 1961 (Table 12). The dollar cost of imports to Kalymnos and Kos rose nearly 500 per cent in the last ten years (Table 13). The most pressing economic problem in Greece is the unfavorable trade balance,[9] which reached $620

[9] The adjusted trade balance used here refers to the difference, in United States dollars, of imports over exports after receipts from tourists and overseas migrants' remittances have been entered.

Table 12

Use of Electricity on Kalymnos

Year	Households	Kilowatt Hours	Cost (Drachmas)
1961	2,632	1,101,532	1,530,002
1965	3,629	1,710,329	2,271,736
1969	4,841	2,800,000	3,650,000

million in 1968. This was nearly $75 in the red for every man, woman, and child in the nation. On Kalymnos, on the other hand, the trade balance was about $120 in the black of hard, convertible foreign currency for every one of the island's inhabitants, or $600 per family.

The prosperity is translated into building construction. Currency devaluations have made Greeks wary of banks and savings accounts. Rising labor

Table 13

Imports into Kalymnos
and Kos, 1959–1969*†

Year	Amount (in dollars)
1959	462,868
1960	595,490
1961	553,685
1962	651,872
1963	903,864
1964	829,284
1965	1,580,502
1968	2,154,126
1969	2,256,313

* Source: Chamber of Commerce, Kalymnos–Kos.

† Between 1959 and 1961 the dollar value of imports to the two islands rose 48 per cent. Because the Chamber of Commerce does not keep separate records for the two islands, the figures are relative for each island rather than absolute. Personal interviews with the customs house manager on Kalymnos indicate the cost rise of imports in this period are at least the average for the two islands.

costs (up 10 per cent in 1969) and the need to provide every daughter with a house for her dowry have practically made piecemeal construction a cultural tradition. As soon as money is accumulated, land is purchased. When enough money is reaccumulated a foundation is laid, and so on. A never-ending series of government lotteries is in constant competition with brick and mortar for the public sector's liquid resources. Kalymnians paid nearly $2.5 million for 1,923 building permits between 1966 and 1969.

There are three main reasons for the continuing prosperity of Kalymnos: (1) favorable customs-tax laws, (2) government support of job and revenue-producing public works, and (3) the diversification of the economy, including the reorientation of sponge fishing.

When the Dodecanese were passed to Greece by the United Nations in 1948, the government in Athens passed special tax laws to permit the importation of foreign products to the Dodecanese at greatly reduced rates of duty. Gasoline costs 90 cents a gallon in Athens, the highest price in non-Communist Europe. It is 59 cents in the Dodecanese. Gold, textiles, appliances, foodstuffs—all are at least 20 per cent less in the Dodecanese than in the rest of Greece. Mainlanders are not allowed to buy major items in the Dodecanese and take them home without paying duty. But they can order finished clothing of highly prized English or Italian cloth and they can vacation on the islands where prestige liquors like Scotch whiskey are half or less than in Athens.

In 1968 the twenty-year tax law expired; it had been designed to stimulate growth and tourism and it had done its job very well. It was renewed. Rhodes is one of Greece's main tourist attractions. Kos, the home of Hippocrates, has developed tourism to the point where it has replaced the tomato crop as the largest industry. Kalymnos is beginning to get the overflow, especially the young foreign tourists looking for "off the beaten track" islands. An estimated 10 million drachmas came into Kalymnos in 1968 from tourism (Koundouris, 1968). That figure will probably double in the next five years. This will result partly from the completion of new dock facilities begun in 1965. The first stage was completed in 1967 and permitted direct landing of ocean-going liners. Prior to this, passengers debarked onto small dinghies at sea, which shuttled them to the island. Departures and arrivals at the port of Kalymnos were up 25 per cent between 1967 and 1970, according to the harbor master.

The dock facilities are indicative of a continuing governmental interest in the development of a Kalymnian infrastructure. Since 1960, a 12-kilometer road was paved to Vathy (Figure 3). Another road is being extended to Emborios, though the population between there and Myrthies is less than 100 persons. The Boubalis hospital was nationalized in 1967, and since then has been totally remodeled and stocked with modern equipment at national government expense. A phone system was built linking every village, including Telendos and Pserimos, with Pothea. Two new schools were constructed and a third renovated. Direct loans have been extended to private and municipal contractors to build tourist accommodations. And all this has gone on through vast political changes at the national level from right to left to extreme right again in less than ten years.

Kalymnos and all the Dodecanese play an important role in the defense of Greece against Turkey. Though the two nations are NATO allies, nightly watches are manned to this day in the Dodecanese against possible attack from the Turkish mainland. There can be no doubt that Greek governments of all political leanings see the development of a Dodecanese infrastructure as having military value.

The social and economic value of such development though is probably just as important. In a country where one fourth of the population lives in the capital, high priority is given to the growth of secondary population centers and the improvement of life in rural areas to cut down internal rural–urban migration. Kalymnos is particularly important, because it is a symbol of pride and virility, with undeniably romantic attributes deriving from the intrepid behavior and casualties of divers. More obviously, the sponge industry is a source of $1.5 million to $2 million a year in hard foreign currency. For this reason the central government undertook to save the sponge industry in the crisis of 1970. Though they were unable to negotiate licenses for the boats to go to North Africa, several permits were secured for work in Italian waters near Sicily and Corsica. Subsidies were also offered to break the market deadlock. Captains with sponge fished in 1969 outside Greek waters were given from 70 to 170 drachmas per kilo of sponge (depending on grade) by the Agricultural Bank. The balance of the captains' price was paid by the buyers. The bank is also undertaking a loan program to aid in the wholesale purchase of sponge expedition supplies by the Captains' Coopera-tive on Kalymnos; the loans for expedition expenses are being increased and interest rates lowered in an effort to break the buyer–captain–diver debt cycle. Further, in an attempt to get the sponge operations modernized techno-logically, loans are now offered for diving equipment purchases at from 2 to 4 per cent interest. The truly remarkable events of the past few years, however, may indicate that the government will not have to subsidize the industry for very long.

The economy of Kalymnos is booming. Capital production was $4.5 million in 1968 (Table 14).

In 1969 the Agricultural Bank of Kalymnos lent over $660,000 to the commercial fishing fleet, and officials say this industry will certainly grow. Remittances nationally averaged $30 for each resident Greek in 1968. On Kalymnos the figure was $138. Before 1950 the sponge industry was 60 to 70 per cent of the Kalymnian economy. Today it is only 30 per cent, but it is still the largest single item in Table 14. Three factors account for the continued vigor of sponge production and sales, in spite of synthetics, lack of licenses, and the shortages of labor: (1) the Bodrumi sponge industry, (2) the opening of the Japanese markets, and (3) a major technological and social structural change in Kalymnian sponge operation.

Table 14

Kalymnian Economy, 1968

Source	Amount ($)	Per Cent of Total
Agriculture†	500,000	11
Tourism‡	333,000	7
Commercial fishing	533,000	12
Remittances	1,800,000	40
(merchant marine: $1,000,000, 22% of total; migrants:§ $800,000, 18% of total)		
Sponge sales	1,333,000	30
Total	4,499,000	100

* From Koundouris, 1968.

† Mostly the citrus exports from Vathy Valley.

‡ Not counting income derived from expenditures of several hundred non-Kalymnian students at Kalymnian high schools or incomes of doctors, lawyers, or dentists derived from non-Kalymnians.

§ There are currently an estimated 2,300 Kalymnians in Australia and 3,000 more in America, Canada, West Germany, and the Bahamas.

Where business is involved, political and cultural animosities can be put aside. Kalymnian imports from Turkey were valued at $45,000 in 1959. In 1965, the year of the first sponge crisis, this rose to nearly $500,000. The simple fact is that Kalymnian merchants can sell all the sponge they can get, if it is cost-competitive. Table 15 shows the drastic profit cuts absorbed by buyers on Kalymnian sponge between 1960 and 1969. Profits similar to those

Table 15

Buyer's Profits, 1960 and 1969

Year	Kilos Sold (Captains to Buyers)	Average Price per Kilo ($)	Export Value per Kilo ($)	Gross Mark-up (%)	Overhead (%)	Net* (%)
1960	44,000	14.56	20.55	41	22	19
1969	47,000	20.46	28.20	38	30†	8

* This average does not reflect the differences among buyers on their profits from loans to captains.

† Reflecting higher wages, increased social security benefits, higher interest on financing, and increased freight and insurance costs.

Table 16

Sponge Production by Type of Boat, 1957–1969

Year	Type of Boat	Number of Craft	Crew			Production (Kilos)	Value ($)	Market Price per Kilo ($)
			Divers	Deck	Total			
1957	Skafandra	24	255	268	523	32,834	660,000	20.10
	Fernez	8	69	85	154	9,812	145,600	14.83
	Nude	11	46	11	57	3,296	40,000	12.14
	Total	43	370	364	734	45,942	845,600	18.40 Avg.
1960	Skafandra	18	201	218	419	30,904	473,333	15.32
	Fernez	8	69	67	136	10,116	130,000	12.85
	Nude	9	45	13	58	3,132	40,333	12.88
	Total	35	315	298	613	44,152	643,666	14.57 Avg.
1965	Skafandra	14	117	120	237	19,361	333,333	17.22
	Fernez	11	77	89	166	12,541	193,333	15.42
	Nude	7	42	15	51	5,911	70,000	11.84
	Narghile	3	8	6	14	771	7,667	9.94
	Scuba	2	14	15	29	1,981	30,000	15.14
	Dredge	4	-0-	12	12	695	11,667	16.78
	Total	41	258	257	515	41,260	646,000	15.66 Avg.

Year	Method							
1967	Skagandra	10	83	75	158	16,944	313,600	18.51
	Fernez	6	44	47	91	8,336	159,800	19.17
	Nude	10	77	19	96	10,583	151,533	14.32
	Narghile	7	25	11	36	5,526	94,806	17.16
	Scuba	-0-	-0-	-0-	-0-	-0-	-0-	-0-
	Dredge	6	-0-	18	18	920	23,833	25.91
	Total	39	229	170	399	42,309	743,572	17.57
1969	Skafandra	7	59	62	121	11,870	272,233	22.93
	Fernez	10	68	83	151	14,230	288,967	20.31
	Nude	15	96	47	143	13,877	257,233	18.54
	Narghile	5	17	20	37	4,688	81,667	17.42
	Scuba	1	10	6	16	1,312	32,000	24.39
	Dredge	6	-0-	18	18	1,390	37,333	26.86
	Total	44	250	236	486	47,367	969,433	20.47 Avg.

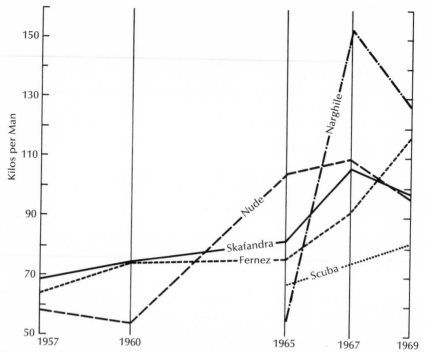

FIGURE 4. Individual sponge production by year and type of equipment.

of 1960 are reported for Turkish sponge processes on Kalymnos and sold on the world markets.

Meanwhile, the opening of markets in the Far East has given a new lease on life to sponge production. These markets require a low-grade species known as *fino-mantapas*, which are readily fished in Greek waters at all depths. One result of this has been indiscriminate deep-water dredging which is very destructive of the ocean environment. A more fortunate effect has been the resurrection of nude diving, along with a modified *fernez* technology called *narghile*, and the abandonment of the mutually exploitative, counterproductive *platika* system. Table 16 shows the results of this latest shift in technology.

The *narghile* system is named after the traditional Turkish water pipe smoked in the Dodecanese until very recently. The divers wear a wet suit, lead belt, weights, flippers, and a mask. Air is delivered to the mask through a thin hose from a small compressor, independent of the boat's motor. The diver cruises the bottom horizontally rather than on foot as the *skafandra* and *fernez* divers do. The method is thus particularly suited to the rough underwater terrain in Greek waters.

The *narghile* and nude-diving systems are inexpensive to initiate and maintain. As Table 16 and Figures 4, 5, and 6 show, they are very effective as well. The rapid development of these types of operations since 1965 has been in direct

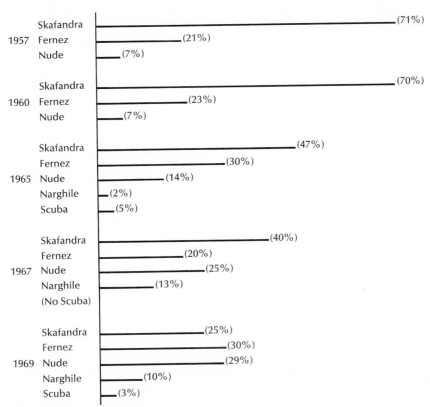

FIGURE 5. Type of diving equipment in use by year.

proportion to the disappearance of the *skafandra* and *fernez*. Those works depended on chicanery, intrepidity, and financial juggling. The new operations using *narghile* equipment and nude divers are staffed by youth from Pserimos and Telendos and other isolated parts of Kalymnos. They rely on commonality of residence and family ties to maintain an equitable share system. They operate on trust and cooperation, rather than on suspicion and invidious competition. Their record of production amply demonstrates the power of this social change. Production effectiveness is further enhanced by the fact that nude diving precludes the bends.[10]

[10] It has recently come to my attention that a similar technological change was made on Cyprus at an earlier date. Cypriot fisheries data show a very erratic industry on that island from 1900 to the present. Fifteen *skafandra* and *fernez* boats were operative in 1934 with only three nude-diving works. In 1948, twenty-eight nude operations and two *skafandra* and *fernez* boats fished. There is no record of the number of divers involved, but in 1948 the thirty boats fished 3,794 kilos of sponge. In 1964 there were still twenty-eight boats (including six *skafandra* and *fernez*, only two nude-diving boats, and twenty *narghile* vessels) which produced 6,976 kilos of sponge. The Cyprus fisheries, however, (1) did not operate

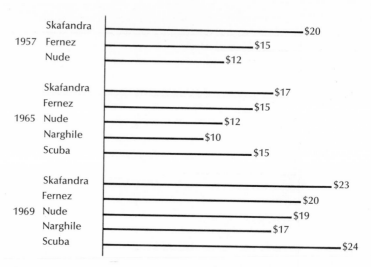

FIGURE 6. Average price per kilo for sponge by year and method of retrieval.

The success of the new boats has ushered in a new era on Kalymnos. If this era is to be marked by fewer deaths and paralysis, it is certainly not going to be characterized by lack of color. In 1970 a wedding was held on Pserimos in the best sponge-diving tradition. Five hundred dollars was spent on music alone in the three-day, nonstop fete. It reminded Kalymnians of the "old days," when divers lit cigarettes with 1,000-drachma notes.

If buyers can continue to find markets for competitively priced marine sponges, then the old spirit and culture of the "island of the sponge fishermen" should continue to provide Kalymnos with a colorful source of income for many years.

---

on a *platika* like that of the Kalymnians, (2) mostly fished in Cypriot waters with periodic stops at home port, and (3) were never a very large or important focus of the economy or social order of the island. For certain purposes a study of social change, if any, accompanying the shift in technology from *skafandra* to nude to *narghile* on Cyprus would make an interesting control case.

12

TECHNOLOGY AND SOCIAL CHANGE:
Some Concluding Observations

Human culture history of the past 2 million years is, in broadest perspec-tive, a story of technological change, interwoven with the biological modifications that produced the modern form of *Homo sapiens*. Of course, much of human history must be told in terms of technology because that is what we have—the material *things* resulting from human activity. But most anthropologists would agree that the crucial turning points in our history have almost always been closely related to technologi-cal developments. Prehistorians look for the earliest stone tools that mark the predawn moments of a distinctly human way of life. The great eras of prehistory (the Paleolithic and Neolithic) were first given names in terms of man's tool-making choices, although anthropologists now prefer to define them with reference to subsistence technology.

The development of food production technology through domestication of nutritionally valuable plants and animals was probably the most fundamental of all man's technological breakthroughs. Sometimes this series of innovations is referred to as the "Neolithic Revolution," even though it was a gradual process lasting several thousand years. The point that is emphasized when the word *revolution* is used is that the pace of technological and social change in the dawning of Neolithic times con-trasted sharply with the glacially slow accumulation of technological heritage of the Paleolithic. Also, when food production technology had taken hold, a chain reaction of other technological developments followed at an ever-quickening speed. The transformation in food pro-duction was followed by the development of metallurgy, invention of the wheel, perfection of systems for writing and recording information, and other technical innovations which had powerful effects on human culture.

In a remarkably short time, from the perspective of man's evolutionary history, the face of the world changed; as populations rapidly expanded into new food-growing regions, city-states were created, and wars were fought for empire. A few thousand years later major culture changes were set off by technological developments in sailing ships and other means of transport. Innovations in navigational instruments (especially the astrolabe) were of great significance in bringing about a new Age of Discovery beginning in the fifteenth century.

The continuing escalation of human population and the transformation of social systems was quickened again with the development of steam and internal combustion engines, bringing on the industrial revolution; and in most recent times the proliferation of atomic-powered and computer-automated technologies marks the frantic metamorphoses of the Atomic Age. Throughout history technological developments have led men to pursue new kinds of constructions and destructions. Indeed, in recent years we have become fearful that "our technology is overwhelming us" —that the machines are becoming the masters of our destinies and the man-created system of gadgets, engines, devices, and structures is ruining us through pollution of the environment and disorganization of our social, cultural, and political institutions.

In the background looms the darkest fear of all—that our technological capability for thermonuclear destruction will bring about an end to *Homo sapiens*. This point reminds us sharply of the interaction between technological development and man's biological career. A push of the thermonuclear button could suddenly end that special trail of biocultural evolution that started two or three million years ago with a seemingly innocuous precocity in tool-making.

Of course it is a kind of word play to think of machines and technical structures "controlling the lives" of men. Men build the machines and other technological projects, and decide about their maintenance, utilization, and control. And changes in social ideologies and political systems, too, have large effects on human culture history. The decline of the Roman Empire, the Great Crusades, and more recent events such as World War II and the Soviet–U.S. diplomatic confrontations cannot be considered simply reflexes of particular technological events. Rather they are historical developments arising from complex social, cultural, and ecological interactions. Recognizing the importance of technological factors in causing sociocultural change does not force one to espouse a complete technological determinism. Man's biocultural evolution is far too complicated a process to be subsumed under single-factor explanations.

The cases of technological innovation that we have put together in this volume are far from an exhaustive sampling of the "types" and situations of technological change. At this point, however, we feel that what is needed is careful, long-term study of selected technical developments in such a manner that useful predictive models can be generated. A major practical goal of such research is to produce information and analyses that could contribute to more intelligent policy-making about our technology.

The comments that we will offer here in summarizing our case studies are not intended as a theoretical model of general technological change. In order to stimulate such efforts we want to suggest some lines for future research effort, based on our study of these preliminary empirical materials.

LARGE-SCALE TECHNOLOGICAL MODIFICATION AND MICROTECHNOLOGY

The contrast between these two major categories of technological change seem to us very important. In the discussions about these materials during the symposium of the American Anthropological Association Meeting, San Diego, 1970, we noted that in the case of large-scale technological enterprises (dams, factories, new cities, and so on) there is constant reference to the "planners," the "government officials" and other agents who consciously put these construction projects in motion and direct their completion.

Our examples of microtechnological developments, on the other hand, involve the spread of consumer goods, usually through already established commercial channels. In these cases there are no "planners" or policy makers, although the cumulative effects of many individual consumer acquisitions may have consequences as far-reaching as those of a large-scale technical project.

Compared to the things and gadgets of "microtechnology," large-scale environmental modifications often involve the planned and unplanned reallocation of scarce local resources. Land space is required for the construction site, and in most cases there is a considerable impact on local water resources. In the case of dams (see Doughty; Scudder and Colson) the physical effects of the water barriers include the inundation of lands which were previously available for other purposes. In the case of a new community (e.g., Ciudad Industrial) the land space pre-empted from local populations may be smaller, but there are a number of other effects on local resources, not the least of which is the reallocation of large amounts of water to provide for the needs of the new urbanites.

Large-scale technological development often requires population movements. In the case of the Kariba Dam, people had to move to new lands, because their home territories were inundated. The new city of Ciudad

Industrial was made possible by shifting a sizable population to what was once a wide-open cactus-and-maguey-dominated tract.

Another common feature of this type of technological change is the creation of a new social system for maintaining the newly created facility. Dams, factories, and other such enterprises require systems of surveillance, repair, and continuing attention. Thus practically any large-scale technological creation brings with it a *new* social system, including a direct communications link to the (usually urban) center from which the development emanated. Another way of looking at this feature is to note that governmental and private commercial planners seldom leave their creations in the hands of local populations. They impose *themselves* directly and permanently on the local people in connection with their continuing use of the new facilities.

In the promulgation of large-scale projects there usually are important differences between governmental planners and private entrepreneurs. Commercial operators generally make their decisions largely in economic, monetary, terms. They seek profits and locate factories or other enterprises accordingly (e.g., Henderson, the sugar factory in British Honduras). Often, of course, the private entrepreneurs are constrained to some extent by the dictates or wishes of governmental agencies.

Governmental agencies, on the other hand, often pursue policies that are more complex than those of private commercial interests. Thus, the new city of Ciudad Industrial in Mexico (see Poggie) would probably have taken a somewhat different form (most likely in a quite different location) if it had been a private commercial development. The actions of the city and factory managers in aiding community development in surrounding rural towns (see pp. 32–34) are most readily explained as a reflection of the broader political policies of the Mexican government planners. Governmental programs have been known to locate enterprises in areas that involved distinct economic risks, because "noneconomic" factors play major roles in the policy decisions of states and nations.

Microtechnological developments *usually* involve commercially distributed *things* or gadgets that become the property of individual local people. There is thus a sense in which the local people appear to "have a choice" in the matter. In the case of snowmobiles (Pelto and Müller-Wille), the spread of the machines throughout various arctic populations is, in a sense, brought about by the accumulated individual decisions of the purchasers. Also, the "decision" to bring about the technological change cannot easily be charged to some distinct policy-making agency. In fact, no general decision is involved. Commercial operators try to maximize sales of their products, but they usually do not make a general decision in the form of, "Let's convert the winter transportation system of ———— (community) to snowmobiles."

The purchasers of the new vehicles make their individual decisions about owning and using snowmobiles for their personal purposes, but they do not foresee or intend the consequences which must inevitably follow if a large number of individuals in the community each makes the same decision.

Microtechnology, then, takes its character from a quite different pattern of decision making than that involved in the building of a dam or factory. The influence of the new technology spreads gradually, unplanned and undirected, and each subsequent development is a result of the trial-and-error adaptive decisions of numbers of people. The new technical device is tried out in new tasks ; new models are introduced ; problems are detected, and ad hoc decisions are made concerning each problem as it arises. In the case of the snowmobile, it did not take long to discover that large game (bears, deer, moose, elk) had little chance of escaping from the drivers. In Finland the bear population was very severely decimated in a single season before legislatures could act to make hunting from snow-mobiles illegal.

Because microtechnological items do not involve big construction projects in the affected communities, there is usually no direct effect on employment opportunities. In contrast, large-scale environmental modifi-cations by their very nature offer work opportunities for *somebody*, although the workers may be largely imported from other areas. In the case of Ciudad Industrial skilled labor was imported from the outside but less skilled labor was recruited locally, and over time there has continued to be some growth of economic opportunities brought about by the industrial complex. This, in fact, was one of the elements in the original policy decision, which was based on a need to improve economic con-ditions in the region.

Although both Ciudad Industrial and the sugar factory in British Hon-duras involved the creation of permanent wage-labor opportunities, many large-scale technologies (e.g., dams, highways, waterworks) require large numbers of workers only during the construction phase and very few afterward. Such a situation may result in the development of a semi-skilled and skilled work force that works itself into a state of unemploy-ment as the project is completed. In a situation where such a temporary work force occurs (e.g., the Peruvian dam project), some of the most important unanticipated consequences may involve the future activities of the work force. As Doughty notes, a not unlikely result is large waves of urban migration. There is also a strong possibility of some political ferment emerging from the thwarted expectations of the ex-workers. The skilled *agents provocateurs* in the world are probably already onto the idea that political agitation may be especially successful around nearly completed construction sites.

Large-scale technological projects usually attract considerable attention at the time they are in planning stages, hence they are somewhat more likely to be studied than are microtechnological developments. In fact, most small-scale material innovations are likely to be completely ignored by ethnographers. In those cases in which certain consumer goods are perceived to have had substantial cultural and social consequences, the realization of these effects usually comes too late to permit a full study of the sequences in the innovation.

Without attempting anything like a full inventory of microtechnologies worthy of study, some especially interesting items may be mentioned. There is a whole series of technical gadgets that are generally thought to reduce the burdens of housework for females. In Mexico, for example, the advent of electrically powered corn-grinding mills (run as small commercial enterprises) appears to have had a major impact on women's food preparation schedules (cf. Foster, 1967:52). Charles Keyes reports similar dramatic effects from the introduction of rice mills in the villages of north Thailand (personal communication). Bottled-gas stoves, blenders, sewing machines, washing machines (and laundromats), and refrigerators are but a small part of the new household technology that deserves careful study. The spread of modern power tools, including chain saws, acetylene torches, and other equipment in rural areas is also an unstudied but important facet of recent technological change.

Bernard and colleagues have made preliminary studies in Idaho that indicate the major role of technological innovations in changing the life styles and social patterning of people involved in the logging industry.

TECHNOLOGICAL CHANGE AND THE CASH ECONOMY

In all the cases in this book, and probably in the majority of situations involving technological change, the effect on the local population includes an increase in felt needs for cash incomes, usually accompanied by a corresponding erosion of the subsistence economy. In the macrotechnological cases the new experience with wage labor, some of it permanent, leads to an increased purchasing of consumer goods and an upward spiraling of cash hunger. Microtechnological items are in their nature consumer goods and require direct outlay of cash. Bicycles, radios, flashlights, lanterns, television sets, and the long list of other consumer items are among the things that young men have in mind when they migrate to temporary wage work in distant mines, mills, and towns; and they are the items that lure marginal agricultural producers to sell their small stores of grain for a bit of cash.

In some cases the rise in cash needs is startling. In the case of the snowmobile, the initial cost is many times the price of anything that most arctic people have ever had occasion to purchase, and the cost of maintenance and gasoline (see page 176) is staggering in comparison with the former state of the local economy. No wonder Lapp skeptics say, "Those machines are eating the reindeer."

Increased needs for cash have some predictable (and many unpredictable) further consequences. In most cases there will be some increased migration to places where cash can be earned in wage labor. In populations of any size it is a fair bet that there will be some rise in theft and other crimes, reflecting the fact that some members of the population find themselves unable to obtain the desired money through legal means. General increases in commercial activity, in the form of new stores and trading posts, new types of traveling vendors, and the innovation of new types of salable items are a usual result. Among the Lapps, for example, the need for more cash has led to small-scale vending of refreshments and other minor goods, sale of reindeer antlers and hides, and, especially, widespread hiring of snowmobile transportation for persons and goods. In fact, many snowmobile owners in Lapland would probably be unable to keep their machines if they did not sell transportation services to friends, neighbors, and "foreign" travelers.

The ramification of effects from a general "cashizing" of the economy has not been traced out in anything like the full detail that is needed for anthropological theory. Anecdotal accounts from various ethnographies make it clear that increased use of cash in traditional communities is often seen as a negative feature by anthropologists. For example, proliferation of money transactions is sometimes cited as a factor in the breakdown of extended kin ties and dependencies. The subject is hardly limited to cases of technological change, but it clearly deserves careful study as one of the major consequences of technological development.

TECHNOLOGICAL CHANGE AND SOCIAL STRATIFICATION

Practically every technological change results in the intrusion of some new *things* into a particular region, along with some shifts in social and economic relations. As already pointed out, the new technology may involve new wage-labor and other employment opportunities, as well as increases in the numbers of government administrators in the area. Secondary service occupations may develop, and usually there is an expansion of commercial activity, regardless of the type of technological change.

All such technical–economic additions can be looked at from one point of view as new exploitable resources. (This does not imply that the technical–economic additions are invariably "good for" the local people.

The changes may indeed be quite maladaptive from the over-all point of view, yet some important changes in exploitable resources still occur.) The questions may then be raised : Who is able to take advantage of the new opportunities? Who profits from the changes? And what are the effects on patterns of socioeconomic stratification?

In practically any region or population there are some individuals and groups who have a disproportionate share of scarce local resources, including political power. In some situations the "local elites" are only slightly better off than their neighbors (e.g., in relatively egalitarian communities). In many areas, however, there are privileged classes, castes, or other categories of persons who are set apart from the rest of the local population by their firm grip on land, animals, and other economic resources, as well as their control of political machinery.

Because they have the socioeconomic means to experiment with new opportunities, the people who *are already in positions of advantage* in the local socioeconomic hierarchy can be expected to take advantage of the newly introduced resources. In addition to possessing "risk capital" for exploiting new resources, they are often in favorable positions with regard to information sources. They are often more articulated to systems of communication.

Several of our cases in this volume involve some shifts in the patterning of socioeconomic stratification, and the tendencies evident in these cases suggest a hypothesis :

The direct and indirect economic and social effects of technological change will lead, in most cases, to increased socioeconomic stratification—that is, increases in inequalities of resource allocation within the local population and region.

A possible exception to this general tendency may be found to occur in cases in which the *pre*technological situation was already characterized by a rather great differential between high and low socioeconomic strata.

In the cases in this book, as in all situations of complex social change, it is difficult to separate "cause" and "effect." The introduction of new technology sets other changes in motion, and these in turn have widely ranging further effects. However, in a number of our cases here, the increase in social stratification is so marked and occurs in such widely different sociostructural situations that we feel "causality" can be provisionally identified.

The case of snowmobiles among arctic peoples is illustrative, although the exacerbation of socioeconomic stratification is not inevitable in all arctic populations. Among the Lapps, ownership of the snowmobiles is very costly, yet it confers economic advantages to those who can afford to own the vehicles. Trends now apparent in parts of Lapland suggest that an economically deprived class of families (without snowmobiles and without reindeer) is emerging as a result of the "snowmobile revolution." In the North American arctic, evidence of increases in social stratification brought about by snowmobiles has been reported by researchers in Pond Inlet and the Mackenzie Delta region (see pp. 187, 181). In these cases not all persons or families can afford to buy the machines, and their ownership confers significant economic advantages on those who *can* afford them. On the other hand, Peter Usher reports from very recent research on Banks Island in Canada that no such socioeconomic stratification appears imminent among the Eskimos there. The same general situation is reported for Noatak in Alaska by Edwin S. Hall. In both these cases it appears that levels of affluence are sufficiently high that *all* persons who desire the vehicles can afford to purchase and maintain them.

Among the effects of the new sugar factory in British Honduras, Henderson notes that those villagers who got into cane production at an early stage appear to have gained some economic advantages, and they tended to be people who were in an advantageous position before the advent of the sugar-cane industry in the area. The individuals who did not reach an economically viable level of cane production may be the first generation of a new "rural proletariat," working for wages for the cane growers and for the cane company. The result again is an increase in socioeconomic differentiation in local communities affected by the new technology.

Scudder and Colson describe the first stages of what appears to be the rise of a privileged group of producer-entrepreneurs in the Kariba Dam area. Once again the successful early innovators appear to be derived from an already established local elite (see Scudder and Colson, pp. 63–64). They are described as having had more education than their fellow villagers, and they were already experienced in dealing with government officials.

The massive urban migration that followed after the Huaylas Dam project in Peru probably obscured some of the effects on socioeconomic stratification, but we note (Doughty, pp. 118–20) that the people in the province of Huaylas gained much more economic advantage from the hydroelectric plant than did those of neighboring provinces. The situation seems to be one in which social differentiation, at least in part, took on a regional structure, rather than a marked intracommunity differentiation.

Bernard notes that the ups and downs in the sponge industry on Kalymnos can be absorbed in various ways by the moneyed boat owners. The lower-class divers, on the other hand, have little flexibility of adaptation, hence technological changes maintain and even accentuate the structure of inequality (Bernard, 1967).

Honigmann's description of new housing for Eskimos in northern Canada also supports the hypothesis that social stratification is increased by technological development. In this case the social differentials between owners of new houses versus those of relatively inferior houses seem to be most visible in people's life styles. The physical and economic character- istics of the modern homes encourage (perhaps even cause) changes in various aspects of life style. Child training, for example, tends to be different when there are clean floors and expensive fixtures to be main- tained. The social differentiation reflected in the new arctic houses follows lines of economic inequalities that were already present in these com- munities (e.g., differences among Eskimos, whites, Indians, and Metis, pp. 231–34).

Thus, in each of the cases in which socioeconomic differentiation is increased by the new technology, the effects seem to occur along lines that were already at least weakly present in the pretechnological social situation. That is, an incipient elite or economically advantaged category of local people is in a position to take early advantage of the new techno- logical situation. They are first to acquire the new machines, gadgets, or jobs. In the British Honduras and Kariba examples, they were the first to get into production of the new crops. Often these first-comers derive extra advantages from being first. Late-comers to the technological changes may experience serious disadvantages from a changed price and cost structure, as in the case of the cane growers.

Ciudad Industrial may be at least a partial exception to our generalization. Social stratification in the Los Llanos region involved marked socioeco- nomic inequalities in the days before the advent of the industrial city. The peasant farmers of the region are very poor, whereas the small number of merchants and *rancho* owners form an economically and socially privileged stratum of people with high prestige and a way of life that differs markedly from that of the *campesinos*. These social differences are, of course, a part of the legacy of the old prerevolutionary *hacienda* system, a legacy not entirely removed by the land reforms of the revolution.

In this pattern of socioeconomic stratification the new jobs and op- portunities of Ciudad Industrial appear to result in a development of a middle class of workers to fill partially the gap between the elite families and the peasants. Research on local conceptions of social prestige in the region makes it clear that the workers of the area occupy a middle range of prestige in the over-all hierarchy (Simon, 1968). The special features of policy in the industrial city, including the restrictions on commercial activity and tight control of housing, seem to have precluded the possibility that the local elite could gain large new socioeconomic advantages. The main gains in socioeconomic status have occurred among the workers, many of whom have been able to rise from a previously poverty-stricken agricultural way of life.

The situation in Ciudad Industrial appears to be quite special and unusual in many respects. Ordinarily one would expect that a class of manager- bureaucrats would become the new local elite. But the managers and bureaucrats of Ciudad Industrial find themselves so close to Mexico City (ca. 50 miles) that their social activities, as well as their principal residences, can be maintained in the city. They are outsiders to the Los Llanos region, and do not seem, therefore, to constitute a visible new elite in the local social system.

Charles Erasmus has reported an apparently similar trend in social stratification arising from technological developments (mainly in the form of extensive irrigation) in the Mayo-Yaqui area of northwestern Mexico. In place of the traditional dual society composed of a few rich elite families and many poor people, "a substantial middle class seemed to be growing up between the social extremes" (Erasmus, 1961 :183). Although this "filling in" of the middle of the social hierarchy is apparently quite noticeable in the towns and small cities of the area, rural populations, comprised mostly of Indians at the bottom of the socioeconomic ladder, may not be participating very much in this upward mobility. ". . . the most prosperous farmers are invariably townsmen . . . and are members of the highest class" (p. 186). Thus, technoeconomic development in the Sonora region may, in fact, be widening the gulf between rural Indians and the Spanish-speaking townsmen, even though a much enlarged and mobile middle class is also resulting from the greatly increased resources of the area.

The dramatic social effects of large-scale technology in the Valle de Bravo region (west of Mexico City) represents an extreme case. There the construction of a hydroelectric dam created an impressively beautiful resort area which has attracted rich people from Mexico City to build costly homes in the area. Thus, a new category of very wealthy elite has appeared on the scene, for whom the not particularly prosperous local Indians and mestizos serve as construction workers, repairmen, and domestic servants. Certainly in this case there has been an augmenting of locally relevant social inequalities.

In general, anthropologists have seriously neglected the study of social stratification. Interesting and theoretically important studies (e.g., by Sahlins, 1958 ; Plotnicov and Tuden, 1970 ; Fried, 1967) are among the relatively rare exceptions to this tendency. Much work needs to be done on the general study of social inequalities and their institutionalized patterning. The cases of technological change we have looked at here suggest that social stratification is a crucial element in understanding the processes of local adaptation to introduced technological features.

TECHNOLOGICAL CHANGE AND MICROCOSM– MACROCOSM ARTICULATION

A major consequence of almost all technological changes in rural areas is a great increase in articulation to the "world out there." The case of the

Bikinians is the extreme example; every technological and social change in their situation has put them further down the road toward a social-welfare-like dependence on the American technological–cultural order that controls their lives.

The case of the Kalymnos sponge divers also illustrates an ever-increasing economic articulation that comes with technological change. Oscillations in the technosocial patterning of sponge fishing reflect a continuing tightening of the linkages between the local scene and distant parts of the world. New technical developments among Florida and California skin divers ; fluctuations in the London sponge market ; and modifications in (e.g., West German) synthetic sponge production are only the more obvious of the many events of the wider world that have quick reverberations in Kalymnos.

Many of the causes of the increased dependencies are obvious. Gasoline motors and other fossil-fuel-propelled vehicles and motors require the establishment of regular supply services. In the Far North, for example, the commercial activities of organizations such as the Hudson's Bay Company become more and more crucial as outboard motors, chain saws, snow-mobiles, rough-land motorcycles, and other motor-driven devices are accepted as essential equipment by arctic and subarctic peoples. The employment opportunities created by factories, new cities, and hydro-electric systems bring people into closer articulation not only to govern-mental agencies but with labor organizations and other specialized associations of the world community.

Manning Nash, in his *Machine Age Maya* (1958), has described the coming of labor unions and political party influence to the Guatemala Indian community of Cantel, where a textile plant had been established. The same kinds of political party activity and labor organization extensions are manifested in Ciudad Industrial in Mexico, and in the new city of Ciudad Guayana in Venezuela (Peattie, 1968). Similar extensions of union activities, national cooperative organizations, and other elements of macrocosm social organization are also visible in the case of the sugar factory described by Henderson.

The unusual situation of Mauritius deserves special attention. In this case the island population's entire technological and social history is a chronicle of the various contacts from the wider world. The population crisis that has developed there in recent years is a reflex of the "eliminate malaria" campaign made possible by the powerful effectiveness of DDT, an American technological spin-off of World War II. Although the people and politicians of Mauritius are fully aware of the crisis their population explosion has created, the introduction of population-control technology is to a considerable extent caused by influences from thousands of miles away, especially organizations such as the International Planned Parenthood Federation. The solution that individuals and families in Mauritius will seek in their struggle for survival will surely involve large-scale migration to other parts of the world, thus increasing their interconnectedness with the rest of our "world-island."

Migration to other regions, especially to urban centers, is one of the main side effects of technological development and change. Whether it is because of new needs for cash; new aspirations for regular wage work developed during temporary employment on dams, bridges, or other constructions; or displacement caused by the inundation of homelands, the resulting city-ward migrations provide another strand in the ever-increasing articulation to the wider macrocosm. Many individuals shuttle back and forth between city and homelands, in response to job opportunities and also in response to social needs and patterns in home villages. Urbanizing workers return home for major fiestas or life-cycle rituals; they send gifts, money, and information to those who have remained at home; and they often persuade their younger brothers and sisters, or perhaps the whole family, to join them in the metropolis. It should be apparent that such increases in city-rural contacts through labor migration in turn causes further technical changes to be introduced in the home regions, along with all the other social, cultural, and psychological effects.

TECHNOLOGICAL CHANGES AND THE PHYSICAL ENVIRONMENT

Several of the cases in this volume involved extensive changes in the physical environment resulting from technological innovations. The Kariba Dam example is particularly instructive. Stopping a flow of water to create a large artificial lake obviously has a powerful effect on the environment. But Scudder and Colson point out that the effects on the environment have included many totally unforeseen problems, the most striking of which is probably the changed patterns of tsetse fly infestation. Changes in precipitation, vegetation, animal populations, and human settlement patterns all have a marked impact on subsistence patterns, health problems, and other features of human adaptation.

In the case of the new sugar factory in British Honduras, the technological construction did not itself directly "cause" changes in land use and ownership patterns. However, the new possibility for sugar-cane production was seized on by the government and local people as a justification for land reallocation and a large shift in land-use patterns which will, in turn, have powerful effects on flora and fauna as well as other features of the environment.

We do not have to travel to the Arctic to see the environmental impact of snowmobiles. Throughout the northern tier of the United States, as well as in Canada's populated regions, the advent of snowmobiling has had serious (usually detrimental) effects on the environment. Vegetation is mowed down, game animals are overhunted (legally and illegally), new kinds of roads and trails are created, and patterns of human use of backlands have changed markedly because of snowmobiles. Legislatures in the affected areas have had to enact complex new regulations in an attempt to stem the ecological impact of the machines. Previously inaccessible lakes are being exploited ; previously unreachable and rare animal populations (e.g., the few remaining wild horses in Montana) are made vulnerable ; and an entirely new kind of contamination, noise pollution, will bring about unknown effects on the health and behavior of the animals and humans of arctic and other northern wilderness areas.

Until very recently the ecological effects of technological change have been very little studied by anthropologists or anyone else. The rapid increase of interest in the study of environments, fueled by our concern about environmental deterioration, should produce a growth of interest in such research. Plant and animal ecologists (including geographers) have the most knowledge and technical skill for identifying and measuring changes in biological environments, but all of the situations of technological change examined in this volume point to the complexities of social and cultural factors that influence patterns of reaction to technology; in the untangling of these complexities, anthropologists should have an important role to play. The contribution of anthropological research to such environmental studies will, we feel, be more successful if we focus much more attention than heretofore on the technological features of general sociocutural and economic changes.

Our very preliminary survey has convinced us that much needs to be done if we are to develop useful guidelines for understanding the role of technological developments in rural regions. We would go so far as to say that the penetration of modern technology into traditional rural communities is the largest single factor accounting for the pace of sociocultural change in most parts of the nonindustrialized world.

If anthropologists are to make significant contributions to the study of technological processes, a very considerable increase in methodological rigor is necessary. Statements about costs and profits, changes in time allocations, and choices among alternative actions require careful quantification of data. As our awareness of complex secondary effects develops, we must be prepared to follow the reverberations of particular technological innovations into diverse and complex realms, and with greater time depth. It will require long-term studies to do justice to the complexities of technological effects. Scudder and Colson's years of work in the Kariba Dam area provide a model that should be more widely emulated.

Although the collection of carefully defined numerical data is essential for the study of some facets of technological development, such statistical work is far from providing an adequate basis for understanding the interactions between technological and social processes. Carefully descriptive work is needed to provide the "contextualization" for assessing the relationships of technical developments to other aspects of culture and society. To throw light on the human side of technological change, especially from the perspective of the people affected by such changes, we must study the cognitive, "ethnotechnological," and psychological dimensions of individual projects and products. Too frequently it appears that technological studies have been concerned with profit-and-loss economics and "modernization" from the outsider's point of view, rather than with the interpretations used by the affected populations to define their situations and formulate adaptive strategies. It has been the special concern of anthropologists to explore that "actor's point of view" in situations of sociocultural change. This perspective, if used in judicious combination with effective quantitative observations, can add the vital humanistic dimension to technological studies.

It is possible that anthropologists have shied away from studies of technological development because of a fear that such research, in its concern with technical and material things, would be "dehumanizing." And a study of technological processes that is concerned only with technical and economic effects would indeed fall very short of the kind of integrative and holistic study that we need in order to gain perspective on man's environmental crisis.

René Dubos, in *So Human an Animal*, expressed this need for a broader perspective when he wrote, "We may hope eventually to develop techniques for predicting or recognizing early the objectionable consequences of social and technological innovations so as to minimize their effects, but this kind of piecemeal social engineering will be no substitute for a philosophy of the whole environment, formulated in the light of human aspirations and needs" (Dubos, p. 237).

BIBLIOGRAPHY

Agapitides, S.
1950   La population du Dodecanese. *Bulletin de l'Institut International de Statistique*, No. 2, XXXII:412–20.

Anderson, D. E.
1918   *The epidemics of Mauritius*. London: H. K. Lewis.

Aronson, S. H.
1952   The sociology of the bicycle. *Social Forces*, 30:305–12.

Barnwell, P. J., and A. Toussaint
1949   *A short history of Mauritius*. London: Longmans Green.

Barth, F.
1967   On the study of social change. *American Anthropologist*, 69:661–69.

Beejadhur, A.
1935   *Les indiens à l'île Maurice*. Port Louis: La Typographie Moderne.

Benedict, B.
1957   Factionalism in Mauritian villages. *The British Journal of Sociology*, No. 4, VIII:December.
1958a Education without opportunity. *Human Relations*, No. 4, XI.
1958b Cash and credit in Mauritius. *The South African Journal of Economics*, No. 3, 26:September.
1961a *Indians in a plural society*. London: H.M.S.O.
1961b Mauritius at the crossroads. *The British Journal of Sociology*, No. 4, XXI:December.
1962   Stratification in plural societies. *American Anthropologist*, No. 6, 64:December.
1965   *Mauritius: problems of a plural society*. London: Pall Mall.
1967   Caste in Mauritius. In *Caste in overseas indian communities*, B. M. Schwartz, ed. San Francisco: Chandler.
1970a Pluralism and stratification. In *Essays in comparative social stratification*, L. Plotnicov and A. Tuden, eds. Pittsburgh: University of Pittsburgh Press.
1970b Population regulation in primitive societies. In *Population control*, A. Allison, ed. London: Penguin Books.

Bernard, H. R.
1965   Greek sponge boats in Florida. *Anthropological Quarterly*, April, 1965.
1967   Kalymnian sponge diving. *Human Biology*, May, 1967.
1967   Economic innovation and cultural conservatism. *Paper at AAA meeting* Washington, D.C.
1968   Kalymnos: economic and social change on a Greek sponge fishing island. Unpublished Ph.D. dissertation. Ann Arbor, University Microfilm.

333

Billiard, A.
1822   *Voyage aux colonies orientales*. Paris: La Librarie Française de l'avocat.

Blair, C. P.
1964   Nacional financiera: entrepreneurship in a mixed economy. In *Public policy and private enterprise in Mexico*, Raymond Vernon, ed. Cambridge, Mass.: Harvard University Press.

Bradfield, S.
1963   Migration from Huaylas: a study of brothers. Unpublished Ph.D. dissertation, Cornell University, 51ff.

British Naval Intelligence
1944   Dodecanese handbook, A.M.P.O. London

Brookfield, H. C.
1957   Mauritius: demographic upsurge and prospect. *Population Studies*, No. 2, XI: November.
1959   Population distribution in Mauritius. *The Journal of Tropical Geography*. 13: December.

Brouard, N. R.
1965   Population and family planning in Mauritius: a historical review. In *Family planning review, 1957–1965*. Port Louis: Standard Printing.

Campbell, J. K.
1968   *Modern Greece*. New York: Praeger.

Caverhill, W.
1969   New housing for northern Indians. *North 16* (Nov.–Dec.), 8–12.

Clark, C. C.
1969   Problems of communication in rural Africa. *Canadian Journal of African Studies*, 3: 223–31.

Colson, E.
1960   *Social organization of the Gwembe Tonga*. Manchester: Manchester University Press for the Rhodes–Livingstone Institute.
1962   Trade and wealth among the Tonga. In *Markets in Africa*, P. Bohannan and G. Dalton, eds. Evanston, Ill.: Northwestern University Press, 601–16.
1963   Land rights and land use among the Valley Tonga of the Rhodesian Federation: the background to the Kariba resettlement program. In *African agrarian systems*, D. Biebuyck, ed. New York: Oxford University Press, for the International African Institute, 137–56.
1964   Social change and the Gwembe Tonga. *Human Problems in Central Africa*, No. 36:1–10.
1966   Land law and land holdings among the Valley Tonga of Zambia. *Southwestern Journal of Anthropology*, No. 1, 22:1–8.

Coulter, G. W.
1967   What's happening at Kariba? *New Scientist*, December 28.

Damas, D.
n.d.   Taped interview in 1968 (see acknowledgment).

Davenport, W.
1960   Marshall Islands Navigational Charts. *Imago Mundi*, Bobbs-Merrill Reprint Series in the Social Sciences, XV: 4–48.

Dodecanesian National Council
1943   *The Dodecanese Islands*. New York: The Dodecanesian National Council.

Doob, L. W.
1960 Becoming more civilized: a psychological exploration. New Haven: Yale University Press.

Doughty, P. L.
1968 *Huaylas: an Andean district in search of progress.* Ithaca: Cornell University Press.

Dowling, M. A. C.
1953 The malaria eradication experiment in Mauritius, 1948–1952. Final Report by the Officer in Charge. Port Louis. Mimeo.

Drucker, P.
1950 The ex-Bikini occupants of Kili Island. Pearl Harbor. Typescript.

Dubos, R.
1965 *Man adapting.* New Haven: Yale University Press.
1968 *So Human an Animal.* New York: Scribner.

Eisner, T., A. van Tienhoven, and F. Rosenblatt
1970 Population control, sterilization, and ignorance. *Science,* No. 3917, 167: January 23.

Erasmus, Charles
1961 *Man takes control.* Minneapolis: University of Minnesota Press.

Ervin, A. M.
1968 *New northern townsmen in Inuvik.* Ottawa: Mackenzie Delta Research Project, Northern Science Research Group, Department of Indian Affairs and Northern Development, Publication MDRP 5.

Fagan, B.
1967 The Iron Age People of Zambia and Malawi. In *Background to African evolution,* W. W. Bishop and J. Desmond Clark, eds. Chicago: University of Chicago Press, 659–86.

Fallers, L. A.
1955 The predicament of the modern African chief: an instance from Uganda. *American Anthropologist,* 57:290–305.
1959 Despotism, status culture and social mobility in an African kingdom. *Comparative Studies in Society and History,* 2:11–32.
1961 Ideology and culture in Uganda nationalism. *American Anthropologist,* 63:677–86.

Fallers, M. C.
1960 *The Eastern Lacustrine Bantu* (Ganda, Soga). London: International African Institute.

Fishel, J.
1964 The brave experiment. Honors Thesis. Bloomington: University of Indiana.

Foster, George M.
1967 *Tzintzuntzan.* Boston: Little, Brown.
1969 *Applied anthropology.* Boston: Little, Brown.

Francis, K. E.
1969 Decline of the dogsled in villages of arctic Alaska: a preliminary discussion. *Yearbook of the Association of Pacific Coast Geographers,* Vol. 31:69–78.

Freeman, M.
n.d. Taped interview in 1968.

Fried, Morton
1967 *The evolution of political society.* New York: Random House.

Friedl, E.
1959   Dowry and inheritance in modern Greece. *Transactions of the New York Academy of Sciences*, XXII, ser. 2.

Gans, H. J.
1967   *The Levittowners*. New York: Pantheon Books.

Gay, J., and M. Cole
1967   *The new mathematics and an old culture: a study of learning among the Kpelle of Liberia*. New York: Holt, Rinehart and Winston.

Gerlach, L. P.
1963   Traders on bicycles: a study of entrepreneurship and culture change among the Digo and Duruma of Kenya. *Sociologus*, 13:32–49.

Gold, G. L.
1968   Commercial elaboration and development in a region of Mexico. In *Social and cultural aspects of modernization in Mexico*, Frank C. Miller and Pertti J. Pelto, eds. Mimeo. Minneapolis: University of Minnesota.

Government Bulletins
1961   Boletín de estadística Peruana. Perú Ministerio de Hacienda y Comercio, Dirección Nacional de Estadística y Censos. No. 5, IV:778.

Government Reports
1958   Report of the commission appointed to inquire into the circumstances leading up to and surrounding the recent deaths and injuries caused by the use of firearms in the Gwembe District and matters relating thereto. Lusakan Government Printer.
1965   Cotton growing in Zambia. Department of Agriculture. Lusaka.

Graburn, N. H. H.
1969   *Eskimos without igloos*. Boston: Little, Brown.

Graves, T. D., N. B. Graves, and M. J. Kobrin
1969   Historical inferences from Guttman Scales: the return of age-area magic? *Current Anthropology*, 10:317–27.

Guemple, L.
n.d.   Taped interview in 1968.

Guy, T. and M.
1968   *Île Maurice: régulation des naissances et action familiale*. Lyon: X. Mappus.

Hall, Edwin S.
n.d.   Tape-recorded interview concerning the introduction of snowmobiles in Noatak, Alaska.

Harlow, H. F.
1953   Mice, monkeys, men and motives. *Psychological Review* 60:23–32.

Hickerson, H.
n.d.   *A survey of the villages of British Honduras: the northern Maya area*. Unpublished manuscript.

Hill, R.
n.d.   Taped interview in 1968.

Hines, N. O.
1962   *Proving grounds; an account of the radiobiological studies in the Pacific, 1946–1961*. Seattle: University of Washington Press.

Honigmann, J. J., and I.
1965   *Eskimo townsmen*. Ottawa: Canadian Research Centre for Anthropology. University of St. Paul.
In Press   *Arctic Town*.

Housing Survey, District of Mackenzie, Inuvik Region
1966 Fort Smith, Industrial Division, Northern Housing Section, Department of Indian Affairs and Northern Development.

Hunt, J. McV.
1965 Intrinsic motivation and its role in psychological development. In *Nebraska symposium on motivation*, D. Levine, ed. Lincoln: University of Nebraska Press.

Inkeles, A.
1967 Becoming modern. Paper presented at Michigan State University.

Jones, G. D.
1969a Los Caneros: sociopolitical aspects of the history of agriculture in the Corozal region of British Honduras. Ph.D. dissertation, Brandeis University. Ann Arbor, University Microfilms.
1969b Sociopolitical adaptations to sugar cane production: comparative implications. Paper presented at the 68th Annual Meeting of the American Anthropological Association, New Orleans, 1969. Unpublished ms.

Kahl, J.
1959 Some social concomitants of industrialization and urbanization. *Human Organization*, 18:53–74.
1968 *The measurement of modernism*. Austin: University of Texas Press.

Kasperson, R. E.
1966 *The Dodecanese: diversity and unity in island politics*. Chicago: The University of Chicago Press.

Kerr, G. B.
1969 Selected bibliography in communication. *Canadian Journal of African Studies*, 3:248–56.

Kilbride, P. I.
1968 Perceptual abilities and acculturation among rural Baganda. Paper presented at the Meeting of the American Anthropological Association, Seattle, Washington. Mimeo.

Kilbride, P. I., and M. C. Robbins
1968 Linear perspective, pictorial depth, perception and education among the Baganda. *Perceptual and Motor Skills*, 27:601–602.
1969 Pictorial depth perception and acculturation among the Baganda. *American Anthropologist*, 71:293–301.
1968 with R. B. Freeman, Jr. Pictorial depth perception and education among Baganda school children. *Perceptual and Motor Skills*, 26:1116–18.

Kiste, R. C.
1967 Changing patterns of land tenure and social organization among the ex-Bikini Marshallese. Unpublished Ph.D. dissertation, University of Oregon.
1968 Kili Island: a study of the relocation of the ex-Bikini Marshallese. Department of Anthropology, University of Oregon.

Koundouris, E.
1970 *Study of sponge fishing on Kalymnos* (in Greek). Kalymnos, privately printed.

Kramer, A., and H. Nevermann
1938 Ralik-Ratak (Marhsall-Insein). In *Ergebindisse der Sudsee Expedition 1908–1910*, G. Thilenius, ed. Hamburg: Friederichsen, de Gruyter and Co.

Kuczynski, R. R.
1949 *A demographic survey of the British colonial empire*. Volume II, South Africa

High Commission Territories, East Africa, Mauritius, Seychelles. London:
Oxford University Press.

Leysne, H. W.
1952   Food for Kili. Micronesian Monthly Trust Territory of the Pacific Islands.

Lotz, J. R.
1962   Inuvik, N. W. T., a study of community planning problems in a new northern
town. Ottawa: Industrial Division, Department of Indian Affairs and
Northern Development. Mimeo.

Luce, R. W.
1958   Report to the government of Mauritius on employment, unemployment, and
unemployment in the colony in 1958. Port Louis: Mauritius Legislative
Council, Sessional Paper No. 7 of 1958.
1958   The Luce report: a time for decision. Port Louis: Mauritius Legislative
Council, Sessional Paper No. 8 of 1958.

McClelland, D.
1961   *The achieving society.* New York: D. Van Nostrand, 399–400.

McElroy, Ann
1968   The effects of urbanization on Eskimo child life and personality. *Working
Paper No. 2, Urbanisation in the Arctic and Subarctic.* Chapel Hill, N. C.:
Institute for Research in Social Science.

Mafeje, A.
1969   Large-scale farming in Buganda. In *The anthropology of development in
Sub-Sahara Africa*, D. Brokensha and M. Pearsall, eds. Monograph No. 10,
The Society for Applied Anthropology.

Manners, R. A., and J. H. Steward
1953   The cultural study of contemporary societies: Puerto Rico. *American Journal
of Sociology*, 59, 2:123–30.

Mansoor, I. M.
1965   A social evil. In *Family planning review, 1957–1965*. Port Louis: Standard
Printing.

Markwith, C.
1946   Farewell to Bikini. *National Geographic Magazine*, 90:97–116.

Martinez, G. M.
1966   La hačienda y el ejido en Teotihuacan y su contorno. Paper read at the XI
Mesa Redonda de Antropología, Sección de Etnología y Antropología
Social, México, D.F.

Mason, L.
1950   The Bikinians: a transplanted population. *Human Organization*, 9:5–15.
1954   Relocation of the Bikini Marshallese: a study in group migration. Unpublished Ph.D. dissertation, Yale University.
1958   Kili community in transition. *South Pacific Quarterly Bulletin*, April.

Mauritius
1955   Report of the committee on population, 1953–54. Port Louis: Mauritius
Legislative Council, Sessional Paper No. 4 of 1955.
1956   Natality and fertility in Mauritius, 1825–1955. Central Statistical Office.
Mimeo.

Mauritius General Election
1967   Commonwealth No. 3. London: H.M.S.O.

Mauritius Reports
1965 Report for the year 1963. London: H.M.S.O.
1968 Report for the year 1966. London: H.M.S.O.
1970 Report for the year 1967. London: H.M.S.O.

Mauritius Slave Trade: Minutes of Evidence
1826 B.P.P. 90, Feb. 17, 1827.

Mead, Margaret
1956 *New Lives for Old*. New York: W. W. Norton.

Meade, J. E., and others
1961 *The economic and social structure of Mauritius*. London: Methuen.

Meade, Lt. H. C.
1946 Operation Crossroads: resettlement of Bikini population. Report on Administration of Military Government for the Month of March, by the Island
Commander, Kwajalein, to Commander Marianas.

Micronitor
1970 Marshall Islands Weekly Newspaper, Majuro, Marshall Islands, Vol. 1,
No. 32, April 18.

Milbert, M. J.
1812 *Voyage pittoresque à l'Île de France*. Paris: A. Nepveu.

Miller, N. N.
1969 Current research in rural sociology and communications. *Canadian Journal
of African Studies*, 3:237–39.

Mintz, S.
1956 Canamelar: the subculture of a rural sugar plantation proletariat. In *People
of Puerto Rico*, J. H. Steward et al. Urbana: University of Illinois Press,
314–417.
1959 The plantation as a sociocultural type. In *Plantation systems of the new
world*. Washington, D.C.: Pan American Union.

Mintz, S., and E. R. Wolf
1957 Haciendas and plantations in Middle America and the Antilles. *Social and
Economic Studies*, 6:380–412.

Moore, W. E.
1963 *Social change*. Englewood Cliffs, N.J.: Prentice-Hall.

Moyer, B. S.
n.d. Taped interview in 1970.
1970 Wage labor and ski-doos. Paper presented at the Tenth Annual Meeting of
the Northeastern Anthropological Association, Ottawa.

Müller-Wille, L.
1970 Snowmobiles: technological change in the Arctic. Paper presented in the
Seminar für Völkerkunde (University of Münster).

Müller-Wille, L., and P. J. Pelto
1971 Technological change and its impact in arctic regions: Lapps introduce
snowmobiles into reindeer herding. *Polarforschung* (W. Germany), 41.

Mumford, L.
1934 *Technics and civilization*. New York: Harcourt Brace.

Mundale, C.
n.d. Personal communication.

Myres, L.
1944   See British Naval Intelligence.

Nag, M.
1962   Factors affecting human fertility in nonindustrial societies: a cross-cultural study. New Haven: Department of Anthropology, Yale.

Nash, M.
1958   Machine age Maya: the industrialization of a Guatemalan community. Memoir No. 87. American Anthropological Association, Vol. 60, No. 2, Part 2.

No author
1964   Censo general de población VIII, México, D.F. Secretaría de Industria y Comercio, Dirección General de Estadística.

Peattie, L. R.
1968   *The view from the barrio*. Ann Arbor: The University of Michigan Press.

Pelto, P. J.
1962   Individualism in Skolt Lapp society. Suomenmuinaismuistoyhdistys Kansatieteellinen Arkisto Monograph 16. Helsinki, Finland.
1966   Adaptation to cultural stress: suggestions for research. Paper presented at symposium on the Inter-Relation of Biological and Cultural Adaptation. Burg Warternstein: Austria. Ditto.

Pelto, P. J., M. Linkola, and P. Sammallahti
1968   The snowmobile revolution in Lapland. *Journal of the Finno-Ugric Society*, 69:1–42.

Perlman, M. L.
1970   The traditional systems of stratification among the Ganda and Nyoro of Uganda. In *Social Stratification in Africa*, A. Tuden and L. Plotnicov, eds. New York: Macmillan.

Philips, R. A. J.
1967   *Canada's North*. New York: St. Martin's Press.

Pike, N.
1873   *Sub-tropical rambles in the land of the Aphanaptery*. London: Sampson Low, Marston, Low and Searle.

Plotnicov, Leonard, and Arthur Tuden
1970   *Essays in comparative social stratification*. Pittsburgh: University of Pittsburgh Press.

Poggie, J. J., Jr.
1968   The impact of industrialization on a Mexican intervillage network. Ph.D. dissertation. University of Minnesota.
1969   and Frank C. Miller. Contact change and industrialization in a network of of Mexican villages. *Human Organization*, Fall 9969, No. 3, 28:190–98.

Prentice
1963   Cotton growing in Northern Rhodesia. *Empire Cotton Growers Review*.

Prentout, H.
1901   L'Île de France sous Decaen. Paris: Hachette.

Provins, K. A., C. R. Bell, S. Biesheuvel, and W. T. V. Adiseshiah
1968   The cross-cultural measurement of perceptual and motor skills in relation to human adaptation. *Human Biology*, 40:484–93.

Rapaport, A.
1969   House form and culture. Englewood Cliffs, N.J.: Prentice-Hall.

Reina, R.
1967 Milpas and milperos: implications for prehistoric times. *American Anthropologist*, 69:1–20.

Richard D. E.
1957 United States Naval Administration of the Trust Territory of the Pacific Islands. Washington, D.C.: U.S. Government Printing Office.

Richards, A. I.
1966 The changing structure of a Ganda village: Kisozi 1892–1952. East African Studies No. 24. Makerere Institute of Social Research. Kampala, Uganda.

Riesenberg, S. H.
1954 Report on visit to Kili. Trust Territory of the Pacific Islands. Office of the High Commissioner. Typescript.

Robbins, M. C., and R. B. Pollnac
1969 Drinking patterns and acculturation in rural Buganda. *American Anthropologist*, 71:276–85.

Robbins, M. C., A. V. Williams, P. L. Kilbride, and R. B. Pollnac
1969 Factor analysis and case selection in complex societies: a Buganda example. *Human Organization*, 28:227–34.

Roberts, G. W.
1954 Some aspects of mating and fertility in the West Indies. Population Studies, Vol. 8.

Robertson, R. G.
1967 The coming crisis in the north. *North*, No. 2, 14:44–53.

Rodgers, W. B.
1967 Household atomism and change in the out Island Bahamas. *Southwestern Journal of Anthropology*, 23:244–60.

Rogers, E. M.
1962 *Diffusion of innovations*. New York: The Free Press.
1969 *Modernization among peasants: the impact of cummunication*. New York: Holt, Rinehart and Winston.

Romney, D. H. (ed.)
1959 Land in British Honduras: a report of the British Honduras land use survey team. London: H.M.S.O. Colonial Research Publications No. 24.

Roscoe, J.
1911 *The Baganda*. London: Frank Cass and Co., Ltd.

Sahlins, Marshall
1958 *Social stratification in Polynesia*. Seattle: University of Washington Press.

Sammallahti, P.
1969 Moottorikilkan taloudelliset ja sosiaaliset vaikutukset. *Lapinkansa*, daily newspaper of Rovaniemi, Finland. July 2.

Schiller, R.
1968 Snowmobiles: the cats that conquered winter, *Reader's Digest*, 90:49–54.

Scudder, Thayer
1960 Fishermen of the Zambezi. *Human Problems in Central Africa*, No. 27:41–49.
1962 *The ecology of the Gwembe Tonga*. Manchester University Press for the Rhodes-Livingstone Institute.
1965 The Kariba case: man-made lakes and resource development in Africa. *Bulletin of the Atomic Scientist*, December:6–11.

1966 Man-made lakes and population in Africa. In *Man-Made Lakes*, R. Lowe-McConnell, ed. New York: Academic Press, on behalf of the Institute of Biology.

1966 Man-made lakes and social change. *Engineering and Science*. No. 6, XXIX: 18–22.

1968 with D. Brokensha. Resettlement. In *Dams in Africa*, N. Rubin and W. M. Warren, eds. Frank Cass and Co, 20–62.

1968 Social anthropology, man-made lakes and population relocation in Africa. *Anthropological Quarterly*, No. 3, 41:168–176.

1969 Relocation, agricultural intensification, and anthropological research. In *The anthropology of development in Sub-Saharan Africa*, D. Brokensha and M. Pearsall, eds. The Society for Applied Anthropology, Monograph No. 10, 31–39.

In Press Ecology and development: the Kariba Lake Basin. In *The careless Technology: Ecology and International development*, M. T. Farvar and J. Milton, eds. New York: Natural History Press.

Shear, T. L.
1941 The Greek Dodecanese. In *Greece: 1821–1941*. New York: American Friends of Greece. Reprinted by Dodecanesian National Council.

Siegel, S.
1956 *Nonparametric statistics for the behavioral sciences*. New York: McGraw-Hill.

Simon, B.
1968 Social stratification in a modern Mexican community. Paper read at the 1968 Annual Meeting of the Central States Anthropological Society in Detroit, Michigan.

Simpson, E. N.
1937 *The ejido, Mexico's way out*. Chapel Hill: University of North Carolina Press.

Smith, D.
n.d. Tape-recorded interview, 1970.

Smith, L.
n. d. Tape-recorded interview, 1970.
1970 The mechanical dog team: the ski-doo in the Canadian arctic. Paper presented at the Tenth Annual Meeting of the Northeastern Anthropological Association, Ottawa.

Smith, R. F.
1969 Comments on the use of pesticides in California. Statement prepared for presentation to the California Senate Agriculture Committee, June 19.

Social Benefit Programs for Residents of the Northwest Territories
1967 Sessional Paper No. 8, 1963. Council of the Northwest Territories, Debates, 34th Session, March 6–April 10, 1967. Three volumes. Ottawa: Commissioner of the Northwest Territories.

Southwold, M.
1965 The Ganda of Uganda. In *Peoples of Africa*, J. L. Gibbs, ed. New York: Holt, Rinehart and Winston.

Spier, R. F. G.
1968 Technology and material culture. In *Introduction to cultural anthropology*, J. A. Clifton, ed. Boston: Houghton Mifflin.

Stevenson, D.
n.d.   Tape-recorded interview, 1970.

St. Pierre, J. H. B.
1800   *A voyage to the Isle of France.* London: Vernor and Hood.

Thompson, C. T.
1969   *Patterns of housekeeping in two Eskimo settlements.* Ottawa: Northern Science Research Group, Department of Indian Affairs and Northern Development. Publication NSRG 69–1.

Titmuss, R. M., and B. Abel Smith
1961   *Social policies and population growth in Mauritius.* London: Methuen.

Tobin, J. E.
1953   The Bikini people, past and present. Majuro: Marshall Islands. Mimeo.
1954   *Kili Journal.* Majuro: Marshall Islands. Mimeo.

Toussaint, A.
1954   *Early American trade with Mauritius.* Port Louis: Esclapon.

Usher, P.
1966   Banks Island: an area economic survey, 1965. Report of the Department of Indian Affairs and Northern Development. Reprinted in 1968.
n.d.   Tape-recorded interview, 1968.
n.d.   Tape-recorded interview, 1970.
1970   The use of snowmobiles for trapping on Banks Island, N.W.T., Paper presented at the symposium on Technology and Social Change, AAA meeting, San Diego.

Wagley, C., and M. Harris
1955   A typology of Latin American subcultures. *American Anthropologist*, 57: 428–51.

Wallace, A. F. C.
1958   Study of processes of organization and revitalization of psychological and sociocultural systems. In *American Philosophical Society Yearbook*, 1957. Philadelphia: American Philosophical Society.
1961   *Culture and personality.* New York: Random House.

Wambaugh, S.
1943   The Dodecanese Islands. In *Greece of tomorrow.* New York: American Friends of Greece. Reprinted by Dodecanesian National Council.

White, R. W.
1959   Motivation reconsidered: the concept of competence. *Psychological Review*, 66:297–33.

Whiteford, A. A.
1964   *Two cities of Latin America: a comparative description of social classes.* Garden City, N.Y.: Doubleday.

Wiens, H. J.
1962   *Atoll environment and ecology.* New Haven: Yale University Press.

Wilson, G., and M.
1945   *The analysis of social change.* London: Cambridge University Press.

Winkler, Captain
1899   On sea charts formerly used in the Marshall Islands, with notes on the navigation of these islands in general. Washington, D.C.: Smithsonian Annual Report.

Wolf, E. R.
1959   Specific aspects of plantation systems in the New World: community sub-cultures and social class. In *Plantations systems of the new world*. Washington, D.C.: Pan American Union.

Yatsushiro, T.
1963   *Frobisher Bay 1958*. Ottawa: Northern Science Research Group, Department of Indian Affairs and northern Development. Publication 63-6.

Young, F. W.
1964   Location and reputation in a Mexican intervillage network. *Human Organization*, 23:36–41.

Young, F. W., and R. C.
1960   Two determinants of community reaction to industrialization in rural Mexico. *Economic Development and Culture Change*, 8:257–264.
1962   Key informant reliability in rural Mexican villages. *Human Organization*, 20:141–48.
1962   Co-occupational role perceptions in rural Mexico. *Rural Sociology*, 27:42–52.
1966   Individual commitment to industrialization in rural Mexico. *American Journal of Sociology*, 31:373–83.
1967   Toward a theory of community development. In *The challenge of Development*, Richard J. Ward, ed. Chicago: Aldine Press.

Zambia Mail
1970   Getting busy with cotton. January 27.

Zirounis, M.
n.d.   To dendro tis zois. Kalymnos. Privately printed.

INDEX